RETHINKING
TRAGEDY

RETHINKING TRAGEDY

Edited by Rita Felski

The Johns Hopkins University Press

Baltimore

© 2008 The Johns Hopkins University Press
Essays by Rita Felski, George Steiner, Simon Critchley, Kathleen M. Sands, Page duBois,
Joshua Foa Dienstag, Elisabeth Bronfen, Heather K. Love, Michael Maffesoli,
and Terry Eagleton © 2004 by *New Literary History,* The University of Virginia
All rights reserved. Published 2008
Printed in the United States of America on acid-free paper
2 4 6 8 9 7 5 3 1

The Johns Hopkins University Press
2715 North Charles Street
Baltimore, Maryland 21218-4363
www.press.jhu.edu

Library of Congress Cataloging-in-Publication Data

Rethinking tragedy / edited by Rita Felski.
p. cm.
Includes bibliographical references and index.
ISBN-13: 978-0-8018-8739-0 (hardcover: alk. paper)
ISBN-13: 978-0-8018-8740-6 (pbk.: alk. paper)
ISBN-10: 0-8018-8739-9 (hardcover: alk. paper)
ISBN-10: 0-8018-8740-2 (pbk.: alk. paper)
1. Tragedy—History and criticism. I. Felski, Rita, 1956–
PN1892.R46 2008
809'.9162—dc22

A catalog record for this book is available from the British Library.

*Special discounts are available for bulk purchases of this book. For more information, please
contact Special Sales at 410-516-6936 or specialsales@press.jhu.edu.*

For Ralph Cohen,
with the greatest admiration

Contents

Rita Felski Introduction 1

Defining Tragedy

George Steiner "Tragedy," Reconsidered 29

Simon Goldhill Generalizing About Tragedy 45

Wai Chee Dimock After Troy: Homer, Euripides, Total War 66

Kathleen M. Sands Tragedy, Theology, and Feminism
in the Time After Time 82

Joshua Foa Dienstag Tragedy, Pessimism, Nietzsche 104

Rethinking the History of Tragedy

Page duBois Toppling the Hero: Polyphony in the Tragic City 127

Martha C. Nussbaum The "Morality of Pity":
Sophocles' *Philoctetes* 148

Simon Critchley I Want to Die, I Hate My Life—
Phaedra's Malaise 170

Tragedy and Modernity

David Scott Tragedy's Time: Postemancipation Futures
Past and Present 199

Stanley Corngold Sebald's Tragedy 218

Olga Taxidou Machines and Models for Modern Tragedy:
Brecht/Berlau, *Antigone-Model 1948* 241

Timothy J. Reiss Transforming Polities and Selves:
Greek Antiquity, West African Modernity 263

Contents

Tragedy, Film, Popular Culture

Elisabeth Bronfen   Femme Fatale—Negotiations of Tragic Desire   287

Heather K. Love   Spectacular Failure:
The Figure of the Lesbian in *Mulholland Drive*   302

Michel Maffesoli   The Return of the Tragic
in Postmodern Societies   319

Terry Eagleton   Commentary   337

Notes on Contributors   347

Index   351

RETHINKING
TRAGEDY

Introduction

Rita Felski

To rethink tragedy is, of necessity, to acknowledge a history of prior thought. Indeed, the magisterial bulk and the sheer weightiness of that history cast a long shadow over the present. The subject of tragedy has preoccupied a formidable range of thinkers, from Aristotle to Hegel, from Schopenhauer to Lacan. Moreover, while the writing of tragedy may have waned in recent times, readings of tragedy have proliferated. Greek tragedy, in particular, is frequently hailed as an exemplary source of insight into ethical and philosophical questions; in its very remoteness from the present, it throws light on the dilemmas and contradictions of modernity. As Dennis Schmidt has argued, the growing self-doubt of philosophy and the questioning of reason, analytical method, and conceptual knowledge as primary values have much to do with the turn to tragedy as the form that most eloquently dramatizes the stubborn persistence of human blindness, vulnerability, and error.[1]

Beyond the philosophical engagement with tragedy and the tragic extends a vast corpus of literary criticism and interpretation. Widely considered the most prestigious of art forms, tragedy has inspired endless and interminable commentary. Gathered together in their entirety, these definitions and discussions of tragedy, along with the detailed exegeses of its Greek, Shakespearian, French classical, and modern exemplars, could easily fill a bookstore. It is only in recent years, as critics have challenged the automatic deference and pre-eminence accorded to works of the canon, that interest in tragedy has waned, yet such a change of fortune is more evident in English departments than in comparative literature and continental philosophy, where tragedy continues to occupy a prominent place.

To speak of "new" tragic theory in the context of such a *longue durée* of critical reflection is to risk charges of hubris. There is a danger of assuming, in a manner all too easily exposed as smug and naive, that our own historical moment is uniquely equipped to transcend the benighted errors and obfuscations of the past. Surely the sedimented weight of so many centuries of sustained thought is not to be casually dismissed. Can we so easily move beyond an intellectual horizon that forms the invisible

1

backdrop for our own reflections on tragedy as epigones and latecomers? It is precisely such miscalculated confidence and its consequences that is an abiding subject of tragedy. Rather than breaking free of the past, the tragic protagonist finds himself entangled in its meshes; the weight of what has gone before bears down ineluctably on what is yet to come. You may think you are through with the past, writes Simon Critchley in this volume, but the past is not through with you. And yet a rethinking of tragedy is surely beginning to take place, even if hindsight may reveal it to be more indebted to its precursors than it now realizes.

Conventionally, scholars have distinguished between three kinds of meaning and usage clustering around "tragedy" and "tragic": the literary, the philosophical, and the vernacular. The first of these has the most venerable lineage. In ancient Greece, observes Glenn Most, tragedy refers to literature rather than life; it is a genre rather than an idea, a form of dramatic poetry governed by certain conventions rather than an aspect of philosophy or a rendering of the irresolvable contradictions of human experience. (Insofar as Greeks deduced broader meanings from tragic form, Most remarks, such meanings were political rather than philosophical: "not so much metaphysical anxieties about a human's place in an unintelligible universe, as rather the political tensions between the individual and the community associated with Athens' rapid and controversial democratization.")[2] Aristotle, for example, conceives of tragedy as a natural species of poetry, defined by formal and textual criteria rather than by philosophical content or broader cultural resonance. Hence his focus on the immanent organization of the tragic work of art and the qualities of the tragic hero, rather than the social, ritualistic, or theatrical dimensions of tragedy. Aspects of such a taxonomic approach persist into modernity, most famously in the doctrine of the three unities promulgated in the seventeenth century, but also in those modern discussions of tragedy that stipulate formal or thematic criteria, such as poetic language or a high-born hero, as non-negotiable conditions of the genre.

The idea of the tragic, by contrast, is a thought pattern forged in the crucible of German Romanticism. Friedrich von Schiller is often hailed as one of the most influential architects of the view that human existence is essentially tragic, epitomizing a painful and irrevocable schism between the individual and the world in which he finds himself stranded, a theme that will be subsequently pursued and elaborated by Schlegel, Schelling, Hegel, Schopenhauer, and Kierkegaard. This view is in turn premised on large-scale processes of secularization, disenchantment, and individualization that make it possible for human beings to think of themselves as caught up in conditions of isolation and existential homelessness. The idea of the tragic thus drifts free of the genre of tragedy and acquires a general theoretical salience and metaphorical power as a prism through which to grasp the antinomies of the human condition. The paradox ensues whereby philosophers of tragedy turn to Greek exemplars to provide independent support and evidence for their arguments, even as they annex the history and practice of tragedy to serve their own theoretical ends. What renders the tragic so resonant to modern theory, as Vassilis Lambropoulos points out, is its gesturing toward what lies beyond the limits of human understanding, its ability to play an "ethical role without acquiring a fixed moral value."[3]

Classicists have often protested such conflations of tragedy with the modern idea of the tragic as leading to distortions or anachronistic misreadings of Greek tragedy. Moreover, as Olga Taxidou remarks, the philosophical appropriation of tragedy may minimize its aesthetic qualities and entirely overlook its theatrical, performative, and embodied dimensions: "In approaching tragedy philosophical thinking treats it in the best scenario like a realist novel and in the worst as a philosophical treatise that uses human examples."[4] Some of the most influential commentaries on Greek tragedy, however, while acknowledging the irreducible otherness of Greek society, have also succeeded in bringing out some striking commonalities between Greek preoccupations and our own, whether in terms of a shared "linguistic turn" or an overlapping cluster of ethical and political concerns.[5]

Finally, there is the vernacular use of "tragedy" and "tragic," ubiquitously applied to car accidents, the death of children, and most recently to events such as 9/11. When it crops up in ordinary conversation or popular journalism, "tragic" may imply an intended association with *Othello* or *Oedipus*, or a metaphysical lesson about the inescapability of suffering, but it need not do so. Often, as Terry Eagleton remarks, when people describe something as being tragic, they mean nothing more than "very sad." Unlike most theorists of tragedy, Eagleton takes pains not to dismiss such everyday usage as misguided; indeed, he suggests, scholars might do well to allow it more credence, given the sheer impossibility of coming up with a substantive definition of the tragic that can satisfactorily account for all known examples of tragic art. Poking holes in various literary and philosophical attempts to define tragedy, Eagleton leaves us with what he describes as a "theory in ruins," even as he insists that renewed attention to the tragic can help revitalize a critical tradition

3

that, in its current political or postmodern guises, routinely trivializes or underplays the experience of human suffering.[6]

It is against such a backdrop of established usage that a rethinking of tragedy is beginning to take shape. This nascent shift in critical sensibility consists, I want to suggest, of several distinct strands. One group of scholars wants to revise—and revive—tragedy by disentangling tragic art from the idea of the tragic and its Romantic and existentialist connotations. Tragedy has often been conceived as an exalted form that transcends the mundane world of politics and concerns itself only with the loftiest of concerns. The most powerful version of this thesis is Steiner's often cited *The Death of Tragedy.* The incandescent energies of tragedy, Steiner declares, flare up at only a few moments in time, such as fifth-century Athens and sixteenth- and seventeenth-century Europe. Even here, there are only a handful of works that are authentically tragic (much of Shakespeare, Steiner concludes, is too hopeful). Thus tragedy is synonymous with the bleakest form of metaphysical pessimism. It depicts man as an unwelcome guest in the world and teaches us that it is better never to have been born. Nourished by a sacred and hierarchical cosmology, the tragic flame splutters and dies in the inhospitable air of our secular, democratic times. Tragic terror and exaltation are utterly at odds with modern optimism, our sturdy and unquenchable belief that all problems can ultimately be fixed. "More pliant divorce laws could not alter the fate of Agamemnon," writes Steiner; "social psychiatry is no answer to *Oedipus.*"[7] Tragedy underscores the hopelessness of our attempts to remake the world.

Steiner's book set the tone for subsequent debate, even if some scholars took issue with his historical claims about tragedy's demise. Hence the fortunes of tragedy suffered a precipitous decline with the rise of political criticism in the 1980s and '90s. The Brechtian account of tragedy soon became a commonplace: tragedy takes on the role of ideology in cloaking the historically contingent in the mantle of the eternal and inevitable. Tragedy was perceived as the enemy of politics in promoting a sense of hopelessness, fatalism, and resignation. "The most influential kinds of explicitly social thinking," writes Raymond Williams in his summary and critique of this view, "have often rejected tragedy as in itself defeatist. Against what they have known as the idea of tragedy, they have stressed man's powers to change his condition and to end a major part of the suffering which the tragic ideology seems to ratify."[8]

Thus critics of differing theoretical and political persuasions were united in their perception of the essential nature of tragedy, even as they valued this nature differently. Such a consensus has now collapsed. The view that tragedy deals with the solitary suffering of a Promethean hero and eschews the mundane world of politics is, according to some scholars, a historically specific reading of tragedy rather than the definitive encapsulation of its essence. Raymond Williams was one of the first to argue that modern critics had projected the individualist and existentialist philosophies of their own time onto the entire history of tragedy as a genre, thereby misrepresenting key aspects of that history. Of course, it may be difficult to avoid all such acts of anachronistic attribution; revisionist readings of tragedy are also, in their own way, beholden to the hopes and beliefs of the present. But it is becoming more apparent that the genre of tragedy—even if the definition is limited to such uncontroversial cases as Greek drama, Shakespeare, or French classical tragedy—contains some remarkable variations in its aesthetics and politics and that we cannot afford to be overly confident about what tragedy is or must be. "Tragedy is then not a single and permanent kind of fact," writes Williams, "but a series of experiences and conventions and institutions."[9]

For example, some feminist scholars were quick to endorse a view of tragedy as entailing the fall of a solitary "great man" and consequently dismissed tragedy as a genre preoccupied with the heroics of masculine overreaching. Such a description may have a limited purchase in the case of Shakespearean tragedy, but it fails utterly in explaining Greek texts that are thickly plotted with internecine strife and familial intrigue. Greek tragedy is centered in the family and the *polis* rather than the individual; its preoccupation with issues of desire, sexual conflict, adultery, gender inequality, mother-child relations, and similar themes overlap at many points with feminist concerns. Moreover, as both George Steiner and Judith Butler have pointed out, our view of Greek tragedy is heavily influenced by the dominance of the Oedipus myth, a dominance largely due to the cultural impact of Freud. What if we were to reinstate *Antigone* as the exemplary Greek tragedy?[10] Or *The Bacchae,* with its episodes of gender ambiguity, female erotic frenzy, and ritualistic dismemberment?

"More Greek tragedy has been performed in the last thirty years than at any point in history since Greco-Roman antiquity," writes Edith Hall.[11] That classic tragic art has come to seem more resonant, alive, and contemporaneous than modern tragic theory seems sufficient cause to reconsider certain commonplaces of criticism and to look afresh at the history of tragedy. Yet even as the ideas of many scholars of tragedy are being subjected to wholesale scrutiny and reassessment, one thinker has been spared. The recent rehabilitation of Nietzsche is striking; once scorned by classicists for his idiosyncratic and inaccurate interpretations of Greek culture, Nietzsche is now hailed as an inspirational figure and guide to rethinking tragedy. The very untimeliness of Nietzsche's ideas have rendered them newly timely; his vision of tragedy as forged in the crucible of collective frenzy, orgiastic coupling, and rapturous self-loss offers a provocative challenge to the received view of Greek antiquity as the cradle of Western civilization and an epoch of enlightened serenity.[12]

Nietzsche's hope that opera could become the tragic form of his own time speaks to the second strand of critical revisionism. Here the issue is not a rereading of Greek plays but a concerted effort to rethink the definition of tragedy from the ground up and to expand the corpus of what counts as tragic art. What are the most salient and distinctive features of tragedy? Is there a necessary connection between tragedy and drama or can tragedy appear in diverse genres? Are there distinctively modern, or postmodern, forms in which a tragic sensibility can be expressed? The debate about whether the novel can be a genuinely tragic form has been going on for some time, with mixed results.[13] Yet there is virtual silence on the relationship between tragedy and another major modern art form: film. The archives of film theory and criticism have, it seems, virtually nothing to say on this question. And yet the genre of *film noir,* to take just one example, would appear to have much in common with tragic art: moral ambiguity, a movement toward catastrophe that blurs the distinction between agency and fate, and a pessimistic sensibility that renders the workings of the world opaque and impenetrable.[14]

Why has film criticism so studiously avoided the subject of tragedy? The very modernity of film as a medium undoubtedly fueled a belief that new criteria were needed for its evaluation and that a genre with its origins in antiquity could only be outmoded or irrelevant. The avant-garde sensibility and Brechtian convictions of a generation of *Screen* theorists also conspired to render the subject of tragedy off-limits for an influential cohort of film scholars. And yet film studies has been assiduous in its attentions to a closely related genre. While literary critics ranked tragedy far above the debased form of melodrama, film scholars carried out the opposite maneuver, paying scant attention to tragedy while elevating melodrama to a position of previously unimaginable critical prestige. In particular, the rediscovery of the films of Douglas Sirk, along with the growth of feminist interest in the "women's weepies" of the 1940s and '50s, inspired a wealth of writing on melodrama and its subversive potential.

This writing helped, however unwittingly, to throw the very distinction between tragedy and melodrama into crisis. Conventionally, melodrama is assumed to depict a morally legible universe, dwelling on crisis and catastrophe only to submit them to the ordering hand of providence. It assigns individual characters an unambiguous role in the Manichean struggle of good versus evil, virtue versus vice. The heightened expressiveness of melodrama leaves nothing unspoken; its characters, writes Peter Brooks, "name without embarrassment eternal verities," speak in the register of exaggeration, overstatement, and absolutism.[15] By contrast, tragedy is prized for its refusal to offer clear-cut solutions and absolute judgments; according to Hegel's influential thesis, it stages a conflict between competing rights rather than between right and wrong. Such a conflict, moreover, is often enacted in the divided desires and psyche of a single protagonist rather than being parceled out among a dramatic cast of allegorical types. Robert Heilman writes: "It is in tragedy that man is divided; in melodrama, his troubles, though they may reflect some weakness or inadequacy, do not arise from the urgency of unreconciled impulses. In tragedy the conflict is within man; in melodrama, it is between men, or between men and things."[16]

Such a distinction seems plausible as a way of distinguishing between different ways of representing suffering. And yet the question of whether a text is to be classified as ambiguous or straightforward, whether it renders the world opaque or immediately legible, is not always self-evident or easily settled. Thus rereadings of Sirkian melodrama revealed a richer and more complex aesthetic structure than was originally recognized; its intensified symbolism, fractured, disjunctive rhythms, and elaborate orchestration of visual effects combined, critics argued, to create a powerful sense of the doomed and claustrophobic qualities of American domestic life in the 1950s. In spite of adhering to conventional Hollywood production values and often-formulaic plots, Sirk's trademark techniques of stylistic flamboyance and aesthetic excess cast the values and attitudes of his time in a deeply ironic light. Noting that such films portray "the impossible contradictions that have turned the American dream into its proverbial nightmare," Thomas Elsaesser concludes that the "best American melodramas of the 50s [are] not only critical social documents but genuine tragedies."[17]

Film critics did not, however, extend such isolated observations to a sustained reassessment of the generic distinctions between tragedy and melodrama and the relationship between them. Is melodrama opposed to tragedy? a subset of tragedy? the modern version of tragedy, as Peter

Brooks has argued? Or is the very distinction between tragedy and melodrama tenuous or even untenable? In a recent comparison of Visconti's *Death in Venice* and Sirk's *Imitation of Life,* Ben Singer points out that the former film is conventionally seen as tragic and the latter as melodrama. Why, he wonders, is the work of art-house favorite Visconti never classified as a melodrama, given its heavy reliance on pathos and the grotesque in its portrayal of the doomed nature of unrequited love? Conversely, why is classic Hollywood film never discussed under the sign of tragedy, even when, as in the case of Sirk, it avoids the polarization of melodrama and presents the quintessentially tragic scenario of morally ambiguous characters torn apart by their allegiance to competing values?[18]

In such cases, we might conclude, formal criteria carry less weight than social presuppositions and ideological judgments. Tragedy's association with elite art is now so strongly established that the idea of a modern popular tragedy—and its possible realization in Hollywood film—has been virtually unthinkable. Moreover, while the doomed passion of a German intellectual in *Death in Venice* easily lends itself to reflections on the tragic truths of the human condition, Sirk's focus on the conflicts between mothers and daughters has the effect of dragging a text downward, ensuring its inclusion in the "lower" genre of melodrama. In critical decisions about what counts as tragedy, judgments about subject matter—its weightiness, seriousness, and universal import—are often as salient as questions of form, such that attention to the feminine and domestic has often disqualified texts from being considered tragic. Mary Ann Doane writes: "The dilemmas of the mother are rarely tragic; they are much more frequently contextualized in the mode of melodrama."[19] As our assumptions about the moral dignity and seriousness of persons change, so too may our view of what counts as tragic art.

Who, then, can be a tragic subject? What categories of person are to be included under such a rubric? Such questions speak to the final aspect of rethinking tragedy. According to a well-established thesis, the death of tragedy is linked to the democratization of literature and life that engenders a new focus on everyday life and ordinary individuals. Tragedy, by contrast, requires protagonists that are, in Northrop Frye's words, the "highest point in their human landscape."[20] The tragic hero, Frye writes, allows his servants to do his living for him; he is a semidivine figure, inscrutable and ferocious, wrapped in the mystery of his communion with something beyond. And according to Steiner, the elevated social status of the tragic protagonist is not a peripheral detail but an essential precondition of the form. "There is nothing democratic in the vision of tragedy. The royal and heroic characters whom the gods honour with their vengeance are set higher than we are in the chain of being."[21] This distance is the source of tragic awe, shrouding the suffering of an individual in exemplary public significance. Thus, even as tragedy is seen to transcend politics, its very existence depends on a specific organization of political life.

Terry Eagleton, however, makes an alternative case: modernity, rather than destroying tragedy, may be the precondition for universalizing tragic potential. Democracy, after all, does not guarantee happiness, but promises at best the pursuit of happiness, a pursuit that can all too easily result in disastrous judgments, Faustian over-reaching, or the agony of being torn apart by conflicting desires or values. As Eagleton points out, only with freedom does the tragic gulf between desire and realization become possible. While this freedom may be far from absolute, modern history extends the promise of self-actualization to an ever-widening circle of persons, thereby multiplying the opportunities for human agency, miscalculation, and error, while simultaneously underscoring the painful schism between incandescent dreams and insurmountable social circumstance. Even as modernity lays out its enticing promises of progress, freedom, and amelioration of injustice, the often spectacular failures of such promises throw a melancholy cast over much of the literature and art of the modern era. Indeed, the twentieth-century tradition of critical theory will often recast the history of modernity as an essentially tragic narrative of unending exploitation, alienation, and catastrophe.

Freud is also one of the most influential architects of the modern tragic sensibility, proposing that irresolvable conflict and unsatisfied desire are not temporary conditions but make up the very substance of what it means to be human. In this democratized vision of suffering, the soul of a bank clerk or a shop girl becomes a battleground on which momentous and incalculable forces play themselves out. Once limited to the role of comic stooges or one-dimensional symbols of social problems, lower-class individuals could now appear in art as many-shaded subjects driven by ambiguous yearnings and contradictory desires. Steiner writes of Greek tragedy: "There are around us daemonic energies which prey upon the soul and turn it to madness or which poison our will so that we inflict irreparable outrage upon ourselves and those we love."[22] Such words seem equally suited to much of the literature of modernity, even if we no longer subscribe to a cosmology of semidivine heroes and belief in fate. The gods come down to earth; it is now the ineluctable power of social forces or unconscious desires that carry the tragic protagonist where he or she does not want to go. As Benjamin Constant remarked in his comments on modern tragedy almost two centuries ago, "the social order, the action of society on the individual, in diverse phases and diverse epochs, this network of institutions and conventions, which envelops us from our birth and is not broken until our death" is "entirely equal to the fatality of the ancients."[23]

A number of mid-twentieth-century literary critics, drawing largely on Freudian and existentialist themes, sought to make the case for a distinctively modern tragic literature. It made little sense, they argued, to invoke archaic notions of the sacred or social rank; in modernity, the tragic protagonist is Everyman rather than a great man, even as tragic extremity springs from the mundane rather than being opposed to it. "A tragic hero," David Lenson concluded, "may be drawn from any class, race, region, sex, or occupation."[24] And yet to look back on this criticism from the standpoint of the present is to be struck by its uniform vision of the tragic subject. The same handful of texts recur again and again in critical discussion: *Moby-Dick, Death of a Salesman, The Plague, Waiting for Godot,* and *Endgame,* the texts of Kafka and Faulkner. Neither Edith Wharton's Lily Bart nor Ralph Ellison's invisible man, for example, ever appears in these discussions of the modern tragic sensibility. While Greek tragedy commonly cast women and foreigners in the role of tragic protagonists, the roll call of modern tragedies often seemed to convey a tacit belief that a tragic subject could only be a white male.

This is not to suggest that each and every portrayal of subaltern suffering should henceforth be reclassified as tragic. Revisionary criticism, no less than traditional criticism, must confront the task of delimiting its object; a category made infinitely elastic because of nervousness about exclusion will soon be depleted of effectiveness as an analytical tool. If all descriptions of unhappiness or affliction were to count as tragic, the canon of tragedy would extend almost as far as the canon of writing. In fact, as I have noted, the word "tragic" is often used in everyday speech to describe a wide span of accidents, calamities, and mishaps, from the trivial to the catastrophic. But "tragic" is also an aesthetic term that refers to a distinctive forming of material; here it describes not just suffering but a particular shape of suffering.

It is, of course, the specifics of this shape that are the source of dispute. Critics are divided as to whether tragedy requires verse, gods, a chorus, catharsis, dramatic form, great men—and above all, whether it exists only in art or also in life. And yet the contentiousness of these disputes may obscure some significant agreements and commonalities of view.

For example, critics of differing methodological and political stripes concur that tragedy undermines the sovereignty of selfhood and modern dreams of progress and perfectibility, as exemplified in the belief that human beings can orchestrate their own happiness. In confronting the role of the incalculable and unforeseeable in human affairs, it forces us to recognize that individuals may act against their own interests and that the consequences of their actions may deviate disastrously from what they expected and hoped for. Exposing the limits of reason, the fragility of human endeavor, the clash of irreconcilable desires or incommensurable worlds, the inescapability of suffering and loss, tragedy underscores the hopelessness of our attempt to master the self and the world. Dennis Schmidt writes: "In tragedy we are reminded that we live in a world that is not of our own making or control and yet a world to which we are answerable."[25]

As this reference to answerability suggests, it is not that tragedy replaces the idea of individual sovereignty with the inexorable unfolding of a predetermined pattern. Such a possibility is belied by the dramatic power and presence of its protagonists; it is hard to conceive of Antigone or Hedda Gabler as pawns being pushed about on the chessboard of fate. Indeed, if there were no possibility of acting otherwise, tragedy would be evacuated of much of its anguish and terror. Rather, as many critics have noted, what distinguishes tragedy is an uncanny unraveling of the distinction between agency and fate, internal volition and the pressure of external circumstance. According to Jean-Pierre Vernant and Pierre Vidal-Naquet, "the same character appears now as an agent, the cause and source of his actions, and now as acted upon, engulfed in a force that is beyond him and sweeps him away."[26] Northrop Frye observes that "tragedy seems to elude the antithesis of moral responsibility and arbitrary fate."[27] And Schelling writes in an earlier moment of "an actual and objective conflict between freedom in the subject on the one hand, and necessity on the other, a conflict that does not end such that one or the other succumbs, but rather that both are manifested in perfect indifference as simultaneously victorious and vanquished."[28] It is this uncertain causality that engenders the moral ambiguity of tragedy; the ethical imperative and yet the impossibility of gauging to what extent individuals can be held accountable for actions that wreak catastrophe on themselves and the world.

Such qualities help to render the topic of tragedy newly timely, possessing obvious relevance, for example, to the rethinking of agency in the wake of poststructuralism. To recognize the ways in which actions are shaped by forces beyond the individual's control or awareness is not necessarily to deny personhood but to expose the insufficiency of modern ideals of autonomy and rationality. Tragic works from *The Bacchae* to *Beloved* offer powerful meditations on the ambiguities of causality and the complex intertwining of internal motives and external imperatives. Conversely, popular politics—including the rhetoric of both social movements and mainstream politicians—has often preferred the register of melodrama. To portray one's own side as helpless and virtuous and one's opponent as powerful and evil is to harness a rhetoric geared toward triggering outrage at the spectacle of injustice.[29] Tragedy has none of the same sharply honed sense of purpose and clarity of judgment. And yet, as several contributors to this volume emphasize, tragedy is not opposed to politics, but only to a politics that draws its strength from moral and metaphysical absolutes.

Moreover, this unsettling sense of a blurred boundary between structure and agency, between freedom and fate, should not be seen as an extraordinary experience but rather as thoroughly mundane. Not a condition limited to princes or prelates, it pervades our experience of being in the world at an elemental level. Martha Nussbaum makes the point well:

> . . . that much that I did not make goes towards making me whatever I shall be praised or blamed for being; that I must constantly choose among competing and apparently incommensurable goods and that circumstances may force me to a position in which I cannot help being false to something or doing some wrong; that an event that simply happens to me may, without my consent, alter my life; that is equally problematic to entrust one's good to friends, lovers, or country and to try to have a good life without them—all these I take to be not just the material of tragedy, but everyday facts of lived practical reason.[30]

In most cases, of course, such everyday facts will not unleash the prolonged anguish and catastrophe that is the stuff of tragedy. But it is because of our routine experience of the limits of our own agency, the inevitability of conflict, the constant possibility of acting badly or wrongly, the plurality of incompatible goods—the impossibility, in other words, of "having it all,"—that ancient tragedies still have contemporary resonance.

Indeed, there is some irony in the fact that tragedy, often chastised in English departments for its evasion of the political, is now attracting interest among political theorists. Peter Euben and Christopher Rocco argue that Greek tragedy is good to think with, that it offers perspicacious insights into the politics of rationality that press beyond the false polarizations evidenced, for example, in the debates between Habermas and Foucault. In the plays of Sophocles or Euripides, they argue, we find uniquely sophisticated meditations on the compromised nature of reason, the dilemmas of democracy, the politics of knowledge, the intertwining of barbarism and enlightenment. Even as Greek tragedy diagnoses the dangers of intellectual hubris, single angles of vision, and attempts at theoretical mastery, even as it faces up to the waywardness of language and depicts a world riven by agonistic politics and Dionysian turbulence, it also underscores the inescapability of epistemological reflection and the ethical urgency of claims to justice. Well in advance of Adorno and Horkheimer, Greek tragedy thus offers a prescient and far-reaching meditation on the dialectic of Enlightenment.[31]

That tragedy and politics are far from opposed is also confirmed by literary reckonings with the legacy of slavery that have emerged from the African diaspora in the United States and the Caribbean, many of which draw heavily on tragic topoi. While the figure of the "tragic mulatto" has sometimes been dismissed as a sentimental stereotype, for example, Werner Sollors argues that the authentically tragic aspect of this figure should be taken more seriously. There are, he argues, striking parallels between Greek tragedy and the literature of slavery and segregation: issues of obscure origins, interfamilial strife, and impossible conflicts of allegiance. Race is one way in which tragic consciousness is played out in the modern world.[32]

Tragedy has also proved a fertile source of inspiration for writers on the African continent, as evidenced in such texts as Wole Soyinka's *The Bacchae of Euripides,* Athol Fugard's *The Island,* and Tayeb Salih's *Season of Migration to the North.* While the history of tragedy has sometimes been used to advance claims for the purported superiority of the Western tradition, these postcolonial revisions unsettle such dogmatic polarities and self-serving claims, using tragic form to illuminate the catastrophic consequences of Western racial politics. According to David Scott, a tragic aesthetic may also serve as a valuable corrective to current trends in postcolonial theory. Refuting any notion of human beings as rational persons in control of their own destiny, tragedy resists the lure of Romantic dreams of progress, reveals the past to be thoroughly enmeshed in the present, and undercuts clear-cut oppositions between coercion and resistance. In questioning the distinction between modernity and its others, tragedy serves an important role in "reorienting our understanding of the politics and ethics of our postcolonial present."[33]

This rethinking of tragedy in various forms and guises allows us to push beyond the tri-partite definition of tragedy and the tragic that I alluded to at the start of my essay and that has long framed critical discussion. Thinking of tragedy as a mode offers several advantages in adjudicating the question of tragedy's historical transformations. A more elastic term than "genre," "mode" lends itself especially well to the complicated history and vicissitudes of tragic art. Modes are adjectival, remarks Alistair Fowler, denoting a selective group of features rather than a text's overall defining structure; the term thus draws our attention to the hybrid, mixed qualities of genres.[34] This adjectival usage can emancipate us from prescriptive taxonomies in literary criticism that persist in equating the tragic with a now virtually defunct form of poetic drama. At the same time, we can avoid lapsing into the generalities often associated with the idea of the tragic in philosophy, where the particulars of tragic art are too easily transmuted into a series of broad-brush claims about the pathos and horror of human existence. Conceiving of the tragic as a mode also gives us a more selective rubric than its everyday use to mean "very sad"; it directs our attention to the formal particulars that render sadness tragic—details of plot and structure, characterization and language, what I have called the shape of suffering—while still allowing us to enfold multiple media and forms within its purview.

In this regard, we can agree with Steiner that tragedy as a certain type of dramatic form is now in eclipse, while noting the persistence of a tragic mode in modernity, often realized in forms (film, philosophy) that are not usually associated with tragedy. Indeed, Steiner's own later writings, tending as they do toward an increasingly somber and melancholic engagement with the numinous, might well be described as tragic in this sense. The "death of tragedy" thesis may clarify why traditional tragedies are no longer being written, but it cannot explain why they are still being read, watched, performed, revised, and invoked (a question that Steiner pursues in *Antigones,* where he addresses the persistence of tragic myths and archetypes). From the standpoint of a strong historicism, tragedy could only be of antiquarian interest, a musty cultural relic as remote from the concerns of late modernity as humors or phlogiston. That this does not seem to be the case suggests that we need to acknowledge generic continuity as well as generic change.

The achievements of postcolonial theory include its powerful critique of models of homogeneous, discrete, self-enclosed space and its elaboration of notions of hybridity, translation, and global flow, which can deal more adequately with the complexities of cultural transmission.

We surely need similar models for thinking about the cross-temporal movement and migration of texts. Recent work in literary studies has enriched our sense of the historical provenance of works of art; but its distaste for the language of the eternal and universal has often resulted in an equally limited insistence that texts be wholly explicable by the time-bound conditions of their origins. The result is a notion of history as comprising a series of separate, unrelated slices or segments—what Wai Chee Dimock calls "synchronic historicism" and Henry Staten "an atomizing periodization of the diachronic flow"—that is unable to account for the ways in which texts persist and signify across time.[35] Such a process of historical quarantine has the effect of turning texts "into fossils to be examined and labeled, rather than voices that might in any way speak back—indeed, might speak back to the very procedures used to make sense of them."[36] This response seems especially impoverished in the case of tragedy, which assumes very different forms across the contingencies of history and time but which also undermines the progressivist logic of modern thought, serving, as Kathleen Sands writes in this volume, to "disrupt and defy the narration of time as meaning."

The following essays on rethinking tragedy begin and end with the work of two influential thinkers whose views could hardly be more divergent. George Steiner's discussion of what he calls absolute tragedy emphasizes its links to a political elite, its metaphysical grandeur, and its irrevocable pastness. For social theorist Michel Maffesoli, by contrast, the tragic is quotidian, popular, and contemporary, epitomized in the practices of present-day youth culture (raves, drug-taking, popular music). The modern project of individual *Bildung* and social progress, argues Maffesoli, is giving way to a renewed tragic consciousness, embodied in an ethics and aesthetics of the moment, a fascination with extremity and excess, and a surrendering of the self to impersonal forces. The other essays in this collection, stemming from scholars working in literature, classics, philosophy, anthropology, film studies, theology, and political theory, offer equally diverse perspectives on the value of tragedy, the contemporaneity of the tragic, and the task of rethinking what tragedy might mean today.

In his essay, Steiner reflects on *The Death of Tragedy* more than forty years after its publication. Noting the radical indeterminacy of "tragedy" and "tragic," he seeks to delimit these terms not through fruitless attempts at formal definition but by elucidating a common core of suppositions. According to Steiner, this core consists of a sense of ontological homelessness, of "alienation or ostracism from the safeguard of licensed being." In returning to his earlier arguments, he concedes that such a condition of fundamental estrangement and primordial suffering is not superseded by modernity but continues to mark the thought of thinkers such as Marx, Freud, and Lévi-Strauss. Acknowledging the historical variety and fluctuation of tragic forms, he notes that "with few exceptions, 'tragedy' after Goethe perpetuates itself in prose fiction, in opera, in film, in reportage." Yet Steiner also insists on a fundamental difference between such modern expressions of the tragic and what he calls the "absolute tragedy" of the Greeks, which is marked by a radical pessimism alien to both Christianity and atheism.

According to Simon Goldhill, this reading of Greek tragedy as the quintessential vehicle of a tragic worldview finds little support in the culture and writings of ancient Greece. Its appearance is notably more recent, forged out of Kantian beliefs about the disinterestedness of art combined with the historical influence of a Romantic Hellenism that came to regard Greek tragedy as a privileged aesthetic object, the epitome of all that is transcendental, sublime, and universal. In its modern reception, Greek tragic art has thus been stripped of its historical and political meanings and viewed as a purely metaphysical meditation on the nature of the individual, the family, or the state. What are the theoretical and political stakes of such attempts to generalize about tragedy? Greek tragedies, it turns out, are themselves replete with sophisticated reflections on the benefits and risks of generalization, questioning the value of the exemplary even as they also blur the line between the universal and the specific. Goldhill is far from suggesting that we give up all attempts at generalizing—an impossible task—but he wants our readings of Greek tragic art to do justice to both its political meanings and its transhistorical resonance without resorting to premature judgments about what tragedy really is or should be.

Wai Chee Dimock invites us to expand our conception of the tragic to include natural disasters and nonhuman actors, including, most recently, the devastation wreaked by hurricane Katrina. The destruction of cities enacts death, suffering, and deprivation on an unimaginable scale, epitomizing a lack of proportionality that does not lend itself to a humanist calculus of guilt and responsibility. That we do not hesitate to use words such as "tragic" in everyday speech to describe such catastrophes suggests that our scholarly definitions of tragedy may be too constrained; indeed, the history of Greek theatrical performance authorizes an alternative view of the tragic as a collective event, a mass experience rather than an autonomous work of art. Turning to *The Iliad,* Dimock suggests that it renders the destruction of Troy akin to a natural disaster; massed forces of soldiers stretching as far as the eye can see come together to form an aggregate, a collective being, that is something other than human in its sheer size and scale, that surges forward like an inexorable and unstoppable hurricane. Both epic and tragedy, Dimock proposes, contain images of collective destruction that threaten our very notion of the person, that gesture toward the obliteration of populations without discrimination, that assimilate the social world to the domain of physics and its implacable conversion of human beings into matter. Both natural disaster and social catastrophe bear witness to impersonal forces that exceed the human in wreaking a homogenizing logic of destruction.

Kathleen Sands pursues her conception of tragedy by examining its relation to Christianity and by reassessing feminist rejections of the tragic. In a useful clarification of the distinction between tragedy and trauma, she notes that "tragedy, as an aesthetic form, consigns trauma to a ritual space where, rather than being silently reenacted, it is solemnly voiced and lamented." As a form that acknowledges the brokenness of the world, tragedy resists moral certainties as well as purely aesthetic interpretation, forcing us to face a negativity so radically other—and yet so disturbingly close—that it overwhelms our understanding. Sands considers the tragic dimensions of Christian theology, as manifested in its conceptions of evil and its vision of a fallen world, but she believes that such elements are ultimately sublated in a narrative of redemption at the end of time. Sands detects a similar evasion of the tragic in feminist theology and feminist thought more generally. Acknowledging the good reasons why feminists might be suspicious of tragedy (including women's long association with fallenness and with self-sacrifice), she also shows how feminism's refusal of tragedy and its dream of social perfectability relies on a questionable metaphysics, in which injustice is viewed as a form of falsehood and suffering as a parenthetical and temporary condition.

Joshua Dienstag dissents from those scholars of tragedy who see tragic pessimism as synonymous with the bleakest anguish and unutterable despair. He points out that the philosophy of pessimism has received scant attention from scholars and that pessimism is commonly understood as an undesirable psychological trait or as entailing an apolitical or politically conservative stance. Dienstag fleshes out Nietzsche's ideas about pessimism to arrive at very different conclusions. Pessimism, he argues, arises out of a sense of the contingent, time-bound nature of existence, as caught up in an inexorable flux of creation and destruction. In Greek tragedy, it is symbolized in the figure of Dionysus, who epitomizes

17

a wisdom that is collective and popular rather than individual, who does not counsel quietism or despair but stands for a joyful embracing of what is in the face of the instability and perishability of all things. This tragic pessimism does not die in modernity but assumes vital new forms in both art and philosophy, as in the writing of Camus and Arendt. The pessimistic spirit, concludes Dienstag, is restless and radical, unlikely to be enamored of the status quo; it does not oppose politics, even as it chastens any form of politics that seeks to ground itself in narratives of perfectability and progress.

The next section of *Rethinking Tragedy* revisits tragic texts of the past to reflect on their current resonance. Page duBois voices a vigorous critique of various misreadings and misuses of Greek tragedy. Not only is the genre of tragedy commonly reduced to the single example of Oedipus (or, more rarely, Antigone) but it is also widely associated with a constellation of aesthetic clichés: the great man, the fatal flaw, the fall. Moreover, theorists from Hegel to Lacan and Butler zero in on the fate of the tragic protagonist, interpreting Greek tragedy via quintessentially modern ideas about the primacy of the self. Dubois seeks to challenge such anachronistic interpretations and to defamiliarize Greek tragedy by emphasizing its aesthetic strangeness and remoteness from our own time. She highlights three key aspects of this tragic aesthetic: the omnipresence of slaves and of political debates about slavery; the role of mourning, loss, and lamentation; and the polyphonic, richly heterogeneous qualities of tragic language. In epitomizing a historically distant, alien form of life that is not centered on the individual self, she suggests, Greek tragedy may paradoxically be newly pertinent to our own time.

Martha Nussbaum tackles the relations between tragedy and ethics by reading Sophocles' *Philoctetes* in relation to classical and modern debates about the value of pity. It is, she observes, the pity play par excellence, a drama bent on triggering compassion in the viewer through its remorseless multiplication of the sources of Philoctetes' suffering. "In a manner unparalleled in Greek tragedy," she writes, "Sophocles shows us the texture of a life at the margins of life," vividly underscoring the harsh realities of permanent hunger and thirst, of social isolation, of unremitting physical pain—conditions that have afflicted and continue to afflict much of the world's population. Noting that pity has often made critics nervous, calling forth charges of excessive soft-heartedness, partiality, even effeminacy, Nussbaum weighs up the various indictments of pity by the Stoics, Nietzsche, and others. Reading such charges in dialogue with Sophocles' text, she presents a qualified defense of pity as an emotional response to representations of suffering with ethical and political value.

Simon Critchley pursues the question of the tragic by turning to the work of Racine. In a careful delineation of Phaedra's malaise, of a tragic subjectivity riven by the twin torments of conscience and desire, Critchley invokes the idea of unhousedness, of the belief that "being is not our home." Phaedra's languor stems from her sense of imprisonment in an alien body as well as in a monstrous and inescapable past; her overwhelming fatigue stems from her thrownness, her facticity. Drawing much of his vocabulary from Heidegger and Levinas, Critchley also suggests that this sense of existential lack, of originary inauthenticity, lies at the heart of Christian thought. "For what is hereditary sin but the claim that the being of being human is originally constituted as a lack, as a radical indebtedness to a past that cannot be made up by the subject's own volition?" Describing how the metaphysics of Jansenism permeate Racine's tragedy in its refusal of life in the world and its invocation of a hidden, watchful, God, Critchley argues that *Phaedra* epitomizes a form that has often been deemed impossible: Christian tragedy.

The next cluster of essays pushes debates over tragedy toward an explicit engagement with history and the politics of modernity. For David Scott, the issue of time is especially salient. What defines our present moment, he proposes, is the crumbling of a progressivist view of history, a dwindling confidence that time can be marshaled into a redemptive narrative of emancipation and overcoming. Hence the renewed timeliness of tragedy as a form that casts all such hubris-laden plotlines into doubt, that draws attention to the force of the unforeseeable while also underscoring our inescapable entanglement in the past. Comparing the two editions of C. L. R. James's *The Black Jacobins* throws an intriguing new light on contrasting emplotments of history and time in postcolonial politics. Inspired by the revolutionary and black nationalist hopes of the 1930s, James's original account of the Haitian revolution is cast in the form of a heroic Romance, depicting a world-historical battle between slavery and freedom. Revised in the changed historical circumstances of the 1960s, the second edition interpolates six new paragraphs that cast Toussaint Louverture as a tragic figure, his fate epitomizing the painful dilemmas and irresolvable contradictions experienced by colonized peoples struggling against a history of colonial enlightenment. A tragic sensibility, Scott concludes, may inspire a more self-reflexive politics attuned to the ambiguous and complex relations between time and action, intentions and contingencies, determination and chance.

Stanley Corngold approaches the question of tragedy and modernity via an engagement with the writings of W. G. Sebald. These works strive to register the enormity of the destruction inflicted on the human and natural worlds in modern times, especially in the context of recent German history, even as they bear witness to the shortfalls of memory and the inevitable and risky falsifications of fiction making. Corngold invites us to think of the tragic not in terms of the usual criteria of plot or character but as a matter of *style:* in the mood-saturated qualities of Sebald's prose he finds a confusion of feelings, a mournful amazement, a melancholic, dust-laden ambience that captures the tonality of the tragic in our own times. Syntax offers an oblique way of conveying an experience of historical catastrophes too big to report, too vast to be faced full on. Out of this close attention to Sebald's texts, Corngold draws out "ten items toward a revised thesis on modern tragedy" that speak directly to the question of what tragedy means today.

The work of Bertolt Brecht, as noted earlier, is often seen as the antithesis of a tragic sensibility, thanks to Brecht's Marxist commitments and his famously skeptical attitude toward catharsis and traditional aesthetic experience. Olga Taxidou challenges this received view through a reading of the *Antigone-Model 1948,* a record of Brecht's reworking of Hölderlin's version of *Antigone,* photographed by Ruth Berlau. Here, she argues, we see a more nuanced and sophisticated engagement with Greek tragedy than Brecht is usually given credit for, even as Brecht modulates the received philosophical readings of Antigone by underscoring her theatricality and her embodiment, casting new light on the relations between mourning, gender, and the law. The image of Helene Weigel as Antigone bearing a door on her back is a classic Brechtian gestus that combines ritual and history, the textual and the material, actor and object, highlighting the anomaly of a female body on stage within a dramatic tradition once composed entirely of male performers. Brecht's reworking of past tragic texts fuses rationalism and violence, humanism and barbarism, in the attempt to find a theatrical form that can register the modern experience of historical catastrophe.

Timothy Reiss juxtaposes commentary on Plato and Greek tragic drama with a reading of some recent West African plays. What these disparate texts have in common, he argues, is a conception of a human agent that is strikingly different from modern Western ideas of the solitary self as revealed in conventional theories of the tragic. Rather, Greek culture gives us a view of the person as embedded in multiple circles of being from the familial to the cosmic; to be human, in this light, is to be present for others, to exist in collective and communal webs of meaning. African revisions of tragedy since the 1960s also question Western notions of agency, intention, and individuality; plays by John Pepper Clark-Bekederemo, Wole Soyinka, and Ola Rotimi, among others, revise and rework Greek tragic myths to new political ends while drawing on conceptions of embedded personhood that are analogous, in certain respects, to those of Greek culture. This is not to imply that African texts embody some authentic realm of tradition outside of Western modernity but to attend to a complex blend of indigenous histories and transcultural interchanges that has shaped the distinctive qualities of African tragic art and that underscores the provincial nature of many arguments about tragedy.

The final cluster of essays moves the conversation about tragedy toward film and popular culture while pursuing further the question of who can be a tragic subject. In her reading of *Double Indemnity,* Elisabeth Bronfen reassesses the significance of the femme fatale of *film noir.* A figure such as Phyllis Dietrichson is often read by feminist critics as a stereotype of feminine evil or as a symptom of male anxiety, possessing no agency or independent reality of her own. Such a reading, Bronfen suggests, unwittingly replicates the fetishistic gaze of Phyllis's lover and coconspirator, Walter Neff, who is unable to acknowledge her existence as a distinct and separate human subject. Drawing on Stanley Cavell's discussion of misrecognition as a structural element of tragedy, Bronfen shows how *Double Indemnity* repeatedly stages such moments of misrecognition, as the hero turns away from the femme fatale or refuses to meet her gaze, leaving the viewer to decode the ambiguous emotions that are registered in her facial close-ups. Bronfen proposes that the femme fatale should be seen as a prototype of modern feminine tragic subjectivity. Neither a helpless victim nor a transgressive subject, she acknowledges her own fallibility and flawedness, accepts responsibility for her actions, and is willing to face death as the consequence of her desires.

Heather Love takes up the motif of the tragic lesbian, situating homosexuality in relation to what she calls the modern tragedy of social types. Invoking Terry Eagleton's discussion of the *pharmakos,* or scapegoat, she notes that modernity creates new symbols of abjection, figures whose very being is seen to crystallize an all-pervasive condition of lack and failure. "Nothing befalls them; because their very existence seems tragic, not only every catastrophe but every passing disappointment takes on the character of a curse, and seems to arise from within rather than without." The fate of the *femme damnée* is preordained by a familiar script that depicts female homosexuality as a doomed condition. Against those who would dismiss such images as retrograde residues of the bad old days before Stonewall, Love insists on their continuing resonance in psychic and social life. Pursuing this theme via a reading of *Mulholland Drive,* she shows how David Lynch's film explores the interconnection of tragic and comic versions of female same-sex desire, revealing lesbian identity to be caught up in a sedimented history of fantasies and myths. The current disavowal of the tragic lesbian stems from the willed repression of a past that nevertheless continues to haunt the present.

The question of tragic temporality is also central to the final essay. Michel Maffesoli's work is widely read and discussed in Europe, although not quite so well known in the United States. In this translation from his recent book, *L'Instant éternel: Le retour du tragique dans les sociétés postmodernes,* Maffesoli develops a diagnosis of the present that draws on the earlier arguments of *The Shadow of Dionysus, The Time of the Tribes, The Contemplation of the World,* and other works not yet translated into English. According to Maffesoli, the project of modernity, defined as a future-oriented faith in individual development and political transformation, is inexorably reaching its end. Against those who lament this sign of the apathy of the young or mourn the loss of history in the society of the spectacle, he urges us to take seriously the current transvaluation of cultural values. An orientation to the future is giving way to an immersion in the present; individual existence is being replaced by affiliation with the group (the postmodern tribe); there is a widespread fascination with religiosity, mysticism, myth, and the supernatural (the "New Age"), as well as with violence, excess, and the glamour of self-destruction, whether simulated or real. These cultural symptoms, argues Maffesoli, point to a widespread resurgence of the tragic in its Nietzschean sense; living for the moment, recognizing the precariousness and vulnerability of existence and the limits of human agency, and yet affirming life in the face of death with exuberance and passion. Against moralistic and ascetic interpretations of tragedy, he argues that in ancient Greece and in our own time, "the culture of pleasure goes hand in hand with the tragic sense of destiny." Maffesoli's provocative recasting of the idea of the tragic invites us to look not to high art but rather to much-maligned aspects of popular culture—rock concerts, senseless violence, the worship of celebrities—for the reincarnation of the spirit of Dionysus.

This collection of essays, then, leaves us with a vision of tragedy that is both recognizable and alien, both familiar and strange. No longer a sacramental relic, a safely distanced object of veneration or disdain preserved in past time, the tragic is shown to persist—against official ideologies of utopian optimism and political perfectability—into the present. The world of Antigone or Phaedra is utterly remote from our world, and yet such historical disjunctures may coexist with flashes of illumination and unexpected connections across time. To rethink tragedy is to create such new constellations of thought; in the juxtaposition of Racine with Levinas, Antigone with *film noir*, the friction created by the jagged edge of historical difference sparks fresh moments of revelation and insight. The death of tragedy is not so much an incorrect prognosis as an inconclusive one; after all, the dead, as Kathleen Sands remarks, do not always stay in the ground. This recognition of both the perishability and the persistence of the tragic—a form we think we have left behind, yet which continues to haunt us—heralds the rebirth of tragic criticism.

Notes

I would like to thank Ralph Cohen, Gabriel Hankins, Mollie Washburne, and Jennifer Wicke for their invaluable help in the preparation of this essay, and Tom Broughton-Willett for creating the index.

1. Dennis J. Schmidt, *On Germans and Other Greeks: Tragedy and Ethical Life* (Bloomington: Indiana University Press, 2001).

2. Glenn Most, "Generating Genres: The Idea of the Tragic," in *Matrices of Genre: Authors, Canons, and Society,* ed. Mary Depew and Dirk Obbink (Cambridge, MA: Harvard University Press, 2000), 21. For a useful overview of various conceptions of tragedy and the tragic, see also Adrian Poole, *Tragedy: A Very Short Introduction* (Oxford: Oxford University Press, 2005).

3. Vassilis Lambropoulos, *The Tragic Idea* (London: Duckworth, 2006), 10.

4. Olga Taxidou, *Tragedy, Modernity, and Mourning* (Edinburgh: Edinburgh University Press, 2004), 33.

5. See, for example, Simon Goldhill, *Reading Greek Tragedy* (Cambridge: Cambridge University Press, 1986); Bernard Williams, *Shame and Necessity* (Berkeley: University of California Press, 1993).

6. Terry Eagleton, *Sweet Violence: The Idea of the Tragic* (Oxford: Blackwell, 2003).

7. George Steiner, *The Death of Tragedy* (1961; rpt., New Haven: Yale University Press, 1996), 8.

8. Raymond Williams, *Modern Tragedy* (Stanford: Stanford University Press, 1966), 63.

9. Ibid., 45–46.

10. George Steiner, *Antigones* (1984; rpt., New Haven: Yale University Press,

1996); Judith Butler, *Antigone's Claim: Kinship Between Life and Death* (New York: Columbia University Press, 2000).

11. Edith Hall, "Introduction," in *Dionysus Since 69: Greek Tragedy at the Dawn of the Third Millennium,* ed. Edith Hall, Fiona Macintosh, and Amanda Wrigley (Oxford: Oxford University Press, 2004), 2.

12. See, for example, Paul Gordon, *Tragedy After Nietzsche: Rapturous Superabundance* (Urbana: University of Illinois Press, 2001).

13. One of the better books on this question is Jeanette King, *Tragedy in the Victorian Novel* (Cambridge: Cambridge University Press, 1978).

14. See, however, Robert Warshow's "The Gangster as Tragic Hero," in *The Immediate Experience* (New York: Atheneum, 1971).

15. Peter Brooks, *The Melodramatic Imagination: Balzac, Henry James, Melodrama, and the Mode of Excess* (New York: Columbia University Press, 1984), 41.

16. Robert Bechtold Heilman, *Tragedy and Melodrama: Versions of Experience* (Seattle: University of Washington Press, 1968), 79.

17. Thomas Elsaesser, "Tales of Sound and Fury: Observations on the Family Melodrama," in *Home Is Where the Heart Is: Studies in Melodrama and the Woman's Film,* ed. Christine Gledhill (London: BFI, 1987), 67–68.

18. Ben Singer, *Melodrama and Modernity* (New York: Columbia University Press, 2001), 56–58.

19. Mary Ann Doane, *The Desire to Desire: The Woman's Film of the 1940s* (Bloomington: Indiana University Press, 1987), 71.

20. Northrop Frye, *The Anatomy of Criticism: Four Essays* (Princeton: Princeton University Press, 1957), 207.

21. Steiner, *The Death of Tragedy,* 241.

22. Ibid., 7.

23. Benjamin Constant, "Reflections on Tragedy," in *Revolution in the Theatre: French Romantic Theories of Drama,* ed. B. V. Daniels (Westport, CT: Greenwood Press 1983), 107.

24. David Lenson, *Achilles' Choice: Examples of Modern Tragedy* (Princeton: Princeton University Press, 1975), 163.

25. Schmidt, *On Germans and Other Greeks,* 7–8.

26. Jean-Pierre Vernant and Pierre Vidal-Naquet, *Myth and Tragedy in Ancient Greece,* trans. Janet Lloyd (New York: Zone, 1990), 77.

27. Frye, *Anatomy of Criticism,* 211.

28. F. W. J. Schelling, *The Philosophy of Art* (Minneapolis: University of Minnesota Press, 1989), 251.

29. See, for example, Linda Williams, *Playing the Race Card: Melodramas of Black and White from Uncle Tom to O. J. Simpson* (Princeton: Princeton University Press, 2001).

30. Martha Nussbaum, *The Fragility of Goodness: Luck and Ethics in Greek Tragedy and Philosophy* (Cambridge: Cambridge University Press, 1981), 5.

31. Peter Euben, *The Tragedy of Political Theory: The Road Not Taken* (Princeton:

Princeton University Press, 1990); Christopher Rocco, *Tragedy and Enlightenment: Athenian Political Thought and the Dilemmas of Modernity* (Berkeley: University of California Press, 1997).

32. Werner Sollors, *Neither Black nor White Yet Both: Thematic Explorations of Interracial Literature* (New York: Oxford University Press, 1997). See also Kevin J. Wetmore Jr., *Black Dionysus: Greek Tragedy and African-American Theatre* (Jefferson, NC: MacFarland, 2003); Carole Anne Taylor, *The Tragedy and Comedy of Resistance: Reading Modernity Through Black Women's Fiction* (Philadelphia: University of Pennsylvania Press, 2000).

33. David Scott, *Conscripts of Modernity: The Tragedy of Colonial Enlightenment* (Durham, NC: Duke University Press, 2004), 21. See also Ato Quayson, "African Postcolonial Relations Through a Prism of Tragedy," in *Calibrations: Reading for the Social* (Minneapolis: University of Minnesota Press, 2003).

34. Alistair Fowler, *Kinds of Literature: An Introduction to the Theory of Genres and Modes* (Cambridge, MA: Harvard University Press, 1982), 106–11.

35. Wai Chee Dimock, "A Theory of Resonance," *PMLA* 112, no. 5 (1997): 1061; Henry Staten, *Eros in Mourning: Homer to Lacan* (Baltimore: Johns Hopkins University Press, 1995), 16.

36. Jennifer Fleissner, "Is Feminism a Historicism?" *Tulsa Studies in Women's Literature* 25, no. 2 (2002): 48.

Defining Tragedy

"Tragedy," Reconsidered

George Steiner

The semantic field of the noun "tragedy" and of the adjective "tragic" remains as indeterminate as its origin. Colloquial, idiomatic usage attaches "tragic" to experiences, mental or material, which range from triviality—"the cake has burned in the oven"—to ultimate disaster and sorrow. The intentional focus can be narrow and specific, as in "a tragic accident," or undefinably spacious, as in the shopworn phrase "a tragic sense of life." The numerous intermediate hybrids under the rubric of "tragi-comedy" or even "optimistic tragedy," a tag publicized in Soviet parlance, further blur linguistic and existential demarcations.

"Tragedy" in reference to western literature is itself an elusive branch of tangled ramifications. If its roots are to be found in drama, in the scenic enactment of those "goat-songs" cherished by nineteenth-century philologists and ethnographers, its application to other genres may well have been as ancient. The ascription of tragic sentiments to episodes in the Homeric epics appears to have been current. Whether the epithet characterized lyric poetry is not known; but it will pertain habitually to narratives of grief and of death in Ovid or Virgil. As our literatures evolve, the concept of tragedy extends far beyond the dramatic genre. It serves for poetry and prose fiction—for d'Aubigné's *Tragiques* as for Dreiser's *An American Tragedy*. In turn, by osmosis as it were, it permeates the descriptions of ballet, of film. Composers such as Beethoven, Berlioz, Brahms incorporate the marking "tragic" in their compositions. Throughout this seemingly unbounded and mobile spectrum, "tragedy" and "tragic" can lose their sometime specificity. They come to enhance any conceivable nuance of sadness, misfortune, or loss. Dionysian rites of heroic sacrifice—if that is what they were—have all but receded from definition.

At least one classical usage, moreover, suggests that we do not know, at some elemental level, what it is we are talking about. It occurs in *Laws* 7.817b. The context is that of Plato's notorious repudiation of mundane letters, notably drama (the young Plato having himself hoped to be a tragedian). The Athenian informs Clinias that there is no need for writers of tragedy, though they "may be men of genius," in the projected *polis:*

29

> Respected visitors, we are ourselves authors of a tragedy, and that the finest and the best we know how to make. In fact, our whole polity has been constructed as a dramatization of a noble and perfect life; that is what we hold in truth to be the most real of tragedies.

Even allowing for A. E. Taylor's "forcing" rendition of *mimesis* as "dramatization," the passage remains profoundly puzzling. How can the edification of a "noble and perfect life" in Plato's luminous if Spartan commonwealth be construed as "the most real of tragedies"? In what respect are the architects and legislators of this polity tragic authors beyond the claims of any poet? Is there some ineluctable component of tragedy, which is to say of failure and self-deception in the political process itself even here, especially where the latter comes nearest to the ideal? Or is that a modern, illegitimately "psychological" reading? No commentary of which I know is of help. Yet the centrality of the crux in Plato's idiom and sensibility is undeniable. Dante is lucidly helpful when defining *commedia* for us, when giving us to understand why even his *Inferno* is part of a "comedy." Plato leaves us helpless.

Such radical indeterminacies make arbitrary and sterile the innumerable formal definitions of "tragedy" offered since Aristotle. At best, each is only a more or less local classification, a more or less *ad hoc* ruling towards moral, aesthetic, or political ends. Polonius's catalogue of tragical modes captures the fatuity of normative categorizations. There are those, Kafka perhaps, Beckett, who have been inclined to dispense with the term altogether.

Consequently, I prefer not to work with any formulaic, legislative definition of "tragedy" as it is used to label a literary genre. All such definitions, moreover, tend to be variants on Aristotle's *Poetics,* a text which raises far more problems than it solves. What I aim for is a generative nucleus of supposition, of reasoned intuition, a minimal but indispensable core shared by "tragedies" in literature and extending, by analogy, by related metaphor, to other expressive modes.

This nucleus (*Ur-grund*) is that of "original sin." Because of that fall or "dis-grace," in the emphatic and etymological sense, the human condition is tragic. It is ontologically tragic, which is to say in essence. Fallen man is made an unwelcome guest of life or, at best, a threatened stranger on this hostile or indifferent earth (Sophocles' damning word, dwelt on by Heidegger, is *apolis*). Thus the necessary and sufficient premise, the axiomatic constant in tragedy is that of ontological homelessness—witness this motif in Beckett, in Pinter—of alienation or ostracism from the safeguard of licensed being. There is no welcome to the self. This is what tragedy is about.

Different faiths, different mythologies, different scenarios of secular anthropology and psychology, of political theory, provide programmatic narratives of, explanations of, the imperative of primordial guilt. They are as prevalent in modern positivism as they were in archaic hypotheses. The Judeo-Christian and Pauline fable of Adamic disobedience and inherited guilt has darkened the human prospect virtually to our day. It has modulated with intriguing ease into secular and profane models. Marx's 1844 manuscripts postulate a stage in human relations in which the primal exchange of trust for trust, of love for love, became fatally one of property and of money, dooming our species to the treadmill of labor and class conflict. Marx's prophetic rhetoric provides no account of how or when this fall from innocence came to pass. Freud's legend, equally evasive as to time and place, is one of original parricide, of the murder of the father by the horde of his sexually deprived sons, an act which thereafter determined the fulcrum of neurosis and repressed culpability in the human psyche. The *mytho-logique* of Lévi-Strauss, continuous on that of Rousseau, locates our fall in the transition, presumably violent, from an at-homeness in the natural and animal world to an estranged, singular status in "culture." As in the Promethean paradigm, it is man's mastery of fire, his transgression from the raw to the cooked, which has generated a condition at once sovereign and irremediably polemic, at once privileged and accursed. In each of these foundational narratives, the Adamic blueprint, however secularized, is unmistakable. Some distant, dread crime or error, the tension between these two categories being crucial to tragedy (*hamartia*), has sentenced man to the ever-renewed cycle of frustration, of individual and collective self-destruction. An original sin, however defined, has brought torment and (absurd) death into our naked world.

So far as we can tell, this *topos* of original sin and of a legacy of guilt does not figure as such in early Greek mythology. It is the "background noise," to borrow a cosmological term, in myths of human rebellion, of fierce conflict between mortals and immortals. It is the coercive context to the tales of Prometheus, of Tantalus, of Sisyphus. We can make out its lineaments in the sad fable of Pandora's box. If Hölderlin's gloss is correct, human ruin is ineluctably inwoven in man's search for agonistic proximity to the gods. But we do not find the motif in any pure or abstract form. I suspect a missing link.

What is certain is the archaic insight, already current in the sixth century BC (Theognis?) that "it is best never to have been born; that it is next best to die young; that ripeness and longevity are a cruel malediction." It is precisely this axiom, together with the consequences which derive from it, which engender the internal logic of tragedy. It is this paradoxical *credo* which constitutes a "tragic sense of life" together with the articulate voicing and performative demonstration of that sense. Without the logic of estrangement from life, of man's ontological fall from grace, there can be no authentic "tragedy."

When writing *The Death of Tragedy* in the 1950s, I had inferred this categorical imperative but had not underlined it adequately. Where the axiom of human estrangement, of survival itself as somewhat scandalous, is attenuated, where it is blurred by concepts of redemption, of social melioration (an old-age home for Lear), where messianic intervention is harnessed, we may indeed have serious drama, didactic allegory of the loftiest sort, lament and melancholy (the *Trauerspiel* analyzed by Walter Benjamin). But we do not have tragedy in any absolute sense. We have contamination by hope—*le sale espoir,* as Sartre memorably put it. Absolute tragedy, whether in Euripides' *Bacchae* or Kafka's parable of the Law, is immune to hope. "Not to have been born is best." The rest is, very much in Dante's sense of *commedia,* "tragic-comedy," however bleak.

Thus a core of dynamic negativity underwrites authentic tragedy. It entails a metaphysical and, more particularly, a theological dimension. Hence the perennial engagement of philosophy with tragic drama, an engagement more persistent and searching than that with any other aesthetic phenomenology. From Plato and Aristotle to Hegel and Kierkegaard, from Kierkegaard to Nietzsche, Freud, and Benjamin, philosophic analysis has argued the legitimacy of tragedy, the paradox of pleasure derived from the tragic. Beyond any other genre outside the philosophic dialogue itself, as we find it in Plato or Hume, tragedy has been the meeting point between the metaphysical and the poetic. Heidegger dramatizes this congruence when he asserts that western thought has turned on a choral ode in Sophocles' *Antigone.* What needs to be precisely understood are the connotations of the metaphysical and the theological in this context.

The proposition that human existence is alien to innocent being, that men and women are unwelcome guests errant—note the presence of "error" in that word—on the earth, comports a metaphysical implication. It presumes that there are nonhuman agencies hostile or at best wholly indifferent to intrusive man. It posits, as current idiom has it, the "Other." Social and economic at the outset, in Rousseau and Marx the concept of alienation has acquired a specific gravity, an ontological weight illustrated by absolute or pure tragedy. A legacy of guilt, the paradoxical, unpardonable guilt of being alive, of attaching rights and aspirations to that condition, condemns the human species to frustration and suffering, to being tied to "a wheel of fire." Our existence is not so much a "tale told by an idiot" as it is a chastisement from which early death is the only logical deliverance. In Adamic and Calvinist monotheism, punishment emanates from an offended, vengeful deity. In classical mythology, jealous gods exercise their blind or malign cruelties even on their worshippers (this outrage obsesses Euripides). The daemonic, the devilish, is loosed on the city as a whole or on Faustus's midnight.

Philosophically problematic, yet none the less terrifying is the notion, personified in the Roman pantheon, of "ill luck," of inexplicable, arbitrary bad fortune or accident (the tile falls off the roof with historical results) which can eradicate human hopes and endeavors. Aristotle classified contingent disaster as a lesser mode; he saw its melodramatic rather than tragic tenor. In common experience, however, it is the most compelling reminder of the abyss, of that in our works and days which seems to offend forces, be they anarchic, surpassing our own, mocking our foresight. These forces lie in ambush around the next corner or where three roads meet. Triviality triggers the monstrous: had the messenger reached Cordelia's executioners half a minute earlier. . . .

To cite such presences as the daemonic, the "Other," or Poe's "imp of the perverse," to envision them as retribution or misfortune personified, is to speak theologically. It is to postulate as inherent to tragedy and the tragic the apparatus of theological assumptions and values. Tragedians, from Aeschylus to Beckett, have been "doctors of divinity," even where their stance is antinomian or in denial. This is demonstrated, at a dramaturgical level, by their enlistment of the super- or preternatural. The role of the deities in Greek and Roman tragic theater is of the essence. The Weird Sisters in *Macbeth,* the Ghost in *Hamlet,* the swarm out of hell proclaimed on the heath in *Lear,* are no conventional or technical flourishes. They manifest the intrusion of mortal men and women into a spider's web of nonhuman, superhuman agents and voyeuristic watchers whose exact legitimacy and powers may be in question, but whose appalling proximity to fallen mankind is palpable. We call on "Angels and ministers of grace" to defend us, even where the ambiguities of our own theological status press on us. The summit of tragedy in English literature is Faustus's intuition, via Marlowe's speculative and philosophic genius, that a deity capable of forgiving Faustus would be a false god. The

entire reticulation of thought and feeling, of language and gesture com-
pacted in such a moment or in Hamlet's meditation on self-slaughter,
depends strictly and necessarily on theological prerequisites. Though in
some degree internalized and astutely "off-stage," these are operative in
the crystalline clarities of Racine. The horrors of Hippolyte's death at the
hands of Neptune are narrated; this only accentuates the proximity of
the inhuman.

The ebbing of this cardinal dimension and its historical recession from
immediacies of acceptance and of reference are a complicated story. Calvinist predestination, the seemingly inexplicable lottery of programmed
damnation, is a late variant on ancient fatalism. As this reading of fallen
humanity's condition decays into libertarian enlightenment, into the
politics of hope expounded by secular messianism (socialism, the American promise), so does tragic drama in any stringent sense. The redemptive, profoundly sentimental coda to Goethe's *Faust II* may conveniently
date the abstention from, the repudiation of the metaphysics and theology of tragedy as these had been articulated and "bodied forth" since
the fall of Troy. With few exceptions, "tragedy" after Goethe perpetuates
itself in prose fiction, in opera, in film, in reportage. The dissemination
of pressure takes us from a Grünwald Crucifixion, steeped in the heresy
of despair, to a mythological spectacle by, say, Tiepolo, whose aesthetics
are already brilliantly and reassuringly cinematic.

This raises the difficult question whether atheist tragedy is possible.
Again, one needs to discriminate. Among past masters, *professed* atheists,
such as Leopardi or Shelley, are exceedingly rare. Social constraints and
religious despotism made public atheism precarious if not suicidal. But
the grounds for a presence and presentment of the divine in western art,
music, and literature lie much deeper. If western painting and sculpture,
if western music are, as it were, "saturated" by religious occasions and
motifs, the reason is that of a fundamental dialectic. The aesthetic act of
creation (I have tried to show this in *Grammars of Creation*) is experienced
either as a *mimesis,* an *imitation* of the divine *fiat* or as a challenge to it.
These two impulses, imitation and challenge, are often inseparable. For
Tolstoi, at the pitch of creativity God is the jealous bear waiting to wrestle with him in the forest. To Picasso, he is the rival master in the next
room. The music of Bach, that of Schoenberg, is God-possessed. Wittgenstein spoke for countless artists, writers, thinkers when he said that
had he been able to he would "have dedicated to God" his *Philosophical
Investigations.* What other true critic and complete reader have we? asked

Coleridge and Gerard Manley Hopkins after him. D. H. Lawrence spoke of being consumed in God's fire when writing.

Engagements with the eventuality of God can generate reflexes and intonations of the most diverse kind: rage, ecstasy, irony, despair, self-surrender. The plays of Euripides ironize divine intervention, arguing the malignity or even impotence of deities whose ethical perceptions, whose intellectual insights, have begun to lag behind those of *homo sapiens*. *Lear* not only states the likelihood that the gods (God) treat men and women with infantile sadism—"like wanton boys they kill us for their sport"—but that the justified questioning of human beings in innocent agony (Job)—"Why should a dog, a horse, a rat have life? And thou no breath at all?"—is doomed to remain unanswered. Blasphemy, a fundamentally religious mode, characterizes key motions in Jacobean drama that inherit the art of Marlowe. Blasphemy is spelt out in the long-suppressed exchange between Molière's Don Juan and the beggar. Kleist's *Amphytrion* achieves a rare, delicate equilibrium between fury against divine guile and capriciousness on the one hand and a deep apprehension of supernatural mystery on the other. Shelley's *Prometheus* and *Cenci* press claims of human justice, of compassion, of reason against the arbitrary tyranny of the gods and the hypocritical despotism of religious institutions. The *Cenci,* in particular, come closest in our literature to being what Tourneur had entitled *An Atheist's Tragedy:* "Beatrice shall, if there be skill in hate / Die in despair, blaspheming." Yet however bitter the dramatist's dissent from faith, however flagrant his refusal of grace, be it in Aeschylus' *Seven Against Thebes,* in Byron's *Manfred,* or in Artaud's *reprise* of Shelley, the matrix of meaning and of references is theistic. The proximity, the (malevolent) relevance of the divine is manifestly inferred.

So let me ask again: is an atheist tragedy in any strict sense, a tragic vision of the world from which the possibility of God (or the gods) has been excised, feasible?

There is so very little to go on. Where the question of God is an archaic irrelevance, the cardinal axiom of human estrangement from at-home-ness in this world, the dialectic of enmity between human fate and some enigma of culpability at the outset, loses hold. Conflict, whether ideological or social, whether public or familial, persists. It can be of the utmost violence and sorrow. Domestic hatred howls in Strindberg's dramas, in the dynastic and biblical collisions in Racine. Victimization and massacre smolder in the backdrop to Brecht's didactic allegories. But where the issues are secular, where psychological or social melioration and therapy are conceivable, the fundamental construct, however anguishing, is that of "melodrama." Verdi's perplexities over his *Othello*—in certain respects a more coherent, persuasive work than Shakespeare's—make the point. The agnosticism at the core of Iago's "motiveless" sadism struck him as factitious. Hence Verdi and Boito's composition of Iago's *credo,* of the shattering homage to an evil deity.

Repeatedly in Shakespeare, whether on stage or by clear inference and invocation, the fifth act borders on redemption, on a recuperative dawn after the tragic night. Scotland will blossom after Macbeth's death, Cassio's régime will benefit Cyprus, Fortinbras looks to be a sounder ruler than Hamlet would have been. Goethe's errant Faust is gloriously absolved. Are there, then, any plays totally secular, located in a world wholly immanent, yet "tragic" in some essential regard?

Büchner's *Woyzeck* is a singularity of genius. It transpires in a world of which God, if ever He was, is unaware. There is not, as in much great literature, the intimation of a *deus absconditus,* of the "God-abandoned." Such absence yields a potent negative theology itself metaphoric of the tragic. The zero-world in which Woyzeck totters to extinction, in which his deranged tormentors strut, in which children play in a raucous emptiness, is end-stopped at every point. It is an aggregate of suffocation made the more hermetic by the macabre superstitions to which its agents are prey, by Büchner's suggestion that even inorganic matter is hostile to man. Thus the "God-question" does not and cannot arise. Yet the logic of tragic annihilation, of the blank guilt of existence, is coherent and formidably moving.

When "God" is invoked at the close of Yeats's bleak miniature, *Purgatory,* this invocation is made a perfunctory cliché. The irrelevance of God to the dramatic action is complete. It is Yeats's art to adumbrate the supernatural possibilities trapped inside nature, to infer a ghostliness the more maddening because it is altogether psychological:

> The moonlight falls upon the path,
> The shadow of a cloud upon the house.
> And that's symbolical; study that tree,
> What is it like?

To which the sole answer is "no matter what it's like." Symbolism refuses any validation beyond itself. Analogy is, as in the asceticism of Wittgenstein's *Tractatus,* evasion. It is precisely these two rhetorical moves, the symbolic and the analogous, which postulate, which are re-insured by, transcendence. In Yeats, as in Büchner, immanence is vengeful, deriding the vulgar reflex of outward, solacing reference.

Every facet of the question of whether rigorously secular tragedy is possible, of whether "tragedy" is applicable, in any strict sense, to an action and context purged of God, is set out in the plays and parables of Beckett. His language(s) is permeated by scriptural and liturgical reminiscences (*Endgame* turns on the hammer and nails of the Crucifixion). The theological recedes from Beckett's world as does light from a dying star. But the ground-bass, if one can put it that way, is in almost every instance the posing of our question. Beckett asks whether serious drama, whether signifying dialogue (with whom, with what?) is feasible after God. This posterity is at once more diffuse and more ironic than that of Nietzsche's trope. Beckett intimates that He may never have been, and that this refusal to be is irreparably tragic. "He doesn't exist, the bastard." The phrasing is incomparable in its laconic duplicity. The "bastard" does not exist; or, in that nonexistence, malign beyond words, lies the evil and ostracism of man's condition.

Waiting for Godot could not, I believe, have been written without *Purgatory*. Its setting, intonations, and crowded emptiness expand on Yeats's nightmare. With time, it may well be that Beckett's plays (experiments), from *Godot* to the scream of nullity and closing silence of the last parables, will be recognized as the transition into post-metaphysical, post-metaphoric modes. Once Vladimir and Estragon have rung hollow changes on the keywords "illusion" and "hallucination," tragedy, as we have known it since Aeschylus, is of the past.

Absolute or "high" tragedy and its manifold approximations evolved in an ideological and social context. However dissociated from the contingencies and mercies of common daylight, tragedy is never politically value-free. Its decline was concomitant with the democratization of western ideals, with the eclipse of imperative destiny in the power relations between mortals and the supernatural, between men and women and the state. From Aeschylus to Shakespeare, from Sophocles to Racine, high tragedy engages the (mis)fortunes of the privileged, of the princely, of a dynastic elite. The very rubric "tragedy" in its Senecan and medieval demarcation is that of "the fall of illustrious men." Tragedy argues an aristocracy of suffering, an excellence of pain. The point needs to be made accurately. It has nothing to do with social snobbery, with hazard, with fortuitous circumstances of priestly or regal or titled patronage, as pseudo-Marxist chatter would have it. The motives are of the essence.

In its Attic matrix, the seminal myths which underlie tragic drama, notably the Homeric substratum and that of other epic cycles, are peopled by gods and semi-gods, by monarchs, by princely heroes. Theirs are the foundational narratives and exemplary catastrophes. So they are in Shakespearean tragedy and in the courtly sphere of French neoclassicism. These dark happenings are informed by the intuition, more radical than any political prejudice or fastidiousness of spirit, that fate—the gods, an oracular or ancestral malediction, overreaching ambition, madness in a major key—selects for its victims *personae* of condign stature. As René Char majestically put it: "midnight is not in everyman's reach." Obviously all human beings, however humble their condition, however helpless their social milieu, are subject to terror, to injustice, to inexplicable agony. Nothing is louder, if unheard, throughout history than the howl, so often gagged or violently silenced, of the oppressed. Even salesmen undergo heart-rending deaths. The discrimination lies deeper.

In classical mythology, in Renaissance scenarios of history, eminence and the temptations to which it is prone are to the gods, to daemonic agencies on the heath, as is the scent of blood to a shark. As men and women draw closer to the divine, in Hölderlin's reading, that very proximity engenders unbearable tensions, jealousies which have the unforgiving wildness of love. Eminent human beings, says Hölderlin, stand out like lightning rods whom Olympian bolts both irradiate and scorch. When they exercise dominion over matters of state, when they seek to bend history to their will, as do Shakespeare's or Sophocles' protagonists, that in life itself which is envious of man "answers back," fatally. The Promethean impulse in us is at once ineradicable and doomed. Thus Hades itself attends on the self-destruction of Racine's Phèdre, and the universe momentarily holds its breath at the desolation of Bérénice.

Pace the claims of egalitarianism, of "political correctness" (which Lenin would have termed an "infantile disorder"), the perception of the metaphysical, of the agonistic relation to being as these are made explicit and functional in tragedy, is not given to everyman. *N'est pas minuit qui veut* (Char). Tragic experience is a menacing vocation, dying in the tragic vein, as Sylvia Plath proudly confessed, an art. It is not only that the tragic agent enacts his or her vulnerability to the inhuman, to forces transcending his or her control and understanding. He internalizes this paradoxical privilege, making of it a conceptual, self-divisive process. He or she is simultaneously actor and spectator, a duality spelt out in the conceit, ancient as tragic drama itself, of human existence as theatre. Rightly or wrongly, this pitch of self-awareness, of introspective dramatization within an arena of metaphysical forces, came to be ascribed to towering, exceptional personages, to Cassandra, to Orestes, to Ajax, to Hamlet the Dane—to "literate" spirits in the root-sense, difficult to paraphrase, of literacy of consciousness. Social status, a representative role in the community being, in ancient Greece, in Elizabethan-Jacobean England, in the Europe of the *ancient régime,* a virtually self-evident, unexamined correlative.

This literacy generates the idiom, dare one say "idiolect," particular to tragedy. The resort to complex, meta-musical verse forms and a modified epic vocabulary in Aeschylus, Sophocles, and Euripides is no technical accident or auxiliary. It is primary. The discourse of gods and furies, of sovereigns and heroes, is that of a grammar and cadence under extreme upward pressure. Its formal elevation, its prodigal economy, its metaphoric reach tell of a conflictual world, of an often fatal dialectic (dialogue) removed from the waste motions, from the hybrid tonalities, from the hit-and-miss unbending of the vulgate. There are rare, though inspired, patches of prose in midst Shakespearean tragic drama; there is the ominous moment of prose in Goethe's *Faust I.* But the Elizabethan norm is that of the iambic pentameter and its variants. Racine's alexandrines, the incisive symmetry of his (and Corneille's) couplets, constitute a metaphysic of reasoned enclosure and a theory of history and society. The almost incredible sparsity of Racine's lexical means—they amount to roughly one tenth of Shakespeare's—empower a rhetoric of understatement, the Tacitean *litote,* which edge tragedy to the calculated threshold of silence. The tragic counterstatement to Christian guarantees of remission and salvation, as we hear it in the Jansenism of Pascal and Racine, looks to silence. In all these cases, loftiness, complexity, concentration of speech define a tragic vision, a face-to-face encounter with the "greater than man" whose "casting" as in a "cast" of characters, is, again, socially hierarchic. It will not be until *Woyzeck* that lower-class speech, that inarticulacy, articulates the terror and the pity of tragedy. Büchner makes emotions *prosaic* so as to declare a world, a human circumstance, empty of God. Wherever literature attempts to resuscitate high tragedy, in Ibsen's *Brand,* in the orientalizing formalities of Yeats, in T. S. Eliot's *Murder in the Cathedral* and *Family Reunion,* the instrument is that of verse. This is not how common men and women express themselves. Tragic discourse characterizes the few: Seneca's *pauci, aliqui tamen.*

Given these enabling constraints, absolute or high tragedy, as I have sought to define it, is rare. Moreover, consider the psychological cost, the taxation of sensibility. Here is a performative statement of man's unhousedness in the world (*apolis*), of an elemental, non-negotiable enmity between being and existence. Here is an exposition of the belief that it is best not to be born. Absolute tragedy presents men and women whom the gods torture and kill "for their sport," for whom there is no intercession with compensatory justice (whereas Job's flocks are doubled after his trial). Negation is paramount, the "never" in *Lear* being reiterated five times. Nothing but suffering and injustice comes of nothing. In high tragedy, nullity devours as does a black hole. If the cruel visitation of life is inflicted on us, the logic of deliverance can only be that of suicide. How is one to endure this proposition, let alone derive from it aesthetic satisfaction? (Thinkers from Aristotle to Freud have looked for an answer, trying to contravene Plato's prohibition of tragic drama. But their hypotheses remain tentative.) It is not surprising, therefore, that there are few absolute tragedies. What is surprising is that they have been composed and performed at all and that they contain some of the finest poetry and most acute philosophic, psychological insights accessible to the human mind.

The Greek precedent is at once paradigmatic and opaque. Only one trilogy, Aeschylus' *Oresteia,* has come down to us. This makes any evaluation of the intent and impact of all other tragedies hazardous. We simply do not know whether the missing plays would have mitigated or amended the presentment of catastrophe (indeed, did most trilogies dramatize the same mythical ensemble?). In the absence, furthermore, of the satyr plays which served as epilogue to the tragic triad, we cannot judge whether some parodistic counterpoint brought cathartic relief and laughter. With what feelings and vision of things did the audience leave the theater of Dionysus? It is, in consequence, on a provisional basis that one can assign certain titles to the catalogue of absolute tragedy.

Among these are Aeschylus' *Seven Against Thebes;* Sophocles' *Ajax* with its meditation on suicide and his *Antigone* with its descent into live burial (a motif which both Hegel and Kierkegaard regarded as emblematic of tragedy). Aristotle and Goethe took Euripides to be "the most tragic of tragedians," the most despairing. Euripides dwells on divine malignity, on the sadism which daemonic and godly forces unleash upon human beings when these are, by any rational moral estimate, not at fault or only partly so. Hence the horrors perpetrated in *Medea,* in *Hecuba,* in *The Trojan Women,* in *Hippolytus,* in *Heracles,* and the possibly fragmented *Phoenician Women.* Hence, above all, the dark miracle, both theatrically and poetically, of the *Bacchae.* Had we nothing but that play, perhaps the last in the Attic repertoire, we would know of absolute tragedy. Somewhat eerily, the closing scene has survived only in mutilated form. Points of detail are blurred by *lacunae*. But the commanding motion is clear: confronted by human claims to justice, by human pleas for compassion, the incensed deity is bereft of argument. He retreats from one petulant response to the next. The atrocities, the injustice inflicted on the *polis* and its inhabitants are arbitrary, madly disproportionate. They emanate from inexplicable, blind destiny. The gods and the fabric of the world lash out against man and deride his claims to rationality: "Long ago, my father Zeus ordained these things." Or as a guard reportedly said to an inmate dying of thirst in one of the death camps: "Why do you ask for a reason? There is no 'why' here."

As Dr. Johnson reminds us, tragedy is not natural to Shakespeare. The tragic-comic weave of our world, its refusal to be only one thing at one time, possessed his panoptic genius. His immensity is as pluralistic as is human experience itself. Shakespeare knew that there is a revel in the basement or neighboring house at the moment when monarchs murder, that a child is being born in the hour of Hamlet's death. No less than Goethe, Shakespeare flinches from simplifications, from the monotone of the absolutely tragic. I have pointed to the political upbeat which concludes *Macbeth, Othello, Hamlet.* Even in *Lear,* the finale is enigmatically ambiguous. One need not impose a Christian gloss to detect the hints of redemption or repair.

So far as I can make out, we have only one Shakespearean text, almost certainly written in collaboration with Thomas Middleton, which is uncompromisingly tragic: it is that erratic, volcanic bloc, *Timon of Athens.* Here the universe itself is made pestilential; the sun breeds infection; generation is a curse arising out of diseased sex. Murder and betrayal are wasteful anticipations of suicide. Life is "a long sickness" cured solely by death. The decisive move comes at the close. Timon will see to it that his epitaph is made oblivion by the wash of the sea. Of all minds of which we have record, Shakespeare's was the most saturated by words, by all-encompassing syntax. Now Timon proclaims: let "language end." Which, for Shakespeare, is to say, and to say this one time only, "let the cosmos end in mute despair." As it did in the *Bacchae* when human beings are transformed into speechless beasts.

Christianity made total tragedy implausible. Whatever the sorrow or transient injustice, there is, as Milton put it, "no time for lamentation now." The fall of man, pivotal to absolute tragedy, is a *felix culpa,* a necessary prologue to salvation. Goethe's *Faust II* ends by celebrating the Christian contract with hope, its investment in absolution. Goethe's is a

41

reply to Marlowe's *Faustus,* one of the very few tragedies to defy Christo-logical optimism. Marlowe's tremendous intuition that a God capable of pardoning Faustus is not a God whom a free spirit can take seriously, let alone worship, leads to hell and everlasting torment. The reasoned black-ness of Marlowe's dramaturgy, its philosophic dialectic, are profoundly non-Shakespearean. Shakespeare skates the abyss; Marlowe enters it. As does God-denying Shelley in *The Cenci,* an indictment of religious hy-pocrisy, a mapping of gratuitous horror the ironic paths of whose end—Beatrice's "Well, 'tis very well"—comes near to being unbearable. Here, indeed, was "a light to make apparent some of the most dark and secret caverns of the human heart."

Two grim conjectures underwrote Racine's construction of pure trag-edy in what was, after all, an age of post-Cartesian rationality. The first was the Jansenist doubt as to the comforts and therapeutic promises of orthodox Catholicism, the apprehension, voiced by Pascal, that "Christ would be in agony until the end of time." The second was the implacable hypothesis whereby men and women, guilty, damned prior to the com-ing of Christ into our world (a temporality which remains unfathomably "unfair"), would suffer eternity in hell. This supposition ascribed to the *personae* of classic mythology their exceptional doom: Phèdre bears wit-ness:

> Fuyons dans la nuit infernale.
> Mais que dis-je? Mon père y tient l'urne fatale;
> Le sort, dit-on, l'a mise en ses sévères mains:
> Minos juge aux enfers tous les pales humains.
> [Let us flee into hellish night.
> What am I saying? My father holds the fatal urn;
> Fate, they say, has placed it in his severe hands;
> Minos judges in Hades all pallid humans.]

It is an abstention from all outward violence which makes of *Bérénice* what may well be the apex of high tragedy. In this miraculously "composed"—in both senses of the word—and adult drama, there is no thunder on the heath, there are no supernatural apparitions or bloody alarms. The underlying pulse-beat is that of silence: *Lorsque Rome se tait.* The tranquil door to despair, to unendurable and irremediable hurt, is that of valedic-tion. Of the parting from each other and forever of two human beings in overwhelming love. The enforcement of this *adieu*—this word, of course, has "God" embedded in it—banishes life from further meaning. Claudel will make us re-experience the immensity of such farewell in *Le Partage de Midi.* One wonders whether it is the arrogance of understatement, in some ways kindred to Japanese codes of ceremonial suffering, which has made English-language access to Racine so fitful. Even in *Othello,* there is a clown.

Few absolute tragedies after Racine and Büchner. Or variations on previous themes, as in Pinter's fierce readings of *Lear* in *Homecoming,* in O'Neill's and Sartre's reversions to *Oresteia,* or in Athol Fugard's "Antigone" (*The Island*).

The enormity of history after 1914 is self-evident. Historians put at hundreds of millions the sum of those done to death in wars, political and racial slaughter, deportation, famines, concentration camps. There are no certain figures as to the tens of millions murdered by Leninism-Stalinism, by Maoism, and their derivatives. Anywhere between thirty- and fifty-thousand human beings were incinerated in one night in the fire-raids on Hamburg, Dresden, on Tokyo. Nuclear and bacteriological weapons have been used. Across the planet, torture is endemic and officially sanctioned. Arguably the threshold of our humanity, of that which elevated us above the bestial, has been irreparably lowered.

The arts have done their sporadic best to respond. Painters and sculptors have striven to remember effectively: via Picasso's *Guernica* or Giacometti's figures of the living dead. Shostakovitch's quartets and symphonies bear grave witness. Poetry can cite Paul Celan, prose can point to Primo Levi and Chalamov's tales of the Kolyma death-world. With the discretion of the oblique, a number of novels have attempted to imagine the unimaginable, although none has matched Kafka's previsions. Of available media, it is film, both fictive and documentary, which has come nearest. The graphic immediacy of the camera, its free play with time, the resources of montage and collage, relate to the otherwise inconceivable and pulverized as does no other executive form (cf. *Shoah*). Whether the tidal wave of sadistic pornography, of pedophilic images, which now engulfs our visual media reflects a new numbing of sensibility, whether it is the voyeuristic satyr play after the "killing fields," is an unnerving question. What Quine would call "blameless intuition" does suggest that this is so. But what would be conclusive evidence?

It is virtually indecent to envisage high tragedy engaging recent and current events as Greek tragedy engaged the Persian wars or the massacre at Miletus. We distrust the truths of eloquence. Who now shares T. S. Eliot's melancholy conviction that verse drama is the natural, legitimate format of conflict and concentrated sensibility? The aesthetics of conceptual art, the semen on the bedsheet, the creed of the happening, of

43

Merz or the ready-made—reflecting as they do the collapse of agreed values and developing the parodistic genius of Surrealism—are antithetical to high tragedy. Our immediacies are those of derision, of black farce, of the multimedia circus. At some moments of political social crisis, tragedy in its classical mask still provides a shorthand: as the *Trojan Women* did during the Vietnam war, as the *Bacchae* served during the turmoil of the drug-culture and flower children. But these are loans from the museum.

Our anguish, our sense, deep as ever but immanent and psychologized, of a threatening "otherness" in the world, of our exposure to irrational, malevolent misfortune, will persist. But it will find new expressive forms growing, as they already have, out of *Woyzeck,* out of *Godot* and the theater of the absurd. Desiderated: an adequate theory of comedy, of the riddles of grief, singular to man, in the merriment of *Twelfth Night* or the finales of Mozart's *Così fan tutte.* There are hints towards such an understanding at the midnight hour of Plato's *Symposium.*

As is, I see not persuasive grounds on which to retract the case put in *The Death of Tragedy,* 1961 (now, if I may be forgiven for saying so, in its seventeenth language).

Generalizing About Tragedy

Simon Goldhill

Personam tragicam forte vulpes viderat:
quam postquam huc illuc semel atque iterum verterat
"O quanta species," inquit, "cerebrum non habet."
A fox once saw an actor's tragic mask:
He turned it this way and that, once and again.
"What an amazing sight!" he said, "but it's got no brain."

Phaedrus, Fables of Aesop

The long tradition of Western writing about tragedy might make it seem natural for critics and artists to reach toward an abstract and general concept of "the tragic" in their discussions of dramatic literature or of the structured comprehension of the pain and turmoil of the world. Defining "tragedy itself" has become a shared and competitive game (with Schelling, Hegel, Nietzsche, Kierkegaard, Jaspers, and many others as its key players). The lure of seeking such a general and abstract understanding is evident, especially for nineteenth-century German thought and its heirs today. But, as ever, what seems natural has a full cultural history behind it. A broad or more narrowly circumscribed intellectual history can, of course, be written for each of these searches for the tragic essence. Nietzsche's construction of the tragic, for example, has been analyzed within his own growing philosophical thought, within his reading of his predecessors, and as an influence on later writers.[1] But in this chapter I am interested in taking a different tack toward a cultural history of the idea of "the tragic." I explore the prior question of what it might mean to appeal in this way to "the tragic" as an abstract concept: that is, what are the implications and costs of generalizing about tragedy? This chapter explores not only what is at stake in the hypostatization of "the tragic" but also how a more nuanced sense of the exemplary can be traced from within Greek tragedies themselves.

There is a repeated pattern of rhetoric in claims to recognize the truly tragic. It is a familiar and rather easy commonplace to dismiss the modern journalistic love of the term "tragic" as a trivialization, used as it is for any upsetting event from the broken bone in a footballer's foot to

45

the natural disaster of the tsunami. This critical rejection of the journalists' promiscuous recognition of tragedy is part and parcel of an attempt to reserve the vocabulary of "the tragic" not just to denote the grandest genre of the Western theatrical tradition but also to describe and to privilege a particular sense of the human condition: a suffering that sets man against the otherness of the world, "call it what you will: a hidden or malevolent God, blind fate, the solicitations of hell, or the brute fury of our animal blood."[2] Generalizing about the tragic is one strategy for introducing a hierarchy into perceptions of human suffering—downplaying your mundane misery in the name of my truly tragic.

The rhetorical exclusion of the not-really-tragic has deep intellectual underpinnings. One crucial frame for this hierarchizing of tragic experience is Christianity's revalorization of the discourse of suffering [*pathos/ passio*] through the passion of Christ and the martyrdom of his saints. In Christianity, suffering evokes a fully theological perception of the world and of man's place in it, as well as an understanding of the body and spirituality. When suffering becomes so charged a term, there is inevitably a great deal at stake in how pain or misery is narrativized (and valued), and thus policing the tragic becomes in turn far more than a philological nicety. Nationalism in the nineteenth and twentieth centuries (and beyond) also feeds repeatedly on a narrative of the suffering of the people— or, more precisely, on the claim of a specific and special tragic suffering of a particular people—just as bourgeois identity politics so often locates authority in a tale of a group's or an individual's personal suffering. A recognition of "real pain," "genuine suffering," becomes a political self-justification, where all too often the claim to tragedy—the tragedy of the rape victim, the tragedy of illness, the tragedy of the Palestinian people—is an attempt to arrogate an unimpeachable status. There is a politics in defining tragedy that aesthetic arguments about "the tragic" have tended to repress. The rhetoric of suffering is always a weapon in the contests of justice.

The ancient use of the term *tragikos* has a different rhetorical force and quite different intellectual underpinnings. *Tragikos* is used in ancient Greek (first of all) as floppily as "tragic" is in modern journalism. It is used, of course, in a technical sense (as it is in modern English) to apply to any aspect of the dramatic performances of the festival of the Great Dionysia in Athens: "tragic stage," "tragic mask," "tragic costume," and so forth. But when Plato's Socrates refers to "tragic talk" [*tragikôs legein*], "speaking in a tragic manner," he indicates a language that is grander and more pompous than usual.[3] It implies nothing about suffering, but a sense of the majestic or stately. This can be a source of humor, and making fun of tragedy's grandeur is a staple of Aristophanic comedy. In the mouth of the Platonic Socrates, "tragic" marks a wry self-recognition that his language is getting a little overheated. So Aristotle's celebrated definition of tragedy includes the stipulation that tragedy should be expressed "in language which is embellished" (*Poetics* 6.2). A heightened language is integral to tragedy in this definition. In a similar way, many centuries later the Greek novelists reserved the terms "dramatic," "theatrical," and "tragic," for scenes of heightened emotion, usually the conflicting feelings of the novel's characters at some surprising denouement—or for the rhetoric of grief, which some disaster calls forth from the protagonists, highly educated as they are in the formal arts of rhetoric. "The tragic" here implies little more than the grandly poetic and emotional, garlanded with the literary prestige of the classical.[4]

When Aristotle in the *Poetics* calls Euripides "the most tragic" of playwrights [*tragikôtatos*] (13.10), it is therefore difficult to tell how hard the term is to be pressed. At the most basic level, it indicates that Euripides is the poet who produces in his audience the deepest feelings of pity and fear: he is especially emotive. There may be a further implication that Euripides is particularly good at constructing a narrative that ends in extreme and unmitigated misfortune (though Aristotle himself seems to prefer a pattern in which a character is led toward a familial murder that is avoided at the last). But Aristotle also uses the term *tragikos* much as other writers do. He dismisses some metaphors as being "too grand and tragic" for good oratory (*Rhet.* 3.3.4). Even in the *Poetics* his use of "tragic" does not seem to imply a closely defined or theoretically rigorous category. So, when he criticizes the plot device that leads a character knowingly to commit an act of violence against someone who is known, but then retreats from the violence, he explains (14.7) that "this is repulsive and not tragic [*miaron . . . ou tragikon*]: for it lacks suffering" [*apathes*]. The "not tragic" is glossed as that which "lacks suffering," because nobody is the victim of violence and even the violent emotions are held in check. It does not seem to imply a worldview or a metaphysics. In a similar way, the plot that brings a good man into adversity is said (13.2) to be "neither pitiful nor fearful, but repulsive" [*miaron*], just as the "most untragic" [*atragikotaton*] plot, that of a bad man reaching prosperity, is untragic precisely because it is "neither moving, nor pitiful nor fearful." The tragic is linked to the emotional registers of "pity and fear," and Aristotle wants to avoid the "repulsive" but "shows no inclination to enlarge the experience of pity and fear from tragedy into anything resembling a world view."[5] Indeed, Stephen Halliwell persuasively denies that we should be "moving towards a formulation of what Ar[istotle] considered to be the essence of 'the tragic,' taken as a complete vision or experience of at least one face of reality . . . Such an expansion of the idea of tragedy has no place in the *Poetics*."[6]

Aristotle does offer in his typical style an opening and famous definition of tragedy—"the representation of an action which is serious, complete and of a certain magnitude—in language which is embellished in various forms in its different parts—in the mode of dramatic enactment, not narrative—and through the arousal of pity and fear effecting the *katharsis* of such emotions" (6.2). But this is a formalistic definition of the dramatic form *tragoidia:* it indicates that tragedy is drama (an enactment rather than just a storytelling); that its language is heightened (by which he also means it includes song and other lyric poetry, as well as that its diction is grander than usual speech); that it takes as subject matter something that is not flippant, funny, or trivial; that it causes emotional responses in an audience and that such responses have a psychological effect (to offer as neutral as possible a version of *katharsis,* which I will not translate here).[7] Pity and fear are the primary emotions of tragedy, and this is borne out in the comments I have already cited above. It is important that Aristotle does not here mention *pathos,*[8] and at no point in the definition does he give any indication that his definition of tragedy is extendable from the dramatic form to a view of the world or that a view of the world is inherent in or integral to tragic form.

Plato stretches the language of tragedy more than any other Greek writer.[9] In the *Philebus* (50b1–4) Socrates says that "pleasure and pain are mixed not just in drama but also in the whole tragedy and comedy of life." This is the first example in extant literature of the now familiar cliché of life as a tragedy (or comedy). But it is worth noting that this bold metaphor does not specify at all what the tragedy or comedy of life might consist in, beyond a mix of pleasure and pain,[10] and the language is motivated by the immediate context of the discussion of the strange mix of pleasure and pain in drama. Similarly, when the Guardians of the Republic dismiss the tragedians from the *polis,* they say that "we aspire to be the makers of the best tragedy, because our whole constitution [*politeia*] is constructed as a *mimesis* of the finest and best life—which is what *we* count as the finest tragedy" (*Rep.* 7.817b1–8). The Guardians are explicitly in competition with the tragedians, and hence they appropriate the language of tragedy—rather strangely—for their constitution. (It is strange since there appears to be no sense of suffering or misery in the perfect constitution.) This has sometimes been taken to imply that the philosophical worldview is different from the tragic worldview, though it does not progress beyond bald dismissal at this point in Plato's argument.

The long discussion of the censorship of poetry in *Republic* 10 does go on to attack Homer and tragedy for its representation of the world, as part of Plato's establishment of philosophy as a master-discourse over and against all the authoritative languages of the city. But this general case that poetry, in philosophy's austere view, is an inadequate moral representation of the world is the closest we come in ancient Greek writing to using the language of tragedy to construct an abstract view of the world, and even here what is at stake for Plato (apart from the attack on poetry's mimesis) is the failure of poetry to encourage a proper, philosophical self-control [*sophrosune*].[11] Far from introducing a privileged notion of human suffering, Plato dismisses the pathos of tragedy as undignified at best, and at worst as morally corrupting for indulging lazy and destructive emotionality.

In ancient Greek, then, you simply can't say "this event was truly tragic" in order to authorize one form of suffering over any other. The difference from modern usage is striking and significant.

Aristotle's *Poetics,* in short, is a theory of tragedies, not a theory of the tragic. It moves in typical Aristotelian manner from examples toward a general model and puts the general model in a teleological and hierarchical structure, as Aristotle does elsewhere with parts of animals or constitutions of city-states. Tragedy as a form culminates in Sophocles' *Oedipus Tyrannus* and declines through Aristotle's own era, the fourth century. This history remains formal: tragedy declines in its use of character and the chorus, as earlier tragedians had excelled in these aspects of the dramatic art. Aristotle throughout the *Poetics* is in debate with his master, Plato, most obviously in his support for the beneficial educational value of the emotional impact of tragedy. Aristotle's refusal to see tragedy and its conflicts as a threat to the order of philosophy is perhaps the deepest level of his opposition to the Platonic project. As Aristotle defines tragedy, there is no reason to ban it from the city.

Nonetheless, Aristotle is repeatedly taken as the father of the tragic as theoretical abstraction.[12] The complexity of the process by which Aristotle became such an authority after the Renaissance precludes any attempt at a full history here. Terence Cave's magisterial *Recognitions* focuses on one term from the *Poetics, anagnorisis,* and traces its construction in largely seventeenth- and eighteenth-century theoretical manuals, as well as in recognition scenes in drama and other literature.[13] It also treats contemporary theoretical approaches. To discuss the inheritance of even the less scandalous terms of Aristotle's treatise, let alone the whole thesis of the *Poetics,* would require a study of a truly monumental scale. All I wish to do here is to point toward two particular interrelated strands of eighteenth- and nineteenth-century thinking which will help frame my argument about the move toward generalization in discussions of the tragic.

The first concerns the huge influence of Kant and especially the aesthetics of the *Critique of Judgement.* In recent years the third Critique has increasingly been seen as central to Kant's thinking, and Kant's aesthetics has become an intensely debated area.[14] I want here merely to note that the four basic "moments" of the third Critique stand behind a good deal of how Greek tragedy has been thought of as an art object, and, in particular, how a response to a tragedy is formulated as a response to "the tragic." It should be clear that my concern is not with the difficulties or precisions of Kant's argumentation but with the diffuse and sometimes indirect (and even incoherent) influence of Kantian thinking on the criticism of Greek tragedy.[15]

The principle of "disinterestedness," when it is taken to imply a separation from an interest in the good, demands not only a response to form above all but also a rejection of a concern with the political—and, indeed, a rejection of an audience's conflicted engagement with conflicting moral debate in their response to beauty. Judgment should be "universal" and "purposive without purpose" (that is, should attempt to abstract itself from knowledge of the purpose of production) and "necessary"; and this in turn constitutes how the object of studious attention is conceptualized—at least that is how Kant was often read during the nineteenth century (although much modern criticism has worked to break down such barriers between the political, the moral, and the aesthetic in Kant's thinking).[16] The sublimity of tragedy transports its readers into a disinterested contemplation of the universal, the necessary, and the purposive without purpose. That is the power of "the tragic." The abstract and general concept of the tragic allows the Kantian subject to view Greek tragedy as a privileged aesthetic object.

Schelling, whose model of the tragic resonated through nineteenth-century critical language, read and discussed Kant in the 1790s with his student friends Hegel and Hölderlin. His writing demonstrates the Kantian pull on the criticism of tragedy perfectly: "the study of Greek poetry . . . is and always will be the necessary duty . . . of all experts who want to arrive at universal judgements, and of all thinkers who seek to define once and for all the pure laws of beauty and the eternal nature of art."[17] Schelling's language is completely imbued here with Kantian vocabulary and argument. For Schelling, the study of Greek is the necessary duty of those want to fulfill the Kantian ideals of aesthetic judgment. Hegel may have seen Antigone as emblematic of the historically defined moment of "the Greek spirit," and his reading of the play certainly shows how deeply intertwined politics and aesthetics remained. But even as Hegel differs in his aesthetics in this way from Kant, he too strove to construct a universalizing view of *the* family and of *the* state as abstract and general principles—a philosophy of the tragic.

The second strand of eighteenth- and nineteenth-century thought follows on directly from Schelling's Kantianism and concerns Romantic philhellenism and its particular investment in the perfection of Greek art.[18] The tyranny of Greece over the European imagination develops a specific rhetoric of art, a rhetoric for which Winckelmann is integral to the plastic arts, along with Lessing, and for which Hegel, Schelling, and Schlegel have a major impact on the language of literary criticism. In all spheres of the arts, there is an extraordinary emphasis on what Ernest Renan called *"beauté éternelle, sans nulle tâche locale ou nationale"* (an eternal beauty with no stain of the local or the national).[19] Greek art and literature are repeatedly praised as being timeless (as Hofmannsthal wrote of Antigone, "Dies strahlende Geschöpf ist keines Tages!" [This glorious creature belongs to no given time!]).[20] Greek culture speaks across the ages to contemporary artists because it is not limited by the time of its production. It is ageless. Because it is divorced from any sordid or trivial engagement with the mundane, it escapes from the accusation of being tied to the local. Because it is not marked by the disturbing politics of nationalism, it is universal. Greek art epitomizes the transcendental and the sublime and is the standard by which modern art is judged (and judged to fall short): that is what "classic" means.

It is hard for nineteenth-century critics to escape from this framing of praise. So when Matthew Arnold suggests that "an action like the action of the Antigone of Sophocles, which turns on the conflict between the heroine's duty to her brother's corpse and that to the laws of her country, is no longer one in which it is possible that we should feel a deep interest," his worry is aimed precisely at the criticism that the local and the national will prevent an audience from profound concern.[21] George Eliot responded by reasserting that *Antigone* encapsulates "that struggle between elemental tendencies and established laws by which the outer life of man is gradually and painfully brought into harmony with his inner needs."²² She declares that *Antigone* speaks to the "elemental," "the life of man," an abstract and general understanding of human life that precisely transcends the local and the national. It is by virtue of its appeal to the universal and the timeless that Sophocles' play is both attacked and defended.

The examples of such diction could be multiplied dozens of times from both the intellectual leaders of the nineteenth century and from the schoolbooks and journalism of the period. What should be clear even from this very truncated and inevitably oversimplified glimpse is that the prevalent view of the excellence of Greek tragedy (the Greek ideal) is deeply implicated with the Kantian project (German Idealism). Tragedy's timeless sublime engages the reader's sense of disinterestedness, the universal, the necessary, and the purposive without purpose. Tragedy is for contemplation (and the lack of regular performances certainly helped this perspective), and how the beauty of tragedy is expressed strives to embody the ideal of aesthetic judgment expounded by Kant. The difference between the Romantic construction of the tragic and the Greek view of tragedy is marked. Szondi captures the contrast nicely: "Seit Aristoteles gibt es eine Poetik der Tragödie, seit Schelling erst eine Philosophie der Tragischen" (Since Aristotle we have a poetics of tragedy, only since Schelling a philosophy of the tragic).²³

This very brief framing of the nineteenth-century construction of the idea(l) of the tragic allows us to see two different ways of answering the question of how the critical term "tragedy" is used. First, it can be a term of literary history. In this form, "tragedy" becomes a way first of all of constructing a link between Greek tragedy, the Latin tragedies of Seneca, the English tragedies of Shakespeare, the French tragedies of Racine and Corneille, the Norwegian tragedies of Ibsen, and so forth. As with any discussion of genre, this connection must recognize tacit and explicit linkages by the respective artists as well as the genealogical lines drawn by critics. Seneca translates and transforms Greek tragedy into his Stoic milieu, just as Racine and Corneille knowingly respond to both literary tradition and critical exposition of the form of tragedy in their compositions. Each of these authors works with a set of expectations formed in and by a generic history (and most would happily use the term "tragedy" on a title page). When in Seneca's *Medea* we hear *Medea fiam,* "I will become Medea" (171), a threat that is fulfilled at the point of killing her children, when Medea declares *Medea sum,* "I am Medea" (910), Seneca offers us a knowing glance back to Euripides: his readership knows the role model his character is fulfilling. When Shakespeare's Hamlet asks "What's Hecuba to him . . . ?" his reflection on grief displayed at a fiction is a self-reflexive comment on tragic drama for which the reference to Hecuba opens a significant vista back to the Greeks. Although there are innumerable proclamations of the rules of tragedy, the way in which any particular play instantiates a generic affiliation is far more complex than a simple model of law and transgression might suggest. What is at stake in determining the boundaries of the genre of tragedy, as with any such boundary dispute, involves issues of critical authority and ideology, to which we will return shortly. It is enough for the moment to note that the term "tragedy" in this first sense acts thus as a self-conscious marker of generic affiliation.

The second use of the term "tragedy," however, is to promote a particular view of man's place in the world and a particular understanding of the narratives of suffering and conflict. Nietzsche marks the strategic move clearly when he immediately glosses his approach to tragedy with "One of the cardinal questions here is that of the Greek attitude to pain."[24] Such a vision aims to link tragedies not through formal qualities or self-affiliation to a genre but through a shared sense of the order of things. Thus, what links Aeschylus to Ibsen in this account is their shared expression of "the tragic"—an attitude to pain, broadly conceived. "'Tragedy' is a dramatic representation, enactment or generation of a highly specific world-view," writes George Steiner paradigmatically, a worldview that is "summarized in the adage 'It is best not to be born, next best to die young,'" which "entails the view that human life *per se,* both ontologically and existentially, is an affliction . . . The proposition implies that men and women's presence on this earth is fundamentally absurd or unwelcome . . . that our lives are . . . a self-punishing anomaly."[25] There are, states Steiner, few tragedies that capture in full this pure and simple sense of the tragic, but all the more reason to turn back to them and to "be humbled by their strangeness."[26]

What concerns me here is not whether overlapping these two different uses of the term "tragedy" necessarily leads to confusion (it seems clear that part of the self-affiliation to a genre could be precisely through a shared recognition of a view of man's place in the world, in the way that the genre of detective fiction, for example, repeatedly and knowingly utilizes the image of the self-marginalizing and alienated hero or heroine, in conflict with the negotiations and corruptions of society in its institutional forms—hence they are so often unmarried). Rather, the question I wish to explore is how the modern construction of the abstract and general notion of "the tragic" affects—and distorts—the critical understanding of ancient tragedy.

Let us start again with Aristotle. It is striking that the *Poetics* barely mentions the *polis*.[27] This despite the fact that tragedies were performed first and foremost at a festival of the *polis,* the Great Dionysia, and were funded by the *polis;* not only were the playwrights selected and funded by the state, through the process of liturgy, but there was also a fund, known as the theoric fund, which paid every citizen to attend (so that for theater, as for jury service, and, eventually, for the assembly, no one could claim loss of income as a reason not to participate in the political event). What is more, the festival was the largest gathering of citizens in the calendar and was perceived to be a stage for political celebration and display, as well as for the more challenging dramas.[28] It is in part because of the sheer scale and impact of the drama festival on the imaginary of the city that Plato is so intent on banning the tragedians from his Republic. Yet Aristotle has no time for this political framing, and when he dismisses *opsis* (spectacle) as the least important part of tragedy, he is also giving a normative direction, I would suggest, for the whole festival and not just for the staging of plays.

Aristotle's silencing of the civic frame of drama may have several reasons. By the fourth century, tragedy had spread throughout Greece via repertory companies and the building of theaters in other cities.[29] Its fifth-century links to Athens and democracy had been greatly dissipated. Aristotle's major intellectual interest is in the educational benefit of tragedy for the citizen through the staged display of practical reasoning, which is not merely a rejoinder to Plato but also links his ethics and aesthetics in an integral manner. This focus on the individual is also reflected in the treatment of the chorus, which, he notes, should be "handled as one of the actors" (18.7); that is, he makes no mention of the chorus as a collective or as a different authoritative voice of the community in the drama. It has the effect of further reducing any impact of the civic frame. But Aristotle's stance has had a long-term influence on the criticism of tragedy, especially when combined with the Romantic focus on universality and disinterestedness of aesthetic judgment.

The impact of this Aristotelian stance is still powerfully evident in contemporary critical debate. The most significant critical turn in the last thirty years of criticism of ancient tragedy has been precisely the relocation of tragedies within a local and national socio-political context.[30] The critical resistance to such readings has been formulated as specifically Aristotelian in a renewed focus on "tragic pleasure," "emotional response"—and specifically, if often unconsciously, Kantian in its appeals to aesthetic beauty.[31] It is also seen in the selection of texts for critical attention. When Steiner suggests that only some Greek tragedies are tragedies pure and simple, he is following a long tradition of creating a canon within the canon. The plays of Euripides which have the most densely focused political themes—the *Phoenissae* is a paradigmatic example—are rarely treated to extended critical appraisal, let alone praise, in the nineteenth century (and beyond), and are very rarely staged.[32] The *Antigone,* as Steiner has shown so well, is treated as great precisely to the degree that it can be shown to escape the taint of the parochialism of politics, and, as in Hegel's analysis, can enter the abstract and general world of "the family," "the State," "the individual"—as transhistorical categories.[33]

More striking still is the treatment of the *Oresteia.* The trilogy has come to be regarded in the second quarter of the twentieth century as one of the greatest mountains of theatrical achievement. Yet for much of the eighteenth and nineteenth centuries, the *Agamemnon* was circulated and performed separately from the other two plays of the trilogy, and it is a commonplace of criticism that the *Eumenides* is flawed as a play precisely because of its turn to Athenian politics and the messy business of the politicized courtroom. The difficulty of maintaining the universalism and disinterestedness demanded by the tragic, when faced with the threat of civil strife and the frank persuasions of the political solution to the drama, have made it harder to see how the *Eumenides* is a fully integrated conclusion to the tensions set in place by the *Agamemnon.*[34] Yet in the second half of the twentieth century the *Oresteia* has become a necessary masterpiece: in 1991 alone there were more performances of the *Oresteia* in America than in the whole world between 1800 and 1865.[35] The increased recognition of the politics of tragedy in the twentieth century is one major factor in explaining this shift. The two different productions of this trilogy by Peter Stein in Berlin and Moscow, to take merely one celebrated example, were widely perceived to be contributing to the changing politics of Eastern Europe, either side of the collapse of the Berlin Wall and the Soviet Union—and praised and evaluated precisely in such terms.[36]

"The tragic" has been a strategic and persuasive definition that has worked to keep the most evidently and directly political of ancient tragedies from the elite of the great books tradition and that has realigned the political as abstract, transcultural discussion. A corollary of this is that an increased recognition of the political nature of ancient tragedies both changes the critical definition of the canon and changes the evaluation and performance history of particular plays.

Yet this is not a teleological history whereby the modern world triumphs in critical perception over earlier generations' blindnesses. The potential for generalizing readings of tragedy has always been there. As Oliver Taplin has reminded us, ancient Athenian tragedy was almost immediately an exported genre, which spoke across national boundaries, and the plays of the fifth century became repeated and studied classics within fifty years of their first productions—and entered the school system as classics, where they have remained ever since.[37] Tragedy was perceived to be literature to inform and form the imagination: from the beginning, "they [ancient Greeks] believed that tragedy was somehow offering them insights into the human condition."[38] Tragedy is indeed often quoted by other Greek writers as a source of wisdom and understanding, a cultural evaluation that is exploited with brilliantly self-conscious *Witz* by Philostratus in the third century CE, when he has his hero Apollonius of Tyana travel to the mysterious East to seek the ultimate truth from the Sages of the Orient, only to find that they quote Euripides to him. But even as it struggles with insights into the human condition, Athenian tragedy itself is already highly (self-)conscious about the role of the general, the exemplary, and the educational—and exposes it to a probing scrutiny.

Take Euripides' *Electra*. This drama marks its generic affiliations all too clearly. It takes as a subject the central play of the *Oresteia,* the great masterpiece of the previous generation (with which both Euripides and Sophocles were obsessed), and rewrites Aeschylus' dramaturgy with the most outrageous and self-conscious élan. This Electra—whose name means "unbedded"—is married to a farmer (but still a virgin), and thus living in an Odyssean rural hut, far from the political center of the palace, the setting for Aeschylus' (and Sophocles') play. Electra enters carrying a pot to fetch water—a visual memory and parody of the Aeschylean Electra, who entered carrying libations for the tomb of Agamemnon (a site that does not much interest this Electra). The recognition scene brings on an Old Man who has visited the tomb and seen there some offerings. He suggests to Electra that this must be a sign that Orestes has returned, and he proposes that she test his hunch with the Aeschylean recognition tokens. Could she find a footprint or a lock of hair to compare with her own? She dismisses these as ridiculous: Greece is rocky, there won't be footprints, and anyway boys' feet are bigger than girls'. So too boys' hair is rougher than girls', and many members of the same family have different colored hair. When the Old Man asks if there is some weaving by which Orestes might be recognized (a third suggestion, which makes sense only as the third of Aeschylus' tokens: there is no other rationale for it), Electra's misprision is willful and funny (541–44): "Don't you know that I was still a child when Orestes was exiled from the country? And if I could weave a robe, how could he still be wearing the same clothes as when he was young, unless his robe grew along with his body?" Her sarcastic rationalism offers a sophistic critique of the Aeschylean tokens, which are tellingly put in the mouth of an old man. (The "I was too young . . . If I weren't too young . . ." argument is an exemplary Gorgianic *reductio*.)[39] This self-conscious intertextuality is also applied to the markers of genre itself: as Electra is desperately waiting for news of Orestes' encounter with Aegisthus, she worries (759): "We are lost. For where are the messengers?" This is, Electra knows, the moment for a messenger scene. And we duly get one a couple of lines later.

Such self-consciousness is not merely intertextual hooliganism, however. *Electra* is fascinated with the causality of tragedy: how do humans come to commit acts of barbarous violence? It is central to Euripides' play that Electra's rational dismissal of the Old Man turns out to be misplaced: Orestes *has* returned. The failure of her rationality constructs an immediate question for the optimism of fifth-century politics as much as for the new sciences. Democracy depends on the assumption that rational evaluation of rational argument will produce the best decision. Euripides here, as so often, challenges that assumption. As Castor, the deus ex machina, declares of Apollo (1246): *sophos d'ôn ouk echrêse soi sopha* (He is wise / with authoritative knowledge, but his oracles to you were not wise / with authoritative knowledge). Being told authoritatively by a god that god's oracles are not authoritative, although the god is authoritative, opens an irremediable fissure between knowledge and action, which stalls Aristotelian practical reasoning in a swirl of paradox.

It is not merely rational argument as a guide for action that is threatened here. Electra also dismisses the Old Man's arguments because she knows that Orestes would not come back in secret because of any fear of Aegisthus (525). She is clear what heroic action is, and her brother must fulfill this model. Her image of her brother is ruthlessly ironized by Euripides, much as her self-representation as a victim is exposed as a self-serving and manipulative enactment. The timid Orestes is in disguise and in her house as she speaks, just as her own description of herself as forced into humiliating labor is undercut by the Farmer's request that she not fetch water. Euripides explores how constructed images, especially images from the heroic past, are used as motives, guides, and lures for action. So, paradigmatically, the Chorus sings of one of its own mythic narratives (736–44): "That is the story. But it produces scant belief in me—that the golden sun would change its warm seat in the heavens at mortal misfortune for the sake of human justice. But frightening myths for humans are a profit for worshipping the gods." The Chorus tells the story of how the sun changed course in horror at Thyestes' crimes. But the collective, authoritative voice withdraws its belief in its own story: here are Greeks who do not believe their myths, even as they tell them. But, they add, with staggering insouciance, such frightening stories are still useful for religious observance: believe in their efficacy if not in them. As with the deus ex machina, it is when the speaker appears to draw on the position of authoritative wisdom that the gap between knowledge and action is opened most destructively.

The thrust of this questioning—how the exemplary past functions as a model for the present—is most painfully felt at the moment of the matricide itself. The murder happens offstage; we hear Clytemnestra's cry, and then there is a lyric exchange between Orestes, Electra, and the Chorus, which replays the murder. Orestes, horrified by what he has done, relives the scene with bitter despair. Electra, however, recalls how she gave the orders, held the sword, and committed the most terrible of sufferings (1224–26). The contrast with Aeschylus and Sophocles is poignant and precise. In Aeschylus, Orestes, center stage, is faced by his mother, who bares her breast and demands his respect. This prompts the most famous moment of tragic doubt in ancient theater (*Choephori* 899): "Pylades what should I do? Should I respect and not kill my mother?" Pylades' answer—"count all men your enemies rather than the gods" (*Cho.* 900)—is the only speech he speaks, and it acts as the voice of god giving imprimatur to the murder. In Sophocles, the encounter of son and mother happens offstage, but we hear Clytemnestra cry out "My son, pity the woman who bore you!" (*Electra* 1410–11). But we do not hear any response from Orestes. Rather Electra, alone on stage, continues to scream her hatred of her mother, an answer to a figure who cannot hear her. The silence of Orestes, quite as much as Electra's passion, fully dramatizes the horror of an unquestioning commitment to violence. Sophocles displays the silent detachment of extremist violence as the uncanny double of the screams of extremist fervor.[40]

Aeschylus, then, stages a moment of profound doubt followed by an extraordinary reaffirmation of the divine power behind the act of matricide. Orestes, without Electra, who has been sent inside, hesitates and then fulfills god's command knowingly. In Sophocles, the moment of Orestes' decision is both taken offstage and silenced, in order to dramatize the moral consequences of not asking (enough) questions. Electra, alone onstage, offers a verbally violent commentary on the action from which is she separated. Euripides' Orestes has to be forced into the house to kill his mother, and Euripides' Electra, for the first and only time, has her hand firmly on the sword. The moment displays how Orestes' weakness, his inability to stand up to the multiform pressures to do what he knows is wrong, is a contributory factor in the enactment of tragic violence. For Euripides, the myths of the past, the ideological and emotional lures of how to be a hero, combine with a man's weakness to enable a scene of brutal tragedy to take place. The *Electra* explores how commitment to the examples of the past and the lauding of general models of heroism become part of the inexorable, chaotic slide into disaster. Self-consciousness about tragic form is part of this play's exploration of the flaws of critical judgment and the dangerous appeal of self-serving ideologically laden images of the past.

The *Electra* is a play that perfectly conforms to Nietzsche's distaste for Euripides as "the poet of aesthetic Socratism," the poet whose "incisive critical gifts" brought a self-conscious and ironic rationality into the tragic, with disastrous effects for both the Dionysiac and the Apollonian spirit of tragedy. [41] (Perhaps it is no surprise that Euripides' *Electra* awaits its rediscovery in modern theatrical performance, for all that its themes may seem precisely calibrated to contemporary anxieties.) But although the *Electra* may seem to revel with particular verve in its scandalous awareness of itself as tragedy, this sort of challenge to the models of the past as paradigm runs throughout ancient Greek tragedy. Classical Athenian tragedy takes up stories from the epic cycle and from Homer and rewrites them for the fifth-century theater, to speak to a fifth-century audience. The institution of tragedy is a machine to turn epic myth into the myths of the *polis*. A dialectical relationship between heroic past and contemporary world is built into ancient tragedy.

Greek tragedy seeks the general and finds its scope in the common state of mankind. The exemplary of tragedy is to be for all, always: as the Chorus of Sophocles' *Oedipus Tyrannus* sings (*OT* 1186–88), "With your example, yours, Oedipus, I count nothing of the human blessed." Yet not only were Athenian tragedies written for a particular political context, and firmly located within it, but also the plays themselves repeatedly question the value of the exemplary or explore the blurring between the general and the specific. As the body of Ajax lies on stage through the second half of Sophocles' *Ajax,* the debate is precisely whether this corpse is the corpse of a man who deserves respect as all men do or the corpse of a violent traitor, a specific individual who deserves humiliation. Every character in an Athenian tragedy who thinks he can escape from the specific family into which he was born discovers, like Aeschylus's Eteocles, that the curse of the family never leaves. How often are the generalizations of a chorus set in ironic or horrific tension with the action that follows on stage? How often are the moral generalizations of characters on stage revealed as the self-serving rhetoric of the politician?

The consequences of following German Romantic thought into generalizing about the tragic are, then, twofold. First, the hypostatization of the tragic threatens to ignore the socio-political context of tragedies and thus to fail to appreciate how, for example, tragedies address and engage with ancient democratic values. A canon within the canon of surviving tragedies is developed, which distorts our perception of the genre by excluding certain plays and the concerns of those plays from the truly tragic. Ancient tragedy, however, is a highly experimental genre, and the procrustean strategy of defining the tragic and then excluding the material that does not conform to the rules of the tragic is likely to repress the formal innovativeness and dynamic interaction between plays which the genre reveals. Thus, at the most extreme, Euripides, the "most tragic" of playwrights for Aristotle, is the sign of the death struggle of tragedy, a symptom of degenerate culture, for Nietzsche. "The tragic," that is, can distort the historicity of tragedy and the literary history of the genre.

Second, generalizing about the tragic threatens to take the sword to the complex sense within Greek tragedies themselves of the dynamic between generalization and the messy, specific, self-interested turmoil of human activity. Steiner sums up the tragic with the adage "It is best not to be born, next best to die young" and concludes that this "proposition implies that men and women's presence on this earth is fundamentally absurd or unwelcome . . . that our lives are . . . a self-punishing anomaly." Andromache in *Trojan Women* echoes Steiner's words, both for herself and for her sister Polyxena, recently sacrificed at the tomb of Achilles (Euripedes, *Trojan Women,* 636–37): "I declare that not to be born is the same as death, and death is preferable to a bitter life." She concludes that Polyxena is better off than she is, as her sister is at least dead. "As for myself," she finishes (681–83), "I do not even have hope, the last refuge for all humans, nor do I delude myself that I will fare well. It is sweet, though, the seeming." This speech has often been criticized as inappropriate, disappointing, or largely banal. But its very numbness is essential to the drama of the scene. Shortly after it comes the news that her son, Astyanax, will be taken from her and thrown to his death from the city walls. Andromache breaks down into one of the most moving and heart-felt scenes of desperate farewell. She had not before realized how far she was from the depths of sorrow. Even her previous recognition that she will not fare well seems now a pathetic delusion in its inadequacy. Her silent exit realizes Shakespeare's "The worst is not so long as we can say 'tis the worst." The summary adage that Steiner offers is already a cliché, exposed as such in tragedy, an all too easy response that is viciously shown up as hollow by the play's unfurling horror. Andromache's generalization about the hopelessness of her life shows merely that she has not yet grasped where she has actually invested her hope. The audience of this bitter drama may make a range of conclusions about the nature of human life and suffering, but a recognition of the inadequacy of generalizations about the tragedy of life should be part of any such response.

If I were to join the argument about definitions of the tragic, I would want to worry about Steiner's final phrase, "our lives are . . . a self-punishing anomaly," in order to look harder at the idea of self-punishing (especially for a play like *Trojan Women*), and to scrutinize the "our" in "our lives," which threatens not merely to ignore any difference between perpetrators and victims of violence but also to repress the carefully articulated fragility of collective identity in a play like *Trojan Women*. But my own general point has, I hope, been made. The texts of ancient Athenian tragedy repeatedly explore causes of suffering, responses to suffering, misprisions about suffering, and in each of these areas general statements about the nature of human suffering become part of the rhetoric of the play, part of how tragedy happens. How the wisdom of generalizations functions is part of tragedy's questioning.

"'The tragic' is a central concern to anyone who wishes to come to terms with tragedy, Greek or other."[42] I have suggested that one crucial move toward coming to terms with "the tragic" is to historicize the term and thereby to see what the consequences are when it is applied with its full panoply of German Romantic associations to the genre of ancient Athenian tragedies. The challenge for the critic remains to pay due attention to the specific socio-political context of ancient drama, while recognizing the drive toward transhistorical truth both in the plays' discourse and in the plays' reception. This double attentiveness should in turn inform each stage of the literary history of the genre—the fragmented and incremental development of the genre through social institutions of theatre, self-affiliation of writers, and the strictures of critics. Here too the local, the political, and the polemical are in tension with the grandest gestures toward the *longue durée* of the genre of tragedy. At each stage, tragedies and "the tragic" are in a productive and dialectical tension, a tension for which the idea of "the law of the tragic" and its failing/succeeding test cases is likely to prove an unwieldy and distorting methodological model. What's more, Greek tragic texts relentlessly shine a harsh light on the platitudes and general wisdom with which its characters try to come to terms with the political turmoil and personal suffering with which they are faced. There is a message there, too, about the humbleness with which we might stand as critics before the tragedies of ancient theater: before we write a sentence that begins "the tragic is . . . ," "the essence of tragedy is . . . ," we should recall how often ancient tragedies show up the inadequacy of such generalizations as a response to the violent narratives of human conflict.

Notes

1. Exemplary here is M. S. Silk and J. P. Stern, *Nietzsche on Tragedy* (Cambridge: Cambridge University Press, 1981).

2. George Steiner, *The Death of Tragedy* (London: Faber & Faber, 1961), 9.

3. *Republic* 413b4: "but I run the risk of speaking tragically." Cf. ibid. 545e and *Meno* 76e.

4. Froma Zeitlin's Sather lectures deal with this with her customary intelligence and perception; their publication is eagerly awaited.

5. Stephen Halliwell, *The Poetics of Aristotle. Translation and Commentary* (London: Duckworth, 1987), 126. His views are greatly expanded in his *Aristotle's Poetics* (Chapel Hill: University of North Carolina Press, 1986), where the linkage in Aristotle between ethics and aesthetics is convincingly established.

6. Halliwell, *Poetics of Aristotle,* 126.

7. See Elizabeth Belfiore, *Tragic Pleasures: Aristotle on Plot and Emotion* (Princeton: Princeton University Press, 1992), for a good account of the difficulties of this passage. See also Halliwell, *Poetics of Aristotle,* 168–201.

8. On the importance of pathos in Plato, and Aristotle on tragedy, see Thomas Gould, *The Ancient Quarrel Between Poetry and Philosophy* (Princeton: Princeton University Press, 1990).

9. For a full discussion with bibliography see Stephen Halliwell, "Plato's Repudiation of the Tragic," in M. S. Silk, ed., *Tragedy and the Tragic* (Oxford: Oxford University Press, 1996); See also Dorothy Tarrant, "Plato as Dramatist," in *Journal of Hellenic Studies* 75 (1955): 82–89.

10. Itself a familiar notion powerfully and paradigmatically expressed in the famous scene of Priam and Achilles in *Iliad* 24, 524ff.

11. See Gerald Else, *Plato and Aristotle on Poetry* (Chapel Hill: University of North Carolina Press, 1986); Penelope Murray, *Plato on Poetry* (Cambridge: Cam-

bridge University Press, 1996); Elizabeth Asmis, "Plato on Poetic Creativity," in *The Cambridge Companion to Plato,* ed. Richard Kraut (Cambridge: Cambridge University Press, 1992); G. R. F. Ferrari, "Plato and Poetry," in *The Cambridge History of Literary Criticism,* ed. George Kennedy, vol. 1 (Cambridge: Cambridge University Press, 1989); Andrea Nightingale, *Genres in Dialogue: Plato and the Construct of Philosophy* (Cambridge: Cambridge University Press, 1995), especially 60–92.

12. See Michelle Gellrich, *Tragedy and Theory: the Problem of Conflict Since Aristotle* (Princeton: Princeton University Press, 1988).

13. Terence Cave, *Recognitions: A Study in Poetics* (Oxford: Clarendon Press, 1988).

14. From a huge bibliography, see Howard Caygill, *Art of Judgement* (Oxford: Blackwell, 1989); Paul Crowther, *The Kantian Sublime: From Morality to Art* (Oxford: Clarendon Press, 1989); Ted Cohen and Paul Guyer, eds., *Essays in Kant's Aesthetics* (Chicago: University of Chicago Press, 1982); Henry Allison, *Kant's Theory of Taste: A Reading of the "Critique of Aesthetic Judgement"* (Cambridge: Cambridge University Press, 2001); Christian Helmut Wenzel, *An Introduction to Kant's Aesthetics: Core Concepts and Problems* (Oxford: Blackwell, 2005)—each with further bibliography.

15. A useful start on this is Terry Pinkard, *German Philosophy, 1760–1860: The Legacy of Idealism* (Cambridge: Cambridge University Press, 2002), especially 131–213.

16. Cave, *Recognitions.*

17. Friedrich Schlegel, *Über das Studium der Griechischen Poesie* (1795–97) (*SW* I 207).

18. See from a huge bibliography Eliza Butler, *The Tyranny of Greece over the German Imagination* (Cambridge: Cambridge University Press, 1935); Marilyn Butler, *Romantics, Rebels, and Reactionaries* (Oxford: Oxford University Press, 1981); Timothy Webb, ed., *English Romantic Hellenism, 1700–1824* (Manchester: Manchester University Press, 1982); G. W. Clarke, ed., *Rediscovering Hellenism: The Hellenic Inheritance and the English Imagination* (Cambridge: Cambridge University Press, 1989); David Ferris, *Silent Urns: Romanticism, Hellenism, Modernity* (Cambridge: Cambridge University Press, 2000). I have had my own go at this in *Who Needs Greek? Contests in the Cultural History of Hellenism* (Cambridge: Cambridge University Press, 2002).

19. The phrase is taken from Ernest Renan's celebrated "Prière sur l'Acropole" (1865), published first in *Souvenirs d'enfance et de jeunesse* (Paris, 1883) and many times since.

20. Hugo von Hofmannsthal, "Vorspiel zur Antigone des Sophokles" (1900), *Gesammelte Werke,* ed. Herbert Steiner (Frankfurt a.M.: S. Fischer, 1953).

21. Matthew Arnold, *Poems* (London, 1853), preface, 12.

22. George Eliot, "The Antigone and Its Moral," in *The Essays of George Eliot,* ed. Thomas Pinney (New York: Columbia University Press, 1963), 264.

23. Peter Szondi, *Versuch über das Tragische* (Frankfurt a.M.: Insel, 1961), 151.

See also Albin Lesky, "Zum Problem des Tragischen," *Gesammelte Schriften* (Bern: Franke Verlag, 1966), 213–19.

24. Friedrich Nietzsche, *The Birth of Tragedy*, trans. Francis Golffing (New York: Anchor Books, 1956), 7, taken from *A Critical Backward Glance* (1886).

25. George Steiner, "Tragedy, Pure and Simple," in Silk, *Tragedy and the Tragic*, 535–36.

26. Ibid., 544.

27. Edith Hall, "Is There a *polis* in Aristotle's *Poetics?*," in ibid., 295–309.

28. On tragedy and the city, see Simon Goldhill, "The Great Dionysia and Civic Ideology," in *Nothing to Do with Dionysus?*, ed. John J. Winkler and Froma I. Zeitlin (Princeton: Princeton University Press, 1990); "Civic Ideology and the Problem of Difference: The Politics of Aeschylean Tragedy, Once Again." *Journal of Hellenic Studies* 120 (2000): 34–56; P. E. Easterling, ed., *The Cambridge Companion to Greek Tragedy* (Cambridge: Cambridge University Press, 1997); Eric Csapo and William Slater, *The Context of Ancient Drama* (Ann Arbor: University of Michigan Press, 1995); Peter Wilson, *The Athenian Institution of the Khoregia: The Chorus, the City, and the State* (Cambridge: Cambridge University Press, 2000).

29. P. E. Easterling, "From Repertoire to Canon," in *The Cambridge Companion to Greek Tragedy,* ed. P. E. Easterling (Cambridge: Cambridge University Press, 1997); Oliver Taplin, "Spreading the Word Through Performance," in *Performance Culture and Athenian Democracy,* ed. Simon Goldhill and Robin Osborne (Cambridge: Cambridge University Press, 1999).

30. The influence of Jean-Pierre Vernant and Pierre Vidal-Naquet, *Mythe et tragédie en Grèce ancienne* (Paris: Maspéro, 1972), is fundamental. See Simon Goldhill, *Reading Greek Tragedy* (Cambridge: Cambridge University Press, 1986); Froma Zeitlin, *Playing the Other* (Chicago: Chicago University Press, 1996); David Wiles *Tragedy in Athens* (Cambridge: Cambridge University Press, 1997); Christian Meier, *Die politische Kunst der griechischen Tragödie* (Munich: C. H. Beck, 1988); as well as the works cited in note 23. Many studies of particular plays or authors could be cited here.

31. See, for example, Malcolm Heath, *The Poetics of Greek Tragedy* (London: Duckworth, 1987); Jasper Griffin, "The Social Function of Greek Tragedy," *Classical Quarterly* 48 (1998): 39–61.

32. Exceptions include Günther Zuntz, *The Political Plays of Euripides* (Manchester: Manchester University Press, 1955); Daniel Mendelsohn, *Gender and the City in Euripides' Political Plays* (Oxford: Oxford University Press, 2002), who notes (2) how often these plays are treated as anomalous failures within the tragic canon.

33. George Steiner, *Antigones* (Oxford: Clarendon Press, 1984). On Hegel and Antigone and his use of familial terms, see the fine discussion of Miriam Leonard, *Athens in Paris: Ancient Greece and the Political in Post-War French Thought* (Oxford: Oxford University Press, 2005).

34. Sir Hugh Lloyd-Jones epitomizes this difficulty when he states that

Athene's reason for voting for Orestes—that she supports the male and has no mother—"has nothing to do with the issue being judged" (Hugh Lloyd-Jones, *The Justice of Zeus* [Berkeley: University of California Press, 1971], 92).

35. These figures are taken from Amanda Wrigley's catalogue of performances usefully printed in *Agamemnon in Performance, 458 BC to AD 2004,* ed. Fiona Macintosh, Pantelis Michelakis, Edith Hall, and Oliver Taplin (Oxford: Oxford University Press, 2005).

36. See Anton Bierl, *Die Orestie des Aischylos auf der modernen Bühne. Theoretische Konzeptionen und ihre szenische Realiserung,* 2nd ed. (Stuttgart: M & P Verlag für Wissenschaft und Forschung, 1999). Dimitry Trubotchkin, "*Agamemnon* in Russia," in Macintosh et al., *Agamemnon in Performance,* is disappointing in that it barely mentions Stein.

37. Oliver Taplin, "Spreading the Word through Performance," in *Performance Culture and Athenian Democracy,* ed. Simon Goldhill and Robin Osborne (Cambridge: Cambridge University Press, 1999).

38. Ibid., 55.

39. For a more detailed exposition of this scene and its place in the play, see Simon Goldhill, *Reading Greek Tragedy* (Cambridge: Cambridge University Press, 1986), 245–58.

40. See Simon Goldhill, "Tragic Emotions: The Pettiness of Envy and the Politics of Pitilessness," in *Envy, Spite, and Jealousy: The Rivalrous Emotions in Ancient Greece,* ed. David Konstan and Keith Rutter (Edinburgh: Edinburgh University Press, 2003), and, more generally, Simon Goldhill, "Der Ort der Gewalt: Was sehen wir auf der Bühne," in *Die Gewalt und Ästhetik,* ed. Bernd Seidensticker (Berlin: Walter de Gruyter, 2007).

41. Friedrich Nietzsche, *The Birth of Tragedy,* trans. Francis Golffing (New York: Anchor Books, 1956), 81, 79.

42. M. S. Silk, "General Introduction," in Silk, *Tragedy and the Tragic,* 2.

After Troy
Homer, Euripides, Total War

Wai Chee Dimock

What exactly is tragedy, and how wide is its scope? Is it a staged production or something less choreographed, less confined? Does it have a specific location on the geographical map and one on the map of time? And is it discontinued now, no longer current in the modern world? George Steiner celebrates the genre in *The Death of Tragedy* (1961) but minces no words about its chronological limits. According to him, the dramatic art that flourished in fifth-century Athens is now defunct, with no offspring. Modernity is governed by the idea of progress—the idea that we have an unlimited amount of time on our hands, that the future is both bright and interminable. Greek tragedy offers no such assurance. "The *Iliad* is the primer of tragic art," Steiner writes. "In it are set forth the motifs and images around which the sense of the tragic has crystallized during nearly three thousand years of Western poetry: the shortness of heroic life, the exposure of man to the murderousness and caprice of the inhuman, the fall of the City."[1]

Catastrophe is the concluding act in tragedy, and the genre is dedicated to the idea that this *could* happen, that this *could* be the ending. Human beings get maimed, killed, or are driven mad as their well-being suddenly evaporates. These radical shifts give tragedy its peculiar structure of time. In the blink of an eye, the world is thrown off keel. Everything that once anchored it, everything once taken for granted, is irretrievably lost. How can things get so bad so fast? And what have I done to deserve this? These are the questions urged by Greek tragedy—and with more demonic energy than will ever be conveyed by modern English. The name that Aristotle gives to this phenomenon is *peripeteia*—an abrupt reversal that shatters the world, "a shift of what is being undertaken to the opposite in the way previously stated."[2]

And, after this shattering event, there is nothing more: no further development, no next episode, nothing that would take the plot beyond the devastation and set it on a different track. Greek tragedy is a drama in which time suddenly runs out, in which things shut down much more brutally—and much faster—than we think. Drama with such deadly finality would reappear, very briefly, in the sixteenth and seventeenth centuries. But already it was "rear-guard action," Steiner says, out of place in a world that projects itself cheerfully and endlessly into time.[3] A catastrophe that cuts things short—a "fury without hatred"[4]—is deeply at odds with this future that seems our birthright, our faith that time is our entitlement.

Disproportionate Harm

Catastrophes such as the hurricane Katrina make this birthright much less certain. The water rolls in, and in a matter of hours nothing is as before. Other disasters—from the eruption of Vesuvius in 79 CE to the Lisbon earthquake in 1755—have also destroyed instantaneously, but, for most of us, it is Katrina that dramatizes this to mind-numbing excess. Here indeed is *peripeteia,* but driven by no malice, no intentionality, nothing that allows the disaster to make human sense. It is very much a fury without hatred. And, just as it cannot be told as a tale of targeted violence, neither can it be told as a tale of moral desert. For the hurricane spells doom not for one or two individuals, punished because of some flaw peculiar to them. Instead, the doom here descends on masses and masses of people, with no blame attachable. These people suffer not because they deserve it, not because they are fitly chastised, not because there is any proportionality between who they are and what is coming to them.

It is this lack of proportionality that makes these events *catastrophes* to begin with. Whatever vices the victims might have been guilty of, the disaster that befalls them is of an entirely different order of magnitude. It has nothing to do with any rational measure of their lives. And, if they happen to be killed, that rational measure is further rendered meaningless, for everything ends in an instant, dispatching each victim just like every other. Catastrophes of this sort make a mockery of punitive justice, for the destruction here is random destruction, indiscriminate, and therefore also destroying in excess, wiping out human beings not as human beings but simply as physical matter. All natural disasters destroy in this way. The year 2005 is a standout in the variety it offers: not only hurricanes but also the earthquake in Pakistan and the aftermath of the Indian Ocean tsunami. Katrina is especially instructive, however, for its disproportionate harm happened to fall on an entity with a special importance to humans. It is the destruction of this entity that Steiner singles out as the burden of the Athenian *tragoidia:* the fall of the City.

It is tempting to call the fate of New Orleans the updating of an ancient genre. And yet, this latest installment is not an easily recognizable successor to the works of Aeschylus and Sophocles or of Shakespeare and Racine. Katrina is, of course, not a play. It was not written, not produced, not performed for any purpose that we can see. And, while it is hard to say how many were in the cast, one thing seems clear: the protagonist, though equipped with a name, cannot be taken—even remotely, even metaphorically—as a rational agent. What sort of analytic language can capture this kind of plot, featuring a large-scale, nonhuman actor, on the one hand, and large-scale human casualties, on the other? In everyday speech, of course, we never hesitate to use the word "tragedy" for what happened to New Orleans. What exactly does the word mean, used in this way? What relation does it have to its original usage? And how does it extend, complicate, or muddle up the more technical definitions?

Raymond Williams begins with these questions in *Modern Tragedy* (1966), his tribute to the genre's ongoing and undiminished importance. "We come to tragedy by many roads," Williams writes. For some, tragedy is "a body of literature, a conflict of theory, an academic problem." For others, it is a "common name . . . for other kinds of event—a mining disaster, a burned-out family, a broken career, a smash on the road." Those of us "trained in what is now the academic tradition" tend to be "impatient and even contemptuous of what they regard as loose and vulgar uses of 'tragedy' in ordinary speech and in the newspapers."[5] But there is no reason why the loose and vulgar uses should not be taken as a heuristic advantage. For the broad currency of the term points to a phenomenal field of equal breadth: not supervised, not executed according to a blueprint, not always happening inside a theater, and much closer to the experience of uncontrolled harm human beings have always known.

Rather than limiting tragedy to an artistic genre—written by a playwright and performed on stage—it is helpful to loosen up these criteria, giving it much broader scope. For tragedy does not always hinge on human authors and human victims. It is bound by neither stage nor script. As a structure of undeserved harm, it has a tally sheet extending across the entire biosphere, not stopping at any point in the life of our species and not stopping with our species, either. Its unscheduled arrival points to a dimension of the world beyond human calculation, though rarely without human input. Catastrophe is not something we can anticipate, calculate, or wrap our minds around: its radius seems broader than human cognition itself. Producing untold casualties, and all happening inside a tiny window of time, it seems to come with the worst possible combination of the large and the small, mocking our sense of magnitude as well as our sense of sequence. One way to think about tragedy, then, is to see it as a particular kind of irony—an irony of scale—one that arises when the gravest consequences fall where our cognitive powers are least adequate, and with the maximum damage being done within the minimum interval of time.

Seen in this way, Greek tragedy gives us a useful language to think about physical events that are massively abrupt and laterally injurious. The prime example of this is, of course, climate change and global warming, very much an irony of scale in the sense that, even though the effect on humans is drastic, it is no more than a switch from one physical condition to another, a switch that is the by-product of processes that are themselves neutral, such as melting glaciers and rising sea levels, which, in turn, are the by-products of other processes that are also neutral, such as the changing composition of atmospheric carbon dioxide. Without warning, and often from the side, we are constantly being assimilated into the physical world. This assimilation rests on a small critical threshold, a tipping point as abrupt as it is violent, with sweeping consequences registered across the board. This is the structure of *peripeteia,* and no genre is better equipped to instruct us than Greek tragedy.

Tragedy and the *Polis*

Much is gained, in short, by making tragedy coterminous with the well-being of the entire world. George Steiner, while ostensibly writing its obituary, has in fact gone a long way toward this democratizing of tragedy, offering up new demographics, not to say new operating theaters. He looks back to fifth-century Athens, but he also looks forward to developments since: "I have seen a documentary film showing the activities of a Chinese agricultural commune. At one point, the workers streamed in from the fields, laid down their mattocks, and gathered on the barrack square. They formed into a large chorus. . . . The ceremony closed with a recital of the heroic death of one the founders of the local Communist Party. He had been killed by the Japanese and was buried nearby. Is it not, I wonder, in some comparable rite of defiance and honour to the dead that tragedy began, three thousand years ago, on the plains of Argos?"[6] What is interesting here is not only the relocation of tragedy to a new continent but also a new emphasis on the size of its cast, the aggregate numbers that make up its ranks. To see tragedy from the standpoint of the Chorus—made up, in this case, of Chinese agricultural workers—is to have a different sense of what the genre entails. It is to have a different sense of the dramatic form itself: less individualistic, less pivoted on solo players, and more of a group performance, taking place in a theater not strictly enclosed, not set apart from the rest of the population, and sharing more or less the same footing with the assembled audience.

Tragedy in ancient Greece did exist on such a footing. As Oddone Longo points out, "in the archaic period, until the end of the sixth century, tragic performances took place in Athens on an *orkhestra* in the Agora; it was only at about the beginning of the fifth century that a theatrical space, with provisional (wooden) structures, was arranged on the south side of the Akropolis."[7] The tragic theater began not even as a "theatrical event" but as part of the customary goings-on in the city, taking place in the agora, or marketplace, the usual place of assembly. There was neither stage nor auditorium and no sharp dividing lines between the actors and the public. Even after a more formal space was set up, tragedy remained less a discrete production than part of a public processional, with every citizen in attendance. "The more we learn about the original production of tragedies and comedies in Athens," John Winkler and Froma Zeitlin write, "the more it seems wrong even to call them plays in the modern sense of the word." These tragedies took place in a five-day festival known as the City Dionysia. Athenian audiences did not buy tickets on their own, as modern theatergoers do, to see a show put on by strangers, in the company of strangers. Instead, "the price of a ticket was distributed by each local town council [*deme*] to the citizens in good standing on their records; theater attendance was thus closely linked to citizenship. What is more, the audience sat in the open-air theater below the Akropolis in wedge-shaped sections designated for each of the ten political tribes . . . composed of the same few thousands of active citizens to be seen at any important public meeting."[8]

The group distribution of tickets and the seating of the audience make it clear that tragedy was an exercise in collectivity. It was a civic gathering, not unlike the gathering at the law court or the popular assembly. The audience for all three was the same and played an active part on all three occasions. At the dramatic festival, during what Simon Goldhill calls the "preplay ceremonies," it was the audience that took over. Goldhill points out that "the four moments of ceremony preceding the dramatic festival were all deeply involved with the city's sense of itself. The libations of the ten generals, the display of tribute, the announcement of the city's benefactors, the parade of state-educated boys, now men, in full military uniform, all stressed the power of the *polis*, the duties of an individual to the *polis*. The festival of the Great Dionysia is in the full sense of the expression a civic occasion, a city festival. And it is an occasion to say something about the city, not only in the plays themselves. . . . This is fundamentally and essentially a festival of the democratic *polis*."[9]

Tragedy was without question under the city's sponsorship. But did this make it a mouthpiece of the sponsor, an official voice? Or was there some distance, some irony even, between what the city demanded and what tragedy seemed bent on offering? Classicists disagree on this point. And their disagreement centers largely on the status of the Chorus, the most distinctive feature of tragedy, embodying the most obvious matrix for collective expression. Jean-Pierre Vernant, in his influential account, sees tragedy as a divided form, divided between the Chorus, on the one hand, and a highly individualized protagonist, on the other. According to him, the protagonist is "always more or less estranged from the ordinary condition of the citizen," and it is the job of the Chorus, as a "collective and anonymous presence," to "express through its fears, hopes, questions, and judgments the feelings of the spectators who make up the civic community."[10] The voice of the Chorus is the official voice, the voice of the presiding social order. John J. Winkler goes one step further. For him, the Chorus speaks not only for the social order but specifically the order of the fifth-century Athenian empire. Tragedy was a quasi-military induction ritual, an "ephebes' song," performed by a segment of the male population getting ready for manhood, getting ready for war.[11]

John Gould, however, while also associating the Chorus with a collective voice, has a radically different understanding of *which* collectivity it represents. He points out, first, that city sponsorship, as far as it went, extended only to the solo players but not to the anonymous Chorus, since only the actors playing the protagonists received pay from the city. Quite aside from this mundane but not insignificant detail, two other structural components of tragedy seem to work against the Chorus's supposedly official capacity. The first is the foreignness of its voice: "The song of the chorus is expressed in a language yet further removed, in its non-Attic dialectical colouring as well as in its diction and syntax, from the formalized 'speech of the city' given to the actors who play the heroic protagonists: it is, for its Athenian audience, an alien and strangely 'distant' tongue."[12] Secondly, by shifting our attention away from the two most canonical plays—Sophocles' *Oedipus Rex* and *Antigone*—and looking, in particular, at a range of works by Euripides, Gould points out that the social and political standing of the Chorus was often as tenuous as the sound of its speech:

The chorus, with only two exceptions in the surviving plays, enacts the response to events, not of representatives of the citizen body, but precisely of those whom the democratic city of Athens and its institutional core of adult, male citizen-hoplites has defined as marginal or simply excluded from the voice of the "people." The tragic chorus is characteristically composed of old men, women, slaves, and foreigners (the last often non-Greeks as well as non-Athenians). By combining two or more of these categories to produce a chorus, say, of female non-Greek slaves, the chorus may indeed be perceived by the citizen audience as doubly, or even triply, marginal.[13]

Nonhuman Actors

Where exactly did the Chorus stand: emotionally, linguistically, and demographically? Was it an official voice speaking from a securely normative position, or was it more abject, more vulnerable? *The Death of Tragedy* was written prior to this debate, and Steiner cannot possibly be taking sides. However, he does seem to be leaning in one direction when he cites, as the "primer of tragic art," not one of the canonical tragedies, but rather a work that would seem to belong to a different genre altogether, namely, Homer's *Iliad.* In what sense is this epic an instance of the tragic? What does this imply about the relation between these two genres, and their relative capacity for representing harm? Given the obvious absence of the Chorus in the epic, is there some feature here that might serve a parallel function? If so, what does this say about the nature of collectivity in each genre?

The *Iliad,* being an epic, and a war poem to boot, is a chronicle of the many rather than of the one. It is a poem of large numbers, and a poem that meditates on the nature of large numbers. Book Two, for instance, features not only the famous catalog of ships but also a series of extended metaphors likening the assembled armies to many things—nonhuman things—also appearing in aggregate forms:

> As ravening fire rips through big stands of timber
> high on a mountain ridge and the blaze flares miles away,
> so from the marching troops the blaze of bronze armor,
> splendid and superhuman, flared across the earth,
> flashing into the air to hit the skies.
>   Armies gathering now
> as the huge flocks on flocks of winging birds, geese or cranes
> or swans with long lancing necks—circling Asian marshes

round the Cayster outflow, wheeling in all directions,
glorying in their wings—keep on landing, advancing,
wave on shrieking wave and the tidal flats resounds . . .
    The armies massing . . . crowding thick-and-fast
as the swarms of flies seething over the shepherd's stalls
in the first spring days when the buckets flood with milk—
so many long-haired Achaeans swarmed across the plain
to confront the Trojans, fired to smash their lines. (2.539–59)[14]

A raging fire, flocks of shrieking birds, and swarms of buzzing flies—
these are the aggregate forms that the Greek army resembles. And it resembles these things because the process of aggregation has also turned
it into a different kind of entity, fundamentally different from any of
its members. Homer is emphatic on this point. The army, as a military
organization, is a marvelous thing, a new species of being. It is invented
by humans, to be sure, but once it goes into the world it has a life of
its own, a function of its scale. That scale is such that, in its norms of
behavior, it can only be described as a nonhuman actor. For the Greek
army exists for one reason alone. Its sole purpose is to crush its enemies,
to break down their resistance, to "smash their lines." It is entirely appropriate, then, that this species of being should be referred to as the
armed *forces,* because that is what it is: a mechanical agency, operating
for the most part in the domain of physics, obeying only physical laws.
It belongs to a different taxonomic order from the soldiers who make
up its ranks.

   The *Iliad* is a poem about what this nonhuman force can do to a human
city. The epic not only puts that city in its title, it does so using a foreign
word, "Ilium," rather than the Greek word, "Troy." Ilium, or Troy, is of
course no ordinary city. It is the most tragic on record. Of all the cities to
have been razed to the ground, destroyed to the point of no return, this
is the one that has somehow stuck in our collective memory, giving a
durable name to the fact that an entire population, an entire way of life,
can be literally, physically wiped out. The legend of the Trojan War did
not begin with Homer. When the Homeric epics were composed, around
the eighth century BCE, this literature was already well under way. In
the *Iliad,* it looms large, not as a terminal catastrophe (which the epic
apparently does not allow), but as a litany of deaths in combat: routine,
almost unsurprising, lamented, but also more or less taken for granted. It
is this litany that defines the nature of the collective in the Homeric epic.
And its effect is felt not only as an *incremental* attrition—the death of one

soldier here, one soldier there—but also as an *exponential* undoing of the human world, a deep and fundamental erosion of the social fabric, one that leads to an even more chilling "fall of the city."

It is this deep and fundamental erosion that makes war act and feel like a natural disaster. If the blurring of the boundaries between the human and the nonhuman begins with the visual resemblance between the army and flocks of birds and swarms of flies, it ends with an image of war that crosses over almost completely onto the nonhuman side, acting mechanically, indiscriminately, and always in excess, like a physical force, like the storm surge of a hurricane:

> As a heavy surf assaults some roaring coast,
> piling breaker on breaker whipped by the West Wind,
> and out on the open sea a crest first rears its head
> then pounds down on the shore with hoarse, rumbling thunder
> and in come more shouldering crests, arching up and breaking
> against some rocky spit, exploding salt foam to the skies—
> so wave on wave they came, Achaean battalions ceaseless,
> surging on to war. Each captain ordered his men
> and the ranks moved on in silence . . .
> You'd never think so many troops could march
> holding their voices in their chests, all silence,
> fearing their chiefs who called out clear commands,
> and the burnished blazoned armor round their bodies flared,
> the formations trampling on. (4:489–502)

As we have seen, Homeric metaphors are typically elaborate and long drawn-out. In this case, the extended metaphor of the surging ocean is especially apt, since the physical movement of the "battalions ceaseless, / surging on to war" is exactly like the physical pounding of wave on wave. It is a commonplace, of course, to say that war dehumanizes, that the soldiers who are deployed are deployed not as volitional actors but simply as logistical units. Homer's emphasis is more idiosyncratic and even bleaker. In his account, what subsumes each of the soldiers, what turns them into mechanical parts of the armed forces, is not the actual fighting itself, and not even the loudness of the battle cries, but rather the eerie silence that accompanies their prewar march. As he says, you should not think, with so many men marching, that there would be no noise whatsoever. But that is indeed the case. Each of the soldiers seems to have lost his tongue. Silence enshrouds each of them. It is this silence that turns the Greek army into a brilliant visual tableau, a sea of bronze armor flashing, but with the sound completely cut off, not a single word coming from the mouths of the soldiers.

The *Iliad* is often read as a heroic epic, celebrating manhood proven on the battlefield. What is dramatized here is something different. We might think of it as the underside of the poem, a kind of unheroic counterrhythm to the brilliant solo performances of Achilles and Hector. It is this that gives the epic the structural equivalent of a Chorus and makes it a prototype for Greek tragedy, where the Chorus will emerge as a full-fledged component of the dramatic structure. To emphasize the kinship between epic and tragedy is to emphasize the importance of large numbers as the register of harm in both of them. It is these large numbers, in their cowed presence, that gives a special meaning to being a "casualty" of war. For the extinction of sound is not incidental but elemental. A silent world is a damaged world, a world in which human beings live only a kind of half-life, existing only as a spectacle but not as audible words. The heroic warriors *are* audible in the *Iliad;* it is only the aggregate masses that are not. That silence "tragedizes" the epic, making it a dark predictor of the fate of the city. The Greek polis—the seat of democracy—has already died even before Troy falls. It dies each time a nonhuman actor remakes the world in its own image, each time it turns the sound-producing tongue into a dumb blankness.

To see the human voice itself as a casualty of war is to have a different sense of its scale of destruction. That scale is mind-boggling, given the small beginning. War is not only a force in this sense, operating in the domain of physics, it operates, more specifically, as a *nonlinear* system, which is to say, as a set of outcome entirely out of proportion to the initial input. Homer writes: "Strife, only a slight thing when she first rears her head / but her head soon hits the sky as she strides across the earth" (4.481–516). The tiny thing that is war will not stay tiny for long, for she will inevitably undergo a rapid scalar expansion, swelling to colossal heights, lording it over all of us. Seen from this perspective, the Homeric epic is less about human heroes than about the nonhuman actor they set loose. Simone Weil, in her astute essay on the *Iliad* (written in the summer and fall of 1940, after the fall of France in World War II), points out that "the true hero, the true subject, the center of the *Iliad* is force. Force employed by man, force that enslaves man, force before which man's flesh shrinks away. In this work, at all times, the human spirit is shown as modified by its relation with force, as swept away, blinded, by the very force it imagined it could handle, as deformed by the weight of the force it submits to."[15]

As a description of *epic,* Weil's comment is new and startling. As a description of *tragedy,* however, it is all too recognizable. For tragedy has always answered to just this description: it is indeed a genre dominated by force, force that enslaves us, blinds us, sweeps us off our feet, and deforms us. Rather than seeing this as a later development, sui generis, Weil's reading of the *Iliad* suggests that this has been long in the coming, that force has been the subject of poetry from the very first and will probably remain so till the end of time. Beginning with the Homeric epic, continuing through Greek tragedy, and extending to our own time, we can trace a long chronology, a continuum of harm that claims as its victims not a handful of protagonists but entire populations, over thousands of years. If this chronology has anything to tell us, it is that, perhaps more than heroes, it is the tragic chorus that we need to attend to. World War II, to take just one example, is very much a tragedy of the chorus, for this is what we might call total war, with massive civilian casualties. The fates of Hiroshima, Nagasaki, and Dresden show, with chilling clarity, what it means when the human world is assimilated, without apology and often without residue, into the combustible world of physics. These cataclysmic assimilations are worth recalling, for in the twenty-first century less dramatized versions seem to have become routine, sometimes with nothing standing between large segments of the human population and the naked laws of physics. This is what we see in Lebanon in 2006, with roads, bridges, and apartment buildings all blown to pieces, as if they had been hit by an earthquake. Homer has already warned us about this, in his image of the Greek army as a force of nature. But the most powerful warning is to come from the Athenian theater, especially in three plays by Euripides: *Andromache, Hecuba,* and *The Women of Troy.*

Tragic Continuum

As their titles indicate, *Andromache, Hecuba,* and *The Women of Troy* are direct descendants of the *Iliad,* beginning where the epic ends. The story is now told from the other side, however, from the standpoint not of the winners but of the losers, those whose life-world has been shattered. The Homeric word that Euripides retains and amplifies is the word δούλιον ἦμαρ (day of slavery). In the *Iliad,* Hector has used this word to describe the terrible fate that, he fears, might be in store for his wife, Andromache (Il. 6.463). Euripides includes this exact word in both *Andromache* (99) and *Hecuba* (55), and, in *The Women of Troy,* Hecuba also uses this word with a slight variation.[16]

Slavery is not just a metaphor but also a literal fact for these women, who become the property of the Greeks after the fall of their city. In *Hecuba,* the Chorus is a chorus of these foreign, female slaves, mourning their loss:

> O Ilium! O my country,
> whose name men speak no more
> among unfallen cities!
> So dense a cloud of Greeks
> came, spear on spear, destroying!
> Your crown of towers shorn away,
> and everywhere the staining fire,
> most pitiful. O Ilium,
> whose ways I shall not walk again!
> At midnight came my doom
> Midnight when the feast is done
> and sleep falls sweetly on the eyes.
> The songs and sacrifice,
> the dances, all were done.
> My husband lay asleep,
> his spear upon the wall,
> forgetting for a while
> the ships drawn up on Ilium's shore.
>
> I was setting my hair
> in the soft folds of the net
> gazing at the endless light
> deep in the golden mirror,
> preparing myself for bed,
> when tumult broke the air
> and shouts and cries
> shattered the empty streets:—
> *Onward, onward, you Greeks!*
> *Sack the city of Troy*
> *and see your home once more!*[17]

This is how things feel on the losing side; we can't have a more bitter taste of *peripeteia.* The Trojans think they have finally won, and they are celebrating, off their guard. It is then that disaster strikes. The Chorus of slave women know this treacherous turn all too well, but they still look back, with futile longing, to the moments just before it happens: the feast over at midnight, the delicious sense of sleepiness, the ritual of getting ready for bed, the reflections of lights in the golden mirror. It is a domestic scene: conjugal, registered at close range, filtered only through the senses. The horror of what follows is that it takes just a second for this small-scale domestic scene to be subsumed in the large-scale handiwork of a non-human actor. No wall is strong enough to keep this actor out, no object is too small for it to destroy. This is what makes war a "totality," a force that assimilates everything in its path. All those things that are in our own image and on our own scale—the room that holds our bed, the net that sets our hair, the mirror that we look into—all these human things will crumble the moment they undergo this assimilation. This is the condition of tragedy, but, if so, it is a condition that is populational rather than individual. Its harm is across-the-board, granting immunity to none.

Euripides' tragedies faithfully reflect this breakdown of immunity, and reflect it, most of all, in the apparent *redundancy* of the Chorus. Rather than occupying a formal space of its own, safe from the devastation, and giving voice to an unthreatened collectivity from that locale, the Chorus is in the thick of it all, indistinguishable from the protagonist. In *Hecuba,* the Chorus, no less than the protagonist, has seen their world come apart. The Chorus, no less than the protagonist, is the subject of *peripeteia* and the victim of the already transpired catastrophe. The clear dividing line between protagonist and Chorus in *Oedipus Rex* or *Antigone* is not honored here. In these war plays, the protagonist, the minor characters, and the Chorus all seem to be on the same footing. Lines assigned to one could have been easily assigned to the other two. *Andromache* opens with an equal exchange between a slave woman and Andromache, once a princess and the wife of Hector but now also a slave. In *The Women of Troy,* the Chorus of slave women simply echoes Hecuba and Andromache as their shared grief rises to a crescendo. It has nothing different to tell us.

This redundancy must have bothered Aristotle. In the *Poetics,* of course, he famously chooses not to dwell on the Chorus at all, dismissing it in a curt one-liner: "The chorus also should be thought of as one of the actors; it should be a part of the whole and contribute its share in the competitive efforts in the manner of Sophocles, not Euripides."[18] Of the three great playwrights, Sophocles is clearly the one Aristotle prefers, the one whose work answers to his definition of tragedy. Euripides is the least favorite. There are many reasons for this, but what this curt one-liner suggests, in any case, is that within the genre of tragedy there is probably not just a single unified practice but rather two opposing conventions, pointing to two almost antithetical functions for the Chorus and two antithetical understandings of harm. In Sophocles, the Chorus and the protagonist are defined by their "competitive efforts." In other words, one is pitted against the other, which allows for a differential axis between the two, with harm assigned to only one side. In Euripides, there is no such differential axis. The result is the loss of a defensible locale and its corresponding perspectival safety. In short, the tragedy that Aristotle does not like is the one that is marked by the breakdown of a system of safeguards, by the lack of distance between the phenomenal world of the observer and the phenomenal world of the observed. Witnessing and suffering are here one and the same.

This alternative conception of the Chorus suggests that the scope of tragedy is an open question from the very first, as is the localizability or containability of harm. In *The Women of Troy,* the concluding exchange between Hecuba and the Chorus offers one reason why harm cannot be contained, cannot be stopped by the guaranteed safety of a contrapuntal structure:

> HECABE:
> > Troy is a beacon!—look! On the hill every house is blazing,
> > Along the crest of the ramparts, over the roofs,
> > The fire rushes and roars in the wake of the spear!
> CHORUS:
> > Troy in her fearful fall has faded, vanished!
> > At the breath of War, as smoke at the beating of wings! . . .
> HECABE:
> > Listen, temples of gods, beloved city,
> > Ravaged with flame, flowing with guiltless blood!
> CHORUS:
> > Soon you will fall, and lie
> > With the earth you loved, and none shall name you!
> HECABE:
> > Dust mingled with smoke spreads wings to the sky,
> > I can see nothing, the world is blotted out!
> CHORUS:
> > Earth and her name are nothing;
> > All has vanished, and Troy is nothing![19]

Fire and wind, earth and water—these elemental forces are the weapons of mass destruction enlisted by war. The assimilation of the human world to the world of physics becomes absolute at this point. This assimilation is not only irreversible—a threshold that, once crossed, will allow for no return—what it further dramatizes is a process downwardly and mechanically homogenized, where manmade disasters will increasingly look and act like natural disasters. If Greek tragedy has always been inhabited by forces both human and nonhuman, in these war plays it is the latter that triumphs, that imposes upon the world its logic of maximum damage in minimum time. Harm here can only be a global field, coextensive with the life-world of both Chorus and protagonist, with no safe haven. This is what Greek tragedy shows us, and, in the twenty-first century, no warning needs to be heard more urgently.

Notes

1. George Steiner, *The Death of Tragedy* (1961; rpt., New Haven: Yale University Press, 1996), 5.

2. Aristotle, *Poetics,* trans. Gerald Else (Ann Arbor: University of Michigan Press, 1970), 35, 52a22–24.

3. Steiner, *The Death of Tragedy,* 292, 342.

4. Ibid., 6.

5. Raymond Williams, *Modern Tragedy,* ed. Pamela McCallum (1966; rpt., Peterborough, ON: Broadview Press, 2006), 33–34. I should point out, however, that Williams is not primarily concerned with Greek tragedy. Terry Eagleton, also not primarily concerned with Greek tragedy, has similarly argued for an important link between tragedy and modernity. See his *Sweet Violence: The Idea of the Tragic* (London: Blackwell, 2003).

6. Steiner, *The Death of Tragedy,* 355.

7. Oddone Longo, "The Theater of *Polis,*" in *Nothing to Do with Dionysus?,* ed. John J. Winkler and Froma I. Zeitlin (Princeton: Princeton University Press, 1990), 16, n7. Longo draws on Frank Kolb, *Agora und Theater* (Berlin: Gebrüder Mann Verlag, 1981).

8. Winkler and Zeitlin, "Introduction" to *Nothing to Do with Dionysus?,* 4.

9. Simon Goldhill, "The Great Dionysia," in ibid., 114.

10. Jean-Pierre Vernant, "Tensions and Ambiguities in Greek Tragedy," in Jean-Pierre Vernant and Pierre Vidal-Naquet, *Myth and Tragedy in Ancient Greece,* trans. Janet Lloyd (New York: Zone, 1988). Vernant also makes the interesting observation that "this dichotomy between chorus and tragic hero is matched by a duality in the language of tragedy. . . . It is the language of the chorus, in the chanted passages, that carries on the lyrical tradition of a poetry celebrating the exemplary virtues of the hero of ancient times. For the protagonists of the drama the meter of the passages of dialogue is, on the contrary, close to that of prose." See *Myth and Tragedy,* 34.

11. John J. Winkler, "The Ephebe's Song," in Winkler and Zeitlin, *Nothing to Do with Dionysus*, 43. Peter Wilson, following Winkler's lead, further emphasizes the importance of aristocratic patronage and display. See his *The Athenian Institution of the "Khoregia": The Chorus, the City, and the Stage* (Cambridge: Cambridge University Press, 2000).

12. John Gould, "Tragedy and the Collective Experience," in *Tragedy and the Tragic: Greek Theatre and Beyond,* ed. M. S. Silk (Oxford: Clarendon Press, 1996), 219. Also pertinent here is Page duBois's spirited essay "Toppling the Hero: Polyphony in the Tragic City," *New Literary History* 35, no. 1 (2004): 63–82.

13. Gould, "Tragedy and the Collective Experience," 219–20.

14. Homer, *The Iliad,* trans. Robert Fagles (New York: Penguin, 1990), 2.539–59. All references to this translation will be cited by book and lines in the text.

15. Simone Weil, *The Iliad: or, The Poem of Force,* trans. Mary McCarthy (Wallingford, PA: Pendle Hill, 1945), 3.

16. Richard Garner, *From Homer to Tragedy: The Art of Allusion in Greek Poetry* (London: Routlege, 1990), 165.

17. Euripides, *Hecuba,* trans. William Arrowsmith, in *Euripides III,* ed. David Grene and Richmond Lattimore (Chicago: University of Chicago Press, 1958), 48–49, ll. 905–32. All further references to this edition will be cited by lines in the text.

18. Aristotle, *Poetics,* 56a25.

19. Euripides, *The Women of Troy,* trans. Philip Vellacott (Harmondsworth, UK: Penguin, 1965), 122–23.

Tragedy, Theology, and Feminism in the Time After Time

Kathleen M. Sands

In literary circles, there has been a renewed sense of the tragic, a lament for a sensibility that seems to have gone missing in modernity. Since the tragic itself is all about loss, what we lament is the loss of a sense of loss. This lament for tragedy, no doubt, portends its resurrection. But resurrection, unfortunately, is not entirely good news. As Sethe observes in Toni Morrison's *Beloved,* resurrection just means that "them that die bad don't stay in the ground."[1]

In the wake of the twentieth century, it is modernity—the myth of time as the progress of reason and freedom—that is undergoing a bad death. The resurrection of tragedy is a symptom of a time that sees itself as post-time, whether this takes the form of reactionary antimodernism or of a chastened radicalism. But of course what we are "post" is not time, only a particular myth of time, and this wrestling with tragedy is our search for a new way to tell time's story.

There is an emergent consensus that the decline of tragic literature was regrettable. But there is disagreement, especially between Terry Eagleton and George Steiner, as to whether Christianity, along with modernity, is partly accountable for that decline.[2] Underlying this quarrel, however, is a less articulate disagreement about the meaning and peculiar value of tragedy itself. What is tragedy, or, more precisely, what should it be? What would be good about its resurrection? The chief purpose of this essay is to answer that question. In so doing, the essay challenges the evasion of tragedy in the theological mainstream and in feminist thought. After proposing a normative definition of tragedy in part 1, I argue in part 2 that western Christian theology has both acknowledged tragedy in the fallen world and attempted to resolve tragedy by defending God. However, there are literally the best of reasons for evading the tragic, in particular the apparent tension between a tragic sensibility and a commitment to human liberation. Part 3 of this essay examines this healthy-minded resistance to the tragic as it appears among feminist theologians, and also in a recent work by Carol Gilligan. Nonetheless, I will conclude, it is not for nothing that the tragic persistently reasserts itself in postmodernity, and to live well in this moment the strange fruit of tragedy must somehow be our nourishment.

I. The Meaning of the Tragic

To define tragedy as a genre is a normative enterprise, since genres are normative. In the case of tragedy, the canon typifying the genre is centered on the classical Greek tragedies, but the norms embedded in that canon are not self-evident. We can begin by observing that tragedy concerns not suffering *simpliciter,* or even profound suffering, but the telling of suffering. To define tragedy—to explain what makes a tragedy "successful"—is to discern what makes profound suffering good to tell. The problematics of defining tragedy and of finding meaning in suffering are therefore the same: it is equally perilous to find and not to find meaning in suffering. To find meaning in suffering is in some sense to accept it, enabling the legitimation of suffering that may be unjust or unnecessary. But to find no meaning in suffering is to leave history not only unredeemed but unmourned and forgotten. And so it is with tragedy. If a story is not ultimately tragic, it is not tragic at all; the finality of the loss it narrates is only apparent. Yet ultimate tragedy would seem not only devoid of value but actually destructive of value, and so not worth the telling. Like Job in the presence of God, we rather should close our mouths.[3]

Tragedies are to history as trauma is to time. Traumas interrupt time; they are black holes, not just potholes, in the journey. This is their finality, the feeling of "the end" that circumscribes and sanctifies every profound loss. Yet traumatic finality, just because it feels so absolute, remains unfinished, a "lump in the spirit."[4] It cannot be spun into the fabric of meaning, and so manifests itself as gap or silence. And because it cannot be integrated or expressed, trauma demands reenactment.

In the same way, tragedies are not exactly part of history; they disrupt and defy the narration of time as meaning. But there is a normative difference (which is to say, there *should* be a difference) between trauma and tragedy. For tragedies, if they succeed, change the modality of repetition from act to ritual, from event to narration. Tragedy, as an aesthetic form, consigns trauma to a ritual space where, rather than being silently reenacted, it is solemnly voiced and lamented. Just as marking off the sacred creates the profane, so tragedies mark off trauma and in so doing wrench back from trauma the rest of life, during which time does not stand still and from which swaths of meaning can be made. This modal transposition is the peculiar efficacy of tragedy; it changes trauma into the density around which meaning orbits, held and repelled like planets around the sun.

This normative definition runs against the definition of tragedy as a pessimistic worldview, a definition presumed both by tragedy's theological detractors[5] and by some of its literary proponents, most notably George Steiner. Martha Nussbaum argues persuasively that the Greek tragedies embrace a squabbling plurality of incommensurable goods.[6] If so, it is better to say that tragedies shatter worldviews than that tragedy is itself a worldview. Tragedies are not pessimistic worldviews because they are not worldviews of any kind. On the contrary, they tell of worlds and times that are broken such that no coherent view of them can be had.

Tragedies tell of suffering, but they are something more than *Lebensschmerz*. They are stories that narrate a specifically moral sort of catastrophe. Tragedies record the fundamental contradiction between reality and ideality: life is not as it should be; *we* are not as we should be. This contradiction is the birth trauma of moral consciousness, and each new blossom opens around the knowledge that the contradiction will outlive it. In repudiating some part of reality, some part of ourselves, tragedies convey a prereflective, negative moral judgment. In ordinary speech, the objects of these negative moral judgments are labeled "evil." Tragedies, then, are stories in which the experience of suffering bleeds into the question of evil.

Usually our judgments of evil rely upon what amounts to a metaphysical warrant: the notion that what we judge evil is in some sense less real than what we judge good. But this is just the metaphysical crutch that tragedy kicks out from under us. If life really is not as it should be, then our negative moral judgments lack this sort of metaphysical grounding. We repudiate tragic acts, events, or even persons in full recognition that they have as much reality, as much reason for being, as much ultimacy as anything else. We make moral judgments that are existentially absolute, and yet they are judgments with no absolute grounding. Worst of all, they are judgments against, variously, ourselves, the world, or the divine.

This is the moral catastrophe within the specific catastrophe that a given tragedy narrates. Catastrophes such as killing one's daughter may stay in the theater, but this is the one that follows us home—the catastrophe, not just of innocent *suffering,* but of innocent *fault.* Tragic actors are morally faulted, yet in a way that could not have been avoided. And when we behold that fault and judge it, we simultaneously partake in it.

So the faultedness, for all of us, is also an injustice we suffer. This is the heart of tragic fault: to affirm our value is at once to stand against our-selves, and to affirm the world is at once to stand against it—not against our selves or the world *in toto* but against a brokenness that is, in the manner of trauma, ultimate.

Tragic fault is the birth trauma of moral consciousness, but the labor, in this case, comes after the birth. And the labor will be permanent, be-cause the wholeness we can make will only be partial and provisional. Tragedies advance the uneasy intuition that the true and the good are neither identical to each other nor coherent within themselves. "Is there no means to speak us fair, and yet tell the truth? It will not hide, when truth and good are torn asunder."[7] Seen in the dark light of tragedy, the world promises to be valuable only so far as we make good on our truth claims, and to be intelligible only so far as we make true what we envi-sion as good.

The plurality of goods, within tragic narratives, is a function of their location within this world. Tragic conflicts might dissolve in eternity or utopia, but in this world there is a plurality of incompatible goods. In the Greek canon, there are conflicts (to name just a few) between familial bonds and civic obligation, Dionysian passion and Apollonian reason, law and love. But such conflicts exist in the present as well as the past, and they come not just in matched pairs but in unruly bunches. In polit-ical life, sexual life, even in the management of one's daily schedule, we have to do with values that are as likely to pull in different directions as to overlap. Given this diversity and incommensurablity of goods, we will make choices that injure our lives and characters in fundamental ways. We will do so by choice, yet we will not be able to avoid these choices.

The diversity and incommensurability of goods implies also the plu-rality of truth. For if goods are diverse and incommensurable, they each may have their own reasons. Economic development may militate against the health of the environment, national security against personal liber-ties, a successful career against a happy love life, and so forth. More dis-turbing, the same goes for the things we judge evil. "It is commonplace," Terry Eagleton writes, "to speak of war as meaningless. . . . [but] war is all too rational, at least in one somewhat shriveled sense of the term."[8] Whether we contemplate war, patriarchy, slavery, the maldistribution of wealth, or banal cruelty, each demonstrates daily that it has reasons of the most enduring kind. Like plural goods, these disvalues create their own rationalities, their own worlds, and their own histories.

A moral sensibility forged in these conflicts is as different from moralism as tragedies are from morality plays. Because tragedies long for lives that are integrally good, they draw no bright line between character and happiness, between doing good and faring well. And because the goods comprising an integral life and community are not innately harmonious, tragedies concern moral suffering and failure rather than moral success. In tragedy, the grays, blacks, and whites of moral abstraction are colored with the passions, sorrows, and fears of lived experience, and goodness involves not only obligations, virtues, rules, and acts, but also imagination, creativity, desire, and the constant undertow of loss.

Just as tragedy saves us from moralism, so it saves us from the facile aestheticism in which suffering belongs to a pattern that is "ultimately" beautiful. That vantage point, surely, is available only to those who can afford the most comfortable seats. In tragedy, however, beauty is no mere *objet d'art*. It is more like the loveliness of the sycamore trees in which Morrison's Sethe watched black children hang, a loveliness she recalls with a certain horror, disclosing as it did the indifference of trees to the children who hung in them.[9] Just as tragic suffering is moral suffering, so tragic beauty is a suffering beauty that, like Sethe's, comes from growing into one's scars. Yet this beauty—whether remembered, imagined, or only longed-for—alone makes it palatable for the world to go on revolving around unfathomable loss.

This encounter with the unfathomable points to a third dimension of the tragic—in addition to the moral and the aesthetic, the mystical. In tragedies, there is the terrible clarity of having gotten to the bottom of things, only to discover that the bottom is bottomless. With a bracing certainty, we know ourselves to be encountering something that we cannot know. Tragedies, when they work, rivet us at the brink of this sort of abyss; we neither are able to fathom it, nor to look away. Christian theologians have called this state a limit experience.[10] But theologians, sanguine souls, most often think of the limit as good, as in Anselm's famous definition of God as "that than which nothing greater can be conceived."[11] Anselm felt his definition to be in and of itself a proof of God, because its meaning was grasped not through cognition, but through mystical apprehension of a greatness beyond cognition.[12] But there are negative limit experiences as well—that than which nothing worse can be conceived. Tragedies are full of them, history is full of them, and the explosion of them throughout the twentieth century has set a period after modernity, killing the myth of time as progress and sending us in search of another way to tell time's story.

Wherever one sits, the sight of such an abyss does not generate beauty or meaning; instead, with incomparable intensity, it generates the desire for them. Precisely by uncovering moral lack, tragedies nurture moral desire. A friend of mine was a child in the Netherlands during World War II. As his family teetered on the edge of starvation they would read cookbooks and imagine fabulous dishes that they could not possibly acquire the ingredients to make. Perhaps this is how tragedies work. They feed hunger, approaching meaning and beauty *via negativa,* the way mystics may approach the sacred.

II. The Evasion of Tragedy in the Christian Theological Tradition

Debates about Christianity and tragedy concern more than the meaning of Christianity; they also concern the inscrutable meaning and the peculiar value of tragedy, and of the time-after-time called postmodernity.

For George Steiner, whose magisterial work on the subject helped to ignite the current interest, tragedy conveys "a metaphysic of desperation," a view of the world in which, as Sophocles wrote, "it is better not to have been born," normatively embodied in five Greek tragedies.[13] In Steiner's view, tragedy declined because the two major worldviews of the modern West, Christianity and Marxism, are both hopeful and thus antitragic. For Steiner, tragedy is a sort of antidote to modernity; tragedies paint a world in which rationality does not reign supreme and in which "there is nothing democratic" (241). The world of tragedy, in Steiner's view, was hierarchical, and within this world everything from earth to heaven was connected. Indeed, the loss of common meanings and public art forms is for Steiner a main reason for the demise of tragic literature in modernity.

Terry Eagleton's disagreement with Steiner concerns, among other things, the meaning of modernity and the prospects for meaning after modernity. He faults Steiner and other proponents of tragedy for opposing modernity's salutary products, in their apparent preference for hierarchy over equality, fate over freedom, suffering over progress. To valorize tragedy after a century that has seen more of it than perhaps any other betrays, in Eagleton's view, an elitist disregard for real suffering.[14] But Eagleton is struggling as much against the postmoderns who negate tragedy as against the countermodern connoisseurs with a taste for other people's suffering. Against the latter he repudiates absolutism of the hierarchical, authoritarian sort, but against the former he insists that there is something absolute in history—in Adorno's words, "the absolute of suffering" predicated on the "permanent structures of our species-being" (xii). Indeed, for Eagleton, postmodernism represents a demonic, nihilistic negation of meaning, the opposite of the tragic, rightly understood, yet leading to a political indifference not unlike that which results from the countermodern valorization of the tragic (260, 263). Tragedy, for Eagleton, tells of absolutes, but these are what could be called negative absolutes, absolute losses borne by the powerless, propertyless "losers" of history, whom the Bible calls the *anawim*. [15] On behalf of history's losers, the Bible commands in Eagleton's reading an absolute faith, "the faith of political revolution" (296). That is an act of faith that postmoderns no longer seem prepared to venture, and that countermoderns never ventured in the first place.

In regard to Christianity, Eagleton's disagreement with Steiner is fundamentally a disagreement about the meaning and value of tragedy. For Eagleton, clearly, the point of recognizing tragedy is in some way to ameliorate it. Therefore the fact that Christianity and Marxism are ultimately hopeful worldviews does not, in Eagleton's mind, make them antitragic (10, 30). "It is the tragic that Christianity and Marxism seek to redeem, but they can do so only by installing themselves at the heart of it" (40). With Eagleton, one certainly can question the point of nostalgia for a world or at least a worldview imagined to be not better but actually worse than what we have now. Certainly it is unimaginable that a Sophocles or a Shakespeare, on completion of a tragic masterpiece, would have reflected with a sigh that it will all have been worthwhile if even a single audience member can be made to despair of life. But that does not resolve the extreme difficulty of expressing how tragedy is and is not ultimate, or as Eagleton puts it, how it is that "only by accepting [the worst] as the last word about the human condition can it cease to be the last word" (37). Eagleton attempts to express this through the Marxist distinction between "exchange value" and "use value." The redemptive value of historical suffering, he argues, is not an "exchange value" that can be calculated instrumentally or projected teleologically, and revolutionary redemption does nothing to wipe out the "use value" (though "use cost" might be more accurate) of the suffering itself (37–39).

Appropriately enough, Eagleton's account of Christianity as historical faith in and on behalf of the *anawim* resonates for many nonelite Christians both in the present and in the past. However, nonelites are not the authors of texts and creeds, and so Steiner's is a more precise account of theology's response to tragedy. Within the theological tradition, tragedy is a subspecies of the problem of evil, and evil must be resolvable given the presumed nature of God as all good and all powerful. Since Leibniz, this defense of God in the face of evil has been known as "theodicy,"[16] but the motif of defending God, if not the term, goes to the foundations of western Christian theology. For tragedies tell a story about time that is the polar opposite of the story told by classical Christian theism in which goodness will be victorious "in the end." Theistic faith is precisely the conviction that tragedy is only apparent, and that the losses told in tragedies are not really ultimate. However, these losses are only non-ultimate if the world and history themselves are not of ultimate value to us. Conversely, if we place ultimate value on humanity as it exists in the world and in history, tragedy is the price of the ticket.

But the theological defense of God has not been for God's sake alone. Whatever God's vulnerabilities, theodicy's human function is to legitimate normative claims by reducing good and evil to truth and falsehood. Good, in other words, is held to possess a kind of truth that evil ultimately lacks. Deployed theistically, this enables moral or political proposals to be justified as the nature or will of God. However, this pattern of legitimation can be deployed equally effectively under the aegis of humanism, where the good is ontologically rooted in human nature, or under the aegis of scientific rationalism, where the good is ontologically rooted in the natural order of the world. In each case, moral and political claims are founded on what could be called a positive absolute. Whether this positive absolute is God, humanity, or nature, the pattern of legitimation it upholds is authoritarian and antirational. This is not despite its appeal to an absolute reason, but precisely because any positive absolute will substitute legitimation for explanation, assertions for proposals, and authority for deliberation and choice.

Christian theology has defended God by relying on two interlocking ways of thinking about evil. One is usually known as the privation theory; the other is usually associated with metaphysical dualism. In both, divine goodness is the primal, ultimate reality, and goodness—at least "in the end"—is all powerful.[17] And in both, theistic faith overcomes tragedy.

The privation theory contends that God is Being itself and Being is good. Evil thus becomes, quite literally, nothing. Despite all appearances to the contrary, what seems evil has no ultimate being or power. The privation tradition, because it conceives reality as a single intelligible whole, is also a rationalistic tradition. Its goal is to understand evil rather than simply to repudiate it. To understand is to identify, beneath apparent evils, underlying causes that are good; to correct evil is to activate this goodness, which is understood to be the real truth of things.

The goodness of all things carries also the promise/threat that all things might be equal. Early medieval Christianity avoided this possibility by combining the privation theory with the Neoplatonic "chain of being,"[18] in which degrees of goodness were at the same time degrees of being. The chain of being thus provided a universal intelligibility that simultaneously rationalized a universal, hierarchical order. By modernity, when the principle of equality had displaced hierarchy, this ontology lost its remaining scraps of plausibility. However, this did not mean the demise of the privation tradition, the heart of which is not hierarchical order as such but the principle of universal intelligibility. In modernity, reason would lose the metaphysical resonance of Logos and would become instead methodological and formal, attested more in historical processes and in uniform procedures than in dogmatic verities. But modern rationalism, just as much as ancient rationalism, remained committed to the principle that evil is only apparent: there is no violence or conflict that does not have good reasons at its root.

Of the two theories, privation is the more rationally compatible with Christian monotheism, which admits no truth beside the one, good God. However, rationality is not the only driving interest of Christian morality and politics, and not even of Christian thought, given its moral and political interests. Alongside its commitment to comprehend all, Christian thought also carries the persistent impulse to cast what it deems evil into the darkness beyond ordinary comprehension. This moral impulse is the permanent wellspring of dualism, and from it flows the second, complementary conception of evil in Christian theology. In dualistic thinking, evil cannot be explained away in terms of the good; instead, evil possesses a life and logic of its own.

Ancient and medieval dualisms went on to elaborate metaphysically the nature and origin of evil, its relation to good and its destiny for final extinction. Like the chain of being, metaphysical dualism declined in modernity. Moreover, rationalism rather than dualism has been modernity's overriding theme. But just as the rationalism that drives the privation theory is still with us, so is the moralism that drives dualistic thought. In modernity and postmodernity, both continue to tightrope their way through history, albeit without a metaphysical net. In contrast to elaborate ancient and medieval cosmologies, contemporary dualism can present itself simply as a naïve, even sentimental, moralism.

The "axis of evil," now an underlying principle of U.S. foreign policy, is an important illustration. In ancient systems such as Zoroastrianism or Gnosticism in its many forms, it would have been necessary to offer a cosmogonic account of how the evil nations became so and a teleological prognosis of their final demise. American foreign policy, though sadly lacking the intellectual energy of these ancient schemes, works on the same premise: evil has its own *raison d'être*. Evildoers do what they do simply because they are evil. The word *evil* does not simply articulate a moral judgment; it becomes an ontological explanation.

Despite the logical tensions between them, the deeper link between privation and dualism is that both reduce moral judgments to metaphysical judgments, and through this reduction both legitimate moral claims. In each case, evil boils down to two metaphysical questions. Does evil exist? And, if evil does exist, how does its existence relate to the existence of the good? Privation and dualism give opposing answers to the first question, and only for dualism is the second question a question at all. Nonetheless, both stem from faith in a single, absolutely transcendent Good, which necessarily produces an Other. Rationalism hides its others behind the idea that everything is constituted by a goodness that, while present in different measures, is one and the same. But the otherness of rationalism shows itself on closer inspection to be absolute, for the difference between the unconditional being of God and the contingent being of everything else is infinite. Conversely, the twoness of dualism cannot but be undermined by the notion that only one of its two ultimate principles is good; goodness remains the primal and ultimate reality.

Because of this interdependence, rationalism and dualism are functionally complementary. Rationalism dominates systematic theology, particularly the theology of God. But dualistic tones have more often dominated popular Christian piety and ethics, and *contra* Eagleton, this simple twoness has exerted substantially more power over the Christian imagination than has the bewildering manyness of tragedy. The two patterns collude in the evasion of tragedy. Under threat, rationalist liberality hardens into dualist authoritarianism, and dualism, in generous times, softens into a more integral picture of reality.

The notions of original sin and a fallen world, which comprise the official theological worldview of the Christian West, seem to be tragic but are actually deft syntheses of rationalism and dualism. In the fallen world, classically described by Augustine, sin and evil do seem to exert forces of their own. Despite their ultimate unity in God, the real and the ideal are radically nonidentical in this world, and evil, for the time being, is mightily true. The goods of life, although each deserving a place within the glorious chain of being, cannot in this life be made to fit together without sacrifice and loss. The desires of fallen humanity, though ultimately reaching for the *summum bonum,* cannot be trusted, but are wont to waste themselves among the lower goods. And the will, though theoretically free, contracts like that of the addict toward the vanishing point.[19] For fallen humanity, the proper hierarchy can only be maintained by force and even violence, and this force has to be applied both to the human soul and to the body politic.[20] Human character is innately flawed and blameworthy, yet it is not in our power, individually or collectively, to make it otherwise. And we are strangely innocent of this fault that was scripted before any of us stepped onstage.

This is the state of fallen humanity and the fallen world, and it bears many marks of the tragic—innocent fault, incommensurable goods, vanishing freedom, sacrifice, and fated violence. Nonetheless, the story of the fall as told by Western theology has a moral, and the moral is not tragic. For tragedy is predicated on the assignment of ultimacy to this world. But for Western theology, the fact that the inviolable hierarchy of being seems to have come undone in this world, that evil exerts a power that it cannot not, metaphysically speaking, possess—all this is evidence that the world we experience cannot be the ultimate or original reality but must be a distortion, fallen away from its own true being. To describe the ultimate truth, western theology continued to rely on the privation theory: ultimately, God must be all in all, and all must therefore be good. Within that eternal goodness, the fallen world—that is, history itself—became a mere parenthesis. The story of the fallen world, thus parenthesized, was not tragedy but dualism—the temporary, distorted appearance of evil in a reality that is finally good and of twoness in a reality that is finally one.

Although the rationalistic response to evil was, for the Christian West, perfectly adequate to describing ultimate truth, it was not adequate to the task of redemption, which remained beyond human powers. Indeed, redemption remained beyond history, as apocalypse and eschaton. This was inevitable given the logic of Christian theism, for to demand that history have an end that is unambiguously good is also to demand that history have an unambiguous end. The cost of repudiating tragedy, then, was that it became intolerable to imagine a world that goes on beyond and despite tragedy.

III. The Feminist Evasion of Tragedy

Western theology's response to tragedy, I have argued, has been determined by its management of the problem of evil. Women have been particularly victimized by this, because they virtually have been identified with evil in the theological tradition. In its more dualistic moments, Christian thought has cast women as demonic, for example, Tertullian's characterization of women as "the devil's gateway"[21] or the maxim of the Dominican witch-hunters that "all witchcraft comes from carnal lust, which is insatiable in women."[22] In theology's more rationalistic moments, women have been positioned not as evil but merely as inferior, created for the lower rungs of the hierarchy of being.[23] This was firmly articulated by Augustine when he wrote, reflecting on Genesis 2, that due to the nature of the human [read: male] mind, woman is the image of God only when joined with her husband, but a man, quite on his own, is a complete image of God.[24]

In response to the identification of women with evil or lesser goods, Christian feminists have framed trenchant critiques of both hierarchicalism and dualism. However, few Christian or other religious feminists have noticed that those traditional responses to evil are skewed precisely because they are designed to evade the tragic. To the contrary, feminists—and this applies both to scholars of religion and other theorists—typically perceive their traditions not as evading the tragic but as unduly exacerbating it. In this respect, then, many feminists remain critical revisers of modernity and do not participate in the postmodern or countermodern rediscovery of the tragic.

Much of this feminist critique is more than deserved, especially concerning the tragic canon and the elaboration of tragedy into a worldview. But to recognize the tragic defined in the normative way proposed in this essay is neither to support the particulars of the canon nor to endorse a totalistic worldview of any kind. Tragedy, I have proposed, is the necessity of making moral judgments that are existentially but not metaphysically absolute. To say we have no *absolute* grounds on which to build our lives of course is not to say we have no grounds at all. Life in view of tragedy does not become a castle in the air, but it does become a raft on rough waters, to be navigated with imagination and practical wisdom. Feminists have plenty of those assets, but when it comes to authorizing our moral and political claims, we often have wanted more. Both in religion and in other fields, many feminists want to legitimate normative claims with reference to metaphysical absolutes. And this reduction of the moral to the metaphysical, as I have argued, is the chief reason for the repudiation of the tragic in the West.

Feminists are quite right to critique the tragic canon, however. Since tragedies are stories about irresoluble conflicts and profound loss, it matters which stories, and whose, are diagnosed as tragic. To begin with an illustration from beyond religious feminism, we can consider *The Birth of Pleasure,* in which psychologist Carol Gilligan incisively analyzes and rejects the Oedipus tragedy.[25] Oedipus, Gilligan argues, is a founding myth of gender and sexuality in the West, and under the influence of Freud was elevated to science. Gilligan contends that the *Oedipus* cycle, the *Orestia,* and other classic tragedies are really stories of trauma—experiences of suffering so shocking and injurious to our natures that the psyche responds with dissociation (6). In this light, tragedy appears to be not a means of expression but a means of repression, reinstating loss rather than healing it.

The normative distinction that I have proposed between tragedy and trauma is not persuasive to Gilligan, at least not in reference to these stories. This is partly because of the content of the stories themselves. Oedipus makes the story of sexual love into a struggle between two men over one woman. As Gilligan shows, it is a story of patriarchy, in which all relations are locked into hierarchical patterns of domination and subordination. Since equality cannot happen in such a story, neither can authentic encounter happen. Love becomes a blind and blinding force that must wither in the light of day. Desire is cruelly punished in the man and in the woman does not even appear, since she is significant not as one who desires but only as the object of male desires. And pleasure, although it was the flame toward which the story moves, is snuffed out in the telling.

Among religious feminists, only a few have addressed explicitly the theme of tragedy,[26] but there is a standard feminist critique of the fall story, with its unmistakably tragic notion of innate or "innocent" fault.[27] While innate fault is theoretically applicable to all humans, feminists know that experientially it is most gripping for those who are victimized by violence or abuse. Indeed, the internalization of evils whose origins are external is a hallmark of abuse. From this vantage point, the notion of innocent fault resembles nothing so much as a theology of victim-blaming.

The ideals of sacrificial love and substitutional atonement, derived from the view of the world as fallen, also have been subjected to extensive feminist critique. Since humans as a species are morally flawed in the worst way, we cannot save ourselves; God himself [sic] must drop in and do it for us. Incarnate in Christ, God becomes the perfectly innocent victim upon whom the sins of the world are loaded. And it is not only the sufferings of the world that are loaded on the victim but the world's fault; Christ "is made into sin" for our sake. These too are classically tragic themes. Christ vividly reiterates the *pharmacon* of ancient Greece and the *anawim* of the Bible—the masses who not only suffer for the sins of the powerful but are blamed for those sins as well.[28]

Christ, as sacrificial victim, becomes a model for how other humans should suffer, and this is the point at which the theology of atonement becomes particularly destructive for women under patriarchy and other victims of history. Supplemented by the theology of sacrifice, innocent suffering and innocent fault become not lamentable conditions but ideals to be embraced and cultivated. Feminists observe that sacrifice is self-giving without reciprocity or justice, and to define love in this way is to mistake love for violence.[29] Defilement—being "made into sin"—is an overpoweringly negative theme in the lives of women whose traditions have symbolized as female everything seen as demonic or inferior—the body, the passions, sexuality, or simple willfulness.[30]

In addition to criticizing the contents of the tragic canon, feminists also have criticized the elaboration of tragedy into a view of the world. The most pernicious feature of this worldview, for feminists, is the very hierarchicalism admired by Steiner. Gilligan's critique of tragedy in *The Birth of Pleasure,* for example, is rooted in her earlier rejection of hierarchical value systems or developmental schemes in which the morality of women was cast as categorically inferior.[31] In the case of Christian feminists, the critique of hierarchy applies both to the fallen world and to created nature as envisioned by the theological tradition. Since for Western theology, hierarchy is part of nature as divinely intended, there is no injustice in this pattern of domination. Nor is it unjust when, in the fallen world, hierarchy must be maintained by force or violence. In fact, to rebel against hierarchy, to exorcise its justifying ideologies—in other words, to struggle for liberation—becomes in this worldview the very essence of sin.

In addition to tragic hierarchicalism, religious feminists also have repudiated the notion that suffering is perennial and rooted in the nature of things. Feminists and others concerned with human liberation know that this tragic fatalism is how historical injustices normally are justified. Moreover, tragedies (as usually read) tell of suffering as a universal condition, while liberation rests on the analysis of how suffering is differentially distributed along with power. Tragedies focus on the past, which is definitionally unchangeable, rather than on the present or the future, and they lay guilt for what has already happened rather than imagining ways to be responsible for what is yet to come. Tragedies imply that there is something intrinsically wrong with nature, the cosmos, and even with the divine. Feminist and other liberation theologians can only be repelled by such tragic worldviews and they insist, quite appropriately, that what is most wrong with human life lies not in nature or God but in societies that can and do change.[32]

Gilligan's critical vision also extends beyond the particulars of the canon to tragic sensibility as such. Based on her work as a psychotherapist, she notes that for many women stories of pain and loss are more compelling than are stories of pleasure. However, as Gilligan illustrates with case studies, stories of pain and loss only make sense in view of the pleasures and desires that were at stake in them. Pleasure, then, is the epistemological key: it is pleasure that explains loss and it is the recovery of pleasure that leads people out of the deadness of trauma and back to emotional life. Tragedies, in Gilligan's view, lock up loss and throw away the key. They record pain and shame but disclose nothing of the pleasure that was made to suffer or the desire that was made to regret its own existence. In Gilligan's view, then, tragedies dissociate from suffering and reinforce trauma. So she sets out, as she says at her book's beginning, "to imagine an escape from tragedy" (19). Rather than attempting to move through the tragic, Gilligan suggests, "the road leading to the birth of pleasure skirts the tragic love story."[33]

Religious and other feminists are of course right to insist that no particular social ills, however ancient or recalcitrant, need to be thought of as unchangeable; at propitious times and places, they can be made to give way. Hence the importance of examining critically which conflicts are told as tragic here and now, to what audience. However, while particular social ills need to be questioned, this does not justify an antitragic dream of social perfectibility. Feminists are wrong if we assume that tragedy as such is obviated when judgments about evil are directed against society rather than against nature or when we move from a hierarchical to an egalitarian view of the world. Quite the opposite may be so. The modern dream of social perfection, in which many feminists continue to share, is in fact a vestige of metaphysical dualism; it tacitly assumed that imperfection and limitation applied only to "matter" and not to "spirit." That was why society, once distinguished from nature, began to be conceived without limits. Once this old infinitism is relinquished, however, the world of history and society discloses itself as a field of possibilities that are large but shockingly finite and often profoundly conflictual. Transposing our vision of human prospects from nature to sociality, then, does not erase the tragic; instead, like a disease that has survived inoculation, it springs up in even more virulent forms.

The subject of dualism brings us to the main and most problematic reason for feminist repudiations of tragedy—the desire to provide metaphysical warrants for normative claims. Feminists recognize metaphysical dualism, with its devaluation of the body, sexuality, and history, as an ideological enemy. But they have continued to rely on another kind of dualism—the moral dualism in which the good has an ontological status that evil lacks. This desire to invoke authority of the most absolute sort is especially hard to resist for religious feminism, which indicts the patriarchal language of good and evil yet wants to do so in the very name of God.

Within Christian feminism, these metaphysical warrants so far have assumed three basic forms. One is an ideal of justice that transcends history. This is perhaps the most widespread metaphysical warrant in Christian feminism, appealing as it does to women of color and women in the two-thirds world.[34] A second warrant is a transcendent ideal of nature, where hierarchical domination itself is seen as humanity's fall away from creation as divinely intended. Christian feminists who are most at home in the European theological tradition are most likely to deploy this sort of warrant.[35] The third common metaphysical warrant in feminist theology is also nature but nature apprehended as an immanent ideal, available in women's deeper experiences and in communion with the extra-human world. This is common among Christian feminists interested in women's spirituality, as well as in religious feminists who have left the biblical traditions in favor of Goddess spirituality.[36] Carol Gilligan appears to share this approach, for example, when she characterizes pleasure as "ontological true north" or distinguishes the false voice imposed on girls by patriarchy from the true voices and true love that emerge in feminist theater and other forms of consciousness-raising.[37]

Whether the metaphysical warrant is justice or nature, in all these cases feminists conceive injustice as a species of *falsehood*. Tragedy, by the same move, is rendered at worst penultimate. But tragedy is the price one pays for placing ultimate value in this world, and it is a price that liberation-minded theologians ought to be ready to pay, committed as they are to return from the other-worldliness of the tradition to this world and its history. The same would seem incumbent upon feminist theorists such as Gilligan, who are pledged to return from the airy universals of patriarchal thought to the thicket of practical cares and face-to-face relationships. The evasion of the tragic sets feminist work at cross-purposes with itself: on one hand, there is a returning to the biosphere, the body, history, sexuality, and human community; on the other hand, there is a repeated flight from this world in search of metaphysical absolutes.

Christian feminists, like the tradition before them, have transposed ethics into metaphysics—that is, they have attempted to authorize claims about how the world should be by reducing these normative claims to claims about ultimate reality. That which is judged evil is cast as a distortion, deprivation, or destruction of the real. And if normative claims can be justified in this way, there will be no tragedy, for no genuine good will be ultimately lost, and in the demise of evils, there will be nothing to mourn.

But metaphysical warrants, while they may provide legitimacy, add nothing to intelligibility. Absolutes can inspire action, but they generate no strategies or tactics; they may offer authority of the highest sort, but in so doing they detract from rational deliberation. This is easy to see when we recall the kinds of metaphysical warrants upon which Christian feminists have relied. Everyone is for "justice" in the abstract, but we disagree vigorously about the content of what is just. If I identify my own political program with God's justice, I plant the flag of authority at the summit of my own viewpoint, but others, unless they are already in my company, have little clue how I got there and no idea how to follow me. The same applies to nature, the other most popular metaphysical warrant among Christian feminists. As feminists should know, "nature" is anything but obvious, anything but "natural." It is the most ideological of terms, used always to ratify moral positions where one has arrived by other means.

Feminism, Gilligan wisely proffers, is about democracy, participation in the decisions that shape one's life. If so, it is not enough for theologians to provide, however authoritatively, a feminist version of right and wrong. It is not enough to receive the "right" answers to normative questions; people need the power and ability to produce answers for themselves. Besides availing women of better theological answers, theologians therefore should do what everyone's grade school math teacher exhorted—"show your work." To show the work of theology, we have to explicate how power over norms is exerted and contested, how norms change in time and space, how normative decision-makers are challenged or displaced. We have to offer, in other words, not legitimation but historicization, not a preformed set of postpatriarchal norms but the power to analyze, contest, and create norms.

IV. Conclusion

The work of making norms is the work of making worlds, and in this work, loss can be a field in which meaning is found and a material from which it is built. But everything depends on knowing that we have lost and knowing what we have lost. In "Mourning and Melancholia" Freud distinguished between losses in a way that may be instructive here.[38] Mourning, he said, was triggered by plain, external losses, and the ego became reconciled to those losses by learning, gradually, that it can derive satisfaction from alternative objects. But the mystery of melancholia is that the loss generating it is invisible. It could be said of the melancholic, as of modernity in relation to tragic forms, that the loss itself has been lost.

Detractors of tragedy such as Carol Gilligan think the tragic stories of the West induce something like melancholia—a deadened, self-blaming emotional state in which loss itself is lost. But tragedy ought to uncover the grief and the pleasure; ought to be, in other words, not a symptom of melancholia but a vehicle for its healing. And even for its detractors, tragedy tends to return, just as it returns in the lamenting of its loss. Even Gilligan, despite her many denunciations of tragedy as such, allows that it may be necessary "to go into the heart of tragedy in order to find a path that leads back to pleasure."[39]

But to heal is to uncover, not recover, a loss—to recognize the loss precisely as such. The melancholic, said Freud, has lost something, but rather than lose the desired object, she attempts to become it. In the process, however, she also ingests her hostility at the lost object, and this hostility, now directed against the self, becomes the "critical agency" that Freud would later term the "superego." In melancholia, then, the sense of something gone missing in the world is displaced by the feeling of inadequacy in oneself.

If tragedy is, as I have suggested, the birth trauma of moral consciousness, then it is not surprising that tragedy would reassert itself now. At the dawn of modernity, with the death or eclipse of God, morality was ingested and became humanism. In the dusk of modernity's many moral catastrophes, we can only hope, as Freud did for the melancholic, that we might come in some way to prefer ourselves to our ideals.

For Gilligan and other detractors of tragedy, healing comes by the reclaiming of pleasure and desire. Pleasure is entombed by grief, she argues, and only by finding the pleasure can we know what the grief was about. Gilligan is right about finding the pleasure, and it also would be right to say that postmodern melancholia can be healed only by remembering the moral desire for a human community that is integrally good. But pleasure, resurrected, does not come up in the same condition as it went down, because it has been to the netherworld and back, and grief still clings to it. Nor can moral desire come up in the same condition it went down before Auschwitz, Hiroshima, or September 11, 2001, and the ensuing state of permanent war. So it may be hard to tell the difference between this twice-born longing for the good and actual despair, just as it is hard to tell the difference between the flight from tragedy and the impulse to liberation.

But there is a difference, and in that difference lie the peculiar moral, aesthetic, and mystical values of tragedy. If tragedy can succeed—that is, if profound suffering can be made good to tell—that can only be because we know that we have lost and what we have lost. The losses at stake in tragedy, I have suggested, are fundamentally moral losses—lost ideals about ourselves, the world, and God. To uncover tragedy is, at once, to confront the crushing limitations of humanity and to reignite the desire for lives and selves that are better. It is not a loss we have gotten over, nor ought we to keep trying.

Notes

1. Toni Morrison, *Beloved* (New York: New American Library, 1987), 188.

2. George Steiner, *The Death of Tragedy* (New Haven: Yale University Press, 1980); Terry Eagleton, *Sweet Violence: The Idea of the Tragic* (Oxford: Blackwell, 2003).

3. In his book on Job, Gustavo Gutiérrez suggests that closing the mouth also would have been a better response for the unhelpful friends of Job, and a more fitting response to the plight of the poor than is theological speculation. Gustavo Gutiérrez, *On Job: God-Talk and the Suffering of the Innocent,* trans. Matthew O'Connell (Maryknoll, NY: Orbis Books, 1989), 76, 103.

4. A translation/description of the Korean word "han" by theologian Chung Hyun Kyung. See Chung Hyun Kyung, *Struggle To Be the Sun Again: Introducing Asian Women's Theology* (Maryknoll, NY: Orbis Books, 1990), 43.

5. Perhaps the best illustration of this theological polemic against tragedy is Reinhold Niebuhr, *Beyond Tragedy: Essays on the Christian Interpretation of History* (New York: Charles Scribner's Sons, 1937). See also Paul Tillich, *Systematic Theology* (Chicago: University of Chicago Press, 1957), esp. 1.253–54; 2.132–34; 3.38–39, 92–94, 244–45.

In recent decades, theological works on the tragic are more favorable to the topic. However, while recognizing a tragic dimension to existence, they reject a tragic worldview as contrary to the Christian worldview. See for example Edward Farley, *Good and Evil: Interpreting a Human Condition* (Minneapolis: Fortress Press, 1990).

Tragedy, most Christian theologians argue, should not be a worldview. This is a position with which I agree. However, I argue that tragedy shatters worldviews and thus represents a threat to a Christian worldview that theologians have not digested. Moreover, the motif of theodicy (the defense of God) continues to drive most theological responses to the tragic. See for example Wendy Farley, *Tragic Vision and Divine Compassion: A Contemporary Theodicy* (Louisville: Westminster/ John Knox Press, 1990) and Marjorie Hewitt Suchocki, *The End of Evil: Process Eschatology in Historical Context* (Albany: SUNY Press, 1988). While Wendy Farley sees theodicy as compatible with a tragic sensibility, I argue that they are effectively opposed. Finally, although virtually all contemporary theologies reject metaphysical dualism, they continue to rely on a moral dualism in which good and evil are ontological categories. This, I argue below, is an even more persistent motive than is the defense of God for the evasion of the tragic.

For a detailed discussion of theology and the tragic, see Kathleen Sands, *Escape from Paradise: Evil and Tragedy in Feminist Theology* (Minneapolis: Fortress Press, 1994).

6. Martha Nussbaum, *The Fragility of Goodness: Luck and Ethics in Greek Tragedy and Philosophy* (Cambridge: Cambridge University Press, 1986).

7. Aeschylus, *Agamemnon,* trans. Richard Lattimore, in *Greek Tragedies Volume I* (Chicago: University of Chicago Press, 1960), lines 621–22.

8. Eagleton, *Sweet Violence,* 29.

9. Morrison, *Beloved,* 6.

10. See especially David Tracy, *Blessed Rage for Order: The New Pluralism in Theology* (New York: Seabury Press, 1979), 92–118.

11. Anselm of Canterbury, "Proslogion" in *Anselm of Canterbury: Trinity, Incarnation and Redemption: Theological Treatises,* trans. and ed. J. Hopkins and H. R. Richardson (New York: Harper & Row, 1970).

12. Indeed, the definition was revealed to Anselm as a piece of spiritual consolation in response to a prayer.

13. Steiner, *Death of Tragedy,* xi. Here Steiner also became most explicit about which plays represent "absolute" tragedy: "The Seven Against Thebes, King Oedipus, Antigone, the Hippolytus and, supremely, the Bacchae."

14. Eagleton, *Sweet Violence,* 205–6.

15. Anawim: literally, "the little people"; usually translated as "the poor."

16. G. W. Von Leibniz, *Theodicy: Essays on the Goodness of God, the Freedom of Man and the Origin of Evil,* ed. Austin Farrer (London: Routledge and Kegan Paul, 1951).

17. Philosopher Mary Midgley described what appears to be the same pattern

under the rubric of a "negative" and a "positive" view of evil. See Mary Midgley, *Wickedness: A Philosophical Essay* (London: Routledge, 1986).

18. Arthur O. Lovejoy, *The Great Chain of Being: A Study in the History of an Idea* (Cambridge, MA: Harvard University Press, 1950).

19. On the disordered will, see Augustine, *Confessions,* 7.3,16.

20. See for example Augustine, *City of God,* 19.13, 22.22.

21. For useful summaries of theological misogyny and androcentrism, see Rosemary Ruether, *Sexism and God-Talk* (Boston: Beacon Press, 1983), 94–102, 165–73.

22. From the 1486 manual *Malleus Maleficarum* by Dominicans Heinrich Kramer and Jacobus Sprenger. Cited by Robert Van Voorst, ed., *Readings in Christianity,* 2nd edition (Belmont, CA: Wadsworth Publishing, 2001), 124.

23. Augustine, *Confessions,* 5.10, 7.11.

24. In *De Trinitate* (7.7.10), Augustine wrote, "I have said already, when treating of the nature of the human mind, that the woman, together with her own husband, is the image of God . . . but when she is referred to separately in her quality as helpmeet, which regards the woman alone, she is not the image of God, but as regards the male alone, he is the image of God as fully and completely as when the woman too is joined with him in one." Cited by Rosemary Ruether, *Sexism and God-Talk,* 95.

25. Carol Gilligan, *The Birth of Pleasure* (New York: Knopf, 2002).

26. Wendy Farley, *Tragic Vision and Divine Compassion.* Sharon Welch, though not focusing on the tragedy as a theme, is perhaps the strongest example of a theologian who has absorbed the loss of metaphysical foundations and developed the ethical implications (and the ethical gains) of this loss. See Sharon Welch, *A Feminist Ethic of Risk* (Minneapolis: Fortress Press, 1990).

27. See for example, Rosemary Ruether, *Sexism and God-Talk;* Elaine Pagels, *Adam, Eve, and the Serpent* (New York: Vintage Books, 1989); and Rita Nakashima Brock, *Journeys by Heart: A Christology of Erotic Power* (New York: Crossroad, 1988).

28. This, in addition to the fall story, is an area in which Steiner overlooks the strikingly tragic dimensions of Christian theology.

29. See for example, Jacqueline Grant, "The Sin of Servanthood and the Deliverance of Discipleship," in Emilie Townes, ed., *A Troubling in my Soul* (Maryknoll, NY: Orbis Books, 1993); Carter Heyward, *The Redemption of God: A Theology of Mutual Relation* (Washington, DC: University Press of America, 1982).

30. For insightful feminist critiques of the themes of sacrifice see Darby Ray, *Deceiving the Devil: Atonement, Abuse and Ransom* (Cleveland: Pilgrim Press, 1998); Rita Nakashima Brock and Rebecca Ann Parker, *Proverbs of Ashes: Violence, Redemptive Suffering and the Search for What Saves Us* (Boston: Beacon Press, 2001).

If substitutional suffering is a pernicious ideal for women under patriarchy, it is doubly pernicious for women who are doubly marginalized. Delores Williams argues that the character of African-American women's suffering has been, precisely, that of being forced surrogates. African-American women have been made to stand in for white women (for example, to provide sex for white men) and to stand in for black men (for example, to do "man's work"), Williams argues. For such women, the notion of substitutional suffering is the opposite of salvific; it is a theology of racial and sexual injustice. Delores Williams, *Sisters in the Wilderness: The Challenge of Womanist God-Talk* (Maryknoll, NY: Orbis Books, 1993).

31. Carol Gilligan, *In a Different Voice: Psychological Theory and Women's Development* (Cambridge, MA: Harvard University Press, 1982).

32. For a feminist theology that artfully conveys a tragic sensibility but overcomes these liabilities, see Flora Keshgegian, *Redeeming Memories: A Theology of Healing and Transformation* (Nashville: Abingdon Press, 2000).

33. Gilligan, *The Birth of Pleasure,* 231. This also accounts for Gilligan's preference for the story of Psyche and Cupid to that of Oedipus; it is not just because the content of the former story is more illuminating, but because its genre is nontragic.

34. See Kathleen Sands, *Escape from Paradise: Evil and Tragedy in Feminist Theology,* 55–60. Examples of this approach can be found in Letty M. Russell and others, eds., *Inheriting Our Mothers' Gardens: Feminist Theology in Third World Perspective* (Philadelphia: Westminster, 1988); Ada Maria Isasi-Diaz and Yolanda Torango, *Hispanic Women: Prophetic Voice in the Church* (Minneapolis: Fortress Press, 1992). Susan Thistlethwaite provides an interesting illustration of this approach by a Euro-American theologian who chooses deliberately to avoid the use of "nature" as a theological norm. See Susan Thistlethwaite, *Sex, Race and God: Christian Feminism in Black and White* (New York: Crossroad, 1989).

35. Sands, *Escape from Paradise,* 43–48, 87–113. The theology of Rosemary Ruether is a rich illustration of this approach. See also Letty Russell, *Human Liberation in a Feminist Perspective* (Philadelphia: Westminster Press, 1974) and Heyward, *The Redemption of God.*

36. See Sands, *Escape from Paradise,* 48–54 and 114–36. The thealogy of Carol P. Christ is exemplary of this approach, as are various feminist theologies of eros, in which sexual energy (at least in its "authentic" forms) attunes women both to what is most desirable and what is most real. See Carter Heyward, *Touching Our Strength: The Erotic as Power and the Love of God* (New York: Harper & Row, 1989) and Rita Nakashima Brock, *Journeys by Heart.* For a full critical discussion of feminist theologies of eros, see Kathleen Sands, "Uses of the Theo(a)logian: Sex and Theodicy in Religious Feminism," *Journal of Feminist Studies in Religion* 8 (1992): 7–33.

37. Gilligan, *The Birth of Pleasure,* 159, 107.

38. Sigmund Freud, "Mourning and Melancholia," in *The Standard Edition of the Complete Psychological Works of Sigmund Freud, Volume 14,* trans. James Strachey (London: Hogarth Press, 1957), 243–58.

39. Gilligan, *The Birth of Pleasure,* 56.

Tragedy, Pessimism, Nietzsche

Joshua Foa Dienstag

All the tragedies which we can imagine return in the end to the one and only tragedy: the passage of time.

Simone Weil

Who today would claim the label of pessimist for themselves? We employ the word "pessimism" today largely to name an unhealthy psychological disposition. Like a mysterious tropical disease, pessimism is something we fear to catch without quite knowing what its symptoms are. While tragedy and its history have been the subject of intense academic scrutiny for more than a century, pessimism and *its* history have languished in obscurity. Indeed, it still needs pointing out today that pessimism has a history, and a complicated one at that.

In fact, pessimism is a philosophy—a philosophy at the heart of the debate, both aesthetic and political, about tragedy. Today, "pessimistic" is also a predicate that we are eager to attach to those views we find objectionable. But when Friedrich Nietzsche reissued *The Birth of Tragedy* in 1886, he added the subtitle *Hellenism and Pessimism* and emphasized, in the new introduction, that what he still approved of in the book was its examination of "the good severe will of the older Greeks to pessimism, to the tragic myth."[1] Since that time, the link between pessimism and tragedy, the claim that tragedy is "the art form of pessimism" (*BT* 17), has been the object of a kind of sub-rosa debate in the scholarship on tragedy. It has often been equated (quite wrongly, I think) with the idea that tragedy is distinctly and purely an ancient Greek form of aesthetic activity. And this has been the dividing line between those who have sought to impose strict boundaries on the genre of tragedy and those who have urged a more expansive view. The terms of this debate have, in many ways, changed very little since George Steiner and Raymond Williams set out opposing positions on these questions in the early 1960s.

And yet much of this debate has taken place in ignorance of the pessimistic tradition, or even of the distinctive way in which Nietzsche understood the "pessimism" he ascribed to the ancient Greeks. Pessimism is not a Greek term, of course, and Nietzsche's use of it was an anachronism. But while he did want, with this label, to indicate the distinctive-ness of tragic feeling, his intent was hardly to isolate it in the fifth century BCE. Indeed, Nietzsche's ultimate term for his own (very modern) philosophy is "Dionysian pessimism," where "Dionysus" indicates the ultimate author and actor of all tragedy (*BT* 73). It would be well then for scholars of tragedy to re-examine its relations with pessimism, both to get at the roots of this debate as well as to get some purchase on the question of tragedy's social and philosophical origins.

Much more is at stake than the proper meaning of terms. The continuing political charge in questions of tragedy also finds its genesis here. This is clear enough in Terry Eagleton's recent study of tragedy. For the claim that tragedy issues from pessimism has been linked (questionably, as we shall see) to the claim that the tragic perspective is no longer readily available to us. And this claim has also been linked (again, questionably) to the idea that tragedy is a naturally elitist perspective. Eagleton refers breezily to the "right-wing death-of-tragedy thesis," as if the connection between pessimism and antidemocratic politics were so well-established as to require no explanation whatever.[2] Less blithely, Paul Gordon attempts to liberate a "rapturous" Nietzschean perspective on tragedy from its association with Steiner. It is striking that, in doing so, he specifically denies that Nietzsche's views originate in pessimism; Nietzsche's pessimism, we are told, "is not really pessimism at all."[3] The idea that Eagleton and Gordon share, then, is a simple one: if tragedy is pessimistic, it must lead nowhere, or else nowhere good from a political perspective.

It is this presumption I want to challenge. While Nietzsche's pessimism may not correspond easily to our everyday use of the term, I would argue that it is our blindness about pessimism, combined with our anxiety about it, that are the real stumbling blocks here. "The idea that a pessimistic philosophy is necessarily one of discouragement," Camus once wrote, "is a puerile idea, but one that needs too long a refutation."[4] Taking up Camus's challenge will not only deepen our understanding of tragedy but it will also show that the political implications of pessimism-*cum*-tragedy are not those often assumed. The very fact that Camus, a radical egalitarian, would defend pessimism, gives some indication of its potential to unsettle, rather than confirm, existing political arrangements. To say that tragedy is pessimistic is not to say that it encourages quietism or that it is antidemocratic. In the right hands, pessimism has been—and can still be—an energizing and even liberating ethic. This needs to be taken into account, both in our estimation of tragedy itself, and in our evaluation of Steiner's claims in *The Death of Tragedy* and the many reactions to them.

I.

While the word "pessimism" itself came into widespread use only in the nineteenth century, it clearly names a persistent thought, or set of thoughts, that has recurred often in social and political theory, in tandem with its opposite, at least since the Enlightenment. Leibniz first used the term "optimum," as a correlate to "maximum" (and as opposed to "minimum"), in his *Théodicée* of 1710. French writers then began to refer to his doctrine as one of *optimisme*. The term apparently crosses into English with the popularity of Voltaire's *Candide ou l'Optimisme* of 1759. The first known printed appearance of "pessimism" in English then follows a few decades later, although the context seems to indicate that the term was already in use.[5] Philosophically, however, one might date the emergence of pessimism to the appearance in 1750 of Rousseau's *Discourse On the Arts and Sciences,* with its characterization of modern man as a moral degenerate. While Rousseau's ideas were seconded, in the early nineteenth century, in such works as Leopardi's *Moral Essays* as well as in his poetry, pessimism achieved its brief period of genuine popularity through the work of Schopenhauer, whose *Parerga and Paralipomena* went through many editions after its initial publication in 1851. Thereafter, pessimism, while never a dominant school in philosophy, was a well-recognized position for at least several generations.[6] And this work was part of the context that made possible the literature (for example, Dostoyevsky, Ibsen, Strindberg) which we now readily refer to as pessimistic. What the pessimists share, as I have argued elsewhere, is a view of human existence as fundamentally time-bound and, hence, subject to the vicissitudes of time, lacking in any permanent features.[7] Schopenhauer is perhaps most famous for this view: "*Time* and that *perishability* of all things existing in time that time itself brings about. . . . Time is that by virtue of which everything becomes nothingness in our hands and loses all real value."[8]

Nietzsche's relationship to the pessimists who preceded him was hardly one of uniform celebration. He called Rousseau a "moral tarantula" and although initially inspired by Schopenhauer's philosophy, he eventually dissociated himself from its systematic conclusions (while retaining a respect for its critical spirit). Nietzsche was also unkind toward the pessimists popular in the Germany of his day, especially Eduard von

Hartmann, the prominent Berlin philosopher; Nietzsche called him "completely abysmal."[9] Nietzsche believed that the pessimism of both Hartmann and Schopenhauer led directly to nihilism. Indeed, the very popularity of this form of pessimism in the late nineteenth century was one of the factors that convinced Nietzsche that nihilism would soon enjoy a temporary dominance of European society.

By "pessimism," then, Nietzsche does *not* mean either of two things with which we might be tempted to identify it—it indicates neither a depressive personality nor the philosophy of Arthur Schopenhauer. Indeed, in the same introduction where Nietzsche insists on the pessimistic origin of tragedy, he goes to great pains to differentiate the view he has in mind from that of Schopenhauer, which was at the height of its popularity in Germany when Nietzsche wrote. His own "strange and new valuations," the introduction claims, "were basically at odds with . . . Schopenhauer's spirit and taste!" (*BT* 24). Intermixed with his critique, however, is an account of another kind of pessimism. Nietzsche viewed it as "that courageous pessimism that is . . . the way to 'myself,' to *my* task."[10] Ultimately, he gave his alternative the name "Dionysian pessimism."[11]

II.

The task that *The Birth of Tragedy* set itself was to explain not only the appearance of Greek tragedy, but also its decline in Greek society after Euripides. As is well known, Nietzsche hypothesizes that Socrates' introduction (and Plato's furtherance) of a rationalistic philosophy destroyed the preexisting cultural grounds for Greek tragedy (*BT* 81ff.). But what exactly did Socrates destroy, and how was this possible? Why, in any case, should a philosopher have had the power to affect the theater? The answer lies in the pessimism that Nietzsche associates with the pre-Socratic philosophers and his belief that their ideas reflected the original character of early Greek culture. "Tragedy," as he put it in a note from this period, "is the outlet of mystic-pessimistic knowledge."[12] Pessimism was the philosophical basis for the plays of Aeschylus and Sophocles. This was the wisdom that the pre-Socratics possessed and that later generations first denied and then forgot. Socrates is the agent of this change because his philosophy is essentially *optimistic* (*BT* 91ff.).[13]

Nietzsche did not think of optimism and pessimism as two equal, if opposite, ways of looking at the world, as we might today; rather "pessimism . . . is older and more original than optimism" (*KGW* 4.1.208). Pessimism is the domain of the Ionian philosophers who preceded Socrates and whose teachings we possess only in fragments. Instead of trying to construct a systematic, ordering philosophy, as Socrates and Plato were to do, the pre-Socratics grasped the chaotic and disordered nature of the world and only attempted to cope with it, insofar as that was possible: "Pessimism is the consequence of knowledge of the absolute illogic of the world-order" (*KGW* 3.3.74).

In other notes from this period, Nietzsche first attributes to Democritus the doctrine that "the world [is] without moral and aesthetic meaning" and calls this idea "the pessimism of accidents" (*KGW* 3.4.151). In *Philosophy in the Tragic Age of the Greeks* (written at about the same time as *The Birth* but published only posthumously), he likens Anaximander to Schopenhauer and calls him "the first philosophical author of the ancients." He goes on to describe Anaximander as a "true pessimist" and quotes his only extant fragment to justify the label: "Where the source of things is, to that place they must also pass away, according to necessity, for they must pay penance and be judged for their injustices, in accordance with the ordinance of Time."[14]

In other words, the pre-Socratics, as Nietzsche interpreted them, grasped the animating principle of pessimism: that time is an unshakable burden for human beings because it leads to the ultimate destruction of all things—and that this fate belies any principle of order that may, on the surface, appear to guide the course of events. Of course, whether any of the pre-Socratics would have put things this way is debatable (although Heraclitus, in particular, is certainly often understood in this fashion). What is important here is that Nietzsche understood them to be doing so, that he understood the root of pessimism to be, as he later wrote, "time-sickness [*Zeit-Krankheit*]" (*KGW* 7.2.51). The epigraph from Weil captures the thought exactly: it is the destructive power of time that stands behind any particular cause of suffering in the world.

Nietzsche considered tragic theater to be an outgrowth of this view of the universe as something constantly in flux, constantly in the process of becoming and, thus, constantly in the process of destroying. The ravages of time could not be cured or compensated for through tragedy, only understood: "Tragedy . . . is in its essence pessimistic. Existence is in itself something very terrible, man something very foolish" (*KGW* 3.2.38). Nietzsche rejects the conclusion, popular since Aristotle, that tragedy offers some kind of purification of the emotions generated by the terrible truths of the human condition.[15] He also rejects the idea that tragedies contain some sort of moral lesson meant to instruct us in ethical behavior. Instead, he argues, tragedy simply serves to lay bare for us the horrible situation of human existence that the pre-Socratic philosophers describe, a situation from which our minds would otherwise flee: "The hero of tragedy does not prove himself . . . in a struggle against fate, just as little does he suffer what he deserves. Rather, blind and with covered head, he falls to his ruin: and his desolate but noble burden with which he remains standing in the presence of this well-known world of terrors presses itself like a thorn in our soul" (*KGW* 3.2.38). The tragic outlook is thus generated from a base of pessimistic knowledge. It recommends no cure for the pains of existence, only a public recognition of their depth and power.

From the beginning, too, this view is associated with the Dionysian, "the mother of the mysteries, tragedy, pessimism" (*KGW* 3.3.309). The Athenian public theatrical festivals were known as the Dionysia, and Nietzsche goes so far as to claim the existence of a tradition "that Greek tragedy in its earliest form had for its sole theme the sufferings of Dionysus" (*BT* 73).[16] In Nietzsche's account, Dionysus suffers the prototypical agonies of existence inflicted by time. He is severed from the eternal flux and individuated, then torn to pieces and reunited with the whole: "This view of things already provides us with all the elements of a profound and pessimistic view of the world, together with the *mystery doctrine of tragedy:* the fundamental knowledge of the oneness of everything existent, the conception of individuation as the primal cause of evil, and of art as the joyous hope that the spell of individuation may be broken in augury of a restored oneness" (*BT* 10).

Dionysian suffering is essentially human suffering. In tragedy, this is indicated by a connection between the various elements involved in the public performance of the drama. The tragic hero, to Nietzsche, simply personifies the "Dionysian state" of the chorus as a whole (*BT* 73). The chorus is likewise "the mirror-image in which the Dionysian man contemplates himself" and also "a vision of the Dionysian mass of spectators" (*BT* 63). Thus, actor, chorus, and public are all connected in tragedy through their Dionysian character (*PT* 165). Each is a fragment torn from the whole. Nietzsche is here critiquing, but also reconstituting, the traditional philological stance that the chorus represents the Greek public itself. Although he sharply attacks the original proponents of this view, he, in fact, proposes not to reject it but to modify it. He will accept the connection of citizens and chorus only on the condition that the Greek public is understood as a unique phenomenon, a "Dionysian throng," that is, as a public already infected with the pessimistic wisdom of the pre-Socratics.[17]

Nietzsche's conception is, then, just the opposite of the elitism it is often associated with. Tragic knowledge is not something to which only a privileged few have access. Instead, the tragic theater can function, on his account, *only* when the ethos of pessimism is shared throughout the *demos*. When Nietzsche rails against the "democratization" of taste in post-Socratic Athens, he does not mean the larger population has a natural distaste for tragedy; his complaint is only that the lower classes are particularly susceptible to Socrates' optimism. Appealing to their suffering, it has the effect of stoking their resentments against the rich. (If people were naturally optimistic, Socrates' role would be unimportant. If anything is "natural," it is pessimism, though Nietzsche, who eschews such terms, will only speak of it as "older and more original.") So, he writes, in a lecture on Sophocles, "Tragedy has always contained a pure democratic character, as it springs from the people" (*KGW* 2.3.17).[18]

Against this account of pessimism and tragedy as a kind of Dionysian wisdom, Nietzsche counterposes the new Socratic philosophy, whose characteristic feature now appears to be its optimism.[19] Even while proclaiming its ignorance, Socratic inquiry rejects the pessimistic idea that inquiry, like every human activity, is ultimately doomed: "For who could mistake the *optimistic* element in the nature of dialectic, which celebrates a triumph with every conclusion . . . the optimistic element which, having once penetrated tragedy must gradually overgrow its Dionysian regions and impel it necessarily to self-destruction" (*BT* 91). Socrates does not promise eternal happiness, but he does affirm both that virtue results in happiness and that virtue can be taught—thus happiness theoretically is within the grasp of all.[20] He denies that there is anything ultimately mysterious about life or inevitable about suffering: "By contrast with this practical pessimism, Socrates is the prototype of the theoretical optimist who, with his faith that the nature of things can be fathomed, ascribes to knowledge and insight the power of a panacea" (*BT* 97).

Notwithstanding Socrates' fate at the hands of his fellow citizens, Nietzsche has no doubt that this approach, developed by Plato, was ultimately victorious in its struggle with tragedy: "Optimistic dialectic drives *music* out of tragedy with the scourge of its syllogisms" (*BT* 92). Just as the pessimism of an older generation of Greeks explains the origin of tragedy, so the Socratic turn in Greek philosophy explains its demise. When the population adopted the optimistic perspective, the cultural context for tragedy evaporated (*PT* 161). From Nietzsche's viewpoint, this was anything but a theoretical advance. Greek pessimism had a fundamental honesty that Socratic-Platonic philosophy lacks. This point, in particular, he reemphasized in the 1886 introduction to *The Birth of Tragedy*. While pessimism today, as it was in Nietzsche's time, is commonly associated with ideas of cultural decay, he takes the Greek experience to indicate precisely the opposite: "Is pessimism *necessarily* a sign of decline . . . as it once was in India and now is, to all appearances, among us, 'modern' men and Europeans? Is there a pessimism of *strength*? . . . And again: that of which tragedy died, the Socratism of morality, the dialectics, frugality, and cheerfulness of the theoretical man—how now? Might not this very Socratism be a sign of decline. . . . Is the resolve to be so scientific about everything perhaps a kind of fear of, an escape from, pessimism? A subtle last resort against—*truth*?" (*BT* 17–18).

The Greeks of Socrates' generation could no longer *bear* to live with the brutal truths of the human condition and sought refuge in an optimistic philosophy. To Nietzsche this was "morally speaking, a sort of cowardice . . . amorally speaking, a ruse" (*BT* 18). Either way, it was an active self-deception that made life more tolerable but less genuine. It was a retreat from a real look at time-bound existence to a pleasing fantasy of progress and happiness. Thus, Nietzsche concludes, it is the optimists who are the true harbingers of cultural decline. What else can we call their weakening of resolve in comparison with the stance of the earlier Greeks? Nietzsche's attack on Socrates and Plato is often taken to be a defense of irrationalism, but from his perspective it is they who have retreated from an honest assessment of the world. The pessimistic vision of the world as fundamentally disordered, untamable, unfair, and destructive is the "truth" against which they close their eyes and withdraw to a cave.[21]

III.

Tragic art is the organization of a small portion of an otherwise meaningless world that gives purpose to an individual existence (*WP* 585). It is the attempt to impose a temporary form on the inevitable transformation of the world. Since the world must acquire *some* particular forms in its metamorphoses, art is "repeating in miniature, as it were, the tendency of the whole" (*WP* 617)—only now by an effort of will. Thus, art is not really an attempt to fight the pattern of existence, but rather to shape that pattern into something recognizable, "*to realize in oneself* the eternal joy of becoming—that joy which also encompasses *joy in destruction*" (*TI* 110).

When art assumes this shape, it becomes "the great seduction to life, the great stimulant to life" (*WP* 853). This is *not* to say, however, that such art must be "uplifting" in the conventional sense. Since joy in destruction may be a stimulant to life, even depictions of the most miserable things may be included: "The things they display are ugly: but *that* they display them comes from their *pleasure in the ugly*. . . . How liberating is Dostoevsky!" (*WP* 821). If we can understand *why* an artist like Dostoyevsky, who knows that art is devoid of metaphysical value, would still want to write, then we can understand why Nietzsche thinks pessimism can result in a creative pathos. Similarly, if we can see how tragedy, the "repetition in miniature" of worldly chaos, can represent the liberating "joy of becoming," then we can get a sense for the political productivity of a pessimistic ethic.

The normal situation of an architect, I think, helps us to get some purchase on this: any sane architect must know that no building lasts forever. Built in opposition to nature but using the unstable materials of nature (as, to some extent, every human structure must be), every edifice will be attacked by nature (by wind, by water, by gravity, and so forth) the moment it is completed. Whatever the purpose for which it is initially designed, that purpose will someday be superseded. However beautiful it may seem when erected, it will someday, to another set of eyes, appear ugly. Yet, knowing all this, architects pursue their craft. Knowing that the universe will ultimately not tolerate their work, they continue to organize a small portion of that same universe for local purposes. The lack of an objective or metaphysical meaning for the work is no obstacle; indeed, architects often think of the generation of locally meaningful environments out of natural waste to be a particular goal, a spur to activity.

Dionysian pessimism, then, is an ethos of a similar kind, an art of living.[22] In recommending it as a life-practice, Nietzsche is, in some sense, thereby recommending the practice of life. But since, as he was fond of pointing out, there is really no perspective from which to view life as a whole (whether to deny or affirm it), such an assent can only be a kind of gamble or risk-taking. It is an affirmation in the dark, an approval given in ignorance. Above all, in keeping with the emphasis on the centrality of temporal experience, it is a decision to welcome the unknown future and accept the unseen past, rather than clinging to a familiar present.[23] While other pessimisms (such as Schopenhauer's) also conclude that the universe has no order and human history no progress, Dionysian pessimism is the one that can find something to like about this situation: "My new way to 'yes.' My new version of pessimism as a voluntary quest for fearful and questionable aspects of beings. . . . A pessimist such as that could in that way lead to a Dionysian yes-saying to the world as it is: as a wish for its absolute return and eternity: with which a new ideal of philosophy and sensibility would be given" (*KGW* 8.2.121).

The phrase "fearful and questionable," which recurs frequently in Nietzsche's texts, is carefully chosen to indicate what is at issue here.[24] The aspects of existence that we will have the greatest difficulty grasping and affirming are not the cruel and disgusting; rather, they are those so threatening to our sense of order that we have heretofore denied their very being, so that initially we find them "questionable" or "dubious." Which are these? In *Twilight of the Idols,* Nietzsche ridicules "the almost laughable poverty of instinct displayed by German philologists whenever they approach the Dionysian" (*TI* 108). Why laughable? Because these philologists cannot recognize the "instinct," so to speak, right under their noses. The "Dionysian mysteries" are simply "the mysteries of sexuality . . . the *sexual* symbol was to the Greeks the symbol venerable as such, the intrinsic profound meaning of all antique piety" (*TI* 109). The absurdity of post-Socratic philosophy is ultimately demonstrated in its attitudes toward sex and the body. What ought to be the most obvious and immediate source of knowledge and pleasure is not merely obscured but almost entirely obliterated. Cruelty may be condemned by morality but at least it is acknowledged; sexuality is eliminated from view through a process of "moral castrationism" (*WP* 204, 383). Pessimism, by contrast, puts the terrible power of sexuality at the center of tragic drama.

Sexuality, not cruelty or violence, represents that part of life with which it is most difficult to come to terms. It is the most difficult *not* because it is inherently shameful ("It was only Christianity . . . which made of sexuality something impure" [*TI* 109]). The difficulty lies in affirming the necessity for pain and suffering that accompanies any growth. That is, it involves admitting that we ourselves (and not just the world) are essentially flux and change, as our sexual experiences demonstrate. With its constant dissolution of ego-boundaries, sexuality is more threatening to the optimist than is the human tendency to cruelty. This violation of self—simultaneously painful and pleasurable—is the simplest and best evidence that our own nature is as unstable and tumultuous as that of the rest of the universe and that, therefore, no calculation of our best interest can ever be permanent. It is this situation that tragedy makes visible.

The Dionysian is "the triumphant Yes to life beyond death and change; *true* life as collective continuation of life through procreation"

(*TI* 109). But this can come only at the cost of suffering, as the price to be paid for continuous rebirth: "In the teaching of the mysteries, *pain* is sanctified: the 'pains of childbirth' sanctify pain in general—all becoming and growing, all that guarantees the future, *postulates* pain. . . . All this is contained in the word Dionysus" (*TI* 109). The Dionysian is not *simply* sexuality (Nietzsche is not Freud); rather, the repression of sexuality represents the repression of the "fearful and questionable" as such. (Likewise, Greek tragedies are not *simply* sexual conflicts, though such conflicts are often at the core of them.) Accepting the necessity of pain in a life of growth and change, *setting aside the goal of happiness as the ultimate aim of a human life,* is what the Dionysian "yes" requires. To truly embrace becoming at the expense of being means *to take pleasure in the suffering that accompanies the demise of whatever is.* "The joy of Being is only possible as the joy of appearance[.] The joy of becoming is only possible in the destruction of the actuality of 'Beings,' the beautiful visions, in the pessimistic annihilation of illusions. [I]n the destruction also of beautiful illusions, Dionysian joy appears as its climax" (*KGW* 8.1.114).

The Dionysian "yes" is not a matter of taking a sadistic pleasure in the suffering of others. Rather, it is a decision to value the future over the present. To be glad that ours is a world of becoming, rather than being, means to be glad that things are always changing, that the future is always coming and the present always passing away. It means detachment from whatever exists at present—something that will inevitably appear as callousness towards others: "*Dionysian wisdom.* Joy in the destruction of the most noble and at the sight of its progressive ruin: in reality joy in what is coming and lies in the future, which triumphs over existing things, however good" (*WP* 417). This is what Nietzsche had in mind by such phrases as "*amor fati*" or eternal recurrence. *Not* the idea that we must relive the past again and again, but rather that this pattern of destruction and creation is unalterable and must be borne. And it cannot be withstood by means of faith in progress. We must learn to hope in the absence of an expectation of progress. If this sounds almost nonsensical to the modern ear, perhaps it is because we have been told for so long that progress is the rational thing to hope for.

While no element of our life is unalterable, suffering is the unalterable price to be paid for changing it. It is this condition that we have no choice but to accept as a whole or to reject through the hypocrisy of optimism.[25] In a famous note, Nietzsche embodies the two choices as "Dionysus and the Crucified": "The problem is that of the meaning of suffering: whether a Christian meaning or a tragic meaning." We can surely struggle to alter those elements of life within our purview, but we will still be faced with the larger question where we cannot pick and choose. One alternative is to reject life, and its afflictions, as a whole: "The god on the cross is a curse on life, a signpost to seek redemption from life." The other is to embrace life, with all the suffering entailed, both for ourselves and for others: "Dionysus cut to pieces is a *promise* of life: it will be eternally reborn and return again from destruction" (*WP* 1052). If one accepts the pessimistic assessment of the world as a place of chaos and dissonance, one faces the choice of retreating from it wholesale or embracing it and trying to "let a harmony sound forth from every conflict" (*WP* 852).

IV.

George Steiner, as far as I can tell, did not use the term "pessimism," or its cognates, in *The Death of Tragedy;* but his interpretation has been characterized as pessimistic and, it must be said, with considerable justice—so long as we use Nietzsche's understanding of this term, rather than the conventional one. For Steiner's interpretation of tragedy repeats important elements of Nietzsche's view. First, there is the natural condition of disorder and flux in the world, which is expressed in tragedy: "Tragedy," Steiner writes, "would have us know that there is in the very fact of human existence a provocation or a paradox; it tells us that the purposes of men sometimes run against the grain of inexplicable and destructive forces."[26] It teaches us "of the unfaltering bias toward inhumanity and destruction in the drift of the world" (*DT* 291). As in Nietzsche, tragedy offers no compensation for this—"the wounds are not healed and the broken spirit is not mended" (*DT* 129)—only a controlled repetition of it. Then, there is the historical attack on this pessimism by the forces of optimism and rationality, which occurs outside the theater itself. While Steiner transposes the cultural shift that Nietzsche describes from the fifth century BCE to the seventeenth century CE, the transformation described is the same: "When the new world picture of reason usurped the place of the old tradition . . . the English theatre entered its long decline" (*DT* 23). The culprit is not Socrates, but a Socratic Rousseau, or, rather, "The Rousseauist belief in the perfectibility of man," since "such a view of the human condition is radically optimistic" (*DT* 127–8). More broadly, of course, Steiner claims that it is the rise of the bourgeoisie, the commodification of everyday life, and the final victory of Christian metaphysics that diverted the West from the theater to the novel and from tragedy to melodrama. But it is the optimism that is the common root of such seemingly contrary forces as the Enlightenment, the Church, the market, and even Marxism, that deprives us of the proper context for tragedy.

Like Nietzsche, then, Steiner derives tragedy from pessimism and accounts for the decline of tragedy by reference to the triumph of optimism. But what follows from this account, it should now be clear, need not be a reactionary aesthetics or politics. Whatever Steiner's intent (which I do not pursue here, though I think it has often been oversimplified), Nietzsche's "Dionysian pessimism" is the source of his most radical claims, claims that have, most recently, appealed to a series of radically democratic political theorists. Tracy Strong describes Nietzsche's politics as a "politics of transfiguration," and it is this theme of self-shaping and self-transformation against a tragic background which is the key link between Nietzsche and such figures as Camus, Arendt, Foucault, and William Connolly. Each of these writers has found in Nietzsche a portrait of energetic individuality that can be supportive of democracy while remaining distinct from the liberal assumptions that are often assumed to be a necessary complement to democratic theory. Nietzsche's pessimism does not require elitism, and it does not recommend passivity. Instead, as these twentieth-century inheritors of Nietzsche have seen, it sanctions a process of identity-renovation based not on an assumption of the self's natural integrity but, to the contrary, on an acknowledgment of its fundamental instability and perishability. While acknowledging limits to the human condition, this is a politics of possibility more radical than most. It makes little sense, therefore, to link pessimism (or pessimism-*cum*-tragedy) with conservative politics. The pessimistic spirit is a restless one, unlikely to be enamored of the status quo.

Relatedly, while the derivation of tragedy from pessimism does, as Steiner argued, require marking off a boundary of genre between tragedy and cathartic, but ultimately hopeful, optimistic art forms, such as melodrama, this account should not be taken to limit tragedy to a particular time, place, or (least of all) class of people. To say that not all suffering is tragedy is very different from saying that tragic suffering is rare or specific to particular cultures. Indeed, there are several reasons for thinking that the pessimistic account of tragedy, though not as limitless in its definition of the genre as others, is still an expansive one. In the first place, the insistence on the overpowering force of temporal flux means that there are no permanent cultural conditions to oppose (or foster) tragedy. Rather, it is the lack of such permanence that fosters tragedy. From this perspective, Raymond Williams is right to insist (contra Steiner) that tragedy emerges not from static belief but from "the real tension between old and new," something that occurs in a variety of contexts.[27] Though Nietzsche was no less negative than Steiner on the baleful condition of modernity, he wrote *The Birth* at least in part because he thought the production of a new kind of musical tragedy was possible.[28] And even after he lost his faith in Wagner's abilities in this regard, Nietzsche continued to insist on the *openness* of the future and the potential for both new pessimistic art forms and new forms of life to go with them.[29] When he came to classify Wagner's work as a kind of romanticism and, hence, pseudo-tragic, he turned to other modern works, such as the writings of Dostoyevsky and Bizet's *Carmen*. In the latter in particular, he found the "tragic joke" of our existence so well expressed that he returned to see the opera, by his own account, no less than twenty times (*CW* 157–59).

So, while the pessimistic conception of tragedy may remain hostile to works of easy redemption, there is no barrier to tragedy's appearing in our time or outside of the theater. Indeed, a pessimist must insist on the universal availability of tragic themes, if not on their perennial appearance.[30] Not only did Nietzsche believe his own philosophy was one such manifestation, but he also found writing like Dostoyevsky's to reflect, not nihilism, but precisely a pessimistic ethic. Nor should Nietzsche's labeling of Dostoyevsky (and himself) as "liberating" surprise us. Pessimism is as much an ethic of radical possibility as it is of radical insecurity; indeed, the former is grounded in the latter. It is the lack of any natural boundaries to human character that permits, simultaneously, our capacity for novelty and distinctiveness as well as our capacity for enormous cruelty; we cannot have one without the other. Dostoyevsky's characters sometimes react to this lack of boundaries with actions that are hideous, but this is due to a lack of imagination that does not, on Nietzsche's account, afflict Dostoyevsky himself. Raskolnikov does not define the pessimistic condition; rather, he is its worst possible consequence. But the effect of the book is still liberating, because, like tragedy, it alerts us to, even as it warns us about, the double-edged freedom that is our lot.

Or, perhaps, instead of speaking of freedom as double-edged, we should refer to pessimistic tragedy as teaching the universal, simultaneous presence of freedom and terror in our lives. To political theorists such as Hannah Arendt, the idea that we tread the political arena "without a banister" announces both the danger of totalitarianism and the condition of possibility for true individuality. Modern fascism had demonstrated that there are no innate limits to human cruelty, but our acknowledge-

ment of that fact could, curiously, allow us to reach the equally true conclusion that "with each birth something uniquely new comes into the
world" from which "the unexpected can be expected."[31] Steiner argued
that Greek drama demonstrated the capricious cruelty of the world, as
well as revealing the independence and humanity of those who are the
victims of it. But even a social drama as microscopic and modern (and
bourgeois) as Edith Wharton's *The House of Mirth* (or, I think, the recent
film *Amores Perros*) has the requisite dual sense of freedom and terror.
In both of these, the shape of individuals is most vividly revealed as the
social structures that support them collapse—precisely as in *Antigone* or
Ajax.[32]

This is not the idea that we see the "true" individual in a time of adversity. Rather, it is the view that the sources of individuality and of
that which destroys individuality are the same. From this perspective,
it makes no sense to ask whether the tragic personage is one who willfully separates themselves from their society or whether they are pushed
out by malice or circumstance (neither for Antigone nor for Lily Bart is
there a good answer to this question). To a pessimist, all of these situations arise equally from the fundamental instability of human beings
and human institutions, anchorless in time. We are all equally subject
to the freedom and terror of the tragic situation. And if some stories are
"more tragic" than others, this is due merely to (a) the circumstance that
some situations exemplify a fundamental condition better than others,
and (b) our limited, but real enough, capacity to insulate ourselves from
this circumstance by burying ourselves in a life of conformity. It is one
of the special marks of tragedy, I think, that it often causes us to question
the pursuit of a safe and painless life, even as it *promises* us that in aban-
doning this pursuit we will come to a bad end. In enlarging the envelope
of possible human experience, we will necessarily mark out a unique
path of suffering. Perhaps, instead of "sweet violence," we should speak
of a terror that liberates.

Among political theorists, I think it is Arendt, particularly in *The
Human Condition,* who gives us the best image of a stance that is simultaneously pessimistic, tragic, energetic, and democratic. It has often
seemed difficult to reconcile Arendt's praise for the fiercely agonistic
and individualistic spirit of Athenian democracy (which, to a certain,
limited degree, she saw reflected in American politics) with her critique
of modern liberal institutions, as well as with her long-term historical
dread of the rise of technology and the market. But putting these views

in a pessimistic context helps make sense of them. Modern democracy is, to her, too often optimistic, in the sense that it values the contributions of individuals only insofar as they contribute to a larger process of historical progress. Athenian democracy, on the other hand, lacking a sense of progress, indeed, possessed of the pessimistic belief in the absence of long-term historical patterns, was better able to value individual actions for their own sake. To her, then, it is no coincidence that Athens, the democratic city, is also the city of tragedy. For Athenian democracy treasures, just as Athenian tragedy does, the memory of vital individuals—even when their efforts came to nothing. And Athenian democracy encourages individuals not with promises of progress, but only of remembrance. Similarly, in Camus's *Myth of Sisyphus* we see the attempt to translate a "tragic myth" into an active, democratic political idiom. The futility of Sisyphus's task, we are told, is no obstacle to his embracing it, so long as we understand that futility is the ordinary order of things.[33] Indeed, for Camus, the universality of futility is the basis for a kind of pessimistic equality of citizenship.

Pessimism thus liberates us from a dull submission to a historical meta-narrative that we did not author. It insists that, for better and worse, our lives are not pre-scripted by historical processes or social ties, even as it insists that we act in a context that we cannot control and that therefore we act, in all likelihood, tragically. And yet, as "author," each of us is, like the world that we face, an ever-changing multiplicity with no purpose or desire that is not open to revision, loss, and renewal—most often, but not exclusively, through the medium of eros, which attaches us to others by violating the boundaries of each. Arendt is perhaps more true to this insight than Camus is, in insisting that every political action, no matter how individual in origin, is always an interaction with others. Tragic drama, it is said, truly began to differentiate itself from religious ritual with the introduction of the second actor onto the stage. Likewise, Arendt insists on the condition of human plurality as the starting point for all political reasoning.

The politics of pessimism and tragedy, then, even on an account that insists on some traditional boundaries of genre, are not at all those of reaction or elitism. Indeed, democratic politics require the tragic viewpoint if they are to liberate themselves from the dubious optimistic meta-narratives of modernity. It is this element of Nietzsche's outlook, I would argue, that has so appealed to the contemporary democratic theorists whose work I have hastily described. Pessimism insists on an equality of (tragic) condition; on the ubiquity of flux and eros that frame this condition; on the possibilities and dangers that follow from this; and on the uniqueness of every individual. It does *chasten* politics in that it discourages utopianism; it discounts the belief either in the perfectibility of the species or of our political conditions. But to claim that it deflates our political energies in general is to mistake utopianism for the whole of politics. I have argued, on the contrary, that tragic pessimism liberates us by replacing the pseudo-natural boundaries of self and history with the terrifying limitless horizon of time-bound existence.

V.

Schopenhauer wrote: "The life of every individual, viewed as a whole and in general . . . is really a tragedy; but gone through in detail it has the character of a comedy."[34] While I have taken some time here to defend the association of pessimism and tragedy against misinterpretations of its meaning, I nonetheless do not want to be understood as simply identifying the two. Tragedy may issue from pessimism, but it is not the only thing that can do so. Even before Socrates, there was a Greek comic theater, which, if my argument is to make any sense, must also, in some sense, have been grounded in pessimism. I would argue, furthermore, that we can easily find modern examples of pessimistic comedy; the first in prominence might be *Don Quixote*. But that argument must be the subject for another paper. Failing this, I think it worthwhile to recall the very fine line between tragedy and comedy that Schopenhauer describes. To him, the two genres depict the same human condition, only, we might say, at varying speeds.

Tragedy and pessimism, then, are not one and the same. But there is a strong link between them that has, I have argued, been misunderstood. Pessimism is equivalent neither to ancient Greek theater nor to aristocratic resignation. It does, however, claim to describe the fundamental ontology of the human condition—one of radical insecurity and radical possibility, freedom and terror—that is the potential ground of tragedy. While teaching us the limitations of time-bound life, pessimistic artworks simultaneously describe the potential for distinctiveness and dignity within such a life. Neither is pessimism a mere psychological state; it is, rather, a long-standing philosophical tradition that, though obscure, has a number of modern, democratic proponents. It may be antiutopian, but it is not generally antipolitical, antimodern, or antidemocratic. Tragedy, therefore, can be pessimistic without being dead.

Notes

1. Friedrich W. Nietzsche, *The Birth of Tragedy and The Case of Wagner* (New York: Vintage Books, 1967), 21; hereafter cited in text as *BT* or *CW*, as appropriate.

2. Terry Eagleton, *Sweet Violence: The Idea of the Tragic* (Oxford: Blackwell, 2003), 20.

3. Paul Gordon, *Tragedy After Nietzsche: Rapturous Superabundance* (Urbana: University of Illinois Press, 2001), 22.

4. Albert Camus, *Resistance, Rebellion and Death* (New York: Vintage Books, 1974), 57.

5. See "pessimism," in the *Oxford English Dictionary,* 3rd ed.

6. In the nineteenth century, one would list at least Leopardi, Eduard von Hartmann, and then Hippolyte Taine; in the twentieth, Weber, Horkheimer and Adorno, Camus, Cioran, and so on. Relaxing one's definitions a bit, a much longer list (including such figures as Freud, Heidegger, Unamuno, and Sartre) could be generated. But I cannot take up here the question of the proper boundaries of pessimistic thinking.

7. See Joshua Foa Dienstag, "The Pessimistic Spirit," *Philosophy & Social Criticism* 25 (1999): 71–95.

8. Arthur Schopenhauer, *Essays and Aphorisms* (New York: Penguin Books, 1970), 51.

9. Friedrich Nietzsche, *Beyond Good and Evil* (New York: Penguin Books, 1966), 111.

10. Friedrich Nietzsche, *Human, All-Too-Human* (Cambridge: Cambridge University Press, 1986), 211.

11. Friedrich Nietzsche, *The Gay Science* (New York: Vintage Books, 1974), 331, hereafter cited in text as *GS.*

12. Friedrich Nietzsche, *Werke Kritische Gesamtausgabe,* ed. Giorgio Colli and Mazzino Montinari (Berlin: Walter de Gruyter, 1967ff.), 3.3.73; hereafter cited in text as *KGW* by volume, book, and page numbers.

13. A parallel analysis, but without the emphasis on pessimism, is offered by Tracy Strong, *Friedrich Nietzsche and the Politics of Transfiguration* (Berkeley: University of California Press, 1988), 152ff; hereafter cited in text as *PT.*

14. Friedrich Nietzsche, *Philosophy in the Tragic Age of the Greeks* (Washington: Regnery Gateway, 1962), 45 (see *Werke Kritische Gesamtausgabe* 3.2.312). This is a translation of Nietzsche's German translation of the Greek original, which he slightly adapted to suit his own understanding. A standard English translation of the pre-Socratics renders Anaximander's fragment thus: "And the source of coming-to-be for existing things is that into which destruction, too, happens 'according to necessity; for they pay penalty and retribution to each other for their injustice according to the assessment of Time'" (G.S. Kirk, J.E. Raven & M. Schofield, *The Presocratic Philosophers* [Cambridge: Cambridge University Press, 1983], 118).

121

15. Friedrich Nietzsche, *Twilight of the Idols* (New York: Penguin Books, 1968), 110; hereafter cited in text as *TI;* and *The Will to Power* (New York: Vintage Books, 1967), sec. 851, hereafter cited in text as *WP* by section number.

16. Nietzsche calls this tradition "undisputed," which seems doubtful. Again, however, the accuracy of Nietzsche's construal of the philological literature and traditions is less important here than how these were related to his own views.

17. Nietzsche identifies A.W. Schlegel as the originator of the other view; but, while he proclaims that he gives Schlegel's formulation "a deeper sense," he certainly also exaggerates his own distance from contemporary German thought about the Greeks.

18. Cited in an unpublished paper by Tracy Strong, "The Tragic Ethos and the Spirit of Music," 15. I thank Tracy Strong for sharing this paper with me.

19. My brief account of tragedy has underplayed the role of the Apollinian as a counter-balancing element to the Dionysian. In the context of this discussion, however, it is less salient, since it is the Dionysian element of tragedy that is particularly linked to pessimism and that Socrates is particularly supposed to object to. Though the Apollinian/Dionysian contrast is what the book is famous for, it largely disappears from view after the first forty pages and is replaced by "the new opposition: the Dionysian and the Socratic" (*Birth of Tragedy,* 82).

20. Nietzsche's characterizations of Socrates are given without reference to their source; here it seems clear that he has in mind the conclusions of the Platonic Socrates of *Gorgias, Protagoras,* and *Republic,* that true happiness can come only from virtue and that virtue is equivalent to knowledge; a rather different Socrates could perhaps be constructed from the *Meno* and other early dialogues.

21. I have set to one side here the issue of the anachronism involved in Nietzsche's use of "pessimism" with regard to the Greeks, though I plan to deal with it elsewhere. Suffice it to say that Nietzsche believes that the common axiom of a destructive time-bound existence, shared by figures as diverse as Anaximander and Schopenhauer, justifies the retrospective labeling of early Greek thought as pessimistic. While I would argue that modern ideas of progress and pessimism are distinguishable from the ancient ones, this distinction has more to do with the shape of time predicated by these ideas (rather than time's destructiveness), which is not central to the argument here. Nietzsche, in any case, might deny this distinction or date the emergence of "modernity" to Socrates.

I must also set to one side the question of the "truth" of pessimism to Nietzsche. He does not claim pessimism as a certain product of a deduction, but, rather, as a description of an ontological condition of living that can be grasped through ordinary experience.

22. The phrase "art of living" is from Pierre Hadot (*Philosophy as a Way of Life* [Oxford: Blackwell, 1995], 272), who used it as a description of the intended goal of ancient philosophy, "an exercise practiced at each instant." See also Alexander Nehamas (*The Art of Living* [Berkeley: University of California Press, 1998]), who applies the phrase to Nietzsche.

23. Friedrich Nietzsche, *Thus Spake Zarathustra* (New York: Penguin Books, 1966), 137ff.

24. *Furchtbaren und fragwürdigen* could also be translated as, say, "terrible and doubtful." For other uses of this term, see, for example, *The Will to Power* (852) and *The Gay Science* (370). The phrase always refers to those things that the pessimist can bear the sight of while others cannot.

25. Or suicide. This is perhaps what Camus had in mind when he wrote, "There is but one truly serious philosophical problem, and that is suicide" (Albert Camus, *The Myth of Sisyphus* [New York: Vintage Books, 1983], 3).

26. George Steiner, *The Death of Tragedy* (New York: Alfred A. Knopf, 1961), 128; hereafter cited in text as *DT.*

27. Raymond Williams, *Modern Tragedy* (Stanford: Stanford University Press, 1966), 54.

28. Williams's account of Nietzsche emphasizes this point. See *Modern Tragedy,* 41ff.

29. It is not often noted that Steiner repeats this point in miniature as well. The title of Steiner's book actually overstates his case, for example: "It is not a play but an opera that now holds out the most distinct promise of a future for tragedy" (*Death of Tragedy,* 289).

30. This is also the result, it should be noticed, of Williams's view, for example, "The ages of comparatively stable belief . . . do not seem to produce tragedy of any intensity" (*Modern Tragedy,* 54).

31. Hannah Arendt, *The Human Condition* (Chicago: University of Chicago Press, 1958), 178.

32. Lily Bart, Wharton's protagonist, is slowly stripped of her social standing until she is utterly alone, at which point she dies. But, like, Antigone, she goes "to the halls of Death alive and breathing" (Sophocles, *The Three Theban Plays* [New York: Penguin Books, 1982], 102). *Amores Perros* has multiple, intersecting plots too complicated to describe here, but I believe it too projects an overall ethos of unavoidable doom and simultaneously vibrant life.

33. Camus, *The Myth of Sisyphus,* 119.

34. Arthur Schopenhauer, *The World as Will and Representation* (New York: Dover Books, 1966), 1:322.

Rethinking the History
of Tragedy

.

Toppling the Hero
Polyphony in the Tragic City

Page duBois

In January 1997, at the height of the O. J. Simpson frenzy, I was invited to participate in the local Los Angeles PBS radio show "Which Way L.A.?" hosted by Warren Olney. In my capacity as a classicist interested in Greek tragedy, I was asked to comment on Simpson's trial, then being covered gavel-to-gavel and beyond on local and national television channels. Waiting tensely for my moment, I listened through almost an hour of remarks from criminal defense lawyers, district attorneys, academic legal experts, and participants from the School of Criminology at U.C. Berkeley. When at last Warren Olney came to me for a sort of epilogue, he asked: "Isn't O. J. like the hero of a Greek tragedy, a great man brought low by a tragic flaw?" I knew that he wanted me to expound on the pathos of the spectacle, the tragic dimensions of a man elevated to divine status by the masses and then dragged through the mud as a consequence of his own hubristic overreaching.

Instead, I nervously blurted out that the situation did indeed resemble that of Greek tragedy, but in the sense that the ancient city staged its political and ritual life in public tragic performances. As ancient Athens made itself into a theater, it engaged in political reflection and political education through its worship of Dionysus. The parallel I made with the O. J. Simpson trial focused not on the great man fallen, but rather on the consequences, especially for African-American defendants, in criminal trials all over America. If this particular jury including African-American members acquitted O. J., future juries would react to ensure that other defendants, especially African Americans, would not get off lightly, be acquitted, or saved from life imprisonment or death by lenient jurors. O. J., who could pay for the best criminal defense possible, would be cited as an example by countless prosecutors who would point to the injustice of the verdict. Poor African-American defendants would suffer and be convicted and imprisoned to compensate for a general sense of outrage that O. J. had gotten away with murder.[1]

In this sense, the trial did indeed resemble a Greek tragedy; it was a political spectacle with political consequences. I wish I had talked too about the instability, weirdness, and multiplicity of persons on display in the trial, and how such features, to be found also in Greek tragedy, made it strange and wonderful. I wish too that I had been able, in my remarks on tragedy, swiftly to undermine the triumphalist neoconservative account of the original stability, superiority, and homogeneity of Western civilization, as such an account celebrates what it imagines to be eternal systems of justice, aesthetics, and philosophical coherence.[2] Such complexities proved, of course, impossible in the sound-bite world of NPR.

In popular culture, and in much literary theory as well, tragedy has become something of a dead signifier, connoting only these salient features: the great man or woman, the tragic flaw, the fall. How can such a model come to terms with Greek tragedy, with a lyric ode such as the following verse from Euripides' *Bacchae,* in which a chorus of possessed, maddened, ecstatic Asian women, in fact men costumed as bacchantes, dance and sing of their devotion to the god Dionysus:

> Out of the land of Asia
> Down from holy Tmolus,
> Speeding the service of god,
> For Bromius we come!
> Hard are the labors of god;
> Hard, but his service is sweet.
> Sweet to serve, sweet to cry:
> *Bacchus! Evohe!*[3]

Such moments, with the chorus of male actors dressed as maenads, dancing and singing in ecstasy, with its collective voice and its insistence on another place from which the tragedy addresses its audience, have an unnerving, unfamiliar, untranslatable, and disturbing quality. This is not the familiar tragic hero, faced with an ethical choice, acting with hubris. When coming to terms with the legacy of the tragic, I think we should respect this strangeness, a quality recognized by the maverick Friedrich Nietzsche, who was notoriously repugned by classicists: "The chariot of Dionysus is covered with flowers and garlands; panthers and tigers walk under its yoke."[4]

I am interested especially in the erasure of such moments in accounts of tragedy, in the ways that many heirs of the classical tradition, not just radio commentators but also literary and philosophical intellectuals, when they think about Greek tragedy, see only the great man and his fall, and then adjudicate the value, the "usability" of Greek tragedy in the present on the basis of a partial and reductive account of ancient drama. I want here to consider the history of this issue, and to suggest that reflection on the relevance of Greek tragedy should not be confined to the pathos of the great man, or even that of the everyman who comes to replace him, as we read Greek tragedy now.[5] The focus on the individual, in even the most sophisticated allegories using tragedy, remains a choice that can ignore the dialectic between part and whole, between individual and collective, and erase, polemically, context and history, as we see also in contemporary calls to dethrone individual demonized tyrants such as Saddam Hussein or the forgotten Muammar al-Gaddafi, or in newspaper stories that rely entirely on anecdotes and portraits of individuals to analyze the present. Alain Badiou, for one, laments the return of "humanitarian individualism," the abandonment of "revolutionary Marxism" and "the forms of progressive engagement that it inspired."[6]

Greek tragedy is not just about the great man, or even the little man; part of the problem is the filtering and reduction of the rich and polymorphous heritage of Greek antiquity through centuries of interested readings. And I include one of the earliest readers of tragedy, Aristotle, who interprets the legacy of tragedy in a partial and historically situated way. I will here consider Aristotle's role as an early interpreter of tragedy, and then discuss various modern readers' roles in focusing attention on the tragic hero as well. Then I want to look at other ways of seeing tragedy, of opening it to a more heterogeneous, unstable, polymorphous kind of reading that might well speak to postmodernity, or a globalizing world of increasingly polarized power and powerlessness. My hypothesis is that just as Greek tragedy bore testimony to the beginnings of the formation of the Western subject in the fifth century BCE, so now readers nostalgic for the sovereign subject which developed from this formation anachronistically privilege that subject as they read or watch tragedy. But at a moment when that subject has been called into question by a variety of kinds of fragmentation, dislocation, and difference, we can see in tragedy a much richer and more diverse set of bodies and questions than Aristotle and modernity bequeath to us. If I take a rigorously historicist line here, it is meant to return us to a less partial and reductive view of Greek tragedy, in the name of discovering other kinds of relevance to the present, a moment before the closure of the individual subject that might speak to its dissolution now.

The most influential reader of Greek tragedy is the philosopher Aristotle. Yet Aristotle is remote from the richest and most productive moment of Greek tragic production, his interests in the phenomenon of tragedy are very different from those of the fifth-century citizens of Athens who created the genre, and readers of Aristotle have often misread him. John Jones points out that the probable date of the *Poetics,* Aristotle's principal text on tragedy, is 335 BCE, that is, "when Aeschylus has been dead for rather more than a century, and Sophocles and Euripides . . . for about seventy years."[7] Although for non-classicists this may not seem very significant, given the principle that the more remote things are from us, the closer they seem to each other, in fact the passage of time between Aeschylus's career and Aristotle's formulations matters a great deal in a historicist account of the theorization of Greek tragedy.

Much happened in the meantime between Aeschylus's birth in the sixth century BCE, his first production of tragedy in 499 BCE, his last work produced in Athens, the *Oresteia* of 458 BCE, and the one hundred and fifty years intervening between these events and Aristotle's treatise. Even if we consider the death of Sophocles in 406 BCE as an endpoint to the great age of Greek tragedy, Aristotle, born in 384 BCE, is distant from it. Events, and structural changes, intervened. Athens had fought its rival, the league of states led by Sparta, through the last third of the fifth century and had been defeated. The city then became a subject-ally of Sparta and in 404 an oligarchy, when the thirty tyrants sponsored by Sparta took power over the city. Although democracy was eventually restored, reforms diminished its radical character, transferring legislation from the assembly of all citizens to a panel of six thousand. Struggles for hegemony over the Greek city-states continued in the fourth century, with Athens challenging Sparta in the company of other members of coalition forces, then allying with the Spartans themselves against the rise of Thebes. When Athens sought to restore its empire, its allies rebelled. As Perry Anderson writes, "Thereafter there was no chance of the Hellenic cities generating a unified imperial state from within their midst, despite their relatively rapid economic recovery from the effects of the long Peloponnesian War: the very parity and multiplicity of urban centres in Greece neutralized them collectively for external expansion. The Greek cities of the fourth century sank into exhaustion, as the classical polis experienced increasing difficulties of finance and conscription, symptoms of impending anachronism."[8] To the north, Phillip II of Macedon continued to gain power, finally provoking Athenian fears and eventually defeating Athens at the battle of Chaeronea in 338 BCE. Although the *polis* of Athens survived, it continued in a crucially changed form, no longer a radically experimental and imperially dominant democracy. Athens had begun its transformation into the center of education and culture that it became in the Hellenistic age, after the conquests of Aristotle's pupil Alexander.

Jean-Pierre Vernant argues for the historically specific "moment of tragedy," pointing to Aristotle's temporal distance from this moment: "Within a hundred years the tragic seam had already been exhausted and when Aristotle in the fourth century set out, in his *Poetics,* to establish the theory of tragedy, he no longer understood tragic man who had, so to speak, become a stranger. Tragedy succeeded epic and lyric and faded away as philosophy experienced its moment of triumph."[9] In this account of the sequence of genres, Vernant sees tragedy as only possible in the conditions peculiar to the fifth century BCE, in a "gap" "wide enough for the opposition between legal and political thought on the one hand and the mythical and heroic traditions on the other to stand out quite clearly. Yet it is narrow enough for the conflict in values still to be a painful one."[10]

All the intervening events—the defeat and changes for democracy, the new leagues, the defeat by the Macedonians, and the subordination of Athens to Macedon—affect the position of Aristotle with respect to tragedy. As I have argued elsewhere, Aristotle's is not the attitude of a democratic citizen of Athens towards tragedy as a ritual and political institution of democracy.[11] Although Aristotle was a student of Plato, and sometime resident in Athens, he inhabited Athens as an alien, leaving twice when the political mood of the city seemed dangerous for a philosopher and a Macedonian. His father had been court physician to a Macedonian monarch, and he may have spent part of his childhood in the court at Pella. As the anecdote had it, he left Athens to prevent the Athenians from sinning twice against philosophy, from executing him as they had Socrates, and his antidemocratic attitudes are typical of elite thinkers of antiquity. Aristotle may have tutored the future conqueror and founder of the Hellenistic empire, Alexander, and consistently in his political writings he offered positions critical of democracy.

Aristotle's attitudes toward Athenian tragedy, therefore, must be located within a belated and antidemocratic situation.[12] Mostly apparent in his *Poetics,* a manual for writing or "making" poems, his prescriptions reflect an administrative attitude remote from the highly charged political engagement of Athenian citizens in the new and radical democracy of the fifth century BCE. Whether his use of the term "katharsis" draws primarily on ritual contexts and connotes "purification" or "cleansing," or on medical concepts, connoting "purging," is not for me here the crucial issue.[13] Rather, it is his focus on the management of a population, an attitude very distant in its prosaic and encyclopedic setting from the fervent participation of citizens in the tragic celebrations of Dionysus that were the ancient drama festivals. Simon Goldhill has described the civic and ritual aspects of those festivals, showing how far removed they were from a post-Romantic "literariness," and even from the perspective of the polymath Aristotle. Goldhill reminds us that the Great Dionysia, the principal drama festival celebrating Dionysus, included in the days preceding the performances the escorting of a statue of Dionysus to a nearby village and back, and another subsequent procession involving participants who carried ritual loaves and phalluses, followed by bull sacrifices. In the theater of Dionysus on the day of the performances, the city's generals poured a libation, the names of exceptional citizens crowned for benefiting the city were announced, tribute from the Athenian empire subject states was displayed, ephebes whose fathers had been killed in battle paraded, and according to some authorities, the names of freed slaves were proclaimed.[14] Goldhill concludes: "The theatre was a space in which all the citizens were actors—as the city itself and its leading citizens were put on display" (57).

Aristotle's encyclopedic work on plants and animals, on the histories of philosophy and politics, his manuals on rhetoric and the writing of plays and poems, belong to a different regime of truth than that of the theater of Dionysus in the fifth century, and the intense engagement of the city in its invention of itself as a radical democracy. Aristotle notoriously does not even mention Dionysus in his account of tragedy. As Vernant says, "the city . . . turned itself into a theater,"[15] and Aristotle stands apart from this experiment. His views on catharsis, for example, refer to a disciplining of the social body, directing the reader's attention from the collective towards the individual member of the audience, who experiences a catharsis of pity and fear. The philosopher offers a view of tragedy from the perspective of power, administration, and the cultivation of individual contentment. He assumes a view from above and outside the city, concerned with identifying systems that prevent social disruption and disorder, where tragedy is useful, contra the view of Plato, precisely because it displaces unruly emotion into the realm of art in order to maintain order in the state. Tragedy becomes a site of mastery for the philosopher, who is a manager, analyst, and theoretician of the state and its elite members.

The focus on the individual within tragedy, the great man, who in time becomes everyman, probably begins with a productive misreading of Aristotle. John Jones discusses the importation of the tragic hero into the *Poetics,* "where the concept has no place."[16] In the *Poetics,* Aristotle says that tragedy is the representation of an *action* (*praxis*) that is "heroic and complete and of a certain magnitude (1449b)."[17] There is no mention here of a "tragic hero" or a "fatal flaw." He further says that "tragedy is not a representation of men but of a piece of action, of life, of happiness and unhappiness, which come under the head of action, and the end aimed at is the representation not of qualities of character but of some action (*praxis*)" (1450a). As Jones makes clear: "Mutability is Aristotle's tragic focus, not misfortune" (47). Aristotle explicitly calls into question the focus on the hero: "a plot does not have unity, as some people think, simply because it deals with a single man (*hena*)" (1451a). He praises Sophocles' *Oedipus,* beginning a long tradition of focus on this play, and argues that the best sort of tragedy concerns the mean between worthy and wicked persons, who through some *hamartia,* "missing the mark," fall into misfortune. He also says that character (*ethos*) must be good, but relative to the class of person concerned: "Even a woman is 'good,' and so is a slave, although it may be said that a woman is an inferior thing (*kheiron*) and a slave beneath consideration (*holos phaulon*)" (1454a).

Aristotle's comparative evaluations of epic and tragedy draw on his views concerning the superiority of aristocracy to democracy. He considers the argument that tragedy is *phortike,* "vulgar," compared to epic: "The whole tragic art, then, is to epic poetry what . . . later actors were compared to their predecessors, since according to this view epic appeals to a cultivated audience which had no need of an actor's poses, while tragedy appeals to a lower class [*phaulous*]. If then it is vulgar, it must obviously be inferior" (1462a). Although Aristotle says this is a criticism of actors, not poetry, the vulgar democratic audience of tragedy is a part of the spectacle; Aristotle recommends *reading* tragedies instead of watching actors, obviating the ritual and political circumstances of fifth-century performance. He concludes by conceding that tragedy is the superior form, because of its vividness and economy of length, unity, and effectiveness in producing pleasure (*hedonen*) (1462b).[18] In line with his advice concerning the reading of tragedy is his neglect of the collective nature, for example, of the tragic chorus: "the chorus must be regarded as one of the actors" (1456a). Such a comment reflects the ahistorical nature of Aristotle's experience of tragedy, and it leads to a history of misrecognition.

Jones argues further that readers project a modern self onto Aristotle's treatise: "Probably not much of the ancient tragic experience is recoverable by us, but we can avoid forcing upon Aristotle the local and no doubt transient self of the modern West" (36). Later readers do force upon Aristotle, and tragedy, the "tragic hero" with his "fatal flaw." Influential readings focus not on praxis, on action, nor on mutability of fortune, but on *characters,* transferring to the ancient form what soon becomes a modern, individual, internal, and psychological self. Hegel's reading of the *Antigone* identifies two central characters. As Michelle Gellrich points out, while restoring the notion of conflict to tragedy that is absent from Aristotle's view, "Hegel understands the conflict in pervasively binary terms: Antigone versus Creon, family versus state, female versus male, unwritten divine law versus written civic edicts."[19] In his description of the drama, what matters is the collision between two characters, one identified with the ethical world of the family, the other with the city; Hegel contrasts male and female with a view to their individuation, albeit in the context of their ultimate unity in Spirit: "these two universal beings of the ethical world have, therefore, their specific individuality in naturally distinct self-consciousness, because the ethical Spirit is the immediate unity of the substance with self-consciousness."[20] In the *Aesthetics* he goes further in attributing a romantic self to the characters of drama: "however far the individual and his inner life is the center of the drama, . . . a drama must display situations, and the mood they arouse, as determined by the character of an individual who resolves on particular ends and makes these what he wills in practice."[21]

For Freud, Sophocles' tragic hero Oedipus has the flaw of every man, the desire to kill his father and sleep with his mother; this is every human being's destiny. Freud looks only to the individual as he reads the Greeks. For him, Oedipus stands for each man, and for Greek tragedy itself, in a metonymy that ignores other characters, the chorus, the language, and other myths that serve as the matrix for the very many Athenian tragedies that fall out of the tradition.[22] As confirmation for the crucial role of the Oedipus complex in psychic life, Freud discusses not just the myth, but also tragedy: "What I have in mind is the legend of King Oedipus and Sophocles' drama which bears his name."[23] He argues that Sophocles' work is a tragedy of destiny, and that Oedipus's "destiny moves us only because it might have been ours—because the oracle laid the same curse upon us before our birth as upon him" (296).[24] Freud goes on to consider not another Greek tragedy, but *Hamlet,* citing it as proof of the gathering repression that characterizes the psychic life of mankind.[25]

Jacques Lacan, following Hegel, sees only Antigone, fatally beautiful; she is the death drive, living between two deaths. As a reader of Sophocles he is blinded to all but Antigone: "*Antigone* reveals to us the line of sight that defines desire. This line of sight focuses on an image that possesses a mystery which up till now has never been articulated, since it forces you to close your eyes at the moment you look at it. Yet that image is at the center of tragedy, since it is the fascinating image of Antigone herself."[26] He rewrites Hegel's version of the tragedy to locate conflict not in the antagonism between the two characters Antigone and Creon, but rather as internal to a tragically split and insatiable self. Antigone becomes the sign of death, of the unreachable, the limit of the human, the incest taboo: "Her life is not worth living." "Antigone goes beyond the limits of the human. . . . Her desire aims at the following, the beyond of *Ate*" (263). So he too reads the tragedy, brilliantly, but within a modernity that focuses on the individual and the split, suffering self.

Judith Butler, in *Antigone's Claim,* offers not a reading of Greek tragedy, but a utopian meditation on the place of the character Antigone in the invention of a possible new psychoanalysis, in which the focus would be not on Oedipus, as the father who slept with his mother and killed his father, but rather on Antigone, who reveals a masculine defiance and a culturally unacceptable, even incestuous, desire for her brother.[27] Butler uses Antigone to stand for new forms of family and intimacy and community, forms of loss and lamentation that cannot be assumed into the conventional heterosexual nuclear family. She follows Hegel's reading closely, and also Lacan's, and like them, even as her argument seeks a revolutionary recognition of new families, new forms of affiliation, she concentrates her analysis on the characters in the family, reading the tradition of philosophical and psychoanalytic readings of tragedy rather than the unruly and disturbing thing that is Greek tragedy itself. If I want to restore some of the unmanageability of Greek tragedy, it is in light of such work as Butler's, in other texts she has written, where the historicity, permeability, constructedness and groundlessness of personality and selfhood have been theorized.

Those modern or postmodern readers who are not classicists and who still read *Antigone* as well as *Oedipus Rex* when they consider Greek tragedy, even allegorically, are the exceptions; the other tragedies fall from modern and postmodern view.[28] In *Tragedy and Theory,* a book much influenced by the work of Paul de Man, Michelle Gellrich argues that theory itself produces misreadings of tragedy: "While the sense-making, organizing operations of dramatic theory serve systematic interests, they also perform a definitive cultural function; they so digest tragedy into a form both intelligible and safe that its threatening, enigmatic aspects are transformed" (10–11). This is an illuminating critique, problematic only in that it anthropomorphizes "theory," making it an agent in centuries of reading tragedy. I would rather see the readings of various "theorists" of tragedy historically, from Aristotle to Terry Eagleton, consider the ways in which theories have worked in their historical situations, turn readers' and theorists' gazes away from heroes, male or female, even from characters, and insist again on the "threatening, enigmatic aspects" of tragedy. If we return to Jones's insight concerning the transference of modern ideas of character on to ancient tragedy, to see what else is staged in Greek tragedy alongside the intractable character, the hero, the subject, we discover the threat, the enigma of works of dramatic art that challenge ideas concerning the life centered on the individual self.

I want to point to just three ways in which Greek tragedy exceeds the individual character, the tragic hero, the great man or woman dear to the tradition: in its haunting by the slaves of ancient Greek society; in its access to mourning; and in its presentation of choral song that is necessarily collective, diverse, and heterogeneous.[29] Readings of tragedy that focus on the individual, even the abject, sacrificial *pharmakos,* cannot take account of such moments as this in Euripides' *Hecuba:*

> O Ilium! O my country,
> whose name men speak no more
> among unfallen cities!
> So dense a cloud of Greeks
> came, spear on spear, destroying!
> Your crown of towers shorn away,
> and everywhere the staining fire,
> most pitiful, O Ilium,
> whose ways I shall not walk again!

> At midnight came my doom.
> Midnight when the feast is done
> and sleep falls sweetly on the eyes.
> The songs and sacrifice,
> the dances, all were done.
> My husband lay asleep,
> his spear upon the wall,
> forgetting for a while
> the ships drawn up on Ilium's shore.

> I was setting my hair
> In the soft folds of the net,

gazing at the endless light
deep in the golden mirror,
preparing myself for bed,
when tumult broke the air
and shouts and cries
shattered the empty streets—
Onward, onward you Greeks!
Sack the city of Troy
and see your homes once more!

Dressed only in a gown
like a girl of Sparta,
I left the bed of love
and prayed to Artemis.
But no answer came.
I saw my husband lying dead,
and they took me over sea.
Backward I looked at Troy,
but the ship sped on
and Ilium slipped away,
and I was dumb with grief. (Euripides, *Hecuba,* 905–41)[30]

The anonymous and newly enslaved Trojan women of Euripides' *Hecuba,* a group of men performing as women, sing this chorus, recalling the fateful moment when the city of Troy fell, when these women, speaking as one, became slaves. This song from the chorus evokes the catastrophe of the fall of Troy, with its breached wall and devastation emblematic of the end of civilization for all of antiquity. It also speaks to the disaster suffered by the individual woman; with her husband killed, she herself suffers the social death of enslavement and seeks in the worship of Artemis a return to virginity, to protection from sexual possession by new masters. The choruses of tragedy offer an impressive array of difference, always anonymous, from another group of slave women in Aeschylus's *Libation Bearers* ("From our fathers' houses / they led us here to take the lot of slaves" [77–78]) to the votive slaves of Euripides' *Phoenician Women,* who regret the delay in their arrival at the oracle of Apollo at Delphi: "I came, I left the wave of Tyre, / the island of Phoenicia, / a prize for Loxias, slave to Phoebus' house" (203–5).[31] Not only are these women slaves, they are Phoenicians, not Greek, therefore an anonymous, barbarian, ethnically distinct group, pledged to serve the Greek god Apollo, resident in Thebes because of the genealogical relation of the Thebans to

Tyre. Their voices call up not only the presence in tragedy of barbarians, but also that of the thousands of slaves resident in Athens, in houses and on farms, working in factories and serving citizens.[32]

At many moments in Greek tragedy, the omnipresence of slaves and the horror of enslavement arise in the course of the drama, marking it with the specter of social death, anonymity, and ethnic difference. In Sophocles' *Trachiniae,* the wife of Herakles, Deianeira, about whom some debate has arisen concerning whether she is the "tragic hero," regrets the return of her husband from conquest with a new slave bride. She addresses the chorus, the anonymous women of the city of Trachis:

> Dear friends, while our visitor is in the house
> talking to the captured girls before he leaves,
> I have come out to you, unobserved. I want
> to tell you the work my hands have done, but also to have
> your sympathy as I cry out for all I suffer.
> For here I have taken on a girl—no,
> I can think that no longer—a married woman, as
> a ship's master takes on cargo, goods that outrage my heart.
> So now the two of us lie under the same sheet
> waiting for his embrace. This is the gift my brave
> and faithful Heracles sends home to his dear wife
> to compensate for his long absence! (531–42)[33]

The situation of the new woman is ambiguous; is she a wife or a slave? Deianeira's address to the women of Trachis, the chorus, speaks to the omnipresence of slaves in the houses of the Athenian audience, their sexual availability to citizens, and their effects on relations of power, domesticity, kinship, inheritance, and difference in the city.

Even in the most canonical of Greek tragedies, *Antigone,* second only to *Oedipus Rex* in its overwhelming status for post-Aristotelian and post-Hegelian readers of tragedy, the issue of the ubiquity of slaves in the city emerges ineluctably. As Robert Goheen noted in 1951, the language of slavery in the play is linked to bestial imagery: "In his first speech when Creon describes Polyneices's crimes and concludes by branding him as one who has come 'to feed on kindred blood and lead the remnant into slavery' (202), the mention of enslavement is climactic and presumably is one of the strongest of his charges against Polyneices."[34] Creon uses the language of slavery and the image of a bridle to threaten Antigone; Antigone claims that Polyneices is entitled to burial precisely because he was not a slave; Creon calls his son Haimon a woman's *douleuma,* a "slave-thing" (756).

Rather than focusing solely on the characters' personalities, ethical positions, and destinies, Greek tragedies engage in a complex and often contradictory debate concerning many issues, including slavery, slaves' disturbing presence in the city, the legitimacy of their enslavement, and the possibility of enslavement for free persons represented in the tragic performances and in their audiences. In fact, the inhabitants of cities defeated in war in the fifth century BCE were subjected to death and enslavement, as the historian of the Peloponnesian War Thucydides reports: "Around the same time [421 BCE] during this summer, the Athenians captured Skione by siege and killed the adult males, enslaving the children and women and giving the land to the Plataeans to occupy" (5.32).[35] When the Athenians were at last forced to recognize defeat in the Peloponnesian War, according to the historian Xenophon, they feared retaliation for such brutality:

> As the news of the disaster was told, one man passed it on to another, and a sound of wailing arose and extended first from Piraeus, then along the Long Walls until it reached the city. That night no one slept. They mourned for the lost, but more still for their own fate. They thought that they themselves would now be dealt with as they had dealt with others—with the Melians, colonists of Sparta, after they had besieged and conquered Melos, with the people of Histiaea, of Scione, of Torone, of Aegina and many other states. (2.2.3)[36]

Although ancient playwrights set their tragedies in a legendary past, situations like those represented in ancient Troy saturated contemporary experience. The ubiquity of slaves in the city, some captured in war, made them an inevitable and haunting presence and reminder of the possibilities of disaster in the present.

Nicole Loraux has written about the aspect of ancient tragedy that resembles the oratorio, its moments of grief and mourning, its capacity to call forth sorrow in its spectators, and to console, an aspect she sees as distinct from the political.[37] The theater of Dionysus is not the *agora,* the marketplace, center of civic activity in the *polis;* tragedy is not only political, it is even antipolitical, "anti-politique" in the sense that it goes beyond a city defined by practices of consensus or even by conflict. The city seeks to limit lamentation; tragedy extends it to eternity. Tragedy embodies the oxymoron, the incompatible, playing on the prescriptions and oppositions of political discourse. Loraux argues that lamentation and lyric songs of mourning, the evocation of loss, go against the prescription of the city to forget, and that they bring the spectator to a moment of recognition that exceeds the homogeneous civic community, to an acknowledgement of his or her place among humankind, as mortal (137). This aspect of tragedy is lost too with a focus on characters, character, and ethical choice alone.

Jean-Pierre Vernant argued that the form of tragedy produces a sort of centripetal force, in which the city produces itself, for itself, in the theater. In its engagement with a living past, tragedy expresses itself through a tension between the collective entity that is the chorus, and the characters, played by individual actors. While the characters, names from the legendary past, might be expected to speak in an archaic language, and the anonymous group of persons that resembles the collective of citizens should perhaps speak the language of their day, in fact the reverse occurs, in a chiasmic or centripetal figure in which the choruses sing in archaic lyric language associated with the past, with the aristocratic age, while the characters speak a prosaic language presumably closer to that of the audience.[38] As we accept Loraux's caveat that tragedy exceeds the political and the civic, this aspect of the form of tragedy especially resists assimilation to the familiar. The drama is not a treatise, not a philosophical dialogue, not purely an examination of character and ethical choice. Terrible events occur, characters and chorus are caught up in them, and the strangeness of tragic form is part of the experience of reading or viewing tragedy.

Tragedy probably developed from choral song; the standing out from the chorus by a single character appears retrospectively as the beginnings of drama. Such an occurrence may be said to mark the emergence of a Western sense of "character," the *persona* carved out in the separation of an individual from a collective. Charles Segal pointed to the connections linking writing, literacy, theatrical space, and the developing notion of an interior self in the fifth century BCE:

> The hiddenness of the tragic poet's text in the performance is the negative sign of something always hidden from view, on the other side of the palace wall, which is also the side of the Other. As poet/writer who manipulates real bodies in real space on the stage, the dramatist becomes sensitized both to the invisible graphic space of his text and to the hidden, interior space of the self. What is concealed behind doors and gates—the gates of the palace, of the mouth, or of the body—becomes

the problem of his writerly art. . . . The inner life of the self . . . appears not on the stage but in the behind-the-stage implied by the invisible text. . . . This interplay between interior and exterior space parallels the increasing awareness of the interior realm of the psyche, the individual personality.[39]

Rather than see this as an increasing *awareness* of something already existent, as Segal and Bruno Snell do, I would argue that in tragedy we are witnessing the *construction* of that self, that interiority, that individualism, in a process concomitant with Athenian democratic ideology concerning equality and the interchangeability of citizens.[40]

The radically uneven surface of tragedy, moving as it does from song and dance to speech and back again, makes it different from epic, for example, with its continuous flow of the bard's song, or from lyric, the voice of chorus and singer alone. Choruses in tragedy sing not simply to experience the events for the audience, as Lacan put it, "doing emotional commentary for you," nor do they stand for the citizens themselves, since they often represent foreign, inassimilable persons, slaves, barbarians, or ecstatic maenads.[41] Readings that focus on character, destiny, and ethical choice tend simply to ignore such passages, rendering them invisible, as vestigial remnants of foreignness that deprive the reader of the sense that he or she has mastered tragedy and insist on its radical strangeness and historical distance. Attempts to contain such appearances within civic ideology or the history of absolute spirit must fail; they cannot come to terms with the lyrics' striking strangeness, inassimilability, and representations of difference. The foreign, the collective, the ecstatic, the enslaved are always there, from tragedy's beginnings, disrupting efforts to isolate the solitary, masterly self attempting heroically to grapple with fate.

In a recent essay on the "sociology" of Greek tragedy, Edith Hall offers an important although perhaps overly sanguine interpretation of the diversity on display. Hall observes: "Tragedy offers a range of characters of all statuses from gods and kings to citizens and to slaves, all ethnicities from Athenian, Theban, and Argive Greeks to 'barbarians' (the generic term for non-Greeks) such as Persians and Egyptians, all age groups from babies to the very old, and an overwhelming insistence on the troubled relationships between women and men."[42] She attributes a utopian quality to the presence of women, slaves, and barbarians in tragedy; while they were excluded from public debate in the city, tragedy includes an unexpected array of speakers on the stage. "Tragedy postulates in imagination a world . . . which is 'democratic' in something akin to the modern Western sense; it is a world in which characters of diverse ethnicity, gender, and status all have the same right to express their opinions and the same verbal ability with which to exercise that right" (125). This formulation seems to me to exaggerate the degree to which slaves and barbarians, who usually speak with sorrow, deference, or fear on stage, have achieved a democratic parity with the kings and tyrants of the tragic stage, and to return to an old and familiar model of celebration of the Greek miracle. Tragedy is in fact a site of contradiction and struggle for the city, not perhaps as hegemonically about patriarchal sovereignty as Mark Griffith has argued, but a less ideal space than Hall describes.[43]

If tragedy has something to offer to readers and spectators in the present, it should be more than nostalgia for the private, individual subject of modernity, cherished or lamented by many readers precisely because it is receding in a world of postmodern globalization. Rather, a reading that sees all the differences in tragedy, slaves and free, men and women, kings, queens, and citizens in action, conflicted, contradictory action, can speak to us now. The presence of slaves, the attention to mourning, and the formal complexity of tragedy make it a richer, more contradictory, less familiar object than we are accustomed to find in the pages of Hegel. To read Greek tragedy, tragedy, the tragic, as a discourse on the individual, even one conceived within the narrative of absolute spirit or split by incestuous desire, is to reveal perhaps a nostalgic desire for a sovereign, individual, heroic subject, one who can still make choices, even catastrophic ones, that determine his or her fate, that exhibit will and efficacy now eroded in the face of transnational corporate power. Even as the legacy of modern slavery in the Americas has produced a misrecognition of ancient societies, a failure to see all the slaves of the past, so the disintegrating modern self, the supposedly once-sovereign, individual subject, reads nostalgically for its past in ancient Greek tragedy, which in fact stages very different sorts of struggle and engagement. Just as an analysis of the O. J. Simpson trial would be partial and distorting if it focused exclusively on the tragic hero, his fatal flaw and fall, ignoring the jury, the history of the police and African Americans in the city of Los Angeles, the history of racism, and the past of slavery in the United States, so our readings of ancient tragedy must include more than Oedipus and his family if they are to illuminate our present and our future.

Notes

1. On the criminal justice system in America as the heir of slavery, see Loïc Wacquant, "From Slavery to Mass Incarceration: Rethinking the 'Race Question' in the US," *New Left Review* 13 (2002): 41–60.

2. On these questions, see Page duBois, *Trojan Horses: Saving the Classics from Conservatives* (New York: New York University Press, 2001).

3. Euripides, *The Bacchae,* trans. William Arrowsmith, in *The Complete Greek Tragedies,* vol. 4, ed. Richmond Lattimore and David Grene (Chicago: University of Chicago Press, 1992).

4. Friedrich Nietzsche, *The Birth of Tragedy from the Spirit of Music* [1872], in *Basic Writings of Nietzsche,* trans. Walter Kaufmann (New York: Modern Library, 2000), 37. On this text, see James Porter, *The Invention of Dionysus: An Essay on the Birth of Tragedy* (Stanford: Stanford University Press, 2000).

5. "Among the cultural inventions of mankind there is a treasury of devices, techniques, ideas, procedures, and so on, that cannot exactly be reactivated, but at least constitute, or help to constitute, a certain point of view which can be very useful as a tool for analyzing what's going on now—and to change it" (Michel Foucault, "On the Genealogy of Ethics: An Overview of Work in Progress," in *The Foucault Reader,* ed. Paul Rabinow [New York, Pantheon: 1984], 349–50).

6. Alain Badiou, *Ethics: An Essay on the Understanding of Evil,* trans. Peter Hallward (London: Verso, 2001), 4–5.

7. John Jones, *On Aristotle and Greek Tragedy* (New York: Oxford University Press, 1962), 11.

8. Perry Anderson, *Passages from Antiquity to Feudalism* (London: NLB, 1974), 44. "The Macedonian royal state, precisely because it was morphologically much more primitive than the city-states of the South, was not subject to their impasse and so proved able to overleap their limits in the new epoch of their decline" (45).

9. Jean-Pierre Vernant, "Tensions and Ambiguities in Greek Tragedy," in Jean-Pierre Vernant and Pierre Vidal-Naquet, *Myth and Tragedy in Ancient Greece,* trans. Janet Lloyd (New York: Zone, 1990), 29.

10. Jean-Pierre Vernant, "The Historical Moment of Tragedy in Greece," in *Myth and Tragedy,* 23. On the mutual implication of historical and tragic writings, see C. C. Chiasson, "Herodotus' Use of Attic Tragedy in the Lydian *Logos,*" *Classical Antiquity* 22 (2003): 5–35. Pat Easterling argues that fourth-century tragedy merits attention and should not be ignored simply because none is extant. See Easterling, "The End of an Era? Tragedy in the Early Fourth Century," in *Tragedy, Comedy, and the Polis. Papers from the Greek Drama Conference, Nottingham 18–20 July 1990,* ed. Alan Sommerstein, et al. (Bari, 1993), 559–69.

11. See Page duBois, "Ancient Tragedy and the Metaphor of Katharsis," *Theatre Journal,* special issue on tragedy, ed. David Román, 54.1 (2002): 19–24.

12. Edith Hall takes a more positive view of Aristotle's distance from Athens: "The *Poetics*' near-total displacement of the *polis* from tragedy seems to me to be

an astonishingly original innovation, which adumbrates the incipient and future status of tragedy as an international art-form" (Edith Hall, "Is there a *Polis* in Aristotle's *Poetics*?" in *Tragedy and the Tragic: Greek Theatre and Beyond,* ed. M. S. Silk [Oxford: Clarendon, 1996], 304–5).

13. See Martha Nussbaum, *The Therapy of Desire: Theory and Practice in Hellenistic Ethics* (Princeton: Princeton University Press, 1994).

14. Simon Goldhill, "The Audience of Athenian tragedy," in *The Cambridge Companion to Greek Tragedy,* ed. Pat Easterling (Cambridge: Cambridge University Press, 1997), 56; see also Simon Goldhill, "The Great Dionysia and Civic Ideology," in *Nothing to Do with Dionysos? Athenian Drama in Its Social Context,* ed. John Winkler and Froma Zeitlin (Princeton: Princeton University Press, 1990), 97–129.

15. Vernant, "Tensions and Ambiguities," 33.

16. Jones, *On Aristotle,* 13.

17. Aristotle, *The Poetics,* trans. William Hamilton Fyfe, rev. ed. (London: Heinemann [Loeb], 1932).

18. On tragic pleasure, see F. Decreus, "About Western Man and the 'Gap' That Is Constantly Threatening Him. Or How to Deal with the Tragic When Staging Greek Tragedies Today?" *Euphrosyne* n.s. 31 (2003): 61–82.

19. Michelle Gellrich, *Tragedy and Theory: The Problem of Conflict Since Aristotle* (Princeton, NJ: Princeton University Press, 1988), 46.

20. G. W. F. Hegel, *Phenomenology of Mind,* trans. J. B. Baillie, 2nd. ed. (London: George Allen and Unwin, 1931), 478; translation modified.

21. G. W. F. Hegel, *Aesthetics. Lectures in Fine Art,* vol. 2, trans. T. M. Knox (Oxford: Clarendon Press, 1974), 1160–61. On his admiration for Sophocles' *Antigone,* see pages 1217–18: "This sort of development is most complete when the individuals who are at variance appear each of them in their concrete existence as a totality, so that in themselves they are in the power of what they are fighting. . . . For example, Antigone lives under the political authority of Creon, . . . the *Antigone* seems to me to be the most magnificent and satisfying work of art of this kind."

22. On Freud and the Greeks, see Jacques Le Rider, *Freud, de l'Acropole au Sinaï. Le retour à l'antique des Modernes viennois* (Paris: Presses Universitaires de France, 2002). Le Rider argues that Freud, in his interpretation of Oedipus Rex, conceived himself as an "anti-Nietzsche," unveiling the implicit and hidden Christian assumptions of Nietzsche (157).

23. Sigmund Freud, *The Interpretation of Dreams,* trans. James Strachey (New York: Basic Books, 1965), 294.

24. For a critique of psychoanalytic interpretations of *Oedipus Rex,* see Jean-Pierre Vernant, "Oedipus Without the Complex," in *Myth and Tragedy,* 85–111. See also E. R. Dodds, "On Misunderstanding the *Oedipus Rex,*" *Greece and Rome* 13 (1966): 37–49.

25. See also Theodor Adorno: "At the very outset of the bourgeois age, a play was written in which the category of the bourgeois individual, the autonomous,

independent individual, can be said to have appeared for the first time. I am thinking of Shakespeare's *Hamlet*" (*Problems of Moral Philosophy,* ed. Thomas Schroder,
trans. Rodney Livingstone [Stanford: Stanford University Press, 2000], 112).

26. Jacques Lacan, *The Seminar of Jacques Lacan, Book 7: Ethics of Psychoanalysis 1959–1960,* ed. Jacques-Alain Miller, trans. Dennis Porter (New York: Norton,
1992), 247. Later, he identifies Antigone as "the real hero" (258). Of the chorus he
says only: "In my view, the Chorus are people who are moved. . . . The emotional
commentary is done for you" (252).

27. Judith Butler, *Antigone's Claim: Kinship Between Life and Death* (New York:
Columbia University Press, 2000): "In her act, she [Antigone] transgresses both
gender and kinship norms, and though the Hegelian tradition reads her fate as a
sure sign that this transgression is necessarily failed and fatal, another reading is
possible in which she exposes the socially contingent character of kinship, only
to become the repeated occasion in the critical literature for a rewriting of that
contingency as immutable necessity" (6). "Her [Antigone's] predicament . . . does
offer an allegory for the crisis of kinship: which social arrangements can be recognized as legitimate love, and which human losses can be explicitly grieved as
real and consequential loss?" (24). "Although not quite a queer heroine, Antigone
does emblematize a certain heterosexual fatality that remains to be read" (72).
"If kinship is the precondition of the human, then Antigone is the occasion for a
new field of the human, achieved through political catachresis, the one that happens when the less than human speaks as human, when gender is displaced, and
kinship founders on its own founding laws" (82).

28. In his critique of conservative theorists of the death of tragedy, and of
Butler and other postmodern theorists, Terry Eagleton, writing about tragedy in
Sweet Violence: The Idea of the Tragic, seems ultimately to want to return to a Christian model of sacrifice, in which the meek will inherit the earth. Interestingly,
in his formulation, he follows the influential characterization of Jean-Pierre Vernant concerning "tragic man" and Oedipus. Vernant argues that Sophocles' Oedipus can be illuminated by a consideration of two institutions of the Greek city,
the *pharmakos,* or scapegoat ritual, and the procedure called ostracism. In the
pharmakos ritual, the city selected the most abject of inhabitants, ugly, wretched,
imprisoned victims, beat and drove them from the city's limits, thereby ritually
expelling baseness from the body politic. Eagleton, like many other readers, reads
Vernant on the scapegoat while neglecting his formulations concerning ostracism, which cast light on the relationship between Oedipus and the tyrant, the
most high, the almost god-like ruler of the city. Athens conducted an ostracism, a
sort of anti-election in which the citizens voted every year to expel, in a ten-year
exile, anyone they chose from the democratic city; ostracism has been understood
as a mechanism for ridding the city of those who have become too powerful, in
order perhaps to deflect the envy of the gods, but also to maintain the putative
equality of the citizens and to discourage demagogues or those with tyrannical
ambitions. Vernant writes: "In the person of the ostracized, the city expels what

in it is too elevated, what incarnates the evil which can come to it from above. In the evil of the *pharmakos,* it expels what is vilest in itself, what incarnates the evil that menaces it from below. By this double and complementary rejection it delimits itself in relation to what is not yet known and what transcends the known: it takes the proper measure of the human in opposition on one side to the divine and heroic, on the other to the bestial and monstrous" (Jean-Pierre Vernant, "On the Enigmatic Structure of *Oedipus Rex,*" trans. Page duBois, *New Literary History* 9 [1977–78]: 475–501).

If Eagleton does go beyond the tragic hero, the focus on the individual, and sees the possibilities of transformation in the multitude, he is still caught up in a model of sacrifice based on what seem to me very Christian notions: "there is a sense in which the *pharmakos* is the very paradigm of that nowadays much derided notion, objectivity. To strive for objectivity of judgment in fact demands a fair amount of courage, realism, openness, modesty, self-discipline, and generosity of spirit; there is nothing in the least bloodless about it" (Terry Eagleton, *Sweet Violence: The Idea of the Tragic* [Oxford: Blackwell, 2003], 288–89). The expulsion and destruction of the most high, the powerful who abuse their power, fall from view, and the urging of sacrifice by the low weirdly echoes a certain Christian masochism.

29. On the chorus, see John Gould, "Tragedy and Collective Experience," in *Tragedy and the Tragic: Greek Theatre and Beyond,* ed. M. S. Silk (Oxford: Clarendon Press, 1996), 217–43, and Simon Goldhill's response, 244–56.

30. Euripides, *Hecuba,* trans. W. Arrowsmith, in *Complete Greek Tragedies,* ed. Lattimore and Grene, vol. 3. Martha Nussbaum, who discusses this play in *The Fragility of Goodness: Luck and Ethics in Greek Tragedy and Philosophy* (Cambridge: Cambridge University Press, 1986), typically does not consider the chorus. For a rich, illuminating reading of this tragedy as a whole, see Froma Zeitlin, "The Body's Revenge: Dionysos and Tragic Action in Euripides' *Hekabe,*" in *Playing the Other: Gender and Society in Classical Greek Literature* (Chicago: University of Chicago Press, 1996), 172–216.

31. Aeschylus, *The Oresteia: Agamemnon, Libation Bearers, Eumenides,* trans. Richmond Lattimore, in *Complete Greek Tragedies,* vol. 1. Euripides, *The Phoenician Women,* trans. E. Wyckoff, in *Complete Greek Tragedies,* vol. 4.

32. On slavery in ancient Greece, on slaves' ubiquity and invisibility, and on the impact of American slavery on classical studies in the United States, see Page duBois, *Slaves and Other Objects* (Chicago: University of Chicago Press, 2003).

33. Sophocles, *The Women of Trachis,* trans. M. Jameson, in *Complete Greek Tragedies,* vol. 2.

34. Robert Goheen, *The Imagery of Sophocles' Antigone: A Study of Poetic Language and Structure* (Princeton: Princeton University Press, 1951), 28.

35. Thucydides, *The Peloponnesian War,* trans. Steven Lattimore (Indianapolis: Hackett, 1998). Thucydides cites other such brutal acts of war: 1.114; 2.27; 5.3, 32, 116.

36. Xenophon, *A History of My Times,* trans. Rex Warner (London: Penguin, 1966).

37. Nicole Loraux, *La voix endeuillée: Essai sur la tragédie grecque* (Paris: Gallimard, 1999): "J'aimerais m'attacher à étudier désormais ce qui, sous la figure générique du deuil, résiste dans la tragédie athénienne à l'emprise, omniprésente à Athènes, du politique" (27).

38. Vernant, "Tensions and Ambiguities," in *Myth and Tragedy,* 33–34.

39. Charles Segal, "Greek Tragedy: Writing, Truth, and the Representation of the Self," in *Interpreting Greek Tragedy: Myth, Poetry, Text* (Ithaca: Cornell University Press, 1986), 99–100.

40. See Bruno Snell, *The Discovery of the Mind,* trans. T. G. Rosenmeyer (Oxford: Oxford University Press, 1953); on democratic ideology, see Page duBois, *Centaurs and Amazons: Women and the Prehistory of the Great Chain of Being* (Ann Arbor: University of Michigan Press, 1982). For a critique of readings that focus solely on tragedy, isolated from context, and of Snell's "discovery of the mind," see Leslie Kurke, *Coins, Bodies, Games and Gold: The Politics of Meaning in Archaic Greece* (Princeton: Princeton University Press, 1999), 335–36: "The extended narratives, complex characterizations, direct speech, and animated bodies of tragedy most of all seduce us into a belief in authentic and pre-existent subjectivity ('like our own'), but it is precisely here that we must recognize the culture's most compelling ideological effects. We should perhaps instead see tragedy as a privileged site for competing, multiple constitutions of subjectivity through practice" (335).

41. Pierre Vidal-Naquet, "The Place and Status of Foreigners in Greek Tragedy," in *Greek Tragedy and the Historian,* ed. Christopher Pelling (Oxford: Clarendon Press, 1997), 109–19.

42. Edith Hall, "The Sociology of Athenian Tragedy," in *The Cambridge Companion to Greek Tragedy,* 95.

43. Mark Griffith, "Brilliant Dynasties: Power and Politics in the *Oresteia,*" *Classical Antiquity* 14 (1995): 62–129, and "The King and Eye: The Rule of the Father in Greek Tragedy," *Proceedings of the Cambridge Philological Society* 44 (1998): 20–84. Griffith here uses a modified psychoanalytic model to account for tragedy's representation of monarchy, tyranny, and return to order, arguing that the space of tragedy allows for a play of desires, including an unconscious one on the democratic citizen's part for a childhood governed by a father, and a polity governed by a monarchy, or aristocracy. This is an exciting and provocative argument, which relies for the most part on readings of Aeschylus and Sophocles, more amenable to such claims than the plays of Euripides, stimulating in its willingness to confront a programmatic conservatism in Greek tragedy, which as in Hall's case, is sometimes subject to a familiar idealization, couched in new terms. For an argument against an ahistorical application of psychoanalytic theory to Greek antiquity, now increasingly common, see Page duBois, *Sowing the Body: Psychoanalysis and Ancient Representations of Women* (Chicago: University of Chicago Press, 1988).

The "Morality of Pity"
Sophocles' *Philoctetes*

Martha C. Nussbaum

It was precisely here that I saw the beginning of the end, the dead stop, a retrospective weariness, the will turning against life, the tender and sorrowful signs of the ultimate illness: I understood the ever-spreading morality of pity that had seized even on philosophers and made them ill, as the sinister symptom of a European culture that had itself become sinister.

Nietzsche, *Genealogy of Morals,* Preface, section 5

The savages in North America, we are told, assume upon all occasions the greatest indifference, and would think themselves degraded if they should ever appear in any respect to be overcome, either by love, or grief, or resentment. Their magnanimity and self-command, in this respect, are almost beyond the conception of Europeans. . . . When a savage is made prisoner of war, and receives, as is usual, the sentence of death from his conquerors, he hears it without expressing any emotion, and afterwards submits to the most dreadful torments, without ever bemoaning himself, or discovering any other passion but contempt of his enemies. When he is hung by the shoulders over a slow fire, he derides his tormentors. . . . After he has been scorched and burnt, and lacerated in all the most tender and sensible parts of his body for several hours together, he is often allowed, to prolong his misery, a short respite, and is taken down from the stake: he employs this interval in talking upon all indifferent subjects, inquires after the news of the country, and seems indifferent about nothing but his own situation.

Adam Smith, *The Theory of Moral Sentiments,* V.2.9

The Pity Debate

Pity is problematic. The emotion that lies at the heart of ancient Greek tragedy has provoked intense debate, both in Greco-Roman antiquity and in modern Europe. Some modern philosophers, embracing the general ethos of the ancient Greek tragic poets, hold that pity is a valuable social emotion without which it would be difficult to establish decent political communities. Jean-Jacques Rousseau, devoting an entire book in *Emile* to pity and its social role, connects the emotion strongly to the

148

very possibility of republican government, saying that it brings people together around the thought of their common weakness and vulnerability, in the process undermining hierarchies of title, rank, and wealth. Others, following Plato and the ancient Greek and Roman Stoics—and adding some further arguments of their own—hold that pity saps the civic fabric and produces bad citizens, soft, sluggish, and effeminate.[1]

Sophocles' *Philoctetes* is the pity play par excellence. If most extant fifth-century tragedies do indeed, as Aristotle claims, take the pitiable as their subject matter, showing heroic characters coming to grief in ways for which they are not (or not primarily) blameworthy, the *Philoctetes* appears to be constructed deliberately so as to highlight the prerequisites and workings of the emotion. As Stephen Halliwell puts it, it provides "a remarkable and revealing case of an individual tragedy whose very action comes to revolve around the operation of pity."[2] Pain, sickness, weakness, hunger, cold, isolation, unjust treatment—all these classical occasions for pity, recognized in Aristotle's analysis in the *Rhetoric* (II.8), turn up as features of Philoctetes' life on the island, and they are mentioned again and again. Their seriousness receives great emphasis, especially in the remarkable scene in which Philoctetes suffers a debilitating attack of pain, a scene that may be unique in Greek tragedy, usually so reticent in its onstage depiction of bodily suffering. Similarly emphasized are Philoctetes' blamelessness and the fact, again central to Aristotle's analysis, that any human being might suffer a similar calamity.[3]

Moreover, because we know in this case a good deal about both the epic background and the Philoctetes plays of Aeschylus and Euripides—both of which preceded Sophocles' in date of composition—we can appreciate how fully Sophocles set himself to explore the parameters and occasions of the emotion, accentuating the pitiable nature of Philoctetes' plight and omitting other distracting issues.[4] Unlike his two predecessors, Sophocles chose to make Lemnos an uninhabited island: the Chorus consists of Greek sailors with the arriving expedition, rather than, as in the other plays, local inhabitants. He also, therefore, omits the local character, Actor, whom Euripides represents as providing Philoctetes with healing herbs for his pain. Philoctetes' suffering is thus doubled: to pain and illness is added the suffering of friendlessness and isolation. Sophocles is also the only one of the three who combines the persuading-Philoctetes plot (which involves Diomedes in the epic tradition, though Odysseus is substituted by Aeschylus, and Euripides includes both Odysseus and Diomedes) with the plot in which Odysseus is charged with conveying Neoptolemus to Troy. By thus bringing Neoptolemus and Philoctetes together, Sophocles creates an opportunity for a young and impressionable person to be brought under the sway of pity. We are given a chance to see how the emotion might be connected to choice and action.

Europeans saw that the play was remarkable for its focus on pain and isolation, but on the whole it made them nervous. Adam Smith, praising the play's atmosphere of "romantic wildness, which is so agreeable to the imagination," nonetheless criticized its focus on physical suffering.[5] Only two adaptations from the eighteenth century are widely discussed, one by Jean-Baptiste Vivien de Châteaubrun in 1755 and one by Jean-François de La Harpe in 1783. Lessing, who contemptuously describes Châteaubrun's version in *Laocoon: An Essay on the Limits of Painting and Poetry* (1766), tells us that the French playwright not only softened Philoctetes' suffering by omitting its divine causation, hence its inexorable character, but also provided a sentimental distraction from the themes of pain and isolation. He introduced two characters unknown in all versions of the myth: a princess who just happens to be living on the island and her lady of honor. "All the admirable play with the bow he has left out and introduced in its stead the play of bright eyes. The heroic youth of France would in truth have made themselves very merry over a bow and arrows, whereas nothing is more serious to them than the displeasure of bright eyes."[6] The drama revolves not around whether Philoctetes will be left alone without his bow but around whether Neoptolemus will have to leave without the lovely princess. One French critic even proposed that the newly cheerful play be retitled *La difficulté vaincue.*

Using Châteaubrun as a reference point, Lessing observes that the representation of extreme suffering is controversial in the dramaturgy of his times. Nobody—not even he, he says—is entirely comfortable with the idea that a person who shows that he is in great pain can be a tragic hero. Lessing does not entirely approve of his contemporaries' aversion to displays of pain and weakness, although he owns that to some extent he shares them. We see here, he says, a great difference between ancient Greeks and modern Europeans. European norms forbid weeping and crying as behavior unsuitable for dignified people (and males in particular); Greek norms did not. What was important to the Greeks, he continues, was not to conceal suffering, but, rather, not to be distracted by suffering from proper action.

Contrary to modern norms, he argues, Philoctetes can be a hero because he gives proof of firmness in the midst of suffering by sticking to his underlying views and commitments, in particular his love of his friends and his unwavering hatred of his enemies. Rejecting Cicero's critique of the play for making its hero unmanly, Lessing says that it is proper, indeed, for the (manly) hero to show that he is human and vulnerable: unlike the gladiators in the Roman arena, Philoctetes is "neither effeminate nor callous."[7]

Lessing's defense of Philoctetes is not only (by its own account) an anomaly in the culture of eighteenth-century Europe; it is also quite limited, since Lessing maintains (implausibly) that Philoctetes is not influenced mentally by his pain and insists that he would not be heroic if suffering really did affect his personality. Apart from Lessing, the play found few admirers. Goethe gave it a brief nod of approval in the *Conversations with Eckermann*. On the whole, however, it remained one of the least performed and studied in the tragic canon until relatively recent times and had relatively few modern versions until Seamus Heaney's acclaimed *The Cure at Troy* (1990). It seems, then, worth examining the play in the light of the ancient Platonic-Stoic critique and its modern elaborations, to see whether it contains good answers to the problems that philosophical critics of pity have plausibly raised.

Such an examination will also contribute to recent debates about the democratic character of tragedy. Terry Eagleton's *Sweet Violence*, attacking all theories that see tragic suffering as ennobling or uplifting, insists that tragedy, both on the stage and in the world, begins from the universal "frailty and vulnerability" of the human body, "in which any authentic politics must be anchored. Tragedy can be among other things a symbolic coming to terms with our finitude and fragility, without which any political project is likely to founder."[8] Not surprisingly, the *Philoctetes* is a focus for Eagleton's argument that the confrontation with human pain in tragedy is both immediate and universal. To ask why we feel sympathy for Philoctetes, he writes, is "a pseudo-problem bred by a bogus historicism. We feel sympathy for Philoctetes because he is in agonizing pain from his pus-swollen foot. There is no use in pretending that his foot is a realm of impenetrable otherness which our modern-day notions can grasp only at the cost of brutally colonizing the past."[9]

In a similar vein, Page duBois has argued that Athenian tragedy is democracy's way of staging profound conflicts and vulnerabilities that inhabit its common life; it is not simply about the predicament of the "great man" but also about the situation of the slave and the outcast, about stigma and exclusion. And it focuses relentlessly on grief and mourning, experiences through which the spectator is brought "to a moment of recognition that exceeds the homogeneous civic community, to an acknowledgement of his or her place among humankind, as mortal."[10]

While it is always perilous to offer sweeping generalizations about "tragedy" and "the tragic," the *Philoctetes* is surely a play that leads its spectator to acknowledgment of the horror of bodily pain and of the social isolation that often accompanies it. By bringing its spectator closer to extreme bodily suffering than was the usual Greek norm, it promotes an experience that is in the best sense democratic, one that acknowledges the equal frailty of all human beings and their fully equal need for the goods of life that Philoctetes so conspicuously lacks: food, shelter, relief of pain, conversation, nondeceptive friendship, political voice.

One note before we begin. In most of my writing on the emotion that the Greeks called *eleos* and *oiktos,* I use the English word "compassion," because in a modern context "pity" is frequently associated with condescension and superiority, as the Greek emotion, and Rousseau's *pitié,* were not. Here, because I am planning to stick so close to the Greek terms and the text of the play, I use "pity," as the word is virtually always used to translate *eleos* and *oiktos* into English; it is also, not surprisingly, the word standardly used to render Rousseau's *pitié.* Interestingly, despite these problems, Seamus Heaney sticks to "pity" in his version of the play, rather than using "compassion," perhaps because the latter is a somewhat clunky word for poetic use. Heaney's choice may also have been influenced by the important precedent of Wilfred Owen, who standardly uses "pity" of the emotion with which we acknowledge the common bodily vulnerability of all human beings, utterly eschewing any pride or condescension. Heaney's Sophocles and Owen's war poetry inhabit the same tragic universe, and Heaney may have sought to underline this connection. Perhaps we might even say that "pity" has acquired a poetic tradition in English that is robustly independent of the more Victorian *de haut-en-bas* uses of the term in (some) ordinary usage.

In any event, readers should understand that I am talking about *eleos* and *oiktos,* as Sophocles and, with him, Aristotle understand them.

Pity's Elements

According to Aristotle, whose account of *eleos* in *Rhetoric* II.8 is both a valuable philosophical guide in its own right and an excellent summation of much that we observe in Greek tragedy, pity involves three characteristic thoughts: that a serious bad thing has happened to someone else; that it was not (or not primarily) that person's own fault (the person is *anaitios*); and, third, that it is the sort of thing "that one might expect to suffer, either oneself or someone one cares about" (1385b14–15). Having devoted an entire chapter to these requirements in *Upheavals of Thought*,[11] I shall not dwell on them at length here, except to point out that Eagleton misdescribes my position when he says that I think that you cannot pity someone who brought suffering on him or herself. What I do say is that if we pity in such cases, it is because the magnitude of the suffering is overwhelmingly greater than the magnitude of the fault. Eagleton's own examples fit that analysis well.[12]

The thought of seriousness and the thought of nonfault seem to me just right; the requirement of similar possibilities strikes me as a very usual element in pity, but we should conclude that it is not absolutely necessary, since we pity nonhuman animals without imagining that they are similar in kind to us, and we imagine that a god with no needs pities human beings who are utterly different in kind.[13]

There is, however, another thought that needs to be added to these three in order to make the emotion complete. I call this thought the "eudaimonistic judgment," meaning by this the thought that the person who is the object of pity is an important part of one's own scheme of goals and ends, one's conception of one's own *eudaimonia*. This does not mean that the person is seen as a mere instrument of personal ends: we love and benefit our friends and family members for their own sake. It does mean that the people who will be singled out for pity, as for other strong emotions, are those who are woven into the fabric of one's own life, a part of our sense of what is most important in it. Distant people can be of eudaimonistic relevance in several ways: because the pitier has managed already to concern herself strongly with their well-being; because the pitier attaches eudaimonistic importance to general principles of justice, according to which we have ethical duties to people at a distance; or because, during an episode of deliberation or imagination, the distant people *become* of strong concern to her, although they were not before.[14]

The occasions for pity that Aristotle enumerates read like a plot outline of Sophocles' play. They fall into two groups: painful and destructive things, and bad things for which luck is responsible. (The rationale for the division might be that the bad things in the first group can be deliberately inflicted by another person and need not be caused by luck; if so, old age is misplaced, as are several items in the second group.) In the first group are deaths, bodily damages (*aikeiai*), bodily afflictions (*sômatôn kakôseis*), old age, illnesses, lack of food. In the second group are friendlessness; having few friends; being separated from one's friends

153

and relations; ugliness; weakness; deformity; getting something bad from a source from which you were expecting something good; having that happen many times; the coming of good after the worst has happened; that no good should befall someone at all; or that one should not be able to enjoy it when it does. Philoctetes has every item on this list except old age—including the more unusual ones (getting something bad from a source from which you expected something good; having the good come when it is too late to enjoy it). It is as if Aristotle, who clearly knew the play (since he refers to it in the *Nicomachean Ethics* discussion of *akrasia*) used it as a template for his own discussion. In any case, from this list we can see the extent to which the play provides us with a map of pity and its occasions, as well as the underlying thoughts (seriousness, blamelessness, similarity) that enter into the structure of the emotion.

Arguing Against Pity

The philosophical tradition makes many arguments against the value and appropriateness of pity. We may, however, focus on four, which introduce most of the salient issues. As we shall see, three of the four arguments can already be found in Plato and the Stoics; the fourth chimes in with themes in Stoic ethics, but it is pressed, as such, only in the modern period.

1. Falsity: Pity involves an overestimation of the importance of external goods for people's lives. Pity revolves around various types of pain and deprivation, attributing to them considerable significance for a person's flourishing. So the question immediately arises: Are these matters really important, or not? Nobody, and certainly not Aristotle, would wish to deny that some things for which we pity others are actually trivial and not worthy of our intense concern. Slights to honor, insults, monetary losses—all these, Aristotle holds in his ethical writings, are frequently overvalued. It would consequently be right to criticize someone who asked for pity on account of such relatively trivial matters and to reprove the giver of pity. What is at issue, however, is whether the things that Aristotle lists as the major occasions for pity are worthy of such intense concern. Plato's *Republic* III tells us that the spectacle of Achilles weeping over the death of his friend ought to be stricken from the education of the young in the ideal city, because a good person simply does not think such a calamity very important, believing himself to be sufficient unto himself for well-being (387DE). The Stoics famously develop this position much further, holding that none of life's calamities is properly seen as an occasion for strong emotion. The Stoic who loses a child, a friend, or a city, or who is stricken with pain, will not get upset at these predicaments. Nor will he want the pity of another, which would insult him by wrongly implying that he depends on the gifts of fortune. (The Stoic doctrine of suicide is closely linked to this line of argument, because it assures us that a person can always find an escape from pain if it becomes too intense. Thus, even in such severe cases, there is no occasion for pity.) Both Plato and various Stoic writers associate behavior that rises above pain with manliness, weeping and moaning with effeminacy (e.g., *Republic* 388A).

In ancient Greece, these positions were contentious and, we might say, counter-cultural—although in the late years of the Roman Republic and the early Empire popular sentiments about misfortune and emotion seem much closer to Stoic norms, whether because of antecedent similarities or because of Stoic influence. In eighteenth-century Europe, as Lessing observes, cultural norms have put the expression of strong emotion strictly off-limits for the respectable (noneffeminate) man. For some thinkers, who closely follow Stoic norms, the norm of self-command applies to the inner world as well as to outer displays; to others, somewhat more relaxed, it is all right to have the emotion, as long as one controls its outward expression. (This latter view need not endorse the strong Stoic repudiation of the worth of externals.) One thing that is clear, however, from Lessing's treatise and many other pieces of cultural evidence, is that the face distorted in pain was agreed to be ugly and deeply unheroic; even Lessing hastens to assure us that the Laocoon is admirable because he does not display such a face.

Adam Smith wrestles with these cultural norms, and with the Stoic texts that were his lifelong preoccupation, in a fascinating way. On the whole, he defends the Stoic position on external goods, holding, in consequence, that a good man will not think of life's calamities as occasions for weeping or for the pity of others. In the last edition of the *Theory of Moral Sentiments,* however, published shortly before his death in 1792, he argues that Stoicism goes too far when it urges us not to have pity for the sufferings of our friends and our family. By uprooting these sentiments, Stoicism undermines the bonds that hold families and communities together.

According to Smith, we ought to pity the sufferings of our dear ones. In our own calamities, however, he insists, it is right both to behave like a Stoic and to try to have a truly Stoic inner life.[15] To weep at a calamity is effeminate. Here Smith speaks disparagingly of the French and the Italians. The duc de Biron, he says with fine Scottish contempt, even disgraced himself by weeping on the scaffold.[16] Consider by contrast, he urges, the sublime behavior of the Native American "savages," who greet death with a mocking song and endure with equanimity all the most horrible tortures.[17] The passage that I have cited as an epigraph shows the extent of the fascination these Stoic "savages" held for Smith, a lifelong hypochondriac and constant complainer. They exemplify a norm of manliness to which he is deeply drawn, possibly because it seems so difficult to attain in real life. The passage shows an odd melding of Smith's readings about Native Americans with Stoicism: for the description of how the savages behave during the respite from pain is so close to Tacitus's account of Seneca's behavior during the slow progress of his suicide that it is difficult to think the two unconnected.[18]

Smith's asymmetry thesis is a notable attempt to salvage pity while sticking to Stoic notions of proper manliness. It is not very successful; indeed, it seems quite incoherent. If life's calamities are proper occasions for pity when they strike our friends and family, they are similarly important when they strike us, and we would be right to ask for and accept pity in such circumstances. But Smith's odd thesis is worth mentioning because many people hold it: going through life with dignity intact, for people who have encountered great calamities (people with severe physical disabilities, for example) is often thought to require an extreme Stoical attitude toward one's own misfortunes, while a "softer" attitude is permitted toward the suffering of others.

2. Pity does no good; it is useless moaning and groaning. This objection, pressed often by Nietzsche, is strongly suggested, at least, by the Platonic-Stoic critique.[19] Seneca frequently insists that we do not need pity, or any other emotion, for proper conduct, conduct in accordance with duty. Emotion simply makes us soft and passive, less likely to act well.

3. Pity is closely linked to revenge. A particularly fascinating objection, evident in Seneca but developed most explicitly by Nietzsche, focuses on the commitments to external goods that underlie all the major emotions. If you love one of these uncertain externals, then you are all set up for fear lest it be lost, for grief when it is lost, for pity when others lose such a thing through no fault of their own, for gratitude, when someone helps you get such a thing—and for anger, when someone else willfully damages it. The posture of the pitier seems so nice, so helpful, so full of the milk of human kindness. Consider, however, a person who pities another because he has lost his child (let's say). Such a person is acknowledging in that very emotion that children are really very important. How will this person react if someone damages his own child? A culture of pity is in this way a culture of anger. Seneca knows what he is doing when he urges Nero to avoid the softness of pity, for it lies all too close to the troubling propensities to cruelty that the young man is already displaying. We can make the connection between pity and anger even more direct by thinking about the person who asks for pity: for that person is set up for anger directly, in the very intensity of his concern for the good things that life has taken from him.

4. *Pity is partial: it favors the close against the distant.* This objection is presaged in Stoicism, which urges an impartial concern for humanity as a whole, while depicting pity as focusing on incidents close to the self. Given the egalitarian concerns of eighteenth-century thinkers, however, it gets developed much more fully there, particularly by Smith. He introduces the famous example of an earthquake in China, which will be an object of pity to a "man of humanity" in Europe—*until* he has occasion to worry about something that is really important to him close to home.[20] That worry might be trivial by comparison—the loss of his little finger, as compared to the deaths of "a hundred millions of his brethren." And yet it will extinguish all pity for the large but distant disaster: "He will snore with the more profound security over the ruin of a hundred millions of his brethren, and the destruction of that immense multitude seems plainly an object less interesting to him, than this paltry misfortune of his own." Life provides us with such examples every day.

My own analysis of pity explains this inconstancy in pity better, I believe, than Aristotle's can. In my view, pity requires the thought that the object is among one's most important goals and projects. Distant people can take on such importance through moral education—whether in themselves or through an intense commitment to social justice as an end. But life does not naturally lead people in the direction of such attachments to the distant. We begin, typically, with intense love of a small number of people, and it is only gradually—if at all—that we broaden our emotional lives. For this reason, the morality of pity seems likely to remain an uneven inconstant morality, given to momentary flickers of concern for the distant, who seem really important to us when we hear a vivid story of their plight,[21] and to backsliding when our usual scheme of goals and ends, with ourselves and our loved ones (typically) at the center, reasserts itself.

Are these four objections good ones? Let us now turn to the play, to see whether it suggests some possible responses. I believe that it makes a creative and convincing response to the first and second objections;

it does not fully respond to the third; and it suggests that the fourth is basically correct.

What Sophocles Shows Us

1. Falsity. No drama can precisely refute the Platonic-Stoic argument, because dramas are written about, and for, people who accept a certain conventional view of what is important in life, the very one that the Stoics are trying to dislodge. As Epictetus said, "Look how tragedy comes about: when chance events befall fools." The tragic hero is one such fool, and the pity-feeling audience is a large herd of similar fools. What would be required really to refute the Stoic picture would be a complete ethical theory, plus arguments convincingly showing it to be better than the Stoic view. We would need, as well, a meta-ethical account of the role of common beliefs and intuitions in ethical theory-construction, since most common ways of arguing against the Stoics (by pointing to "our" intuitions) would strike them as suspiciously in thrall to deformed social norms.

What the play does offer, however, is a vivid reminder of some "external goods" that seem very important and a vivid demonstration of how thoroughly those "externals" affect the attempt to live well. If the good life consists in a wide range of actions in accordance with virtue, it appears that it can be disrupted, as Philoctetes' life is disrupted, by isolation, hunger, and pain. Attention is constantly drawn to the way in which every single activity in which Philoctetes engages is mediated, and deformed, by pain. "He comes not with the sound of the pipe, like a shepherd pasturing his flock, but, I suppose, he stumbles under his necessity and cries out with a piercing shout" (212–16).[22] "He would creep now here now there, wriggling along, like a child without the nurse he loves . . . when the spirit-devouring misery (*dakethumos ata*) abated" (701–6). If even basic physical movement is disrupted by pain and disability, then all activities are disrupted—especially when, in addition to pain, one also lives in isolation, with nobody to give one care or even conversation, the other feature of Philoctetes' situation that is most frequently mentioned by the Chorus. The Stoic attempt to maintain that one can act appropriately under the pressures of chance encounters here a serious challenge.

A similar case is made for hunger, around which in many ways Philoctetes' entire life revolves. Left without any source of food, he has to spend his whole day arranging to stay alive, a struggle compounded, once again, by disability and isolation. The drama shows the way in which hunger saps all human projects, something that a prosperous audience might not fully know. Shelter, too, is a focus of pity. Odysseus initially describes Philoctetes' dwelling as cool and pleasant (16–19). When Neoptolemus finds it, however, it is rudimentary, just some pressed leaves and "a cup, made of a single block of wood, the work of a crude workman. . . . Look here![23] Some rags feel warm to the touch, full of the heavy oozing stuff from his sore" (33–39). As for drink, he has to rely on "standing water" (716).

In a manner unparalleled in Greek tragedy, Sophocles shows us the texture of a life at the margins of life, reminding us of daily realities that many poor people experience. Stoics typically do not dwell on this sort of lack. When they talk about poverty, it is genteel poverty: for example, Musonius Rufus, the gentleman farmer, feeling pleased that he has managed to avoid the temptations of the wicked city. Nietzsche, similarly, imagines the life of deprivation as something like the life he leads himself in a *pension* in Sils Maria. Solitude, rejection, simple food and drink, various illnesses—but not exposure to the elements, acute hunger, the absence of fresh water, the need to hunt and catch one's own food, disgusting smells coming from one's own body, severe physical disability affecting mobility itself—all this punctuated by attacks of blinding pain. It seems implausible to maintain that action, and efforts to act, are not severely disrupted by deprivation of this sort. But what is true of Philoctetes because of a rare accident is true, the audience knows or ought to know, of many people around them, much of the time. (What is a siege in wartime—a tactic Athenians loved to deploy—but the attempt to reduce an entire population to unendurable misery, through the force of hunger?)

The Stoics take refuge in the control that each of us allegedly has over thought and effort in the inner world. Even on the rack, they argue, the sage can think well and attempt virtuous actions. It is here that the play makes its most creative contribution to ancient and modern debates, showing us the extent to which deprivation affects the mental life itself. First of all, we learn that Philoctetes has to think all the time of how he is going to get his food; the effort to survive is so difficult and so continual that it threatens to swallow up other thought. "Pitiable alike in his pain and his hunger, he has anxieties with no let-up" (185–87). Second, the Chorus sees that this effort is not a peaceful effort: it introduces emotions of agitation and confusion into the inner world. Philoctetes is "bewildered at each need as it arises" (174–75). His suffering is "spirit-devouring," *dakethumos*. He is as helpless as a child without his nurse. Pain infantilizes. Pain and solitude together also make thinking crude. Philoctetes has not used language for years, and he knows that he is "grown savage," *apêgriômenon* (226). And when pain comes in full force, as the remarkable central scene depicts, it comes perilously close to removing human thought and speech altogether. Philoctetes' metrical cry "*apappapai papa papa papa papai*" (746)—translated, typically, by an inarticulate shout—shows us the razor's edge that separates human beings from other animals: for his cry retains meter and thus a semblance of human ordering, but it has lost syntax and morphology, the hallmarks of human language. Pain can make us less than fully human. The play thus disentangles extreme physical suffering from Smith's romantic fantasy of the noble savage.

Most subtly of all, the play shows us the influence of pain on moral character. Lessing makes things far too easy when he says that Philoctetes remains firm in misfortune. Philoctetes does retain some marks of his former moral character, such as the capacity for friendship that won him Heracles' loyalty. His sufferings, however, have embittered him and made him so suspicious of others that it takes a long time for him to trust Neoptolemus. He trusts him, indeed, only because Neoptolemus claims to be as hate-filled as Philoctetes is himself. And then, having trusted the young man, he is all set up for a disastrous reversal, when the plot to ensnare him comes to light. At this point, hatred and resentment take over completely. His refusal to leave the island to come to Troy, saving others and being saved himself, is viewed by the Chorus and Neoptolemus as excessive and inappropriate, a dwelling on past wrongs that is not right for a noble man. Neoptolemus, having had pity on him and having restored the bow, nonetheless makes a very trenchant criticism of the effect suffering has had on his moral character: "It is necessary for human beings to bear fortunes that are sent by the gods. But those who cling to sufferings of their own choosing, like you, would not rightly receive either sympathy or pity. You have grown wild. You will not take advice, and if someone counsels you, speaking with good will, you hate him and think him an enemy who means you harm" (1317–23). The audience fully understands that the Trojan War would have been lost, and most of the Greeks, including virtually all of the common soldiers and sailors, would have died, insofar as Philoctetes is concerned: only the deus ex machina at the play's end restores the order of history.

In these ways, the play makes a strong case against the Stoics and an even stronger case against Nietzsche, showing that external goods have value for things that the Stoics and Nietzsche themselves greatly value: effort of mind and will, the ability to form projects, and, most important of all, the ability to be a virtuous person, a good friend, and a good citizen. Even though its insistent harping on the importance of the externals that Philoctetes lacks might be dismissed as just assertion of a diseased cultural picture, these "arguments" cannot be dismissed; they cut to the heart of the Stoic critique itself.

2. *Pity does no good.* Is pity just useless self-indulgent moaning and groaning, with no connection to appropriate action? The entire play is a refutation of that contention. Neoptolemus is an easy prey for Odysseus's arguments, because he is young and ambitious. Though basically a fine person, he is prepared to lie and cheat because it will bring victory to his side and glory to himself. What changes his course, returning him to the commitments on which he was apparently raised (to his nature, as he says), is the experience of pity. The play dramatizes this in many ways, not least by putting in Neoptolemus's speeches terms indicative of the pain that he is feeling, in response to Philoctetes' pain. "I have long been in pain" he says (*algô palai*) "suffering at your misfortunes" (805–6). He describes his pity as a *deinos oiktos* that "has fallen upon" him, thus as a powerful and uncomfortable force, not at all soft and effeminate (965). Once he even calls out with Philoctetes' own inarticulate cry, *papai,* expressing the agony of his indecision: "*Papai,* what shall I do from this point on?" (895).

The first result of his pity, insofar as action is concerned, is that indecision itself. Instead of pursuing the plot with his former zeal, he now simply says, "I am at a loss, and do not know what to say" (897). Closely linked to his confusion is self-disgust: "Everything is disgusting when one departs from one's own nature and does things that do not fit it" (902–3). At this point he still tries to execute Odysseus's plan. But his pity prevents him. He turns around and goes back to give Philoctetes the bow, saying, "I go to undo the wrong that I did before" (1224). He rejects his former lies and resolves to treat Philoctetes fairly, as an equal. He will attempt to persuade him to come to Troy to be healed, but he will not force him. There is no doubt that this change, around which the play's entire action revolves, is the result of the experience of pity.

The play thus makes a powerful intervention in the debate between the Stoics and their critics. Seneca repeatedly insists that we can leave the soft emotions behind and still act appropriately; duty is sufficient. Nietzsche follows their line, adding that pity is useful only when it displaces the urge to commit suicide in favor of an urge to understand human misery as profoundly as possible. (He holds this good effect to be rare, though occasionally seen in devotees of Eastern philosophy.)[24] Interestingly, Kant is not so sure. Although he follows the Stoic critique of pity in many ways, he does at one point urge people to go to sickrooms and prisons in order to inspire pity in themselves, since it might provide them with motives to right action that a contemplation of duty all by itself would not provide. Of course it would be better if people did act correctly without relying on emotion, but Kant is interested in getting the right things done for people and thus prefers a motive that is in his eyes imperfect to no motive at all.[25]

The play suggests that there is something about the sheer vividness of seeing another person's plight that powerfully contributes to forming emotions that motivate appropriate action. Modern empirical psychology agrees. In an elaborate series of experiments on the roots of altruistic behavior, psychologist C. Daniel Batson has shown that it is indeed largely true that hearing a vivid account of the story of another person's plight leads to pity/compassion and that pity/compassion leads to helping action. In the typical scenario, subjects (students at the University of Kansas) listen to a story of woe that concerns a fellow student. Some are told to pay attention only to the technical aspects of the broadcast, not its content; others are told to listen to the content and to imagine the situation vividly to themselves. Subjects in the latter group, not the former, report experiencing compassion/pity. What is even more interesting is that in most cases the subjects typically choose helpful actions as a result. Batson is careful to make clear what would be helpful, and he advises choosing something that is not very burdensome (e.g., driving a student with a broken leg to classes for a week). In these circumstances, at least, pity is strong enough to make a difference. We can add that this is a stronger result than it appears, given that the people helped were utter strangers before the experiment and thus not part of the person's own scheme of goals and ends. So the story of woe had not only to engender the three Aristotelian thoughts but also to move the person at least temporarily into the subject's circle of concern. Pity does make a difference.

3. Pity and Revenge. The play does not take issue with the profound Stoic insight that pity is linked to revenge. Indeed, it shows us that the same attachments and commitments that lead Philoctetes to ask for (and receive) pity are also the basis for his vindictive anger against the commanders. Modern readers in particular may feel that, while anger is appropriate, Philoctetes' intense wish for ill to befall them is not. Whatever the difference between Greek and modern views, however, the play shows that Philoctetes goes to excess, even for a Greek, in his devotion to revenge. He threatens to wreck the whole course of history by his bitter intransigence. When we reflect that the world is set right only by Heracles' intervention, we see how destructive revenge can be, for both self and other. There is no doubt that Philoctetes' vindictiveness is closely connected to his high valuation of externals—difficult though it would have been to be a thoroughgoing Stoic in the midst of such extreme deprivation and pain.

The play thus makes us think about the "moral luck" that may lead a good character into excess and deformity, given sufficiently bad experiences. It also asks us how much anger we want in human life, and whether anger can ever be prevented from going overboard. Philoctetes' anger is an intrinsic part of his sense of justice. Indeed, it seems difficult to imagine the demand for justice without anger at treatment such as befell him. More generally, if the lot of people who suffer hunger, disease, and pain is ever to be ameliorated, it probably will not happen without anger at the wrongful acts (the selfishness, the laziness) that inflict these insults on human dignity every day. Nonetheless, his anger is not entirely attractive, and it has its dangers. Thus the play, while not accepting the Stoic/Nieztschean critique, suggests that an important task for the morality of pity will be to place limits on anger and the desire for revenge. It may be helped, in so doing, by a Stoic sense of the equal worth of all human lives: for Philoctetes' excessive anger is surely bound up with his solipsism, with his sense that the fate of the army, of Neoptolemus, of history itself, matters not one whit beside the totally engrossing drama of his own wrong and pain.

4. Partiality. The problem vividly raised by Adam Smith is deeply rooted in the nature of the human emotions. They take up their stand where each of us is, inhabiting the perspective of our own most important goals and attachments. We feel emotions for our own family and not for other people's families, our own group and not another group.

The play shows us this tendency. Neoptolemus is preoccupied with his own success and that of the Greek army. Philoctetes initially figures in his life as a tool to effect his ends. He is not easily moved to pity: when the Chorus utters its first extended expression of pity for Philoctetes, it is with an implicit contrast to Neoptolemus's more detached formulations. "For my part, I pity him," they say (*oiktirô nin egôg'*). They get a cold answer: all of this is the gods' plan, so that the war will not end before it ought to (191–200). It is only when Philoctetes has formed a trusting relationship with Neoptolemus and he has seen the pain with his own eyes that he feels pity—because it is only then that the man is real to him, as a human being whom he knows, a quasi-friend, part of his circle of concern. His moral imagination is stimulated by personal experience, up close: the smells, sounds, and sights of the attack of pain. Sophocles thus suggests that the problem of pity's partiality can be overcome, but only sporadically and unevenly, by ethical experiences that jump-start it by making a person a part of one's scheme of goals and ends at the very same time as the other thoughts constitutive of the emotion are summoned up. We notice that no general ethical principles urging impartiality or concern for the distant are able to assist Neoptolemus here. For their advent we need to wait for Stoicism. Even with a good moral theory, however, human beings who are not Stoics will continue (and, I believe, rightly) to have special attachments to their own immediate context, their own loved ones. In that sense contemporary readers have not transcended the position of Neoptolemus, even though they will have reasons he does not for concern with strangers. The play thus vividly depicts a problem that lies at the heart of our ethical lives today, as we struggle to do justice to the claims of people we do not know.

Even to the extent to which the play shows the overcoming of partiality, it would seem that Philoctetes' heroic status, noble birth, and august destiny are all crucial to his being a focus of concern at all. If it were just some regular human being suffering away on Lemnos, wrongfully abandoned, nobody would be looking for him, nobody would be talking about him, and nobody would care. The democratic audience would be aware, as the Chorus is aware, that Philoctetes' elite status is crucial to the other elite characters' caring about him, and they would be likely to ask, sitting there in the middle of their fellow citizens, how such emotions might be more effectively generalized. The play gives us a fine starting point: the universal vulnerability of the body. It challenges its audience to think of a politics in which this vulnerability does not lead to unequal fates for unequal groups and individuals. Thus it suggests critical questions about slavery, about the status of women, about the treatment of a conquered people. Such questions are more overtly stated in Euripides; but Sophocles knows and stages them too.[26]

Why does the Chorus feel pity more readily than Neoptolemus does? And, since the Chorus is the emotional guide for the audience in this case, why does the audience feel pity when they hear the story of his life, even before they see the man himself? Perhaps these examples will help us understand how an educated pity might overcome the partiality problem. The play shows us that when Neoptolemus's selfish emotions are absent and no particular distraction or impediment is present, human beings have a strong tendency to experience pity when they imagine another person's tale of woe. Sophocles and Daniel Batson are in harmony here.[27] But there are strict limits to the Chorus's compassion. They singled this man out and imagined his tale of woe because he is a noted hero and they had heard his tale before. They attend to him as a person of importance—in a way that they do not, and would not, attend to many thousands of other suffering people. The play is not just Smithian (and Batsonian), showing us that the imagination is fickle and requires the vivid presence of the object of pity and an absence of personal distraction if it is to sustain its imagining. It goes further, suggesting that compassion is in league with hierarchies of heroism and birth. We weep for people whose exploits catch our attention, who are brought before us as fascinating. Such people, very often, will be kings rather than commoners, heroes rather than ordinary foot soldiers. Kings are fascinating and fun, even when they suffer; the ordinary soldier's suffering is boring.

Tragedy, in fact, is an aristocratic art form. Throughout the centuries, people have wept at the predicaments of princes and princesses and refused a similar attention to commoners. Ancient Athenian tragedy was less focused on elite suffering than many subsequent examples in the genre; it devoted considerable attention to the sufferings of women, slaves, and other excluded people.[28] Nonetheless, its protagonists are always among the elite, and the stories that make them interesting are the stories of ruling households.

Could a commoner even be a tragic hero? That question, asked about Arthur Miller's Willie Loman (in *Death of a Salesman)* preoccupied the literary criticism of my youth. No doubt one reason it was posed so frequently was a certain elitism and obtuseness on the part of theorists of tragedy.[29] The problem is not absent, however, in the canonical tragic texts themselves. It is a problem that lies at the heart of tragic pity. Sophocles' play shows us not only what Smith showed—the fickleness and inconstancy of the tragic emotions—but also, implicitly, something more disturbing, of which no doubt Sophocles' audience was not fully conscious, namely, their tendency toward inegalitarian and undemocratic partialities, when fostered by the tragic genre.

The problem of generalizing pity, one of the greatest moral problems of our time, might be thought to be surmountable, since we now have forms of mass communication that make it possible to connect our imaginations to the sufferings of people anywhere in the world. And, despite much critical grumbling about "compassion fatigue," I believe that we do see many good examples of this sort, in which the vivid awareness of distant peoples' plight (victims of an earthquake on the other side of the world, victims of hurricane Katrina, civilians and soldiers whose lives are blasted in war, victims of genocide, women whose lives are deformed by rape and other violence) leads to new concern and to helping action.

Sophocles' play, however, stands as a warning: it is easier for our imaginations to become fascinated by the sufferings of the famous and glamorous. This, indeed, the media also show us every day, as we watch famous trials and ignore the struggles of poor people for basic justice, as the media's choice of which murder victims are even worth our attention reflects antecedent biases of race and class.

How might the modern media solve the partiality problem? As Rita Felski eloquently writes, "No longer a sacramental relic, a safely distanced object of veneration or disdain frozen in past time, the tragic is shown to persist . . . into the present."[30] How, then, can a present in which the obtuseness of an Odysseus is still the norm and the moral sensitivity of a Neoptolemus still the rare exception deal with the problem of pity's unevenness? One easy but relatively superficial solution would be to make sure to focus on examples of suffering that cross lines of class, race, and nation, ensuring that these daily stories of deprivation are told with a vividness and artistry that draws the viewer in. (The films of Satyajit Ray are splendid examples of how a great artist can achieve this. Ray's genius is his ability to make ordinary suffering so utterly particular, so riveting, that a rich American in New York can be connected to the deepest strivings of a rural family in Bengal, despite the utter difference in social and political context that the film faithfully reveals to us.)

There is, however, a deeper problem that the *Philoctetes* and Daniel Batson's work reveal, and we cannot solve it through such great modern democratic tragedies. The problem is that we ultimately need a great deal more than a series of interesting particular narratives if we are to build a world that is fair to the sufferings and the strivings of all. If the "eudaimonistic judgment" about the worth and seriousness of the suffering of distant others is ever to become a stable reality in people's lives, then we have to build structures of attention that ensure that pity will not fade when the story ends or grows stale.

Ultimately, this means that we need to build reliable global institutions.[31] Just as one cannot hope to run a nation on the basis of good emotions—we need a good tax system that will make people pay their fair share even when they are not feeling compassion—so too with the world as a whole: we need institutional ways of ensuring that the global economic order is fair to all and produces decent living conditions for all. That large topic, however, would take us beyond our present theme. What we can say here is that such institutions (like a good welfare system domestically) will never come into being or remain stable unless individual human beings do have, and have often, experiences that link them to the fates of distant people who suffer. Pity is needed to prompt the creation of good institutions and, once they have been created, to sustain them.

We are left with a political and educational challenge. Pity does seem to be both justified (in the central cases) and valuable in prompting appropriate action. It is, however, fickle and in league with hierarchy. How might a society take advantage of the good in pity while cultivating it in an evenhanded way? After all, the common objects of pity are indeed, as Rousseau argued, the common lot of all human beings. In that way the emotion itself gives us a head start. The task of cultivating a truly balanced and equal pity is a daunting one, one that we have not yet fulfilled and have barely attempted. But Sophocles' drama helps us get started, by reminding us that the body's needs for food, drink, shelter, and release from pain, and the bodily human being's needs for friendship, talk, and political voice are both universal and of central significance for all.

Notes

1. I discuss the Platonic critique of pity with reference, as well, to the role of pity in Aristotle's *Poetics,* in "Tragedy and Self-Sufficiency: Plato and Aristotle on Fear and Pity," in *Essays on Aristotle's Poetics,* ed. Amélie Rorty (Princeton: Princeton University Press, 1992), 261–90; the Stoic critique is discussed in *The Therapy of Desire: Theory and Practice in Hellenistic Ethics* (Princeton: Princeton University Press, 1994); the modern debate is analyzed in a general way in *Upheavals of Thought: The Intelligence of Emotions* (New York: Cambridge University Press, 2001), chaps. 6 and 7. I analyze Nietzsche's debt to Stoic arguments in "Pity and Mercy: Nietzsche's Stoicism," in *Nietzsche, Genealogy, Morality,* ed. Richard Schacht (Berkeley: University of California Press, 1994), 139–67, and Adam Smith's fascinating contribution in the forthcoming "'Mutilated and Deformed': Adam Smith on the Material Basis of Human Dignity," part of Nussbaum, *The Cosmopolitan Tradition* under contract to Yale University Press.

2. Stephen Halliwell, *The Aesthetics of Mimesis* (Princeton: Princeton University Press, 2002), 208.

3. See *anaxiou, Rhet.* 1385b14, and "which he himself might expect to suffer, or someone he cares about," 1385b14–15.

4. Dio Chrysostom discusses the three Philoctetes plays in Discourse 52, giving detailed plot comparisons; in Discourse 59 he provides a more extensive paraphrase of the opening scene of Euripides' play. Aeschylus's play is early; Euripides' was composed in 431, Sophocles' in 409.

5. Adam Smith, *The Theory of Moral Sentiments,* ed. D. D. Raphael and A. L. Macfie (Indianapolis: Liberty Press, 1976), 30.

6. Gotthold Ephraim Lessing. *Laocoon: An Essay upon the Limits of Painting and Poetry* (1766), trans. Ellen Frothingham (New York: Farrar, Straus & Giroux, 1968).

7. Ibid., 29.

8. Terry Eagleton, *Sweet Violence: The Idea of the Tragic* (Oxford: Blackwell, 2003), xv.

9. Ibid., xiv. See other discussions of the play at 29 (Philoctetes' suffering is not purposive), 31 (Philoctetes does not bear his pain with stoicism and yet is a tragic character for all that), 280 (Philoctetes is a "monstrous outcast" from human society). See also the discussion of Eagleton's views in Kathleen M. Sands, "Tragedy, Theology, and Feminism in the Time after Time," *New Literary History* 35, no. 1 (2004): 46–47.

10. Page duBois, "Toppling the Hero: Polyphony in the Tragic City," in ibid., 75.

11. Martha C. Nussbaum, *Upheavals of Thought: The Intelligence of Emotions* (New York: Cambridge University Press, 2001), chap. 6.

12. Eagleton, *Sweet Violence,* 154–55; see Nussbaum, "Tragedy and Self-Sufficiency: Plato and Aristotle on Fear and Pity," in Rorty, *Essays on Aristotle's Poetics,* and Nussbaum, *Upheavals of Thought,* chap. 6. Eagleton is familiar with the former, though not, it seems, with the latter.

13. See Nussbaum, *Upheavals of Thought,* chap. 6, where this point is developed at greater length.

14. See "Précis" and "Responses," in book symposium on Nussbaum, *Upheavals of Thought,* in *Philosophy and Phenomenological Research* 68 (2004): 443–49, 473–86, in reply to Deigh.

15. I discuss all the relevant texts in the forthcoming "'Mutilated and Deformed': Adam Smith on the Material Basis of Human Dignity," part of Nussbaum, *The Cosmopolitan Tradition,* under contract to Yale University Press.

16. Smith, *The Theory of Moral Sentiments,* 49.

17. Ibid., 205–6.

18. Smith's source for the Native Americans was apparently a work by Lafitau called *Moeurs des sauvages amériquains,* which depicted the torture scene with a grisly illustration, reproduced in Ian Simpson Ross, *The Life of Adam Smith* (Oxford: Clarendon Press, 1995); it is possible, then, that Smith, focusing on the visual representation, narrates it with language of his own, and thus Seneca manages to creep in.

19. On Nietzsche, see "Pity and Mercy: Nietzsche's Stoicism," in Schacht,

Nietzsche, Genealogy, Morality. Nietzsche here plays on the German term *Mitleid,* noting that it (correctly) implies that there has been a reduplication of suffering, thus making a bad thing worse.

20. Smith, *The Theory of Moral Sentiments,* 136.

21. For experimental evidence on this point, see C. Daniel Batson, *The Altruism Question* (Hillsdale, NJ: Lawrence Erlbaum Associates, 1991).

22. All translations from the play are my own.

23. *Iou iou* probably signifies disgust.

24. See Nussbaum, "Pity and Mercy: Nietzsche's Stoicism," 152, for references.

25. Kant, *Doctrine of Virtue,* Akad. P. 35, see discussion in Nussbaum, *Upheavals of Thought,* 379–83.

26. Here I am in agreement with duBois, "Toppling the Hero."

27. See "Précis" and "Responses," in book symposium on Nussbaum, *Upheavals of Thought,* in *Philosophy and Phenomenological Research* 68 (2004): 443–49, 473–86.

28. See duBois "Toppling the Hero."

29. See the criticisms of Eagleton, *Sweet Violence,* chap. 1.

30. Rita Felski, "Introduction," in *New Literary History* 35, no. 1 (2004), xix.

31. See Martha C. Nussbaum, *Frontiers of Justice: Disability, Nationality, Species Membership* (Cambridge, MA: Harvard University Press, 2006).

I Want to Die, I Hate My Life—
Phaedra's Malaise

Simon Critchley

Faced with the ever-enlarging incoherence of the present, characterised by war without end, the increasingly frantic shoring up of the *imperium,* the deepening contagion of ethnic, religious, and civil conflict, and the fatuous theologization of political life with the categories of good and evil, I would like to turn to seventeenth-century neoclassical French drama, in particular the case of Jean Racine's 1677 tragedy, *Phèdre,* "the masterpiece of the human mind," as Voltaire declared.[1] I must confess at the outset that the reasons for this choice are not entirely clear to me and this essay is not intended as allegory. But I cannot deny that it was written with an eye to the present. I will let the reader make of this what he or she will and turn in detail to the play and its fascinating philosophical implications.

My focus is on the character of Phaedra and the nature of her malaise. I begin by trying to elicit the dramatic pattern of Phaedra's confessions of her desire, a desire that produces a guilty subjectivity that I illustrate with reference to Augustine's *Confessions.* I go on to describe Phaedra's existence as defined by the fact that, unlike the conventional tragic hero, she is unable to die, that existence is, for her, without exit. I pursue this thought by turning to Emmanuel Levinas's brief reading of *Phèdre* and linking it to what is arguably the enabling motif of his work, namely that existence is not the experience of freedom profiled in rapture, ecstasy, or affirmation, but rather it is that which we seek to evade in a movement of flight that simply reveals—paradoxically—how deeply riveted we are to the fact of existence. Counterintuitively perhaps, I try to show how this Levinasian thought has its home in Martin Heidegger's *Sein und Zeit,* in particular in his treatment of the concept of *Befindlichkeit* (state-of-mind or attunement) and its relation to thrownness and facticity. This is the ontological meaning of Phaedra's guilt: one's fundamental self-relation is to an unmasterable thrownness, the burden of a facticity that weighs one down without one's ever being able to pick it up. I try to show how this experience of guilt injects a fearful *languor* into Phaedra's limbs, a languor that I trace to the experience of erotic stupefaction: Phaedra is hypnotized by the desire that she loathes and it is here that she languishes. After linking languor to the concept of original sin, I seek to take seriously the possibility of *Christian* tragedy, that is, an essentially anti-political tragedy that would consist in the rejection of the worldly order and the radical separation of subjectivity and the world. I conclude with a remark as to how Racine's *Phèdre* might lead us to question some of our critical and theoretical *doxai* about the nature of tragedy.

I want to die, I hate my life. Such is the malaise of Phaedra. Yet why does Phaedra feel this malaise? Well, adultery, incest, and murder of an innocent are not mere moral baubles, even for one descended from the line of the gods. Phaedra was the daughter of Minos and Pasiphaë, and granddaughter of Pasiphaë's father, the Sungod or Helios, whose light burns Phaedra's eyes and whose scorching gaze she cannot bear, but from whom she cannot hide. The Sun watches her throughout the play: silent, remote to the point of absence, but of piercing intensity, like the *Deus absconditus* of Jansenism. Her father was King of Crete and later judge in Hades. She married Theseus, King of Athens, who brought her back to Greece after slaying the Minotaur in the Cretan labyrinth. Aphrodite, as she is wont, inflamed Pasiphaë with a monstrous passion for a bull. Daedalus, the artificer, made a hollow wooden cow where Pasiphaë could crouch to be fucked by the bull. From this union was born the Minotaur. It is the overwhelming power of her mother's predestined passion that now flows through Phaedra's veins.

Venus is in Phaedra's blood: it flows through her like a virus, the sickness of illicit erotic desire. With Theseus away for over six months on one of his adventures, she burns with passion for Hippolytus, Theseus's virginal son and her stepson. When Phaedra first saw Hippolytus, she declared, "darkness drenched my eyes." She languishes in dark desire, Venus clawing at her heart, her mother's sin boiling in her blood. Worn down by the guilt of this passion, and the division it creates within her, she resolves to die. This is how we first encounter her in the play, dragging herself into the light to greet her grandfather, the Sungod, for the last time, "Soleil, je te viens voir pour la dernière fois."[2]

Phaedra's silence about her sin is broken on three occasions, in three confessions that mark the dramatic highpoints of the play. Believing Theseus dead and at the promptings of her Iagoesque confidante Oenone, Phaedra with great reluctance confesses her love for Hippolytus:

PHAEDRA:
Tu vas ouïr le comble des horreurs.
J'aime . . . A ce nom fatal, je tremble, je frissonne.
J'aime . . .
OENONE:
Qui?
PHAEDRA:
Tu connais ce fils de l'Amazone,
Ce prince si longtemps par moi-même opprimé?
OENONE:
Hippolyte! Grands Dieux!
PHAEDRA:
C'est toi qui l'as nommé.

[PHAEDRA:
Prepare to hear the crowning woe.
I love . . . I tremble, shudder at the name;
I love . . .
OENONE:
Who?
PHAEDRA:
You know that prince whom I myself
So long oppressed, son of the Amazon?
OENONE:
Hippolytus?
PHAEDRA:
You have pronounced his name.] (1.3)

This is why Roland Barthes calls *Phèdre* a nominalist tragedy.[3] Phaedra's culpability is crystal clear to her from the beginning of the drama; the only issue is getting her to name it, to break her silence. As Theramenes says in the first scene, she suffers from a malady "qu'elle s'obstine à taire." The central issue in the tragedy is the naming of the monstrous, the monstrous desire that produced the Minotaur, the monster that Theseus killed, the desire for his virginal son that now courses through Phaedra's body. She names the truth a second time in a scene of awesome erotic intensity, where Phaedra, in a sort of trancelike rapture, confesses to Hippolytus:

Hélas! Je ne t'ai pu parler que de toi-même.
Venge-toi, punis-moi d'un odieux amour.
Digne fils du héros qui t'a donné le jour.
Délivre l'univers d'un monstre qui t'irrite.

La veuve de Thésée ose aimer Hipployte!
Crois-moi, ce monstre affreux ne doit point t'échapper.
Voilà mon Coeur. C'est là que ta main doit frapper.
Impatient déjà d'expier son offense,
Au-devant de ton bras je le sens qui s'avance.
Frappe. Ou si tu le crois indigne de tes coups,
Si ta haine m'envie un supplice si doux,
Ou si d'un sang trop vil ta main serait trempée,
Au défaut de ton bras prête-moi ton epée.
Donne.

[My foolish heart, alas, too full of you,
Could talk to you of nothing but yourself,
Take vengeance. Punish me for loving you.
Come, prove yourself your father's worthy son,
And of a vicious monster rid the world.
I, Theseus's widow, dare to love his son!
This frightful monster must not now escape.
Here is my heart. Here must your blow strike home.
Impatient to atone for its offence,
I feel it strain to meet your mighty arm.
Strike. Or if it's unworthy of your blows,
Or such a death too mild for my deserts,
Or if you deem my blood too vile to stain
Your hand, lend me, if not your arm, your sword.
Give me it!] (2.5)

Phaedra is making two extraordinary demands here marked by the two monosyllabic exclamations that break up the rhythm of the alexandrine line: "Frappe," "Donne" (strike, give). If Hippolytus will not strike at the monstrous desire within Phaedra with his physical ardor, piercing her heart with his arm as she rises to meet him, then she will take his sword from him and do it herself: "give." She removes his sword from him in a gesture that it would simply be too facile to describe in terms of castration.

Hippolytus—the chaste, the hunter; and Artemis, the goddess of hunting, is also the goddess of chastity—is appalled. He flees. When rumors of Theseus's death come to appear somewhat exaggerated, Phaedra concocts the story that Hippolytus had raped her in order to protect herself. After learning this news from sly Oenone, Theseus banishes Hippolytus, damning him with a prayer for vengeance to the god Neptune. Resolved to tell the truth to Theseus, events take a sudden turn for Phaedra when she learns that Hippolytus, whom she believed indifferent to all women, loves Aricia, last surviving descendent of the line of kings of Athens usurped by Theseus. Hippolytus could love, but loved not Phaedra. Suddenly consumed by jealousy, she stands in silence while Hippolytus is violently and rather operatically drowned by Neptune's sea monster. Phaedra takes poison and, after confessing her guilt to Theseus, dies. Theseus—poor, wooden, uncomprehending, two-dimensional comic-book hero that he is—concludes the play: "D'une action si noire / Que ne peut avec elle expirer la mémoire!" (5.7).[4] He embraces Aricia as his daughter and exits stage left to find his son's body. Such is the story.

She wants to die, she hates her life. But does Phaedra die? Well, yes and no. I would like to look at Phaedra's third and final confession that effectively concludes the drama at the end of act 4—act 5 is little more than dramatic housekeeping, tidying up a few loose ends. Still burning for Hippolytus, Phaedra sees that she has sunk into a web of criminal deception fueled by incestuous desire. In her wretchedness, she turns to face her ancestors, the gods. Let me cite the text in Paul Schmidt's free and muscular rendering and then in the original French:

> Oh, Oenone! . . . am I going mad?
> How can I ask a husband I've betrayed
> To avenge my sinful love for his son?
> I'm sinking in a sea of criminal designs:
> Adultery, incest, and murder of an innocent—
> Tell me to stop! Tell my ancestor the sun
> To burn away my pain to paltry ashes.
> My grandfathers were gods, the stars above
> Shine in the shape of my ancestral lineage;
> The universe is part and parcel of my blood.
> Where can I run? How can I ever get away?
> My father is the fatal judge of Hell,
> What will he do when he sees his daughter confess to crimes that
> Make the demons stare?
> Become my executioner?
> Find me a fitting form of eternal punishment?
> Tell him the family curse lives on.
> Oh god, if only I'd enjoyed my love! Just once!
> To die like this, unsatisfied,
> And full of nothing but remorse!

Que fais-je? Où ma raison se va-t-elle égarer?
Moi jalouse! Et Thésée est celui que j'implore!
Mon époux est vivant, et moi je brûle encore!
Pour qui? Quel est le coeur où prétendent mes voeux?
Chaque mot sur mon front fait dresser mes cheveux.
Mes crimes désormais ont comblé la mesure.
Je respire à la fois l'inceste et l'imposture.
Mes homicides mains, promptes à me venger,
Dans le sang innocent brûlent de se plonger.
Misérable! Et je vis? Et je soutiens la vue
De ce sacré Soleil dont je suis descendue?
J'ai pour aïeul le père et le maître des Dieux;
Le ciel, tout l'univers est plein de mes aïeux.
Où me cacher? Fuyons dans la nuit infernale!
Mais que dis-je? Mon père y tient l'urne fatale.
Le sort, dit-on, l'a mise en ses sévères mains:
Minos juge aux enfers tous les pâles humains.
Ah! Combien frémira son ombre épouvantée,
Lorsqu'il verra sa fille à ses yeux présentée,
Contrainte d'avouer tant de forfeits divers,
Et les crimes peut-être inconnus aux enfers!
Que diras-tu, mon père, à ce spectacle horrible?
Je crois voir de ta main tomber l'urne terrible,
Je crois te voir, cherchant un supplice nouveau,
Toi-même de ton sang devenir le bourreau.
Pardonne. Un Dieu cruel a perdu ta famille:
Reconnais sa vengeance aux fureurs de ta fille.
Hélas! Du crime affreux dont la honte me suit
Jamais mon triste coeur n'a recueilli le fruit.
Jusqu'au dernier soupir, de malheurs poursuivie,
Je rends dans les tourments une pénible vie.

[What am I doing? I have lost my mind!
I, jealous? And 'tis Theseus I implore!
My husband is alive and yet I pine.
For whom? Whose heart have I been coveting?
At every word my hair stands up on end.
Henceforth the measure of my crimes is full.
I reek with foulest incest and deceit.
My hands, that strain for murder and revenge,
Burn with desire to plunge in guiltless blood.
Wretch! And I live and can endure the gaze

Of the most sacred sun from which I spring.
My grandsire is the lord of all the gods;
My forebears fill the sky, the universe.
Where can I hide? In dark infernal night?
No, there my father holds the urn of doom.
Destiny placed it in his ruthless hands.
Minos judges in hell the trembling dead.
Ah! How his horror-stricken shade will start
To see before him his own daughter stand,
Forced to admit to such a host of sins
And some, perhaps unknown even in hell!
What, father, will you say to that dread sight?
I see your hand slip from the fateful urn;
I see you searching for new punishments,
Yourself and your own kin's executioner.
Forgive me. Venus's wrath has doomed your race.
Your daughter's frenzy shows that vengeance forth.
Alas, my sad heart has never enjoyed
The fruits of crimes whose dark shame follows me
Dogged by misfortune to my dying breath,
I end upon the rack a life of pain.] (4.6)

Burning and wretched, she turns to face the Sun, her grandfather. In this movement of turning, she reveals the division at the heart of her subjectivity. Phaedra is watched throughout by the Sun and she is acutely conscious of being watched by this silent, distant, but omnipresent Jansenist God. The Sun is a murderous power, inescapable and distant, a divinity much closer to Yahweh than to an incarnate, loving Christ or any being in the Greek pantheon. As Lucien Goldmann persuasively argues, at the center of the tragic vision of Racine and Pascal is a God who is hidden to the point of absence, who never intervenes in the drama of the world, and yet who watches intensely and who, for the tragic hero, is more present than anything else: "[T]he God of tragedy is a God who is always present and always absent."[5] What Goldmann is bringing to bear on Racine is Georg Lukács's understanding of tragedy in an essay from his first book, *Soul and Form*. The first lines of the essay seem to capture precisely Phaedra's situation: "A drama is a play about a man and his fate—a play in which God is the spectator. He is a spectator and nothing more; his words and gestures never mingle with the words and gestures of his players. His eyes rest upon them: that is all. 'Whoever sees God dies,' Ibsen wrote once; 'but can he who has been seen by God continue to live?'"[6] Phaedra's answer to this last question is a resolute "no," but, as we shall see, it is a negativity that must remain an aspiration.

Against the divinity of the Sun, there is the virus of Venus in her blood, "a cruel God," the darkness of her mother's desire. Phaedra's subjectivity is torn between these two poles, the Sun and Venus, which could be re-described as the call of conscience and the pressure of libidinous desire. But Phaedra's experience of her subjectivity is cosmic, her forebears fill the skies, the universe is constituted by the opposed forces aiming at her tragic destruction. These forces are metaphorically coded in the imagery of light and dark that fills the play. The merciless light of the sun is obscured by the shadow of Venus, producing what Phaedra oxymoronically calls "une flamme si noire," "such a black flame."[7] Phaedra's guilt— and all guilt I would be tempted to add—is experienced as movement, an oscillation between opposites. Guilt is stretched between these two poles of conscience and desire, of the Sun and Venus. It is in this movement that Phaedra's subjectivity is rent.

Phaedra is a paradox: she detests her desire, yet she cannot give way on it; she fears the burning conscience of the Sun, yet she constantly calls to him. The gravity of her desire is constituted by her will to pull free of it in the experience of conscience. The promised ecstasy of libidinous transgression is directly proportionate to the power of moral prohibition. For Phaedra, and this is her paradox once again, her sad heart has never experienced the fruits of the crimes that she has committed. Hers is a sin of the heart, not a sin of the flesh. She never experiences erotic pleasure with Hippolytus, she never couples with the bull like her mother, and the truth is that she could not because her conscience would not let her, not even if some crafty Daedalus built her a wooden engine of disguise. She is unable to sin fulsomely. This is why she ends her life upon a rack of pain. For this, finally and pathetically, she asks forgiveness, in a simple "Pardonne," which echoes and qualifies the "Frappe" and "Donne" of the previous scene.

To my mind, what Racine is dramatizing here is the inner conflict that constitutes Christian subjectivity in Augustine's *Confessions,* a work whose influence on the theology of Jansenism cannot be overstated. Cornelius Jansen's 1,300-page commentary on Augustine was post-humously published in 1640 and quickly condemned as heresy by the Inquisition, the Jesuits, and the Pope himself. In book 8 of the *Confessions,* Augustine describes himself as "still tightly bound by the love of women," which he describes as his "old will," his carnal desire.[8] This will conflicts with his "new will," namely his spiritual desire to turn to God. Alluding to and extending Paul's line of thought in Romans 7, Augustine describes himself as having "two wills," the law of sin in the flesh and the law of spirit turned towards God. Paralyzed by this conflict and unable to commit himself completely to God, these two wills lay waste to Augustine's soul. He waits, hesitates, and hates himself. Seeing himself from outside himself, from the standpoint of God, Augustine is brought face-to-face with his self and sees how foul he is, "how covered with stains and sores" (C 193). He continues, "I looked, and I was filled with horror, but there was no place for me to flee away from myself." But where Augustine finds peace in conversion to God at the end of book 8, Phaedra continues to burn in the dark fire of self-division, unable to free herself.

Such are the fatal circuits of what Foucault would call the Christian hermeneutics of desire opposed to the pagan aesthetics of existence.[9] In a seminar at New York University in 1980, Foucault is reported to have said that the difference between late antiquity and early Christianity might be reduced to the following questions: the patrician pagan asks, "Given that I am who I am, whom can I fuck?" The Christian asks, "Given that I can fuck no one, who am I?"[10] Foucault's insight is profound, but let me state categorically and without a trace of irony that, as a committed atheist, I side with the deep hermeneutics of Christian subjectivity against the superficial pagan aesthetics of existence. The question of the being of being human—who am I?—the fundamental issue of philosophical anthropology that begins with Paul and is profoundly deepened in book 10 of the *Confessions* arises in the sight of God. The problem is how that question survives God's death. This is Rousseau's question in his *Confessions,* it is Nietzsche's question in *Ecce Homo,* and it is Heidegger's question in *Sein und Zeit.*

Everything wounds Phaedra. When she first appears onstage, she is barely able to bear the weight of her body, her knees—trembling—threaten to give way: "mes genoux tremblants se dérobent sous moi" (1.3). Her jewels, veils, and the very braiding of her hair are felt as afflictions. Her first action onstage, in one of Racine's rare stage directions, is to sit, "elle s'assied" (1.3). She experiences her existence as a sheer weight, as the body being pulled to earth by the gravity of erotic desire, the virus of Venus. Existence is not something to be affirmed; nor is it the ground for one's freedom, understood as a projective leap towards the future.

No, life is pain. Destiny is predestined. Existence is thrown. It is to this thrownness, this rack of pain, that Phaedra is *riveted.* She is riveted to herself, to her curse, to the sin that flows in her blood, to the sheer fact of her life. That is the cause of her malaise.

So, where can she hide? Nowhere. What is unique about Phaedra's life—and this is the crucial point for my interpretation—is that it cannot be escaped in death. Death brings no end to her malaise because death, for her, is not an end. In the cruel words of Theramenes in the first scene of the play, Phaedra is "une femme mourante et qui cherche à mourir" (1.1). Her existence is what Barthes calls "une mort-durée."[11] With this in mind, consider again Phaedra's third confessional speech: her ancestors were gods, the sun and stars above shine in the shape of her ancestral lineage, the universe is part and parcel of her blood, her cosmic subjectivity. But if her forbears fill the sky, dividing her guilty subjectivity between conscience and desire, then can she escape into the dark infernal night of Hades? Can she escape from this rack of pain by killing herself? No, because her father is the fatal judge of hell, and holds the urn of doom. And what will he do? Forgive her? Forgive such unspeakable crimes that continue the horror of the family curse? It is hardly likely. Will he kill her? He cannot, as she is already dead. He will therefore have to find some fitting new form of eternal punishment.

If Phaedra's existence is defined by malaise, then this malaise will continue after her death. Which is to say that death is not death, but simply a deeper riveting to the fact of existence and its eternal curse. Phaedra's discovery is death's impossibility. Death is not the possibility of an escape hatch, something she can dispose of through the controlled leap of suicide. Rather, there is a fate worse than death, namely that of an existence without end, whether here—above in the sight of her grandfather, Helios, or there—below at the mercy of her father, Minos. After her death at the end of the play, Phaedra's sufferings will continue only more intensely in the dark suffocacy of Hades. Existence is without exit.

Which raises the following question: if Phaedra does not die, then of which subject is this play the tragedy? Who or what dies in this tragedy? In my view, the corpse on stage at the end of the play is not that of Phaedra, but that of the city, the state, the world. The moral of the tragedy is that life in the world is impossible. I will come back to this.

She hates her life, she wants to die, but she cannot. Learned readers might have noticed that I have been glancing over my shoulder at Levinas while pondering Phaedra's malaise. Levinas cites part of the above passage from Racine—together with Shakespeare's *Hamlet* and *Macbeth* and modern examples from Poe and Maupassant—in his discussion of what he calls the *il y a* in *De l'existence à l'existent:*

> Le ciel, tout l'univers est plein de mes aïeux.
> Où me cacher? Fuyons dans la nuit infernale!
> Mais que dis-je? Mon père y tient l'urne fatale.[12]

For Levinas, Phaedra confronts what he calls "le 'sans issus' de l'existence," the exitlessness of existence. With the *il y a,* Levinas asks us to undertake a thought-experiment, "Let us imagine all beings, things and persons, reverting to nothingness" (*EE* 93). But what would remain after this reversion? Nothing? Levinas's claim is that the very nothingness of all things is experienced as a kind of presence: an impersonal, neutral, and indeterminate feeling that "quelque chose se passe," what he elsewhere calls "an atmospheric density, a plenitude of the void, or the murmur of silence."[13] The *il y a* is this murmuring, the indeterminate sense of something happening in the absence of all things, expressed with the neutral or impersonal third-person pronoun. The present absence of the *il y a* is a descendent of the hidden Jansenist God.

To illustrate phenomenologically the experience of the *il y a,* Levinas writes, "We could say that the night is the very experience of the *il y a*" (*EE* 94). This is what Maurice Blanchot calls the essential or other night towards which the desire of the artist tends. The night into which all familiar objects disappear, where something is there but nothing is visible, the experience of darkness, the density of the void where lucid objectivity collapses into a swarming of points. This is the night of insomnia, the passive watching in the night where intentionality undergoes reversal, where we no longer regard things, but where they seem to regard us: *la nuit me regarde*. This is what Levinas calls "la veille," which denotes both watchfulness and wakefulness, a vigil, a night-watch, but also the state of being on the brink or verge (*EE* 111). Borrowing Blanchot's definition of the artist, we might say that Phaedra is "l'insomniaque du jour," the insomniac of the day.[14] Like all of Racine's tragic heroes, she cannot sleep. During her first appearance on stage, Oenone says, "Les ombres par trois fois ont obscurci les cieux/Depuis que le sommeil n'est entré dans vos yeux [Thrice have the shades of night darkened the skies/Since sleep last made its entry into your eyes] (1.3). One is reminded of Pascal's extraordinarily austere words, "Jesus is suffering the torment of death until the end of time. We must not sleep during that time."[15] These words find a more or less direct echo in Estragon's words in *Waiting for Godot,* in what is possibly the best line ever written: "Was I sleeping while the others suffered? Am I sleeping now?"[16] In her sleeplessness, and on the brink of madness, Phaedra watches wakefully and is watched constantly by the sleepless gods, whether the vengeful transcendence of the Sun or her father's eternal night in Hades.

The mood that accompanies this experience of being riveted to existence is not anxiety or fear, but rather *horror*. As is so often the case, Levinas is using Heidegger as a critical lever to open his own thought. In *Sein und Zeit,* anxiety is the basic or fundamental mood experienced in the face of being-towards-death. Therefore, the most horrible thought would be that of conceiving the possibility of my own death, of that fatal moment when I slip over into nothingness. Against this, Levinas claims that "horror is in no way an anxiety about death" (*EE* 99). What is most horrible, then, is not the possibility but rather the impossibility of my death. "Demain, hélas! Il faudra vivre encore"[17]—such is the sentiment of the world of horror, the world of vampires and zombies, the undead and the living dead. What is truly horrible is not death, but the irremissibility of existence, of awakening underground in a coffin with nobody to hear your sobbing or your fingers scratching on the wood; of being paralysed and speechless while a team of doctors casually discuss what they diagnose as your permanent vegetative state, and so on and so on. Horror is possession by that which will not die and which cannot be killed—something wonderfully demonstrated by Maupassant in his short story "The Horla." Phaedra feels herself possessed by that which she cannot escape, both by the sin of Venus in her blood and the mute presence of the Sun in her conscience. Of course—and this is the entire paradox of horror—what she is possessed by is herself, by her consciousness of sinfulness. The subject of horror is the subject's horror at itself, at that demonic hither-side of itself that it seeks to evade. There is no need for demons—it is the subject itself that is demonic.[18]

Phaedra's horror at herself provokes malaise, but what is it exactly to be *mal à l'aise*? Levinas writes the following in his stunning first original essay from 1935, "De l'évasion": "Le malaise n'est pas un état purement passif et reposant sur lui-même. Le fait d'être mal à son aise est essentiellement dynamique. Il apparaît comme un refus de demeurer, comme un effort de sortir d'une situation intenable. . . . C'est une tentative de sortir sans savoir où l'on va, et cette ignorance qualifie l'essence même de cette tentative" (Malaise is not a state that is purely passive and reposing upon itself. The fact of being in a state of malaise is essentially dynamic. It appears as a refusal to remain, as an effort to leave an untenable situation. . . . It is an attempt to leave without knowing where one is going, and this ignorance qualifies the very essence of the attempt).[19] Thus, malaise is not a passive or quiescent state, it is a dynamic state, even a dramatic state, that arises as a refusal to remain in existence. Malaise is a movement that attempts to *evade* existence. Phaedra is riveted to her existence and this fact provokes a malaise that makes her want to evade it. This is how I understand what might otherwise appear to be her madness: "Insensée, où suis-je? Et qu'ai-je dit?/Où laissé-je égarer mes voeux et mon esprit" [Madness! Where am I, what have I said?/Whither have my desires, my reason strayed] (1.3). She would like to be "insensée," but she is not insane. Madness would be an escape, an evasion from her curse, but she remains tragically lucid throughout.

She wants to die, but she cannot. She would be mad, but remains sane. In the agonizing meanwhile of her suffering, she seeks to evade herself. In what? In death, but she cannot die. In eroticism, but she cannot even commit the sins for which she lacerates herself. In the Wooster Group's extraordinary version of the play, Phaedra is submitted to violent and noisome enemas as if seeking to evacuate and evade her own body. Around her, the other characters abstractedly play badminton. This is the world, it would appear: a distraction, a farce, a comic game. Phaedra tries to play, but lacks the strength even to lift the "birdie" or "shuttlecock" (possibly an even sillier word than "birdie"). Phaedra is enchained to the fact of herself and this is what she wants to evade by fleeing towards the world. Existence, the being of being human, is not something to be embraced, it is rather that in the face of which we take flight towards the world in a movement that Levinas calls "excendence": "Ainsi, au besoin d'évasion, l'être n'apparaît pas seulement comme obstacle que la pensée libre aurait à franchir, ni comme la rigidité qui invitant à la routine, exige un effort d'originalité, mais comme un emprisonnement dont il s'agit de sortir" [Thus, for those needing to evade, being does not simply appear as an obstacle that the free movement of thought would be able to cross, nor as a routine-producing rigidity demanding an effort of originality, but rather as an imprisonment which it is a question of leaving behind] (DE 377). Being is not our home; its house is a prison, the cell of the self constantly surveyed by the murmuring of the *il y a*. This prison is airless and Phaedra is constantly close to asphyxiating. The space of the drama is claustrophobic and enclosed. The tragic hero is a captive. There is no wind and the characters in the drama cannot breathe. One has the sense of the action taking place in a box, a lit-box that is being watched, not just by the audience, but by the players and by the gods themselves. It is a little like the play within the play in Shakespeare's *Hamlet—The Mouse-trap*—an intrigue by which players are caught, guiltily riveted to themselves, where "conscience does make cowards of us all" (3.2, 3.1). After noting that the desire for evasion can "revêt une forme dramatique,"[20] Levinas goes on, "Dans l'identité du moi, l'identité de l'être révèle sa nature d'enchaînement car elle apparaît sous forme de souffrance et elle invite à l'évasion. Aussi l'évasion est-elle le besoin de sortir de soi-même, c'est-à-dire *de briser l'enchaînement le plus radical, la plus irrémisible, le fait que le moi est soi-même*" [In the identity of the ego, the identity of being reveals the nature of its enchainment because it appears under the form of suffering and it invites evasion. Thus, evasion is the need to leave oneself, that is, *to break the most radical and irremissible enchainment: the fact that the ego is itself*] (DE 377). Existence is enchainment not emancipation. Phaedra experiences it as suffering and as the desire to evade oneself, to flee towards the world, to excend herself in empty distraction by playing badminton or whatever. But the movement of flight is held tight by the chain that binds me to myself. Such is the basic fact of the human condition: that I am myself, *hélas!*

Counterintuitively perhaps, the Levinasian thought with which I am trying to understand Phaedra's experience has its home in *Sein und Zeit,* but it is a Heidegger read very much against the grain. It is specifically the concept of *Befindlichkeit* that is of interest here: state-of-mind, attunement or already-having-found-oneself-there-ness. Heidegger's claim is that I always already find myself attuned in a *Stimmung,* a mood or affective disposition. Such a mood discloses me as *geworfen,* as thrown into the "there" (*Da*) of my being-in-the-world. For Heidegger, these three terms—*Befindlichkeit, Stimmung,* and *Geworfenheit*—are interconnected in bringing out the nature of what Heidegger calls *Faktizität,* facticity. Heidegger's early work—and this is a debt that Levinas repays from the first to the last word of his published work, despite his unflinching horror at Heidegger's political commitment—is a hermeneutics of facticity, a description of the everyday ways in which the human being exists.

In being disposed in a mood—and here we begin to hear Phaedra's voice—Dasein is satiated or weary (*überdrüssig*) with itself, and as such its being becomes manifest as a burden or load (*eine Last*) to be taken up. The burdensome character of one's being, the sheer weight of the "that-it-is" (*Das es ist*) of existence, is something that I seek to evade. Heidegger writes, "Im Ausweichen selbst ist das Da erschlossenes" (In evasion itself is the there disclosed).[21] This is fascinating, because Heidegger is claiming that the being of Dasein's *Da,* the there of its being-in-the-world, is disclosed in the movement that seeks to evade it. Evasion discloses that which it evades. It is precisely in the human being's turning away (*Abkehr*) from itself that the nature of existence first becomes manifest. I find myself as I flee myself and I flee myself because I find myself. Heidegger rather enjoys the paradox "gefunden in einem Finden, das nicht so sehr einem direkten Suchen, sondern einem Fliehen entspricht" [found in a finding that corresponds not so much to a direct seeking, but to a fleeing] (*SZ* 135). What is elicited in this turning away of Dasein from itself is the facticity of Dasein's being delivered over to itself (*Faktizität der Überantwortung*) and it is this that Heidegger intends by the term thrownness, *Geworfenheit.*

The parallels between Heidegger and Levinas in the above-cited passages, although striking, should not be overstated. True, the concept of *Befindlichkeit* reveals the thrown nature of Dasein in its falling movement of turning away from itself. But two paragraphs later in *Sein und Zeit,* Heidegger will contrast this movement of evasion with the concept of *Verstehen,* understood as ability-to-be, which is linked to the concepts of *Entwurf* (projection) and *Möglichkeit* (possibility). That is, Dasein is not just thrown into the world, it can throw off that thrownness in a movement of projection where it seizes hold of its possibilities-to-be. This movement of projection is the very experience of *freedom* for Heidegger. Dasein is a thrown project—but where Heidegger will place the emphasis on projection, possibility, and freedom as the essential elements in the movement towards *authenticity,* Levinas might be read as following out another possible trajectory of the existential analytic of *Sein und Zeit.* This trajectory is what might be called "originary inauthenticity." Let me explain myself.[22]

Originary inauthenticity begins by accepting that what I reluctantly confront in my evasive turning away from myself is the fact of my facticity. This stares back at me like an enigma, the enigma of who I am, the past whose opacity constantly threatens to overwhelm me, like the virus of Venus in Phaedra's blood. In the wisdom of Paul Thomas Anderson's 1999 movie *Magnolia,* "You might be through with the past but the past isn't through with you." Originary inauthenticity is the thought that human existence is fundamentally shaped in relation to the brute fact of a thrownness that cannot be mastered through any existential projection. The virile surge of freedom is the mere rattling of bars in a prison cell. Authenticity slips back into a prior inauthenticity from which it cannot escape but which it would like to evade. From this perspective, human existence is something that is first and foremost revealed as a burden, a weight, a load, as something to which I am riveted without being able to know why or know further. This is how we first meet Phaedra in Racine's drama. Inauthentic existence has the character of an irreducible and intractable *thatness,* what Heidegger called "das Daß seines Da." I feel myself bound to "the that of my there," the sheer *Faktum* of my facticity.

Dasein learns to take up this burden in the experience of guilt (*Schuld*), understood as indebtedness (*Verschuldung*) or existential lack. As Heidegger writes in his extraordinary pages on guilt, Dasein is a thrown basis (*ein geworfene Grund*). As this basis, Dasein continually lags behind itself, "Being a basis [*Grund-seiend*], that is to say existing as thrown [*als geworfenes existierend*—one of Heidegger's nicely oxymoronic formulations], Dasein constantly lags behind its possibilities" (*SZ* 284). The experience of guilt reveals the being of being human as a lack, as something wanting. In the light of these remarks, we might say that the self is not, as many would have Heidegger believe (and arguably as he believed himself at the time of writing *Sein und Zeit*), the ecstasy of a heroic leap towards authenticity energized by the experience of anxiety and being-towards-death and consummated in the moment of vision (*der Augenblick*). Such would be the reading of the existential analytic that sees its goal in *autarky,* self-sufficiency or self-mastery. Rather, the self's fundamental self-relation is to an unmasterable thrownness, the burden of a facticity that weighs me down without my ever being able to pick it up. Expressed temporally, one's self-relation is not the living present of the moment of vision, but rather a delay with respect to oneself that is perhaps best expressed in the experience of fatigue and languor. This, I would claim, is the ontological meaning of Phaedra's guilt, its existential movement, prior to any ontic penumbrae.

Phaedra desperately tries to project or throw off her thrownness through life in the world. But this movement of throwing off catches her in its throw and inverts the movement of possibility. She finds herself, mood-wise as Heidegger might have said, riveted to the fact of her self, to her facticity. Phaedra's word for facticity is *blood,* which is not to be understood biologically. Rather, there is a whole metaphysics of blood at work in Racine's tragedy: blood is the existential mark of the past, of one's bindedness to a past that you might think you are through with, but which is not through with you. Contaminated by the virus of Venus that flows in her veins, Phaedra cannot exist in the present, let alone the future of projective freedom. Rather, she is a prisoner of her past, the facticity of her mother's monstrous desire and her grandfather's conscience. Phaedra's present continually lags behind itself. She cannot make up her time. She is always too late to meet her fate and this is why she is so utterly fatigued.

The horror of being riveted to one's facticity injects a fearful *languor* into Phaedra's limbs. The virus of Venus that flows in her blood weighs her down. She writhes, she burns. Her body possesses or is possessed by an unbearable gravity that pulls her earthwards. Languor is her affective response to the exitlessness of existence, to the fact of being chained to herself. What interests me greatly here is the experience of languor as a bodily response to facticity, of the body being coursed through by a desire that is experienced as alien, the virus of Venus in the veins. This desire overtakes me and slows me down, inducing a languid sluggishness, a lethargy, a creeping inertia, a sort of *Trägheit*—which is Freud's word for describing the death-drive, that cosmic-sounding force that provides a compelling analogue to the world of Phaedra's experience.

Languor makes me an enigma to myself. I find myself enchained to a facticity whose very nearness makes me lose focus and unable to catch my breath. I burn, breathless, in my languor. This experience is wonderfully described by Augustine in *Confessions*, book 10, where he is agonizing about the virtue involved in the sensual pleasure of religious music. He writes, and think here of Phaedra's sense of being watched by God, "But do you, O Lord my God, graciously hear me, and turn your gaze upon me, and see me, and have mercy upon me, and heal me. For in your sight I have become a question to myself and that is my languor *[mihi quaestio factus sum et ipse est languor meus]*" (C 262). Augustine's words are cited here in Jean-François Lyotard's remarkable, and remarkably obscure, posthumously published *La confession d'Augustin,* an extremely Christian text for such an avowed pagan.[23] My languor is the question that I have become for myself in relation to the present-absent *Deus absconditus* who watches me, who may heal and have mercy upon me, but whom I cannot know and whose grace cannot be guaranteed. The questions I pose to God make me a question to myself. Lyotard adds, gnomically, "*Lagaros,* languid, bespeaks in Greek a humor of limpness, a disposition to: what's the point? Gesture relaxes therein. My life, this is it: *distentio,* letting go, stretching out. Duration turns limp, it is its nature" (CA 18).

The experience of languor, for Lyotard, is both the body's limpness, its languid quality, and time as distension, as stretching out, procrastination. In languor, I suffer from a delay with respect to myself, my suffering is experienced as what Lyotard calls, in language reminiscent of Blanchot, "waiting": "The *Confessions* are written under the temporal sign of waiting" (*CA* 70). Originally inauthentic, the weight of the past makes me wait, and awaiting, I languish. I grow old, I shall wear the bottoms of my trousers rolled. I am filled with longing. Lyotard, close to dying as he is writing, quotes the above passage from Augustine for a second time, and adds, "*[I]pse est languor meus.* Here lies the whole advantage of faith: to become an enigma to oneself, to grow old, hoping for the solution, the resolution from the Other. Have mercy upon me, Yahweh, for I am languishing. Heal me, for my bones are worn" (*CA* 70).

Phaedra languishes. In an existence without exit, time stretches out and she waits for an end that will not come. She experiences languor as a mental and physical weariness, a sheer fatigue in the face of her thrownness. But her languor also has strong erotic overtones: it is a feeling of dreaminess and laxity, closer to the Middle English "love-longing" and the German *Sehnsucht,* yearning.[24] This is the sort of eroticized sickness that afflicts Troppmann, the hero of Georges Bataille's *Le bleu du ciel,* languishing in his disgrace and burning with hallucinatory sexual desire and thoughts of his own death. The book begins, "I know. I'm going to die in disgraceful circumstances."[25] In Phaedra's confession to Hippolytus, she says, "Oui, Prince, je languis, je brûle pour Thésée" [Yes, Prince, I languish, I burn for Theseus] (2.5). And again, "J'ai langui, j'ai séché, dans les feux, dans les larmes" [I languished, I dried up, in the fire, in tears] (2.5).

Phaedra's malaise is the experience of languor as an affective response to the fact of being riveted to herself. Guiltily bound to the fire of Venus that burns in her blood with the distant Sungod watching impassively, she languishes sensuously in this captivity. Life is a trance for Phaedra, a sort of agonized fainting away that produces moments of erotic stupefaction where she is hypnotized by the desire that she loathes. In this trance, past and present merge and she finds in Hippolytus the image of Theseus, so that when she says to the former that she burns for the latter, then these words are directed to the same erotic fantasm.

If *Phèdre* is a nominalist drama, then there is a name that my entire discourse is dishonestly circling around without discussing, namely *sin.* Might not originary inauthenticity be another name for sin? Is this entire project not therefore an attempt to recover the concept of sin? This remains an open—if not gaping—question.

Immersed as he was in Christian theology, Heidegger's existential analytic is alert to this question and neatly sidesteps it. First, he insists that his concept of falling, *das Verfallen*, should not be understood as a fall from a state of grace to a state of sin (*SZ* 280). Second, Heidegger rather cutely claims that as sin is ontic and the Dasein-analytic is ontological, his concept of guilt proves nothing either *for* or *against* the possibility of sin (listen to the sound of a philosopher eating his cake and having it). Now, such a move would be justified if one could restrict the concept of sin to the ontic domain. But I have my doubts: if the concepts of falling and guilt can be raised to the dignity of ontology, then why not also sin? I do not mean sin as an ontic feature of everyday (im)moral action, but rather as an essential feature of the being of being human. This would exclude venial, mortal, or actual sin, which might indeed be classed as ontic, but include original or hereditary sin, which is a claim about the being of being human. All that I have said about the inauthentic subject finding itself in flight, disclosing itself in its evasive turning away from itself, might be redescribed as an attempt to recover the notion of hereditary sin. For what is hereditary sin but the claim that the being of being human is originally constituted as a lack, as a radical indebtedness to a past that cannot be made up by the subject's own volition? Original sin constitutes the subject in a state of want, as a thrown basis that cannot throw off that thrownness in a movement of free projection. Existence is that load or burden to which I am enchained and in which I languish. I languish in sin, like Oswald at the end of Ibsen's *Ghosts,* whose final Phaedra-like words before he collapses into the languor of his hereditary sickness are "the sun, the sun."[26]

Heidegger, however, comes close to acknowledging the ontological status of original sin in the protocol of a two-part talk given in Rudolf Bultmann's seminar in 1924, "The Problem of Sin in Luther." Although the original manuscript was lost and the short published text is a student transcript written in reported speech and consisting largely of quotations from Luther, Heidegger speaks of the movement of sin as an experience of flight: "He who flees once flees in such a way that he constantly wishes to distance himself further."[27] More intriguingly, Heidegger endorses Luther's critique of the scholasticism of Catholic theology and follows the Protestant emphasis on the ontological centrality of sin, writing that the "the being of man as such is itself sin," and again, "sin is not an affixing of moral attributes to man but rather his real core. In Luther, sin is a concept of existence" (PS 108). The perspective of authentic faith can only be attained when one has fully understood the originally inauthentic being of sin. The difference between Heidegger and Luther consists precisely in the attainability of authentic faith: for Heidegger, it is my ownmost possibility which I can seize hold of by affirming my finitude, whereas for Luther it is God's possibility, namely the giving or withholding of grace.

I would like to conclude with a remark about tragedy and comedy. Racine's *Phèdre* is a tragedy, is it not? Yet, what happens in a tragedy? Why is tragedy tragic? Tragedy is tragic because someone dies, sometimes a whole stageful of personae. If Phaedra is the tragic heroine, then we have seen that her death is at least ambiguous and possibly, on the view argued for in this paper, impossible. She dies, but her existence does not come to an end. It continues in the twilight of Hades with the same awful languor and malaise, the same experience of being riveted to the original sin of who she is, with the gods still watching on. Is Phaedra therefore a tragic figure? One might wonder whether her fate is more tragic than tragedy, inspiring not so much pity and terror as horror.

But, if Phaedra does not die, then of whom is this drama the tragedy? Who is the subject of this tragedy? On this point, Goldmann's interpretation of *Phèdre* proves once again invaluable in leading us back to Racine's Jansenist inspiration.[28] At the core of Jansenism is a refusal of the world and a turning of the subject towards a hidden, watchful God. In what Goldmann calls Racine's "tragedies of refusal," what gets shown is the impossibility and futility of life in the world. What therefore happens at the end of *Phèdre* is not so much her actual death as her death to the world. What Phaedra is forced to renounce is the temptation of life in the world, of the temporary satisfaction of desire, of some sort of contentment.

The world is a farce, a mere bauble, a comic illusion where individuals appear light, empty, and two-dimensional. To a much stronger degree than any other tragedy I know, Phaedra is not only the eponymous protagonist of the drama, but also the only substantial character onstage. The other onstage characters are slight and, indeed, slightly comic: Oenone is little more than a sounding board for Phaedra's essentially solitary dialogues, Theseus is something of a flatfooted oaf throughout, and poor, virginal Hippolytus is an unworthy object of such ferocious desire. Besides Phaedra, the only real characters are offstage: the gods and ancestors to whom Phaedra addresses her monologues. In the face of the farce of the world, it is to the gods that Phaedra is obliged to confess. No one else has the capacity to understand. She is a deep Christian trapped in a superficial pagan world. To this extent, the drama of *Phèdre* once again presses against the limits of the genre of tragedy and one wonders whether its depiction of the world is not in fact closer to Hegel's understanding of the world of comedy as that of illusion, deception, and insubstantiality. At times, Phaedra appears like some lost beautiful soul withdrawn from an uncomprehending world.

This brings me back to the Wooster Group's dramatisation of *Phèdre*—*To You, the Birdie!*—which is deeply comic, often farcical, and where bathos replaces tragic pathos. The weapons of tragedy—swords, shields, and daggers—are comically sublimated into badminton racquets and shuttlecocks. The comic effect is reinforced by the Wooster Group's use of technology, where the performance is punctuated with noises reminiscent of some anachronistic video game or an imagined soundtrack to a silent movie. Unwittingly or not, the Wooster Group are true to the Jansenist inspiration of the play. By playing tragedy as comedy, what is achieved is the radical separation of the character of Phaedra from the noisy and senseless sport of the world that surrounds her.

Is this to say that the tragic, the truly and deeply tragic—the experience of being riveted to the sheer fact of existence, and the games we pursue to evade this fact—is something that can only be played comically? Does the tragic have to be comic for us, here, now, whosoever we are and whatever moment of history this passes for? One might speak of tragic-comedy, after all there are good Beckettian precedents. Is the tragic only tragic as the comic? If it is—and I am inclined to think so—then this is not funny, not funny at all.

This is how I would read another stunning contemporary rewriting of the Phaedra story, *Phaedra's Love* by Sarah Kane from 1996.[29] Turning the previous versions of the play on their head, Hippolytus is here pictured as an inert, heartless, sexual hedonist sprawled on a sofa surrounded by electronic toys, eating hamburgers and crisps while he masturbates pleasurelessly into a sock. After confessing her love for him, Phaedra gives Hippolytus oral sex, after which he reveals both the fact of his gonorrhoea and that he has already slept with Phaedra's daughter. For his sins, he is eventually castrated and disembowelled by Theseus, giving Hippolytus the only glimmer of pleasure that he feels in the entire play. But what I find particularly compelling is the way in which the bleakness of Kane's drama is sustained by moments of deliciously dark humor. For example:

DOCTOR:

Does he have sex with you?

PHAEDRA:

I'm sorry?

DOCTOR:

Does he have sex with you?

PHAEDRA:

I'm his stepmother. We are royal. (*PL* 66)

Or again:

PRIEST:

Love never dies. It evolves.

HIPPOLYTUS:

You're dangerous.

PRIEST:

Into respect. Consideration. Have you considered your family?

HIPPOLYTUS:

What about it?

PRIEST:

It's not an ordinary family.

HIPPOLYTUS:

No. None of us are related to each other. (*PL* 93)

Returning to Racine, but keeping both the Wooster Group and Sarah Kane in mind, it would seem that *Phèdre* is not exactly the tragedy that one might imagine. Something dies, but it is not Phaedra. What dies is the world, and the corpse onstage at the end of the play is not Phaedra's, it is that of the illusion of the polis, the city, the state, the political order. The tragedy here is that of the political order, of Helleno-Hegelian *Sittlichkeit*, or Heideggerian *In-der-Welt-Sein*. As with Milton's *Samson Agonistes*, a tragedy almost contemporary with *Phèdre*, the ship of state is a wreck at the end of the play. Built up through war, conquest, bloodshed, and usurpation, it is destroyed by them too. The moral inference is that life in the world is a game of power, a farce of force, a murderous illusion. It is senseless.

The antipolitical nature of Racine's tragedy is what arguably separates it most profoundly from the entire spirit of ancient Greek tragedy. Attic tragedy dramatizes the *agon* at the heart of the constitution of the political order, whether that between the old and new gods (Orestes versus the Furies) in Aeschylus's *Oresteia* or between the laws of the family and the laws of the polis (Antigone versus Creon) in Sophocles' *Antigone*. The essence of Attic tragedy is the conflict between opposed, yet mutually justified, claims to justice. Such conflict results either in the dissolution of an unjust polis, as is the case with the *Antigone,* or the institution of a new political order of justice, as in the *Oresteia.* Attic tragedy concerns the conflictual nature of political substance. Seen from this perspective, *Phèdre* is something completely different. It is what Nietzsche would see as a monstrous contradiction in terms: a *Christian* tragedy. Antipolitical in its essence, the moral of *Phèdre* is the utter rejection of the temporal world. The true life is elsewhere.

The differences between Attic and Christian tragedy become obvious when one compares *Phèdre* with Euripedes' *Hippolytus.*[30] Although there are many obvious Euripedean borrowings in Racine, it is the additions and subtractions that catch the eye, most strikingly the terrible economy of Racine's verse in comparison to the slight loquaciousness of Euripedes. As the play's title would suggest, Phaedra is more marginal to the action in Euripedes than in Racine, where Phaedra's subjectivity is center stage. The chorus, which plays a large role in Euripedes, is absent from Racine, as is much of the moralizing judgment one finds in the former. The character of the nurse is more central in Euripedes and she is presented as a more caring and interesting character. Also, Hippolytus's loathing of women is much more obvious, which makes his death by a bull emerging from the waves all the more poignant. But the main thematic action is in terms of the divine opposition between Artemis (hunting and chastity) and Aphrodite (eros). Hippolytus is the enemy of the latter and friend of the former and the drama consists in the revenge of Aphrodite, the Cyprian as she is called, upon Artemis. Sin is central to the *Hippolytus* but it is here that the difference with Racine is most clearly marked. Theseus sins in killing his son by bringing down Poseidon's curse upon him, but this sin is *pardoned* and pardon is the central theme of the drama, with characters requesting forgiveness for their actions. This is crystallized in the closing scene, where Artemis appears in a deus ex machina and pardons Theseus in front of his dying son, "Men may well sin, when gods so ordain." This forgiveness is then echoed by the expiring Hippolytus, who breathlessly mutters to his father, "No, you are free. I here absolve you of my death." That is, sin can be forgiven, which is unthinkable in Racine, whereas Phaedra expires asking for but not receiving forgiveness: "Pardonne."

For Racine, only Phaedra lives in the truth. And she lives in the truth by refusing to live in the world. It is the world that dies in the tragedy and Phaedra who lives . . . after a fashion. This gives a very intriguing twist to the Aristotelian conception of tragedy characterized by *peripeteia* and *anagnorisis*. Having resolved to die at the beginning of the play, Phaedra becomes persuaded to live in the world. Her recognition at the end of the play is that this is impossible and she revolves to die once again, only to discover that this is also impossible. Aristotle might understandably have been perplexed.

The truth of subjectivity has to be lived apart from the world. Such is the tragic vision of Jansenism and its many heirs, from Kantian moral autonomy in a political kingdom where means are justified by ends, to Levinas's defense of subjectivity as separation in a world dominated by the political horror of war. There are many other heirs. But how far apart are subjectivity and the world? Here we confront the most acute dialectical paradox of *Phèdre*. If the lesson of Racine's tragedy is that life in the world is impossible, that the true life transcends the world, then I am still obliged to live in the world. The world is the only reality of which I can be sure and there is no question of a mystical intuition or a higher state of authentic awareness within the tragic vision. I live immanently in a world which is real and of which I can be sure, yet I experience a demand for transcendence that exceeds the world, but also my powers of cognition: the incomprehensible source of the moral law in Kant, the transcendent ethical demand of the other in Levinas. Hence the need, in Pascal, for the wager, which is not some intellectual game for a sceptical, urbane, seventeenth-century audience, but is rather the best bet of that which I cannot be sure. The tragic vision is a refusal of the world from within the world, as Goldmann writes, "Tragic man is absent and present in the world at one and the same time, exactly as God is simultaneously absent and present to man."[31]

The human being, like Phaedra, is a paradox: we are ineluctably *in* the world, but we are not *of* the world. That is, *we are not what we are in.* Such is the curse of reflection. We are confronted with a world of things, but we are not at one with those things, and that experience of not-at-oneness with the world *is* the experience of thinking. In other words, the human being is an eccentric creature, an oddity in the universe. Such eccentricity might be described as tragic, but it might be even better approached as comic.

Without God, the drama of Racine's *Phèdre* is reduced to being some story about a crazy woman trying to commit incest at court. We have to believe *that* Racine believed. Yet, what if we do not believe *what* he believed? What if we want to accept a tragic vision without God? Can that thought really be endured? Can it? Really? We will have to find out for ourselves.

Notes

These thoughts were initially prompted by an invitation from Andrew Quick and Adrian Heathfield to respond to the Wooster Group's version of *Phèdre,* entitled "*To You, the Birdie!*" performed at the Riverside Studios, London, May 2002, directed by Elizabeth LeCompte, with Kate Valk as Phaedra and Willem Dafoe as Theseus. I make extensive use of Paul Schmidt's excellently direct unpublished version of Racine's text, prepared for the Wooster Group for the original New York production. Aside from its presentation to generous audiences at London, Cork, New York, and Iceland, this text was the 2003 Simone Weil Lecture at the Australian Catholic University in Sydney and Melbourne. I am grateful to Rita Felski, Rai Gaita, Tom McCarthy, and, in particular, Jill Stauffer and Gabriela Basterra for their responses. All references to *Phèdre* are to the Pléiade edition, *Oeuvres Complètes,* vol. 1, ed. Raymond Picard (Gallimard: Paris, 1950). With minor adaptations, I have used the John Cairncross translation in *Phaedra and Other Plays* (London: Penguin, 1963).

1. All subsequent page references will be given in the text by act and scene number.

2. "Sun, I come to see you for the last time."

3. See Roland Barthes, *Sur Racine* (Paris: Seuil, 1960), 115–22.

4. "With her, such a black act cannot be expunged from memory."

5. Lucien Goldmann, *The Hidden God. A Study of A Tragic Vision in the "Pensées" of Pascal and the Tragedies of Racine,* trans. P. Thody (London: Routledge, 1964), 50, and cf. 36–37.

6. Georg Lukács, "The Metaphysics of Tragedy," in *Soul and Form,* trans. Anna Bostock (London: Merlin Press, 1974), 152. Interestingly, one can also find the words "Whoever sees God dies," without acknowledgement to Ibsen, in Maurice Blanchot's "Literature and the Right to Death," *The Gaze of Orpheus* (New York: Station Hill, 1981), 46.

7. For a helpful discussion of the imagery and language of *Phèdre,* see Edward James and Gillian Jondorf, *Phèdre* (Cambridge: Cambridge University Press, 1994), 19–52.

8. *The Confessions of St. Augustine,* trans J. K. Ryan (New York: Doubleday, 1960), 188–89; hereafter cited in text as *C.*

9. Michel Foucault, *The Use of Pleasure,* vol. 2, *The History of Sexuality,* trans. Robert Hurley (New York: Random House, 1985), 5–6, 11–13.

10. I owe this anecdote to conversations with Bernie Flynn.

11. Barthes, *Sur Racine,* 116.

12. Emmanuel Levinas, *De l'existence à l'existent,* 2nd ed. (Paris: Vrin, 1986), 102; hereafter abbreviated *EE.*

13. Emmanuel Levinas, *Le temps et l'autre,* 2nd ed. (Paris: Presses Universitaires de France, 1989), 26.

14. Maurice Blanchot, *L'écriture du désastre* (Paris: Gallimard, 1980), 185.

15. Cited in Goldmann, *The Hidden God,* 67, 80.

16. Samuel Beckett, *Waiting for Godot,* in *The Complete Dramatic Works* (London: Faber, 1986), 84.

17. "Tomorrow, alas! it will still be necessary to live."

18. I owe this remark to conversations with Rudi Visker.

19. Emmanuel Levinas, "De l'évasion," *Recherches philosophiques* 5 (1935–36): 380; hereafter cited in text as DE.

20. ". . . take on a dramatic form."

21. Martin Heidegger, *Sein und Zeit,* 15th ed. (Tübingen: Niemeyer, 1984), 135; hereafter abbreviated *SZ.* Translated by John Macquarrie and Edward Robinson as *Being and Time* (New York: Harper, 1962).

22. My overall interpretation of Heidegger's *Sein und Zeit* can be followed in more detail in Simon Critchley, "Enigma Variations: An Interpretation of Heidegger's *Sein und Zeit,*" *Ratio* 15.2 (2002): 154–75.

23. Jean-François Lyotard, *The Confession of Augustine,* trans. Richard Beardsworth (Stanford: Stanford University Press, 2000), 18, 55; hereafter cited in text as *CA.*

24. Longing is interestingly discussed by Lukács in "The Metaphysics of Tragedy," 162.

25. Georges Bataille, *Blue of Noon* (London: Boyars, 1979), 23.

26. Henrik Ibsen, *Four Major Plays,* ed. James McFarlane, trans. James McFarlane and Jens Arup (Oxford: Oxford University Press, 1981), 164.

27. Martin Heidegger, "The Problem of Sin in Luther," in *Supplements,* ed. John Van Buren (Albany, NY: State University of New York Press, 2002), 109; hereafter cited in text as PS.

28. *The Hidden God,* 371–91.

29. Sarah Kane, *Phaedra's Love,* in *Complete Plays* (London: Methuen, 2001), 63–103; hereafter cited in text as *PL.*

30. Euripedes, *Three Plays: Hippolytus, Iphigenia in Tauris, Alcestis,* trans. Philip Vellacott (London: Penguin, 1953), 81–128.

31. *The Hidden God,* 60.

Tragedy and Modernity

Tragedy's Time
Postemancipation Futures Past and Present

David Scott

> The time is out of joint; Oh cursed spite,
> That ever I was born to set it right!
>
> Shakespeare, *Hamlet*

I.

Ours, I think, is a tragic time. By this I do not mean merely that we live in a time of moral disasters and political monstrosities—though I think *that* too: we do indeed live in the midst of very palpable barbarism, in the shadow of one of Hannah Arendt's recurring Dark Times, when simple truths are degraded and the light of public reason is very nearly extinguished.[1] But I mean something else, something perhaps at once more *and* less specific than the sorts of impoverishment to which Arendt meant to draw our attention. I mean to refer to something of the quality of our phenomenal *experience* of historical time, our experience, more specifically, of our *present* as time: the present as a plane of temporal intelligibility (the punctual "now") on which the *pastness* of the past (remembered time) and the *futurity* of the future (anticipated time; the time-to-come) are organized and lived in relation to each other. How pervasive the existential sense of it is I cannot empirically say, but it seems to me that we live in a historical moment in which a certain discordance—or displacement—in our experience of past-present-future has occurred or *is* occurring. Like Hamlet's, our time too is out of joint, and it is in this sense of temporal dissonance that I wish to speak of our time as tragic.

There is of course a growing appreciation of the relevance of time to historical thinking in the humanities and social sciences; indeed there is a growing suspicion that the temporalities through which our modernities have organized our collective and individual lives have been disrupted. There is an apprehension, one might say, of *retemporalization.*[2] But I stress here that my concern is not with the now well-known postmodern idea of the simultaneous compression and acceleration of time (some of the political implications of which have been explored, for example, by such writers as David Harvey, Paul Virilio, and William Connolly).[3] It is less speed or intensity or duration that I want to focus on than succession: *time-as-succession*.[4] There is a sense in which the once-familiar temporalities of past-present-future that animated (indeed, that constituted) our historical reason and that therefore organized and underwrote our ideas about historical change—change-as-succession, for example, or change-as-*progressive*-succession, or in its more radical expression, change-as-*revolutionary*-succession—no longer line up quite so efficiently, so seamlessly, so instrumentally, in a word, so *teleologically*, as they once seemed to do. The present-as-time no longer appears—as it was once prominently pictured as appearing—as the tidy dialectical negation of an unwanted and oppressive past; and it is hard to continue imagining the present as though it were merely waiting for its own dialectical overcoming in a Hegelian future-to-come. The rhythms of that relation between past-present-future have been broken, or at least somehow very significantly interrupted. Remains from the past now stick unaccountably to the hinges of the temporality we have relied on to furnish ourselves with the confidence that we are in fact going somewhere other—and better—than where we are. Time has become less yielding now than we have grown to expect that it should be.

The question I have is whether this isn't an experience of time helpfully understood in terms of tragedy; because, arguably, tragedy is a dramatic form attuned to an experience of time in which the future resists being narrated as an unambiguously progressive resolution of the present's impasses. Tragedy offers a reflection on human action that draws our attention toward the relation between time and contingency, between time and the distinctive chanciness of contingency. Embodied intention, tragedy urges, is never completely invulnerable to the unforeseeable and unexpected in time's unfolding and is therefore potentially always exposed to forces and factors beyond human choice and human control. And consequently tragedy puts in doubt the familiar (enlightenment) view of historical time as moving teleologically and transparently from sovereign agency to determinate end, soliciting from us a less assured, less masterful attitude toward prospective futures.

A good deal of contemporary moral, social, political, and cultural criticism is, however, *anti*-tragic in the sense that it is driven by an appeal to an agent who, with conscious intention, and by resisting or overcoming the constraints of *habitus,* makes history. There is a familiar and not irrelevant critical humanism attached to the confident hope in the conscious agency of the subordinate subject resisting dominant power, tilting heroically against the grain of the given. In the best formulations of this idea—or at least the ones that solicit our most sympathetic consideration and even solidarity—this humanism is articulated in the outline of a subaltern subject who, in however small and barely visible ways, contributes to remaking her or his own world *from below*. The formulation of this conception of historical agency is sustained by the well-known constructivist picture of a thin or deontological self—that is to say, a self whose relation to the past is a purely instrumental or utilitarian or contingent (as opposed to constitutive) one.

As Hayden White has famously suggested, in the *mythos* of the West, the story-form of this drama of being human is Romance.[5] But this story-form derives its point in large measure from the assumption of a certain temporality, one that projects an imagined horizon of emancipation for which the subaltern subject longs and toward which she or he strives. The past is there to be overcome on the way to a future waiting just beyond the beckoning horizon. For Romance, in George Steiner's memorable phrase, "Salvation descends on the bruised spirit, and the hero steps towards grace out of the shadow of damnation." In tragedy there are no such consolations. To quote Steiner once more, "in authentic tragedy, the gates of hell stand open and damnation is real. The tragic personage cannot evade responsibility. . . . The redeeming insight comes too late to mend the ruins or is purchased at the price of irremediable suffering."[6] White captures a similar contrast between Romance and tragedy as modes of historical emplotment. Where Romance rides a rhythm of progressive overcoming and ultimate victory over misfortune, tragedy offers an agonic confrontation that holds out no necessary promise of rescue or reconciliation or redemption.[7]

It seems to me that ours is a time in which the story-form of Romance is harder and harder to sustain; the hoped-for futures that inspired and gave shape to the expectation of the coming emancipation are now themselves in ruin; in Reinhart Koselleck's evocative phrase, they are futures past.[8] And this is why a tragic sensibility is a timely one. It is not that a sense of the tragic is bereft of moral and political hope or unmoved by the sufferings that spur the desire for emancipation. Nor is it that a sense of the tragic paralyzes the will to social transformation. Rather, a sense of the tragic doubts the humanist Romance that carries our hopes forward on a progressive teleological rhythm: Dark at length giving way to Light, Evil to Good.

II.

Narrative, as Paul Ricoeur so magisterially explains in his great work on the subject, has been the most apt medium for the linguistic or semiotic embodiment of our experience of time.[9] In thinking about time and narrative—about historical temporality and mimesis—in my own work, I have been concerned with colonial pasts and their aftermaths, specifically, with the colonial slave plantation pasts of the Caribbean and their postemancipation and postcolonial aftermaths. I have been especially interested in the ways in which the pasts of slavery and slave emancipation have been inserted into (have been, indeed, compositionally rendered as central rhetorical elements in) a moral and political story about Caribbean futures. There is an important revisionist chapter in Caribbean historiography in which the reconstructions of the pasts of slavery and emancipation are cast as generative moments in a narrative of anticolonial resistance and liberation. This is a story in which the recovered agency of the slave subject, hitherto suppressed and denied in the colonialist historiography of the Caribbean, is restored to an active, volitional, and therefore meaningful role in figuring a counternarrative of cultural survival and social and political overcoming. In short, in the terms I have already employed, these anticolonial narratives of slavery and emancipation are emplotted in the story-form of Romance. They offer us a vivid picture of a colonial past of negative and repressive power which, quite apart from the truth-value of its historical content, functions formally (that is, narratologically) to secure the temporal rhythm and drive the progressive momentum in which an ignominious past of unfreedom is superceded by—and redeemed in—a glorious future of emancipation.

I have (as I keep saying in many contexts) a doubt about this story. My doubt is not that it can now, in retrospect, be shown to have been empirically wrong all along and that the generation of anticolonial thinkers who formulated its various iterations can now be shown to have been mistaken in their understandings of the past and misguided in their hopes for the future. I want in fact to resist, as far as I can, this sort of *presentist* inclination. Rather, the doubt I have is shaped by my sense of living the disjuncture that I have suggested marks the temporality of the historical present, the sense of living in the ruins of the onetime futures of an earlier generation. As Koselleck reminds, it is in the "succession of historical generations that the relation of past and future" can be perceived as altering.[10]

My doubt, in other words, is shaped by an experience of the displacement of the "horizon of expectation" (this phrase too is Koselleck's) that organized an earlier generation's moral and political imagination of the slave colonial past's relation to the postemancipation and postcolonial future; an experience of the displacement of the temporal rhythms and the sense of destination through which a reconstruction of the colonial slave plantation past enabled the narratological momentum beckoning a new future into the present. In other words, if the anticolonial narrative depended upon a certain temporalization of past-present-future (itself, properly speaking, a retemporalization of an earlier colonial construction of time), the doubt I want to explore is whether, and to what extent, in a present drained of the emancipationist prospects that sustained the efficacy and force of that temporalization, the anticolonial mode of narrativizing the past in the present as Romance continues to be one worth subscribing to. My suspicion is that it is not.

It is this doubt that has drawn me to *The Black Jacobins,* C. L. R. James's great masterpiece of pan-African and anticolonial criticism, first published in 1938.[11] *The Black Jacobins* is the seminal—and perhaps unsurpassed—text in the revision of Caribbean history as a story of anticolonial resistance. In it, as is doubtlessly well known, James tells the magnificent story of Toussaint Louverture and the Haitian Revolution. It is the story of the social and economic conditions under which the eighteenth-century slaves lived and worked; of the outbreak of the French Revolution and its colonial conditions and reverberations; of the slave revolt initiated by Boukman in August 1791; and of the rise of Toussaint of Bréda to supreme leadership over the rebellious forces. It is, moreover, the story of the making of Toussaint Louverture (the Saint who Opens the Way) as a certain kind of subject (one almost obsessively self-conscious and willfully determined) and of his transformation from a man of decisive action into a man assailed by crippling uncertainty. Finally, it is the story of his eventual betrayal by Dessalines, his arrest by Napoleon's brother-in-law, Leclerc, and his deportation into exile and death in France. In short, *The Black Jacobins* is the unparalleled story of black slaves successfully and (as James says), against all odds, wresting their freedom from their white slave masters. This is its canvas.

But anyone who has read it, anyone who has been touched by the rhythms of its passion, by the tension in it of aesthetics and politics, knows that *The Black Jacobins* is more than one of the first great historical accounts of the Haitian Revolution. *The Black Jacobins* is at the same time one of the first great moral-political interpretations of our Caribbean postemancipation futures. Certainly it was for me—as no doubt for others of my generation of Anglo-Creole Caribbeans, the first properly postcolonial generation—a fundamental part of an oppositional education in learning to read the Caribbean past of slavery and emancipation into a revolutionary story of national liberation. But from within the disjunctive temporality of the present, from within a present suffering from what Raymond Williams called the "slowly settling loss of any acceptable future," it is hard to see the conceptual or moral-political purchase of this kind of account.[12] The postemancipation futures imagined by *The Black Jacobins* are now futures past. It is hard not to look back, through the debris of this postcolonial present, at James looking forward out of the constraints and hopes of his colonial present toward the horizon of a future now rapidly becoming a past.[13]

III.

In my view, C. L. R. James's *The Black Jacobins* is an ideal text through which to think some of the conundrums involved in rewriting the history of the postcolonial present; or, to put it slightly differently, to think about time and narrative in the historical criticism of the present *after* colonialism. This is so for a number of reasons. To begin with, unlike Frantz Fanon's *Les damnés de la terre,* for example, *The Black Jacobins* is not primarily a *programmatic* anticolonial text but an explicitly *historical* exercise: its object is historical time (past-present-future); but more than this, insofar as it is constituted as a narrative with a discernible beginning, middle, and end, its *medium* is also time: the story *unfolds* toward a resolution—*in time.* In other words, for my purposes here, one significant virtue of *The Black Jacobins* is precisely that it works through the conventions of a historical discourse (a mode of narrative emplotment) to order a sequence of concrete actions in such a way as to construe a relationship between a remembered past, an inhabited present, and a possible future.

Moreover, *The Black Jacobins* is a work of profound historiographical self-consciousness. In it James agonizes over the problem of the mimesis of historical time. How does one represent the past? To what end? All the significant problems that continue to haunt contemporary historiography—the problem of causality; the relative roles of individual agency and historical structures, great men and social forces; the relation between the "art" of narrative composition and the "science" of theoretical explanation—are problems that James confronted. He did not always adequately address, let alone resolve, them; but he made them visible in their constitutive tension.

Finally and most importantly for what I am after here, in *The Black Jacobins* James is acutely self-conscious of the relation between the modes of historical representation of the past and the *time* of the political *present* out of which he is writing. In the closing paragraph of the Preface he wrote as follows, in a very stirring passage worth remembering:

> Tranquillity today is either innate (the philistine), or to be acquired only by the deliberate doping of the personality. It was in the stillness of a seaside suburb that could be heard most clearly and insistently the booming of Franco's heavy artillery, the rattle of Stalin's firing squads, and the fierce shrill turmoil of the revolutionary movement striving for clarity and influence. Such is our age and this book is of it, with something of the fever and the fret. Nor does the writer regret it. The book is the history of a revolution and written under different circumstances it would have been a different but not necessarily a better book.[14]

A lot of the beauty and brilliance of *The Black Jacobins* is, in my view, contained in this passage. Not only does it announce James's ambivalent relationship to the English Romantics (Wordsworth and Keats in particular), his desire simultaneously to embody and overcome them, it locates him in a very pronounced and palpable way in the political contours of his historical present: the 1936–39 Spanish Civil War (to the discussion of which James contributed in a minor way); the question of the Russian Revolution, its degeneration under Stalin, and its place in revolutionary thinking (memorably, James wrote one of the first histories of the Communist International, *World Revolution*); and lastly, the emergence of an independent international revolutionary movement under the leadership of Trotsky.[15]

Notice that the politics of location being practiced in this passage is not a merely *passive* one. For in suggesting that had he been writing "under different circumstances" he would have written a "different but not necessarily a better book," James challenges *us* (who now read him *under different circumstances*) to ask ourselves how we, from our own historical presents, might retell the story of Toussaint Louverture and the Haitian Revolution. But James does more than merely offer this challenge; he provides us with clues as to what that rewriting might look like. Anybody who reads *The Black Jacobins* today knows that she or he reads a second edition. First published in 1938 (by the houses of Secker and

Warburg in London and Dial in New York), the book was out of print for many years, until it was brought out again in a new edition by Vintage in 1963. The new edition announces itself on the cover as a "revised" edition, but no one so far as I know has inquired into what exactly these revisions are. Or rather, it is typically assumed that the new appendix, "From Toussaint L'Ouverture to Fidel Castro," is the only or at least the most important revision. This, however, is mistaken. There is in fact another set of revisions that is of at least equally far-reaching importance—the changes to chapter thirteen, "The War of Independence." This is the last, the longest, and in many ways the most dramatic and momentous chapter of the whole book. It is the chapter in which everything is coming to a head, in which Toussaint is going to be joined in total war with Napoleon, a war he will at once win and lose, which will bring independence as well as destruction.

But as crucial as this chapter is for the book's overall story, it has scarcely been recognized, much less critically accounted for, that the first six paragraphs of it are fresh interpolations. They do not occur in the first edition of 1938. These passages are of particular interest to me because they are explicitly concerned with the poetics of *tragedy*. (In the late 1940s and early 1950s James, returning to literary and cultural criticism from the minutiae of revolutionary theory and party work, was preoccupied with the relationship between tragedy and history or tragedy and civilization, especially in Aeschylus, Shakespeare, and Melville.)[16] There is an intriguing sense, therefore, in which the 1963 edition of *The Black Jacobins* contains—side by side, so to speak—two contrasting figurations of Toussaint Louverture and two contrasting narrative modes of emplotment of the revolution; what interests me are explorations of the differential temporal work of Romance and tragedy in connecting past-present-future and the uses of tragedy in thinking about the paradoxical yield and limit of enlightenment.

IV.

It is doubtlessly uncontroversial to say that *The Black Jacobins* is principally emplotted as revolutionary Romance. Famously, two books perhaps, more than any others, serve as models for James's historical poetics: Michelet's *History of the French Revolution* and Trotsky's *History of the Russian Revolution*.[17] In view of James's explicit preoccupation with the relationship between the "art" and "science" of historical writing, this is not surprising. Both Michelet and Trotsky, as is well known, had complicated relations to the writing of history, even if they each tended to lean in *one* direction more than the other: Michelet toward art and Trotsky toward science. But like Michelet's and Trotsky's histories, *The Black Jacobins* is a mythopoetic text, less concerned with the details of social history (of the sort, who did what, when, and where), and more concerned with the unfolding of a great moral conflict between adversarial and irreconcilable principles—in this instance, the mortal battle between Slavery and Freedom mapped onto a temporal contrast between Old and New historical orders and harnessed to a momentum of eventual victory of Right over Wrong.

At the same time, *The Black Jacobins* departs from Michelet's and Trotsky's histories in its *heroic* figuration of Toussaint Louverture. Neither Michelet nor Trotsky was very keen on individual heroes. (For Michelet, memorably, if there was a hero at all in 1789, it was the Revolution itself, understood as a kind of metaphysical or spiritual actor; and Trotsky, as much as he admired Lenin, never deified him.) But *The Black Jacobins* is not merely articulated in terms of the Marxist problem of revolutionary agency; it is explicitly written through the myth of the hero. And in this figuration James's sources are partly to be found in the mid-Victorian reverence for the hero and the literary form of the biography. Or to put it slightly differently, both James and Marx are indebted to a wider nineteenth-century moral-aesthetic of the heroic man of action, a moral-aesthetic in which Hegel's idea (in *The Philosophy of History*) of the hero as a World-Historical Individual in whom historical Truth comes to self-consciousness plays a significant role.[18] His legendary racism notwithstanding, the key figure here, I believe, is Thomas Carlyle. In my view, James's Toussaint Louverture is one of Carlyle's "original men," an exemplary and inspiring moral force standing above and beyond the mediocrity of the crowd.[19]

But if these are James's sources, to what *ends* are they being employed? My argument is that the ideological *point* of James's Romantic heroic figuration is vindicationism. *The Black Jacobins* is not merely a Victorian biography; it is a work of black vindicationism in the long tradition from Olaudah Equiano's *Interesting Narrative,* published in 1789, to John Jacob Thomas's *Froudacity,* published in 1889.[20] Moreover, an important strand of this tradition of black Romanticism worked through the example of Haiti and the career of Toussaint Louverture (one of the most famous instances of which was the Rev. James Theodore Holly's 1850 sermon, *A Vindication of the Capacity of the Negro Race for Self-Government, and Civilized Progress*).[21] James's vindicationism, I suggest, was constituted out of a double problem-space: on the one hand, the racism that shaped the white image of the black in the early twentieth century (at the center of which was the contested question of the black's humanity and intellectual achievement); and on the other hand, the colonialist view of the colonized in the interwar years (at the center of which was the contentious issue of the capacity of the colonized for self-government).

The Romantic emancipationist emplotment of *The Black Jacobins* was an answer to these pressing ideological questions, a vindication of the humanity of blacks and their capacity for political self-determination. My doubt, however, is whether these questions continue to be *our* questions, and therefore whether vindication continues to be a mode of response worth advancing. Not, obviously, that either racist assumptions about blacks or Eurocentric ones about the colonized (or ex-colonized) have ceased to exist; but I wonder whether the problematization of colonial racial slavery and postcolonial self-determination ought to continue to be constructed in such a way that the future is conceived as the dialectical negation of the past; or in such a way that the past is perceived as requiring a total overcoming in a utopian future. I read James as struggling with this problem in *The Black Jacobins*. And this is why inquiring into the contrast with the problem-space out of which the new revised edition of 1963 was written is so instructive.

There are two intersecting problem-spaces that are crucial to the context in which tragedy comes to the fore in James's later thinking. One is the collapse (or at least the very considerable dimming) of revolutionary hopes following the Second World War. Like many anti-Stalinist Marxists (most notably those associated with the Frankfurt School), by the late 1940s James was acutely aware that the story of history and change by which he and his colleagues had been guided in their revolutionary activity stood in need of reconceptualizing. World revolution did not materialize, and the Trotskyist left spent much of its time squabbling and splintering. By 1951, of course, James had taken his Johnson-Forest tendency out of the Socialist Workers Party for the last time and written the collaborative text that signaled their departure, *tout court,* from Trotskyism, *State Capitalism and World Revolution* (published in 1950).[22] It is in this period that James returns to explicitly literary-cultural concerns—the novel, Hollywood, comics, and so on—and begins to develop his preoccupation with Herman Melville's *Moby-Dick.* And it is in this context that he writes his *Notes on American Civilization,* in which for the first time he assigns an important role to tragedy as the literary form best suited to capture World-Historical conflict.[23]

The other problem-space is the one defined by the precipitous deterioration of James's hopes for a meaningful decolonization in the Anglo-Creole Caribbean. After an absence of a quarter of a century and on the invitation of Eric Williams, James returned to Trinidad in 1957 to spearhead the reorganization of the nationalist press and to participate in the regional drive for an independent and federated West Indies. But within three years he found his efforts thwarted and derailed as the early radicalism of Williams' famous speech "Is Massa Day Dead?" gave way to the compromise over keeping the U.S. base at Chaguaramas and the betrayal of the federation project. This is the context in which James completes his masterpiece, *Beyond a Boundary* (published in 1963), in which, once again, tragedy is assigned a conceptually generative role.[24]

In short, if *The Black Jacobins* had originally been written and published on the rising curve of revolutionary and nationalist optimism, it was now (in 1963) being reissued in vastly different circumstances: on the one hand, circumstances in which the Cold War had narrowed the room for revolutionary politics; and on the other, circumstances in which national independence was both bringing the curtain down on colonialism and opening toward a future of uncertainty. And this is the context in which tragedy seems to James a helpful way of thinking again about time and mimesis.

V.

In recent years, a number of contemporary writers—classicists such as Charles Segal (in *Tragedy and Civilization*), moral philosophers such as Martha Nussbaum (in *The Fragility of Goodness*), and political theorists such as Peter Euben (in *The Tragedy of Political Theory*) and Christopher Rocco (in *Tragedy and Enlightenment*)—have been exploring in a very fascinating way some of the resources of tragedy as a mode of critical reflection.[25] In my inquiry into the theme of tragedy in *The Black Jacobins*, I am profoundly indebted to this work. For these writers, tragedy offers a reflection on the nature of action, intention, and chance that has implications for how we think about the connections between past-present-future, for how we think of time and change. With different emphases, of course, they see tragedy (Greek tragedy specifically) as raising questions about the relation between the mastery of enlightened reason and human exposure to contingency. Tragedy, they suggest, presents a picture of ourselves as simultaneously authors of our ends and authored by forces and circumstances over which we have little rational control. It is not that tragedy doubts our capacity as world makers or history makers; it is that tragedy doubts whether the rationality involved in agential activity is such as to render us completely immune to the intrusion of misfortune or keep us entirely beyond the reach of chance. What is especially compelling for tragedians, moreover, is that the fact of the plurality of values or ends or goods is not an occasion to affirm a rational calculus on the basis of which to choose the best among rival options. To the contrary, tragedians are interested in those paradigmatic instances in which the plurality of values is such as to make it *impossible* to choose satisfactorily, in which choosing one deeply held value *entails* the loss of some other equally held value. These are circumstances that produce tragic conflict. In their work, therefore, the Hegelian idea of a purposeful History as well as the Kantian belief in the self-sufficiency and autonomy of the self are put into doubt. In short, tragedy complicates our conception of enlightenment, pressing us to see the ways in which reason and unreason, blindness and insight, innocence and guilt, are deeply interconnected.

It is this sensibility that James brings to the revisioned figuration of Toussaint Louverture as a tragic hero in the six paragraphs he added to chapter thirteen of the 1963 edition of *The Black Jacobins*. These paragraphs constitute a reflection on what James thinks of as an authentic tragic dilemma: the conundrum constituted by Toussaint's inability to decide between the choices before him—a return to the past of slavery (which he now knew to be Napoleon's intention) or a future for Haiti without France and the enlightenment she represented.[26] James's reading of this dilemma is explicitly indebted to Aristotle's idea of *hamartia*, or "tragic flaw," and Hegel's idea of "tragic conflict."

In speaking of Toussaint's *hamartia* James emphasizes that it was not a "moral weakness" but a "specific error" that led to his downfall. In so doing James seems to be cautioning against the idea that Toussaint's catastrophic decline and suffering may have been due to a morally unworthy blemish, some corruption of character, or perversity of intention. James says there is none of this. In his view, Toussaint's was more a cognitive error of miscalculation that stemmed from the impossible situation of choice in which he found himself. But it seems to me that that situation of choice was *at once* moral and cognitive inasmuch as Toussaint was obliged to choose between ends that were not simply neutral rivals: a return to slavery or freedom without all that France meant. His dilemma was that any choice would involve for him an incalculable loss. And therefore this miscalculation was not an arbitrary lapse of judgment, a momentary negligence in an otherwise clear and efficient mind. It was not the simple result of poor choice, as though had he the opportunity to do it all over again and with the benefit of hindsight he could have chosen differently, and better. Indeed, to the contrary, for James, Toussaint's error was a *consequence* of his knowledge, not of an *absence* of knowledge.

> Toussaint's error [James had written in the close of chapter 12] sprang from the very qualities that made him what he was. It is easy to see to-day, as his generals saw after he was dead, where he had erred. It does not mean that they or any of us would have done better in his place. If Dessalines could see so clearly and simply, it was because the ties that bound this uneducated soldier to French civilisation were of the slenderest. He saw what was under his nose so well because he saw no further. Toussaint's failure was the failure of enlightenment, not of darkness. It needed another 150 years before humanity could produce and give opportunity to men who could combine within their single selves the unrelenting suspicion and ruthless ferocity necessary to deal with imperialism, and yet retain undimmed their creative impulse and their respect for the attainments of the very culture they fought so fiercely.[27]

It is hard not to recognize the myth-models at work here, Aeschylus' Prometheus and Sophocles' Oedipus (there is in fact little doubt that James had the former in mind). You can feel James struggling here with what Christopher Rocco would call the *paradox* of enlightenment.

Toussaint's dilemma, however, is also the Hegelian one in that he embodies a World-Historical collision between irreconcilable social-temporal orders: an old temporality, represented by New World slavery in its death throes, and a new one being ushered in by the French Revolution. In George Lamming's justly famous discussion of *The Black Jacobins* in *The Pleasures of Exile,* Toussaint Louverture is figured in the image of Shakespeare's Caliban.[28] And this reading (especially since it has been underscored by James's own stage-setting reference to Caliban in *Beyond a Boundary*) has become canonical.[29] I don't entirely disagree with it, since of course it captures nicely the fact that the encounter between Africa and Europe was structured in such a way as to oblige the displaced African to learn—and more than this, learn to *inhabit*—Europe's languages. But in my view there is another Shakespearean figure besides Caliban at work in James's tragic imagining of Toussaint, a figure that explicitly brings into focus the problem of the collision of temporalities at the border of the modern/nonmodern worlds and the making of a subject that embodies this conflicting moment. This is the figure of Hamlet. James's Toussaint Louverture was not only a newly languaged Caliban but also a modernist intellectual, straddling, like Hamlet, a collision of historical times.

James, who was a reader of the great Hegelian scholar of Shakespeare A. C. Bradley and, like him, a Victorian protagonist of character analysis, builds his conception of tragedy around Hegel's understanding of historical conflict or collision; but he also argues that this conflict or collision involved a clash between competing and irreconcilable conceptions of society.[30] In an essay on Hamlet written in the early 1950s, James offered that "all great tragedies deal precisely with this question of the confrontation of two ideas of society and they deal with it according to the innermost essence of the drama—the two societies confront one another within the mind of a single person." It is this attention to the historical location of the distinctive conflicts that particular tragic characters embody that is important to James's reading of *Hamlet* and to his rendering of Toussaint Louverture as a kind of Hamlet.[31] Very much in the spirit of Marxist critics of Shakespeare (I am thinking of Victor Kiernan, for example), James suggests that Hamlet inaugurates a "new type of human being," namely, the modern intellectual, in whom this collision of obligations (the demands of social responsibility, on the one hand, and the individual commitment to freedom of thought, on the other) is at once poignantly conscious and unmasterable.[32] James says: "This colossal change in the organisation of social function was the very basis of individual personality. But from the start it was inseparable from a tension between individual freedom and social responsibility. To the extent that any modern man thought at all, he was subject to this tension. And it was nowhere greater than in the man for whom freedom of thought and speculation became a socialised function—the intellectual."[33] If for the ancient Aristotle thought is subordinate to action, for the early modern Hamlet thought *is* his conception of action.[34]

In my view, it is partly through this Hegelian conception of tragedy as collision, and especially this (Marxist) historicization of the figure of Hamlet as embodying a specific social-temporal mutation, that James seeks to re-imagine his revolutionary hero, Toussaint Louverture. For James, Toussaint, like Hamlet, embodies a social crisis, the collision of embattled and irreconcilable temporalities. Toussaint is *lived* by this historical conflict. Moreover this historical mutation, which he lives as the very integument of his life, has to do specifically with the forms of the *modern,* in this case the externally imposed and reconstituting *colonial* modern. Toussaint, like Hamlet, marks the appearance of a new and modern type of subject, the colonial *intellectual,* whose fundamental relation to the world is a reflective one. (This for James is the decisive difference between Toussaint and Dessalines.) But of course the historical conundrums Hamlet and Toussaint face are not the same. Toussaint's tragedy, the tragedy of his enlightenment, turns on the distinctive character of the structure of power into which he was conscripted and by which he was formed and *through* which he sought to negotiate his way. As a conscripted *object* of a coercive modern power and a would-be modernist *subject* of an embattled intellectual life, he embodied a modern aspiration to freedom (that is to say, an aspiration to a *modern* freedom), imbibed from the pages of the great abolitionist (and friend of Diderot's), the abbé Raynal. There was for him (and James is at pains to emphasize this) no *outside* to his modernity; no *before* to which he could (re)turn for an alternative. But that modernist language of the enlightenment reason of freedom was in an entangled relation to an enlightenment reason of political and economic empire, embodied in Napoleon, which had its own re-enslaving agenda for Toussaint and the men and women he had fought to free. And consequently, Toussaint stood before options—a return to slavery or a future without the sources of enlightenment—which were not of his choosing but which presented him with alternatives that were at once *absolute* (because there was no alternative *but to act,* one way or the other) and *impossible* (because either way he acted was bound to have a catastrophic end).

The moral at stake in James's refiguration of Toussaint as a tragic hero, it is important to see (and this brings me back, a little obliquely, to the question of the present), is not merely about the particularity of this historical instance. Or rather, this particular instance points toward a singular and deeper moral. For James, Toussaint and his predicament are *paradigmatic* of a certain kind of encounter with the modern. Toussaint, James liked to say, was the first and greatest of West Indians. And what he meant by that, I think, is that Toussaint confronted a historical dilemma that has become the inheritance of *all* conscripts of modernity, all those whose modes of life have been so transformed by modern power that they can neither return to the past nor face the future outside the conceptual languages bequeathed by colonial enlightenment. The tragic beauty of Toussaint, first of black colonial moderns, is that he had the courage to face up to this challenge, and he paid for it with his life.

In the additions to chapter thirteen of the 1963 edition to *The Black Jacobins,* therefore, James is offering a reflection on the colonial past that interrupts the anticolonial rhythms of emancipationist overcoming in which past-present-future are aligned in a narrative drama of temporal succession. Toussaint Louverture's embodiment of the violence of the slave past and the revolutionary agency with which he seeks to free himself and his fellows from its embrace and its effects are no guarantee of an unentangled postemancipation future. In the immediate aftermath of the ambiguous national sovereignty of the Caribbean, it is to this intractableness of the past-in-the-present that James seeks to draw our attention: the tragic conundrum constituted by modern power's construction of options that are both ineluctable and paradoxical, at once impossible to disavow and eternally bitter to embrace.

VI.

The Black Jacobins, then, is centrally about time: the temporalities of past-present-future. It is about the chronic instability of these temporalities and the implications for criticism of a displacement of the historical presents in which ignominious pasts are remembered and alternative futures imagined and longed for. The 1963 revisions that bring Toussaint Louverture's tragic dilemma into the foreground of James's great story of the Haitian Revolution (revisions themselves inscribed in a new and unprecedented present in James's life) interrupt the Romantic figuration of the revolutionary hero and the teleological emplotment of anticolonial freedom, offering us a view of Toussaint wrestling with an inextinguishable paradox, itself profoundly a paradox of time—namely, the incommensurable and therefore colliding historical temporalities he embodied and lived as the only reality he knew. Toussaint, James underlines, cannot simply *choose* his way out of the *habitus* that constitutes him, the instinctive fear of slavery's past as much as the instinctive desire for enlightenment's hope.

In tragedy, James seems to suggest, past, present, and future are not successive moments that can be neatly aligned, as though history were heading somewhere—from Despair to Triumph, from Bondage to Freedom—as though the past can be banished by an act of mastering agency. Toussaint Louverture learned the hard way that the past—*some* pasts, anyway—may not be so easily overcome; postemancipation futures may not follow straightforwardly, unambiguously, upon the pasts of slavery. A tragic sensibility, I read James as urging, is one more attuned to the varied ways in which we, like Toussaint, carry the time of our pasts within ourselves as the not-always-legible scripts of our *habitus.* In contrast to the familiar constructivist emphasis on the self as little more than a series of invented and therefore chooseable masks behind which lie an echoless vacancy, the tragic sensibility is poignantly aware of the ineradicable temporal traces, presences, of what we leave behind. Tragedy won't guarantee a radical politics, but it may help us inscribe a more reflexive ethics into the politics we espouse.

Ours is a tragic time. Again, not only in Arendt's sense that we are assaulted by barbarism but also in the sense that the present can't see its way in the exhausted light of the former futures that once secured its destination. A tragic sensibility is timely, therefore, because it is less driven by the confident hubris of those teleologies that once extracted the future (postcolonial and otherwise) so seamlessly from the past, and it is more attuned to the ambiguities and paradoxes of the relation between time and action, intentions and contingencies, determinations and chance.

Notes

1. Hannah Arendt's reflections in *Men in Dark Times* (New York: Harcourt Brace Jovanovich, 1968) on the nature of the ethical and intellectual voice in times of moral disaster were inspired by Bertolt Brecht's famous poem "To Posterity." These reflections have in other contexts been enormously inspiring to me in thinking about one of the most luminous voices of our dark time. See David Scott, "Stuart Hall's Ethics," *Small Axe* 17 (March 2006): 1–17.

2. See, for some notable discussions, the essays collected in John Bender and David E. Wellbery, eds., *Chronotypes: The Construction of Time* (Stanford: Stanford University Press, 1991).

3. I am thinking, for example, of David Harvey, *The Condition of Postmodernity: An Inquiry into the Origins of Cultural Change* (Oxford: Blackwell, 1990); Paul Virilio, *Speed and Politics: An Essay on Dromology,* trans. Mark Polizzotti (New York: Semiotext(e), 1986); and William Connolly, *Neuropolitics: Thinking, Culture, Speed* (Minneapolis: University of Minnesota Press, 2002).

4. I borrow some of the following formulations from my essay, "The Tragic Sensibility of Talal Asad," in *Powers of the Secular Modern: Talal Asad and his Interlocutors,* ed. David Scott and Charles Hirschkind (Stanford: Stanford University Press, 2006), 134–53.

5. See Hayden White, *Metahistory: The Historical Imagination in Nineteenth-Century Europe* (Baltimore: Johns Hopkins University Press, 1973).

6. George Steiner, *The Death of Tragedy* (1961; rpt., New Haven: Yale University Press, 1996), 130, 128.

7. White, *Metahistory,* 8–10.

8. Reinhart Koselleck, *Futures Past: On the Semantics of Historical Time,* trans. Keith Tribe (Cambridge, MA: MIT Press, 1985). This book, as well as Koselleck's more recent *The Practice of Conceptual History: Timing History, Spacing Concepts* (Stanford: Stanford University Press, 2002), have been of considerable help to me.

9. See in particular volume one of Paul Ricoeur's *Time and Narrative,* trans. Kathleen McLaughlin and David Pellaeur (Chicago: University of Chicago Press, 1984), where he sets up the problem of the nature of time and narrative through Augustine and Aristotle.

10. Koselleck, *Futures Past,* xxiv.

11. C. L. R. James, *The Black Jacobins: Toussaint Louverture and the San Domingo Revolution* (London: Secker & Warburg, 1938); hereafter referred to as James, "*The Black Jacobins,* 1st ed."

12. See Raymond Williams, *Modern Tragedy,* rev. ed. (London: Verso, 1979), 209.

13. My book, *Conscripts of Modernity: The Tragedy of Colonial Enlightenment* (Durham, NC: Duke University Press, 2004), obviously forms the basis for this essay, and I repeat here in large part the argument made there. But in the book, the focus on *time* is often muted by my foregrounding of the question of the criticism of the present. The works on which my arguments rest are more extensively referenced there.

14. James, *The Black Jacobins,* 1st ed., viii–ix.

15. See the discussion of this in Scott, *Conscripts of Modernity,* chap. 2.

16. On James's political activity in the U.S. Trotskyist movement, see Scott McLemee and Paul Le Blanc, eds., *C. L. R. James and Revolutionary Marxism: Selected Writings of C. L. R. James, 1939–1949* (Atlantic Highlands, NJ: Humanities Press, 1994).

17. Jules Michelet, *History of the French Revolution,* trans. Charles Cock (Chicago: University of Chicago Press, 1967); and Leon Trotsky, *The History of the Russian Revolution,* trans. Max Eastman, 3 vols. (New York: Simon & Schuster, 1932–33).

18. See, for example, G. W. F. Hegel, *The Philosophy of History,* trans. J. Sibree (New York: Dover, 1956).

19. Thomas Carlyle, *On Heroes, Hero Worship and the Heroic in History* (Lincoln: University of Nebraska Press, 1966).

20. See Olaudah Equiano, *The Interesting Narrative of the Life of Olaudah Equiano,* ed. Angelo Costanzo (Peterborough, ON: Broadview, 2001); and John Jacob Thomas, *Froudacity: West Indian Fables by James Anthony Froude* (London: New Beacon Books, 1969).

21. James Theodore Holly, "A Vindication of the Capacity of the Negro Race for Self-Government and Civilized Progress as Demonstrated by Historical Events of the Haytian Revolution; and the subsequent acts of that people since their National Independence" (1857), in *Black Separatism and the Caribbean, 1860,* ed. Howard H. Bell (Ann Arbor: University of Michigan Press, 1970).

22. C. L. R. James (with Raya Dunayevskaya and Grace Lee), *State Capitalism and World Revolution* (Chicago: Charles H. Kerr, 1986).

23. Published posthumously as C. L. R. James, *American Civilization,* ed. Anna Grimshaw and Keith Hart (Oxford: Blackwell, 1993).

24. C. L. R. James, *Beyond a Boundary* (London: Hutchinson, 1963).

25. See Charles Segal, *Tragedy and Civilization: An Interpretation of Sophocles* (1981; rpt., Norman: University of Oklahoma Press, 1999); Martha Nussbaum, *The Fragility of Goodness: Luck and Ethics in Greek Tragedy and Philosophy* (New York: Cambridge University Press, 1986); J. Peter Euben, *The Tragedy of Political Theory: The Road Not Taken* (Princeton: Princeton University Press, 1990); and Christopher Rocco, *Tragedy and Enlightenment: Athenian Political Thought and the Dilemmas of Modernity* (Berkeley: University of California Press, 1997).

26. C. L. R. James, *The Black Jacobins,* 2nd ed. (New York: Vintage Books, 1963), 289–91.

27. James, *The Black Jacobins,* 1st ed., 241. In the second edition the final sentence of this passage is deleted.

28. See George Lamming, *The Pleasures of Exile* (London: Michael Joseph, 1960), especially the chapter "Caliban Orders History."

29. "To establish his own identity, Caliban, after three centuries, must himself pioneer into regions Caesar never knew." James, *Beyond a Boundary,* unpaginated preface.

30. See, especially, A. C. Bradley, *Shakespearean Tragedy: Lectures on Hamlet, Othello, King Lear, Macbeth* (1904; rpt., New York: St Martin's Press, 1957).

31. C. L. R. James, "Notes on *Hamlet,*" in James, *The C. L. R. James Reader,* ed. Anna Grimshaw (Oxford: Blackwell, 1992), 243–44.

32. See Victor Kiernan, *Eight Tragedies of Shakespeare* (London: Verso, 1996).

33. James, "Notes on *Hamlet,*" 244.

34. Ibid., 245.

Sebald's Tragedy

Stanley Corngold

Although the deliberate strategies of poetic practice enable the compositional unity of formal poetry, we find implied there the fragility of human memory and the destructive entropy of history.

Jennifer Anna Gosetti-Ferencei

There is a country in which only a single group of divinities are worshipped; they are called the clenched teeth.

Franz Kafka

We are at work on a common enterprise: to mark out the features of a modern tragic sense. In this essay I shall refer to the work of those who have already written on modern tragedy—it is a rich accumulation of thought—and especially to the now copious writings of the German prose writer W. G. Sebald (1944–2001), who has much to contribute to this project. Now, one does not come to such an enterprise innocently: every interpreter brings what the philosopher Heidegger calls a "fore-conception" of the very concept he or she means to discover. This could seem like arguing in a circle, but such an impression is unavoidable when one is interpreting other people's words. The task, as Heidegger puts it, is not to "get out" of this hermeneutic circle for the imagined icy air of a presuppositionless science—it is not available in matters of interpretation—but rather to "come into it in the right way," which surely calls for scrutiny of the "fore-structure" of one's understanding.[1] For my part, I understand tragedy in advance as an ensemble of characteristics none of them stable in the reflection on tragedy since Aeschylus. The ensemble includes these features: (1) the drastic, disproportionate suffering of an individual or individuals; (2) capable of reasoning as to design; (3) who judge their suffering as the effect of a cause "high" enough to be intelligible in principle; (4) yet find this cause inscrutable (the lament at undeserved suffering); (5) who then struggle additionally to grasp the intelligibility of that cause; (6) in a community, where the suffering is visible to many and the task of attributing a cause may be undertaken by many. How much of this is present in our current theorizing? What modifications of my fore-conception are required by this work? What modification of this work is required by Sebald?

In approaching the body of thought on modern tragedy that has grown so rapidly in recent years, I will rely on a few felicitous surveys. An essay by Rita Felski reviewing the scholarship on modern tragedy finds the following concordance of views:

> Tragedy undermines the sovereignty of selfhood and modern dreams of progress and perfectability, as exemplified in the belief that human beings can orchestrate their own happiness. In confronting the role of the incalculable and unforeseeable in human affairs, it forces us to recognize that individuals may act against their own interests and the consequences of their actions may deviate disastrously from what they expected and hoped for. Exposing the limits of reason, the fragility of human endeavor, the clash of irreconcilable desires or incommensurable worlds, the inescapability of suffering and loss, tragedy underscores the hopelessness of our attempt to master the self and the world.[2]

Enlarging these categories, Kathleen Sands writes that "the state of fallen humanity and the fallen world," said to arise from notions of original sin, "bears many marks of the tragic—innocent fault, incommensurable goods, vanishing freedom, sacrifice, and fated violence."[3] And she introduces these factors with the crucial proviso: "Tragedy concerns not suffering *simpliciter,* or even profound suffering, but the telling of suffering. To define tragedy—to explain what makes a tragedy 'successful'—is to discern what makes profound suffering good to tell."[4]

Such marks of a theory of tragedy, including the task of giving the account that tragedy "deserves," are visible in many modern works of fiction. They are not so baldly stated there as propositions composing a theory, nor are they found in an only "narrowly defined dramatic genre." Rather, they exist in solution, so to speak, in a variety of works as a "mode, sensibility or structure of feeling."[5] It is precisely here that Sebald has most to contribute to such a theory. He does not write drama: he has written poetry—a vivid, stunning, melancholy book-length poem titled *After Nature,*[6] and he has published nine volumes of prose as well.[7] My essay deals mainly with *Vertigo* (2001), *The Emigrants* (1997), *The Rings of Saturn* (1999), *Austerlitz* (2001), and *On the Natural History of Destruction* (2003).[8] Though some of these writings are like novels and some are like essays, Sebald calls them simply "prose" (in part, a reflex of his shame at what he sees as the trawling for aesthetic effects in other people's suffering). But his prose is anything but simple; it crosses customary genres, embedding, for example, photographs and drawings that bear an only haunting, uncertain relation to his subject matter. His narratives mingle memory, dream, and immediate perception, further braiding the voice of the speaker with the voices of other authorities. Sebald is a challenging modern, and his pertinence to the question of modern tragedy is evident in both his commented histories of suffering and a sensibility that cries out "tragic."

But why turn to so recently discovered a writer as Sebald, when there are many more familiar and assured resources—modern masterworks such as Kafka's *The Castle* or Beckett's *Molloy* or Thomas Mann's *Doktor Faustus*? Except for the contingent—the tragic?—fact of the automobile accident that killed Sebald suddenly in 2001, interrupting the powerful trajectory of his writing that came late in his life, he speaks for "us," he is our contemporary.[9] He is powerful in translation: he has found a transmissible narrative manner that exceeds its local value in German, dreamlike in its vividness and detail, yet coolly hypotactic and dense with historical fact. He renders real places precisely in a mood of universal uprootedness and sober appalledness, and his subject matter is vast: he redreams the nightmare of European ruin and its tributary, colonial ruin. In words of the critic Eric Santner, Sebald's work is "the literary elaboration of an addiction that cuts a new path through the interlacing of history and subjectivity."[10] The word "addiction" picks up the skeptic's epithet "pain junkie," which Sebald has attracted. Since his "history" is mainly, almost exclusively, the *ruin* of peoples, cities, institutions—and individual lives caught up in them—he lets his reader dream the suffering subtended by all that ruin.

A narrator's subjectivity confronted with a large and (at least at first glance, and perhaps forever) senseless suffering takes us to tragedy. And so we will be drawn at once to *what* Sebald says to contribute to the definitions of modern tragedy. He registers the sheer enormity of the destruction inflicted on the human and the natural world in modern times—the numbers of victims, the massiveness of the scale—a seemingly "fated violence" that knows no limits. At the same time, owing to the disproportion, he studies the obstacles in the way of giving a true account of it, so that in his work modern tragedy is inflected as the second-order tragedy of a suffering that cannot be given voice. Sebald did not literally experience the gravest forms of ruin he writes about. Of the disasters closest to his home in south Germany, the Holocaust and the mass incineration of the German cities preceded his coming to full awareness by half a generation. The horrors, as in Africa, of nineteenth-century imperialism in England and in Belgium preceded him absolutely. Under these conditions, his apparently self-assigned task of bearing witness to such destruction could literally endanger his sanity,[11] and Sebald does not hesitate to tell us that his narrator, Sebald's "vice-exister," is forever on the verge. His sanity is threatened by the impossible demand of "remembering" what he has never experienced—for anything less truthful than the bounty of memory would do a disservice to the dead.

Sebald's work is henceforth torn by "incommensurable goods"—the struggle between the need to bear witness to the "fated violence" of tragedy and the factor of writing tragedy—hence, the danger of making *lies* the basis of aesthetic truth. And so we have the continual refrain of the *problem* of memory, its limits, its potential helpers, such as photographs (but they are also only "spectral images" and can mislead); archives of objects (but they are also only "stranded objects," ranging in dignity from the household things treasured by Max Aurach's mother, one of the Jewish subjects in *The Emigrants,* before she was murdered, to objects trailing the negative aura of a simile: I am referring to Sebald's likening the kitschy articles he sees in the antique shop at Theresienstadt, years after it housed a concentration camp, to the wretched cur that has run away from its master). This problem of memory is exemplarily focused in Uncle Ambros Adelwart in *The Emigrants,* who suffers from Korsakov's syndrome, "an illness which can cause lost memories to be replaced by fantastic inventions" (*E* 102). Theses like these are legion in Sebald—he anatomizes personal memory, the memories of other writers, broad swathes of cultural memory, and finds them chiefly derelict—viz., "In the entire history of colonialism, most of it not yet written, there is scarcely a darker chapter than that of the so-called Opening of the Congo" (*RS* 118).[12]

Sebald's tragedy is in great part the tragedy of such fissures in the record: memory is incomplete, and it is unreliable. *Vertigo,* his first long prose work, published in translation in 2001, eleven years after its appearance in German, comes with a title less rich and provocative than the German *Schwindel. Gefühle.* "Schwindel" = "vertigo" but also "swindle"; the period after the word gives "vertigo"/"swindle" the weight of a complete sentence. "Gefühle" = "feelings." The main meaning of the title comes clear in the first of the four pieces composing the work, the novella titled "Beyle or The Remarckable [sic] Fact of Love." This is one of the two pieces, together with "Dr. K[afka]'s Bathing Trip to Riva," in which the first-person speaker, an eternal wanderer with indispensable rucksack, disappears in favor of a more nearly objective third-person narrating the words, feelings, and adventures of other writers—

in the first piece, Stendhal ("Beyle"); in the second, Kafka.[13] The most important of the feelings mentioned in the book's title is defined in the Stendhal-novella as a "vertigo-like [or swindle-like] feeling of a teasing, provocative vexation" (my translation of the hard-to-translate German word "Irritation"). The context of this remark goes straight to our topic. It concerns the "cliffs of fall" in memory—the acute disconnect between what you live and what you remember, between the memory you bring to things when you stand in front of them and what you then actually make of them. If memory is indispensable to the narration of personal history, in a more fundamental sense it is indispensable to experience, since the condition of having experience is the recognition of the items in it. Without memory, experience is shattered in advance, and Sebald is fertile in representing irrational states of self-loss.

The inaugural novella "Beyle" profiles all these elements in varying degrees; but what stands out are the physical suffering that accompanies every one of Stendhal's feints at pleasure and the shattering phenomenology of memory that robs even that grief of a sense of continuous purpose. Stendhal, like Sebald, is expertly aware of "the various difficulties entailed in the act of recollection." He cannot remember anything of the Napoleonic campaign that he took part in as a seventeen-year-old. "At times his view of the past consists of nothing but grey patches, then at others images appear of such extraordinary clarity that he can scarce credit them" (*V* 5).

Consider Stendhal's very disturbing visit to the battlefield of Marengo, which was familiar to him from the stories he had heard:

> Now, however, he gazed upon the plain, noted the few stark trees, and saw, scattered over a vast area, the bones of perhaps 16,000 men and 4,000 horses that had lost their lives there, already bleached and shining with dew. The difference between the images of the battle which he had in his head and what he now saw before him as evidence that the battle had in fact taken place occasioned in him a vertiginous sense of confusion such as he had never previously experienced. (*V* 17)

This vertigo-like (or swindle-like) feeling of a teasing, provocative vexation is owed to what can be called a "commemorative difference." This difference is the motor driving all of Sebald's work. He writes to bear witness—and, in the strongest, most adventurous and personally threatening manner, to bear witness to the complexity of bearing genuine witness—to the horrors littering the geographical and moral landscape of his country and the rest of Europe.

But let us look at this matter in slower motion: we are not yet through with the title. The "swindle," the cheat, may refer to this perpetual disparity between memory, perception, and language, but it may also refer to the sweet cheat of fictive similitude, as such; or, again, to what Sebald, in an essay on the Austrian-Jewish writer Joseph Roth, calls "the substance of life—[that is], all the failed undertakings, all the experienced losses [*Verlustgeschäfte*] that can never again be made good."[14] The feelings of the protagonist and his subjects (such as Stendhal and Kafka—and in *The Rings of Saturn* Thomas Browne, Roger Casement, the Dowager Empress Tz'u-hsi, among many others) might be driven and dominated by precisely this crisis in the knowability of a world consisting essentially of losses, including losses at the level of their knowability, that cannot be made good. This is the sum indicated in advance in the swindle of the title: a knowledge of annihilating violence and then of stories that may only be "about" that shock—that may only circle senselessly around that shock, as Sebald, writing in the first person of a bad time when he did not know which way to turn, discovers, to his amazement, that his seemingly endless, planless wanderings through the inner city of Vienna have had a pattern, after all—only one, precisely delineated pattern, "a sickle to half-moon" shape (*V* 33). Like Sebald's preferred brother and double, Kafka, the world of this writer, as a great writer, is also a "homeland on the moon."[15] But, much, finally, depends on what Sebald can have intended by at once linking and separating, with a period, "vertigo"/"swindle" from "feelings."[16] They set the mood that informs all Sebald's writings—through all its fact and observed history: a sense of mysterious background, inescapably felt through the chief evidence it gives of itself—the minute signs of an incomprehensibly vast destruction of nature and human lives.

I will say one more word about the tragic shortfalls of memory and then something about what remains. There is a decisive passage in *The Emigrants,* where memory as *"Gedächtnis"* (a sort of container of various things memorized and available for recall) is distinguished from memory as *"Erinnerungsfähigkeit"* (the ability to internalize scenes, items, and feelings and then to relive them in the sequence in which they occurred). This latter term, *"Erinnerung"* (personal history, the once spontaneously internalized past) grounds the possibility of narrating the past, its "tellability." But if there is to be such a thing as the narration of the losses suffered by *others*—what Kathleen Sands called others' "suffering good to tell"—then the Korsakov syndrome seems unavoidable, since history writing and by implication tragedy writing requires a "falsification of perspective" (*RS* 125). In this case, tragedy writing would be a kind of fiction writing, and such fiction writing would then have to be seen as a (Korsakovian) *pathology.*

Is there a way out? In considering a "way out," we are reminded that Sebald, not unlike any other interpreter of a text (and unremembered history writing is only another historian's text) is captive of the hermeneutic circle, where no judgment can be obtained that is not predetermined by a "fore-structure" of understanding. Here Heidegger also undertakes to show how the "way out" is actually the right "way in." A valid judgment is obtained when the prejudgment is "worked out . . . in terms of 'die Sachen selbst'"—the very things that are the case.[17] Do we not see Sebald as faithful to this prescription in a tour de force like the following?

> How often . . . had I lain thus in a hotel room, in Vienna or Frankfurt or Brussels . . . listening, not to the stillness, as in Venice, but to the roar of the traffic, with a mounting sense of panic. That, then, I thought on such occasions, is the new ocean. Ceaselessly, in great surges, the waves roll in over the length and breadth of our cities, rising higher and higher, breaking in a kind of frenzy when the roar reaches its peak and then discharging across the stones and the asphalt even as the next onrush is being released from where it was held by the traffic lights. For some time now I have been convinced that it is out of this din that the life is being born which will come after us and will spell our gradual destruction, just as we have been gradually destroying what was there long before us. (*V* 63)

Sebald has not personally experienced "the life being born which will come after us"—these waves of ruin and destruction—but he has intuited them from the phenomenon of traffic, which is, in Heidegger's phrase, the very thing that is the case. But are "fantastic inventions" nonetheless at work in this description? How faithful is this report to Sebald's lived experience?

There is a momentum to these questions. If *Vertigo,* Sebald's first major work, refracts the tragic sensibility through the shortfalls of memory, this sensibility advances dialectically to its close in his late volume *On the Natural History of Destruction* (*Luftkrieg und Literatur* [Aerial warfare and literature—or, more freely, The {absence of all} literature on aerial warfare]). It is about the failure of German writers to have registered in the true detail of its enormity the pulverization and incineration of hundreds of German cities, along with the persons trapped in them, during the final years of the last World War. Following Sebald, you will not find this sort of report in the works of Germany's major postwar writers.

When you do find such mentions, "the real horrors of the time disappear through the artifice of abstraction and metaphysical fraudulence [*Schwindel* = swindle (!)]." But an amateur correspondent—one Harald Hollenstein—wrote him about what his mother had seen in Hamburg.

> She had to go to the Moorweide in a mass transport. There was a bunker, [writes Hollenstein], "built in the middle of the meadow—said to be bombproof, made of concrete with a pitched roof. . . . Fourteen hundred people took shelter there after the first night of terror. The bunker received a direct hit and burst apart. The extent of what happened then must have been apocalyptic. . . . Hundreds of people outside, including my mother, were waiting to be taken to an assembly camp in Pinneberg. To reach the truck, they had to climb over mountains of corpses, some completely dismembered, all lying around on the meadow among the remains of the former bombproof bunker. Many could not help vomiting when they saw the scene, many vomited as they trampled over the dead, others collapsed and lost consciousness. So my mother told me." (*NH* 78)

The point is the detail. This is what was left out of "literature." Sebald explains, "The ideal of truth inherent in its entirely unpretentious objectivity, at least over long passages, proves itself the only legitimate reason for continuing to produce literature in the face of total destruction. Conversely, the construction of aesthetic or pseudo-aesthetic effects from the ruins of an annihilated world is a process depriving literature of its right to exist" (*NH* 53).

Sebald's concept of "unpretentious objectivity," cool matter of factness, corresponds to Heidegger's saving concept of the very thing that is the case. But how is it to be obtained and how demonstrated when the subject matter in question is one to which one has no immediate access? It would have to be found in the truthful narration of an internalized past, stripped of "the inventions of one's fantasy." And what is the appropriate form of truthful narration? The answer lies in a decision as to style. And so we are drawn to *how* Sebald says all this, his manner of narrating, whose distinctiveness is eye-catching the minute one opens his books and notes the *logic* of his page-long sentences (they invite reflection); the *logic* of the interferences of many voices (they evoke a communal project of bearing witness); the *logic* of barely hidden allusions to the works of other writers (they are examples of accuracy taken on faith); the *logic* of embedded citations (the appeal to others' testimony must be exact); and, most strikingly, the *photographs* that adorn these pages, even if they are only occasionally illustrative of the things described in the text above or alongside them (they offer testimony in another medium).[18] All these voices, citations, and images come in from beyond the grave of the present moment of one's reading. And so, if Sebald's plain statements about tragic suffering are so many conceptual gifts to the reader—especially to that reader bent on formulating a theory of modern tragedy—the manner and mood in which they are said is a problem for that reader, the solution of which, if it can be found, would represent a gift returned to the author, a way of defining his tragic sensibility that exceeds his own power of definition—flowing, as it were, above, alongside, and below his explicit statements on tragic suffering.

Sebald's Moods

Sebald's tragic sensibility is one that few readers will not fail to *feel* at once. I use the word strongly and not as a category opposed to *knowing;* it is the "artistic truth" that the aesthetician Jay Bernstein calls "non-truth-only cognition."[19] Learned authority insists on the pertinence of this category; Benjamin and Heidegger have famously formulated the matter. For Benjamin, the poet Hölderlin's odes—"Poetic Courage" and "Blödigkeit" ("timidity" but also "stupidity")[20]—require what he calls *"ein fühlendes Erfassen"* (a feeling mode of comprehension) because "the impenetrability of relation resists every mode of comprehension other than that of feeling."[21] Whence it would follow that only through an initial feeling grasp could one intuit the content of a "diction" of moods. In *Being and Time,* Heidegger lays down a foundation for this claim. In *dichtende Rede* (poetic discourse), he writes, "the communication of the existential possibilities of one's state of mind [one's *Befindlichkeit* or, ontically speaking, one's *Stimmungen,* one's moods] can become an aim in itself, and this amounts to a disclosing of existence."[22] The contents of the mood are certain "existential possibilities," which, in the case we are considering, are the possibilities of tragedy; the view on "existence" disclosed is the view on existence as tragic.

The paper by Eric Santner that I cited earlier identifies the tragic mood as melancholy:

> It generally takes only one or two sentences for a reader to get a feel for the affective atmosphere, the deeply melancholic *Befindlichkeit,* of W. G. Sebald's remarkable work. And indeed, it has become a standard gesture of the already rich critical literature on Sebald to marshal the semantic

field of this resonant word, "melancholy," to capture the specificity of Sebald's voice and the stakes of his literary project. The unavoidability of the question of melancholy in the critical engagement with Sebald's fiction is a function not only of the relentlessly somber tonality of the work and . . . the obsessive preoccupation with death, destruction, and decay . . . ; it has been determined as well by explicit statements by the author himself both inside and outside the body of the major literary works.[23]

But what, now, is the affective content of the mood here termed melancholy? The task of interpretation devolving on readers requires that they give another voice to this sadness, this stupor; and is not, by the way, the photograph in Sebald foremost the photograph of stupor, of what has been so struck, so dazzled by a light that it cannot speak? Roland Barthes wrote, "All criticism is affectionate. . . . This should be carried even further, almost to the postulation of a theory of affect as the motive force of criticism."[24] Criticism is obliged to furnish, in place of affect, another language, another kind of description, and Sebald focuses this requirement for us. He has the ability to make us think of reading him as the task of always going below the narrator's own most explicit account of his concerns, attempting to understand him, first, immediately—as a mode of feeling—and hence (and here I would not like to be misunderstood) as a certain *confusion;* and then, only thereafter, in a way *better than* the narrator, on the model of Friedrich Schlegel's famous aphorism: "To understand someone, one must first of all be cleverer than he, then precisely as clever, and then also precisely as stupid." Schlegel continues: "It is not enough that one understand the true meaning [*den eigentlichen Sinn*] of a confused work better than the author has understood it. One must also be able to know, characterize, and reconstruct [*construieren*] the confusion itself."[25] I must stress that with (Schlegel's) words "stupid" and "confusion," I mean to do phenomenology and not "human values," alluding, a little, to Sebald's own repeated mentions of a "confusion of feelings [*Verwirrung der Gefühle*]," as in one of his main masks, the character named Bereyter, who so much resembles Wittgenstein, in *The Emigrants;* thinking, too, of a phrase from his brother writer J. M. Coetzee's novel *Elizabeth Costello* bearing on the act of writing— "an obsession, an obsession that is hers alone and that she clearly does not understand";[26] and summoning up, finally, from this portmanteau word "stupid" its older sense, "from *stupere,* 'to be stunned, amazed, confounded'. . . . Native words for this idea," the *OED* informs us, "include *dol* (the root of the Ger. *toll* 'mad,' related to the Gk. *tholeros:* 'muddy, turbid')." And, furthermore, until the mid-eighteenth century "'stupid' retained . . . the overtones"—I quote—of being "stunned by surprise, grief, etc." This same Elizabeth Costello says of "the stare that we meet in all the surviving photographs of Kafka[: it is] . . . a stare of pure surprise: surprise, astonishment, alarm."[27] Sebald's text stands to itself in a relation of mournful amazement that takes possession of the reader if he or she will let it.

The crisper version of Schlegel's *Athenäum*-fragment reads: "To understand someone who only half-understands himself, one must first understand him completely and better than himself, but thereafter only half-understand him, only as well as himself."[28] I mean with this "half-understanding" to call attention once again to the phatic element—the bottom half—of Sebald's writing, its being steeped in moods—and moods as such do not speak: they imply a rapturous being-possessed-by being; they are as such stupid and spread confusion—and quite especially the sense of bafflement, of incomprehension that is their basic tonality, which the narrator both produces and registers.

Sebald's prose is not only mutely mood-saturated, so that the reader is on his or her own in offering a redescription; it redoubles this character through "equivalents in the visible world for what you have seen inside."[29] There are many instances of a sort of weather of moods (in German, of course, the word *Stimmung* bridges both domains), weather-phenomena produced by the dissolution into the atmosphere of particles of matter, so that the world is veiled in mist or dust or fog. These particles producing moody weather might further be grasped as the detritus of the past, like the dust dispersed for years by volcanic eruption; and in this domain we have, from *Nach der Natur* on, what Mark McCulloh, the author of a monograph on Sebald, has termed "the ubiquity of the phenomenon of combustion (e.g., starlight, renegade brush fires in the South of France or California, the intentional burning of rainforests in Brazil, the intentional smelting of ores)."[30] All this burning produces smoke: and here we have, especially in *On the Natural History of Destruction,* the murderous dust palls of incinerated German cities and then the famously unnamed in all of Sebald's work, the "suppressed" smoke of the crematoria of the camps. The world's atmosphere is charged with the detritus of past ruin, producing a veil over the present, refracting vision oddly. In a vivid radio interview with Sebald conducted by Michael Silverblatt of *Bookworm,* the latter remarked, "it seems to me . . . there is a ghostly prose here [in *Austerlitz*], dust-laden, mist-laden, penetrated by odd and misdirecting lights; that the attempt here is really to become lost in a fog." This remark immediately prompted Sebald's agreement, and he spoke of his fascination with such "natural phenomena that rendered the environment impossible to see," summoning up then the fog of Dickens' *Bleak House,* also palpable as the dust of past words broadcast through litigation.[31]

The air of moods enveloping Sebald's sentences amounts to a veiling of the sense of sentences, but the effect of these moods is evidently strengthened by a certain "tempo of enunciation." A slow tempo contributes to a melancholy mood; it is built up at the level of form by the slow Stifterian rhythms of Sebald's full-page sentences, with their "elaborated syntax," their pronounced "prosodic rhythms." But it will not be surprising if, under the weight of so much affect, Sebald's prose at times grows agitated. The most striking formal correlative of Sebald's agitation is the vanishing *inquit;* that is, the explicit marker of a citation, of somebody else's voice, tends to disappear at moments in which the narrator is overwhelmed by the truth or power of the other's confession.

The example I have in mind occurs in the Fort Breendonk section of *Austerlitz.* Fort Breendonk is the name of a fortress in Belgium, which the Germans turned into a concentration camp. The narrator enters the former torture chamber, whence a number of homely associations arise; against the background of his growing distress, these images slowly develop and increase in their tempo. The most sinister of them is the washing down of the butcher shop in "W." (Sebald grew up in the town of Wertach in Bavaria), which is associated with the present scene of horror through the "iron hook" that hangs from the ceiling in the Fort Breendonk casemate on a rope. The appurtenances of the butcher shop in memory—a fat hose spurting water on the tiles and a foul-smelling grease soap—point inexplicitly to the business of torture and killing practiced in Fort Breendonk.

We have here the operations of a specific trope (the "half-metaphor," consisting only of its vehicle, its tenor implied), which in a way is a thread that runs through all the major works. The fat hose, the word "spurting," the soap, are the icons of Nazi cruelty culminating in the crematoria, though the Holocaust at large is not named. This sort of trope is found exemplarily in Kafka's "Reflections on Sin, Pain, Hope, and the True Way": "Like a road in autumn. Hardly is it swept clean before it is covered again with dead leaves."[32] *What* is like a road in autumn? It is not named, but one can guess: it is the path that would allow thought to make its way afresh but is cluttered with the leaves of . . . memory, the dead letters of . . . old books. The tenor is not named, as throughout Sebald, the killing camps are not named: Sebald's work as a whole is a vehicle for this unspoken tenor. When asked by Michael Silverblatt about the absence of this supreme horror in his works, Sebald said, in conformity with what he wrote in the earlier pages of the Fort Breendonk scene, "It is impossible to write about such a thing; it's on your mind, but you don't roll it out," although, he went on to say, he has been engaged with such things from the beginning—"persecution, the vilification of minorities. Images of horror militate against our capacity for reflective thinking and paralyze our moral faculties. One must approach these things obliquely." Sebald cites Benjamin for a remark crucial to his own procedure: "A genuine sense of the mysterious is created not through pathos or fanaticism, but by locating it squarely in the mundane."[33] We have, then, in Sebald throughout, a poetry whose subject is missing, the extended metaphor consisting only of the vehicle, its tenor missing. "Memory," Sebald has said in conversation, "does not so much restore the past as take the true measure of bottomless loss. . . . [It] occasions vertigo—a sense of all that has vanished from under our feet—because it reminds us of the missing as well as the found."[34]

Now, in Fort Breendonk, in this particular bundle of agitated sensations, there arises "in some strange place in my head" the association, along with "a nauseating smell of soft soap," of a favorite word of Sebald's father's; the word is *"Wurzelbürste"* (a coarse scrubbing brush) (A 25), one that he, the son, had always found disgusting. Several facts about this sentence seem immediately significant; and in attributing this awareness to the narrator, too, one can sense an almost unbearable weight of significance mounting, both particular to him and of a generally truthful kind. We have this growing meditation on the "unimaginable" suffering of the tortured inmates, suffering inflicted by the *"Familienväter und die guten Söhne aus Vilsbiburg and Fuhlsbüttel* (the good fathers and dutiful sons from Vilsbiburg and Fühlsbüttel)" (A 23); and buried here is a thesis on the materiality of the sign (its "sound-look"), the local and particular origins of words tied to their signifiers, so that for language-acquirers nothing could be further from the truth than the so-called arbitrariness of the signifier. One has the continual sense throughout Sebald that words are things, replete with quite particular associations of the life-world in which they were embedded at the moment of their beginning to matter. They matter in the way they were once (the metonymies of) *matter*. And, listen, too, to the material, phonic anticipation of *"Wurzelbürste-Vater"* (scrubbing brush/father) in the *"Fuhlsbüttel-Vater"*

(Fuhlsbüttel/father), who is an SS torturer. The past survives in associations buried in the sound-look of the language one contingently acquires. There is a second-order, tragic dimension in their persistence and their obscurity, in the fact that they cannot be purged. This is one of the elliptical ways that "the marks of pain which trace countless fine lines through history" (*A* 14) are conveyed.

Under the weight of too much significance, of too much horror, the narrator begins to stagger: "black striations began to quiver before my eyes" (*A* 25). He is the staggering Dionysian, in Nietzsche's words, "the type for whom it is impossible to overlook any sign of an affect."[35] What follows is a sort of barely controlled agitation, a half-page sentence flooded with allusions to his brother witnesses: its swift metaphoricity flows along as a melding of the voices of the narrator, then of Jean Améry, then of Claude Simon, and then of a certain Gastone Novelli.[36] The psychoanalyst Harold Searles wrote about the ability to distinguish between metaphorical meanings and literal meanings: there need to be "firm ego boundaries" in place; but, he continues, "it would seem equally correct to say that metaphor, at least, could never develop if there had not once been a lack of such ego boundaries."[37] Sebald's narrator is Dionysian in his ability to tolerate such a lack; he is touched by Kafka's "longing to extinguish his empirical personality" (*CS* 197). Such egolessness is at once the mark of his agitation and the condition of his inspiration. That is the benefit of the loss of firm ego boundaries: I cite Nietzsche for his semiotic account of being enraptured with the world as text:

> The involuntariness of image and metaphor is strangest of all: one no longer has any notion of what is an image or a metaphor: everything offers itself as the nearest, most obvious, simplest expression. It actually seems, to allude to something Zarathustra says, as if the things themselves approached and offered themselves as metaphors. ("Here all things come caressingly to your discourse and flatter you; for they want to ride on your back. On every metaphor you ride to every truth. . . . Here the words and word shrines of all being open up before you; here all being wishes to become word, all becoming wishes to learn from you how to speak.")

For Nietzsche, for us all, the world is a text requiring interpretation. But seen with wide-open eyes, the world's signs are more than signs: they are vehicles of the things they name, which "ride upon their backs." The impulse of active interpretation is at low ebb. Things ride in on their own names. And these things too are metaphors, they and their meanings ride into the discourse of the inspired speaker. In love, Nietzsche continues, the world's text approaches with the visibility of a loved body; and as around "the high body, beautiful, triumphant, refreshing . . . everything becomes a mirror," all discourse then mirrors, like an aroused lover, the thing, book, or body it is given to understand.[38]

This last part is Sebald with a change of sign; the change of sign is the marker of everything that has happened between the Nietzschean promise circa 1880 of the *Übermensch,* strong in affect, and the wanderer in Europe a hundred years later, when Sebald begins to write. Not the tragic satyr play as Nietzsche knew it but the lament, not high wooing but tenderness for the detail; for the promise is, quite literally, in ruins. Or to return to the particular point: one thing does not ride in to the poet on its name, on one metaphor you cannot ride to every truth; that is the truth of the Shoah.

Like the novelists and memoirists who write about totalitarian terror, such as Jerzy Kosinski, Jean Améry, Primo Levi, and Gregor Rezzori, Sebald accompanies his work with a sense of its extreme difficulty: how can so fragile a thing as personal narration—memoir or first-person fiction— "represent" so vast a suffering? Their works must confront the question of how to describe such things as the bafflement of all ordinary expectations, when banality turns apocalyptic;[39] the unwilled destruction of personality; the loss of homeland; the annihilation of entire peoples. These writers must confront the question of how a *literary* work could be adequate to the main task of enduring, surviving, and bearing witness to such traumas. In a word, bluntly: What has writing got to do with it?

It is not surprising, therefore, to see these authors experimenting with different, oblique, less obvious forms of representation. A stately, melancholy syntax is one of the quieter ways of conveying tragedy too big to report. Another such device is reimagining the archaic in modern dress, a "making it strange" by "making it new." In *After Nature,* Sebald alludes to the burning cities of Germany; there is little of this in the four books following, and then there is a book entirely devoted to this subject, *On the Natural History of Destruction.* It is here that Sebald, for our purposes, comes closest to making an explicit contribution to the theory of modern tragedy.

In my fore-conception of modern tragedy, I spoke about large, disproportionate suffering. In defining modern tragedy, Kathleen Sands, in a previously cited passage, spoke about "fated violence," which I recognize as the source of disproportionate suffering, since here the disproportion is writ large as between suffering that might be intelligible in the light of someone's decision as opposed to violence inflicted for no good reason whatsoever. Sebald situates this tragic aporia in the decision of the British Bomber Command to incinerate the German cities Hamburg, Dresden, Würzburg, Pforzheim, Munich, Frankfurt, and many others, despite solid evidence from early 1944 on that bombing civilian population centers had little or no effect on diminishing the morale of the German people, on hindering industrial production, or on bringing the war to a close one day sooner. Albrecht Speer, the German Minister of Defense, had pointed out a fact not unknown to the British Bomber Command: that strategic bombing of such things as munitions factories, oil refineries, and transportation hubs would have produced an across-the-board paralysis of the German war effort. Nonetheless, this strategic plan was not modified, even as it cost the lives of some sixty out of every one hundred young British airmen (*NH* 17). Why this irrational persistence? It was owed—here, Sebald offers his explanation—

> to reasons largely ignored in the official histories. One was that an enter-
> prise of the material and organizational dimensions of the bombing of-
> fensive . . . had such a momentum of its own that short-term corrections
> in course and restrictions were more or less ruled out, especially when,
> after three years of the intensive expansion of factories and production
> plants, that enterprise had reached the peak of its development—in
> other words, its maximum destructive capacity. Once the matériel was
> manufactured, simply letting the aircraft and their valuable freight
> stand idle on the airfields of eastern England ran counter to any healthy
> economic instinct [*ein gesunder Wirtschaftsinstinkt*]. (*NH* 18)

"Healthy" economic instinct is a piece of wit more acerbic in the German, where it evokes a contrast with the phrase *"gesunder Menschenverstand"* (literally, "healthy human reason," "sanity and reason," or, more simply, "common sense"). Such wit may be a constitutive feature of modern tragedy: it thrives on a sense of the vivid disparity between a reason that might justify suffering (which is not available) and the impulse to cause destructive suffering for its own sake, even when the latter wears the mask of profitability, of "good economic sense," or, worse, of fanatical delusion.

Sebald's narrative continues in a way that throws an interesting light on this tension. The person in charge of the British Bomber Command was Sir Arthur "Bomber" Harris, to whom, writes Sebald, "the Prime Minister [Churchill] expressed certain scruples about the horrifying bombardment of defenseless cities. He [Churchill] consoled himself—obviously under the influence of Harris and his dismissal of any arguments against his policy—with the idea that there was now, as he put it, a higher poetic justice at work and 'that those who have loosed these horrors upon mankind will now in their homes and persons feel the shattering strokes of just retribution'" (*NH* 18). This is the archaic language of tragedy, of the suffering mind attempting to justify its anguish and hitting on a reason. It did not fail, either, to rise up spontaneously among the German survivors of these ruined cities in the language of justified retaliation, an attitude that, as Sebald insistently points out, led to their refusing attention to the real details of their suffering, so that you will find hardly any accounts of it in the literature produced by major German writers after the war.[40]

Ten Items Toward a Revised Thesis on Modern Tragedy

I want to summarize the ways in which a reading of Sebald adds to and also modifies my fore-conception of modern tragedy and the knowledge of the works of others who have written on the theory of modern tragedy.

1. If the discussion about the survival of tragedy into the modern period turns on the centrality to a theory of tragedy of the royal, the sovereign, the superior individual; and on whether tragedy must vanish along with the vanishing of this type in a post-Nietzschean age of the herd, of the common man; then Sebald resolutely takes the side of the common man, enlarging his frame to consider not only masses of ordinary men (the vast multitudes who have gone under) but masses of creatures as well—herrings and moths!

Tragedy has been said to involve "the fall of a solitary 'great man.'"[41] The modern sense of tragedy does not turn on the distinction between the "great" man and any other man and woman. Unintelligible suffering is tragic. Animals—the dog, the Chinese quail—are driven insane through incarceration. Like his *frère semblable* Coetzee, Sebald enlarges our consciousness of the scope of creaturely suffering. The fall down the ontological ladder from the exceptional man and woman extends even to invertebrate creatures.

Tragedy involves suffering that is drastic or disproportionate to common sense as it now affects entire genera, ontological orders of creatures.

2. What, for Sebald, is the form of tragedy without god or gods? If modern suffering is unmotivated and inexplicable, and for that reason

worsened, can the suffering of creatures incapable of reflecting on design—hence, incapable of distinguishing between motivated and unmotivated suffering—be tragic? In Sebald, all creatures suffer. Sebald appears to put these masses of suffering on the same level because the forms of ruin that have afflicted human beings are so vast and senseless that they are all well past the point of being motivated. There was once the wisdom of Yeats's: "There struts Hamlet, there is Lear, / That's Ophelia, that Cordelia"; and though they are passing through a tragic fall, ". . . Hamlet and Lear are gay, / Gaiety transfiguring all that dread."[42] But this play cannot now be played any more gaily by a man or a woman than by a moth or a herring.

3. Tragedy upon tragedy: if, following Kathleen Sands, tragedy is the telling of suffering, then Sebald's tragedy is of suffering that cannot be told, if telling means telling the truth. Modern tragedy is a tragedy of disconnection as between consciousness and self, meaning and reality. Jacques Derrida has shown that the once-firm category of "perception" is untenable; Paul de Man has done the same for the category of "self." In Walter Benjamin's view on modernity, genuine experience [*Erfahrung*] has toppled into specious experience [*Erlebnis*], "the thrill of the hour." Sebald contributes to this series of losses by adding the unreliability of memory while nonetheless fighting a rearguard battle for perception and ethical self-presence. But such self-presence exists in an uneasy relation with the steady sacrifice required from the silkworm-self by its "work of writing." Even while writing, we are creatures of mood and dreams; this makes us forever susceptible to drastic surprises, shocking violence.

4. Sebald communicates an argument about human suffering that figures at the center of the tragic vision and a mood of melancholy appropriate to the fact of human suffering. The argument conveys the gloom arising from the absence in our written records of a response in any way adequate to the enormity of the suffering that men have caused other men, especially in the modern period, where technical ingenuity has supplied ever more destructive weapons to the capitalist drive for exploitation of the earth's resources (including human bodies). He portrays the contrast between the history of suffering actively caused and the relative dearth of witnesses, even of agents, who pass into the anonymity of faceless perpetrators. So many scenes of past suffering in Sebald are empty; time after time he wanders into desolate places where no one is to be seen.

5. Judged by archaic standards, modern tragedy is defective for lacking the dimension of knowing [*anagnorisis*] and full-throated saying.

Sebald resists this conclusion by introducing many interlocking voices as a kind of chorus. In the spirit of Kafka's aperçu, "Only in the chorus might a certain truth may be found," only a collective could give voice to the tragic predicament. We find this collective depicted at the level of content: Sebald quotes the words of writers like Casanova, Stendhal, and Swinburne, and he ventriloquizes writers, most remarkably, Kafka, without attribution. At the level of the detail of style, many voices merge.

But the sufferer remains solitary. It is up to each solitary wanderer to construct his or her witnesses as tradition and commentary—the chorus of voices of those who have borne witness to suffering and the dilemmas of reporting it, understanding it, coming to terms with it. The sufferer is alone in his or her archive.

6. Sebald conjures a sense of pure, "purposeless" evil—purposeless in the pain it inflicts. Where the torturer tortures to no purpose (and that is always the sense of torture), there is no purpose to be discovered, there is no illuminating a purpose that might count as transcendence of the threshold of the suffering body. It follows that knowledge of the harm cannot defray the harm. There is no compensation available. Sebald writes about Jean Améry: "It belongs to the psychological and social state of mind of the victim that what happened to him cannot be made good."[43]

The sense of modern tragedy is of a suffering that cannot be compensated for, that cannot be balanced out, except in a quite perverse though instructive sense. The extraordinarily profitable *balance* sheets of the Belgian Societé Anonyme pour le Commerce du Haut Congo were obtained by an equivalent suffering inflicted on the people of the Congo—a suffering simply tolerated by the indifference of the company stockholders to the "system of forced-labor and slavery" generating its profits. Sebald finds a link between this silence and the silence of German writers about the firebombed cities of Hamburg, Dresden, and many others.

7. In the end German cities were bombed because the mechanism was in place. For the "fate" in "fated violence," read: industrialization, modernization. Modern tragedy is the tragedy of the modern.

8. The best witnessing is the detail. To give detail is to slow down the pace of the narrative. It is a foil against mere rhetoric. It bids concentration. That is why Sebald insists, despite his stated resistance to "images of horror," that the horrors of the incinerated German cities be imagined in detail. That is why he struggles to imagine the horrors of the concentration camp at Fort Breendonk. As a sort of promise of explanation, the detail interrupts the larger narrative, which is one of relentless destruction. In the detail is the hope of justification.

9. Sebald opposes the hectic of modernity, its rapidity—what writers from Goethe to Heidegger and beyond have called the continual undoing of distance [*"Entfernung"*]—with long, hypotactic sentences and embedded *inquits* and citations, requiring an exceptional degree of readerly concentration. In this way he casts an elliptical light on the tragedy of the hectic.

10. Sebald does *not* become infuriated; he is only the vessel of a sort of "traveling fury": it impels his journey to yet another scene of ruin and suffering. His interest in the details of the case is matched by a wide geographical perspective. Modern tragedy calls for scrutiny of the "marks of pain which trace countless fine lines through history" (*A* 14), yes, and also through all the landscapes that modernity has laid waste.

Notes

Epigraphs: Heidegger, Hölderlin, and the Subject of Poetic Language: Toward a New Poetics of Dasein (New York: Fordham University Press, 2004), 251; Franz Kafka, *The Kafka Project,* www.kafka.org/index.php.

1. Martin Heidegger, *Being and Time,* trans. John Macquarrie and Edward Robinson (New York: Harper & Row, 1962), 195.

2. Rita Felski, "Introduction," *Rethinking Tragedy, New Literary History* 35, no. 1 (2004): xii.

3. Kathleen M. Sands, "Tragedy, Theology, and Feminism in the Time After Time," in ibid., 50.

4. Ibid., 42.

5. Elisabeth Bronfen, "Femme Fatale—Negotiations of Tragic Desire," in ibid., 104.

6. *Nach der Natur. Ein Elementargedicht* ("From nature," in the sense of a drawing done "from life": "an 'elementary' poem," in the sense of a poem of and about "the elements") (1989). *Nach der Natur* deals with men in extreme situations—the tormented painter Matthias Grünewald, whose masterpiece is the Isenheimer altar of 1506–15, and the German naturalist Georg Wilhelm Steller, who, in 1741, joined the disastrous Alaskan expedition of Vitus Bering. In Sebald's hands, these icy wastes, writes Kevin Driscoll, figure "as a kind of inverted *Heart of Darkness,* with the lush, brooding blackness of Kurtz's Congo replaced by 'the Bering Sea / where there was nothing and no one but them. All was a greyness, without direction, / with no above or below, nature / in a process of dissolution, in a state / of pure dementia.'" "History Bleakly, Lushly; W. G. Sebald's Posthumous Poems Mix Man and Sharpness," *Washington Times,* November 3, 2002. The poem concludes with episodes from the inner life of Sebald.

7. These works are *Die Beschreibung des Unglücks. Zur österreichischen Literatur von Stifter bis Handke* (1985) (The description of unhappiness: on Austrian litera-

ture from [Adalbert] Stifter to [Peter] Handke); *Schwindel. Gefühle* (1990) (*Vertigo* [2001]); *Unheimliche Heimat. Essays zur österreichischen Literatur* (1991) (Outlandish homeland: essays on Austrian literature); *Die Ausgewanderten. Vier lange Erzählungen* (1992) (*The Emigrants* [1997]); *Die Ringe des Saturn. Eine englische Wallfahrt* (1995) (*The Rings of Saturn* [1999]); *Logis in einem Landhaus. Über Gottfried Keller, Johann Peter Hebel, Robert Walser und andere* (1998) (Lodging in a country house: on Gottfried Keller, Johann Peter Hebel, Robert Walser, and others); *Luftkrieg und Literatur* (1999) (*On the Natural History of Destruction* [2003]); *Austerlitz* (2001) (*Austerlitz* [2001]); *Campo Santo* (2003) (*Campo Santo* [2005]).

8. Titles are given in English in the order in which these translations were published. The dates in parenthesis are the dates of the original German publication. Hereafter, I shall quote from the works as follows: *CS* plus a page number in parenthesis is from *Campo Santo; V* is from *Vertigo; E* is from *The Emigrants; RS* is from *The Rings of Saturn; A* is from *Austerlitz* (2001); and *NH* from *On the Natural History of Destruction*.

9. This is also the view of public intellectuals like James Wood, who terms "Sebald one of the most mysteriously sublime of contemporary writers." For the late Susan Sontag, "*The Emigrants* is an astonishing masterpiece—perfect while being unlike any book one has ever read." In the meantime Sebald has become a chosen possession of academic readers well-acquainted with German, French, and English literature from (at the latest) 1750 on (Sebald's work is saturated with allusions to the canon). And if the circle of these readers crosses with the circle of critics who have promoted his writing (the Nobel Prize–winning novelist J. M. Coetzee, also captivated, belongs to both circles), this adds to his allure. In journals, conferences, and departmental seminars in German, English, and comparative literature, Sebald is being intensively studied.

10. Eric Santner, "W. G. Sebald and the Poetics of Exposure," an unpublished paper delivered at the conference "Democracy/Totalitarianism: Political Theory and Popular Culture in an Age of Global Insecurity," University of Illinois at Urbana-Champaign, April 23–25, 2004.

11. Modern sanity being in any case a touch and go affair, as witness the prison reflections of Casanova, one of the many prisoners—man and animal—whose anguish Sebald depicts: "Casanova considered the limits of human reason. He established that, while it might be rare for a man to be driven insane, little was required to tip the balance. All that was needed was a slight shift, and nothing would be as it formerly was. In these deliberations, Casanova likened a lucid mind to a glass, which does not break of its own accord. Yet how easily it is shattered. One wrong move is all it takes" (*V* 56).

12. Consider Walt Whitman's claim: "All poems or any other expressions of literature that do not tally with their writer's actual life and knowledge, are lies." Cited in Paul Zweig, *Walt Whitman: The Making of the Poet* (New York: Basic Books, 1984), 290.

13. The reader may be interested in my "Tropes in Stendhal and Kafka," *Liter-*

ary Imagination: The Review of the Association of Literary Scholars and Critics 4, no. 3 (2002): 275–90.

14. "Ein Kaddisch für Oesterreich—Über Joseph Roth," *Unheimliche Heimat. Essays zur österreichischen Literatur* (Frankfurt a.M.: Fischer Taschenbuch, 1995), 104.

15. "We [writers] have lost ourselves for the sake of a homeland on the moon." Franz Kafka, *Letters to Friends, Family, and Editors,* trans. Richard and Clara Winston (New York: Schocken, 1977), 204.

16. In Walter Benjamin's phrase, these things "are not separate but they do not mingle." "Goethe's Elective Affinities," in *Walter Benjamin: Selected Works (1913–1926),* ed. Michael Jennings and Marcus Bullock (Cambridge, MA: Harvard University Press, 1997), 1:340.

17. Heidegger, *Being and Time,* 195; *Sein und Zeit* (Tübingen: Niemeyer, 1963), 153.

18. Not trivially, Sebald is besotted by the person and the rhetoric of Kafka. As a professor of literature, he published an essay on a modern tragedy of nonarrival, Kafka's *Das Schloss* (1922); the figure and rhetoric of Kafka otherwise haunt his novels.

19. Jay M. Bernstein, *The Fate of Art: Aesthetic Alienation from Kant to Derrida and Adorno* (University Park: Pennsylvania State University Press, 1992), 3.

20. Both Hölderlin and Benjamin figure in Sebald's *The Rings of Saturn*—Hölderlin explicitly and Benjamin indirectly by means of a symbol. Sebald's narrator wanders through Europe, as did Benjamin, with a characteristic, indispensable rucksack.

21. Walter Benjamin, "Two Poems by Friedrich Hölderlin," in *Selected Writings,* ed. Marcus Bullock and Michael W. Jennings (Cambridge, MA: Harvard University Press, 1996), 1: 24.

22. Heidegger, *Being and Time,* 205.

23. Santner, "W. G. Sebald and the Poetics of Exposure."

24. *The Grain of the Voice: Interviews 1960–1980,* trans. Linda Coverdale (New York: Hill & Wang, 1985), 331.

25. This is the wordier *"Vorform"* of the aphorism, from the unpublished fragments of "Philosophische Lehrjahre"; it is found among the snippets collected under the heading "Form der Kantischen Philosophie."

26. J. M. Coetzee, *Elizabeth Costello* (New York: Viking, 2003), 177.

27. Ibid., 75.

28. *Athenäum*-fragment no. 401. This argument has a precedent in Kant. As Laurence Lampert remarks, "Kant refers to the conflict between Epicurus and Plato as basic, adding: 'Each of the two types of philosophy says more than it knows' (*Critique of Pure Reason* A 472/B500; see also A853/B881). Nietzsche, who is not an epistemological skeptic, suggests that each knows more than it says." *Nietzsche's Task* (New Haven: Yale University Press, 2001), 33.

29. Rainer Maria Rilke, *The Notebooks of Malte Laurids Brigge,* trans. Stephen Mitchell (New York: Vintage Books, 1982), 83.

30. Mark McCulloh, *Understanding W. G. Sebald* (Columbia: University of South Carolina Press, 2003), mxxi.

31. *www.kcrw.com/cgi-bin/db/kcrw.pl?show_code=bw&air_date=12/6/01&tmplt_type=show*

32. Franz Kafka, *The Great Wall of China,* trans. Willa and Edwin Muir (New York: Schocken, 1960), 281. These short texts of Kafka are now entitled, simply, "Aphorisms."

33. McCulloh, *Understanding W. G. Sebald,* 5.

34. "W. G. Sebald: A Profile," *Paris Review* 41 (1999): 278–95.

35. *The Portable Nietzsche,* ed. and trans. Walter Kaufman (New York: Viking, 1954), 520.

36. Michael Gorra astutely observes that throughout *Austerlitz* "Sebald makes no typographical distinction between Austerlitz's words and the narrator's, presenting their conversations without quotation marks and almost without paragraphs; it is as if they have disappeared into each other's voices." This is a marker of the sustained intensity of the relation between the narrator and his double. In "Books and Critics," *Atlantic Monthly* 288, November 2001.

37. Harold F. Searles, "The Differentiation Between Concrete and Metaphorical Thinking," in *Collected Papers on Schizophrenia and Related Subjects* (London: Hogarth Press and the Institute of Psychoanalysis, 1965), 583. Cited in Rolf Breuer, "Irony, Literature, and Schizophrenia," *New Literary History* 12 (Autumn 1980): 118.

38. Kaufman, *The Portable Nietzsche,* 302. I discuss this Nietzsche passage, in so many words, in my *Franz Kafka: The Necessity of Form* (Ithaca: Cornall University Press, 1988), 172.

39. See E. M. Cioran, who speaks of *"ce mélange indecent de banalité et d'apocalypse," Précis de Décomposition* (Paris: Gallimard, 1949), 11.

40. In fact, Sebald suggests, "in Harris a man had risen to the head of Bomber Command who . . . liked destruction for its own sake, and was thus in perfect sympathy with the innermost principle of every war, which is to aim for as wholesale an annihilation of the enemy with his dwellings, his history, and his natural environment as can possibly be achieved. Elias Canetti has linked the fascination of power in its purest form to the growing number of its accumulated victims. In line with this idea, Sir Arthur Harris's position was unassailable because of his unlimited interest in destruction" (*NH* 19).

41. Felski, "Introduction," *Rethinking Tragedy, New Literary History* 35, no. 1 (2004), xii.

42. W. B. Yeats, "Lapis Lazuli."

43. W. G. Sebald, *Campo Santo,* ed. Sven Meyer (Frankfurt a.M.: Fischer Taschenbuch, 2006), 151.

Machines and Models for Modern Tragedy
Brecht/Berlau, *Antigone-Model 1948*

Olga Taxidou

"We know that the barbarians have their art. Let us create another," Brecht triumphantly proclaims in the aphoristic style of the manifesto toward the middle of *A Short Organum for the Theatre* (1947–48). And, of course, the barbarians in this context are "the Greeks." For Brecht, as for most of the European avant-garde, the Greeks and their legacy were part of the failure of the project of Enlightenment, its philosophy, its ideology, and its economies of representation. The quest for a new theater—an Epic Theater in the case of Brecht—had to be defined against the classical, Aristotelian tragic model. However, over the same period, Brecht was working on what was to be his first production after his return to Europe from exile. This was *The Antigone of Sophocles* based on a text by Hölderlin, with stage designs by Caspar Neher. Ruth Berlau was to photograph the process, formulating the first of what was to become a hallmark of the Brechtian project: the *Model.*

This essay proposes to read the *Antigone-Model 1948* together with *A Short Organum,* revisiting that crucial encounter between tragedy and Brechtian aesthetics that has helped create one of the most articulate accounts of the "failure" of tragedy to live up to the demands of modernity. The inappropriateness of tragedy to bear witness to what Brecht (in the same extract from the *Organum*) calls "catastrophe" and its reliance on "Barbaric delights. Human sacrifices all round!" lead Brecht to experiment with the notion of epic, reinvigorating a performance tradition with a long history. This notion of epic was to be sternly anti-Aristotelian, stressing its "newness" in the manifesto fervor of the avant-garde. Its handbook, the *Organum,* was to be combative, lucid, and "crude." However, in the *Antigone-Model* it also finds a tool kit or a *mechane,* as the Greeks/"barbarians" would have it. If we read Brecht's epic theater through the lens of the *Model* rather than solely through the text of the *Organum,* then his relationship with tragedy becomes more complicated, fraught, but potentially more promising in the ways it experiments with the possibility of modern tragedy.

241

After more than fourteen years of exile, after two world wars, Fascism, and the House Un-American Activities Committee, Brecht approached Sophocles' iconic text in an attempt "to make a start somewhere in the general ruin."[1] This encounter exhibits a much more nuanced and sophisticated relationship with Greek tragedy than Brecht is usually given credit for. With their *Model,* more so than with Brecht's interpretation of the play-text (which is based on Hölderlin), what Brecht and Berlau suggest is the possibility of modern tragedy. As a work of art the *Antigone-Model* presents us with a "method,"[2] not an example to be copied or reproduced. As Brecht's friend Walter Benjamin would claim, it embodies not mechanical reproduction but a work that structurally is created on the principle of reproducibility. The impact of the thought of Walter Benjamin, with its emphasis on catastrophe, the ruin, and allegory but also on the possibility of the redemptive quality of art, is felt throughout the *Model.*

The necessity or not of a "model" for modern tragedy takes us back to the original debate on the efficacy of tragedy between Plato and Aristotle. Against Aristotle when it comes to the issue of *katharsis,* Brecht's reading of tragedy is remarkably close to Plato's. He, too, sees its power to distort, arouse, and move, as well as its power to mobilize, reveal, and commemorate. It is its purely theatrical and spectacular dimension that Plato finds objectionable; for Brecht, on the other hand, this dimension becomes a fundamental premise of his whole approach. Plato's antitheatricality is matched by his abhorrence of mourning.[3] The centrality of mourning for tragic form has been stressed by many contemporary classical scholars and anthropologists.[4] Its particular relevance for *Antigone* is something that Brecht engages with both thematically and formally, as his and Berlau's *Model* itself becomes a work of mourning. "It may not be easy," as he says, "to create progressive art in the period of reconstruction. And this should be a challenge."[5]

The emphasis on mourning also highlights the centrality of gender for tragic form. Mourning read both in its historical context and in the context of contemporary neohistoricist and psychoanalytical approaches becomes central to the differentiation, presentation, and representation of gender.[6] Any attempt at a modern tragedy must take into account a long history of performance conventions that deny female performers a presence on stage. Athenian tragedy, in particular, is a homosocial art form, one that displays a difficulty with the female. The convention of men playing women is central to contemporary understandings of the workings of tragedy, not simply as a type of historical pragmatics, but as constitutive of tragic form itself. This classic love/hate relationship with the feminine that Athenian tragedy displays and explores can be read through the workings of mourning, as a civic practice and as a psychoanalytical category, but it may also go some way toward explaining the tense relationship that tragedy has always had with the feminine.

In the figure of Antigone all these issues seem to collide, making her a particularly challenging candidate for the purposes of "reviving" tragedy, particularly after the advent of the early feminist movement and the conspicuous presence of the "New Woman" on the naturalist stage. It is the same figure, however, that proved to be so appealing (in its combination of lawlessness and femininity) to the generation of German philosophers, including Hegel, that Brecht is writing against. For them, in many ways continuing Plato's antitheatrical tradition, Antigone becomes philosophy's designated mourner, there to ritualistically enact the crossing of boundaries (between genders, the borders of the state, life and death), acting as that safety valve that at once tests the limits of the *polis* and helps to restore them, reinvigorated by whatever transgression may have taken place in the interim.[7] I would claim, however, that Antigone viewed as a vehicle for performance, as a "performing machine" (as Brecht's epigone Heiner Müller uses the term), brings into relief the issues of mourning and gender, gender and tragedy, and their complex relationships to the state in a manner that might not seamlessly present her as a heroine or tragic protagonist but, in a way, presents the position she occupies (as performer and as role) as a type of *gestus* of the relationship between mourning, gender, and the law. And this *gestus,* rather than being that of the philosopher (as German idealism would have it) or the patient (as Freud would have it), is that of the actor.

This hypocritical imperative, which restores to the term its meanings of both crisis and critique (and theatricality: *hypocrites* was the Greek term for actors), may help bridge the gap between purely discursive readings of tragedy, which view it as animated philosophy, and historicist ones, which see it in relation to the development of the democratic *polis.* In a sense Plato was right to be suspicious of tragedy and specifically of the body of the actor—hence the negative evolution of the term "hypocrite." Tragedy's power to distort and arouse, influence us, make us think, feel at home or feel strange, relies on the basic principle of embodiment. No matter how much emphasis the traditional view of tragedy places on the power of elevated verse, this power is matched and exceeded by the presence of the actor. Indeed, language and embodiment are usually read in opposition, where the emphasis on high verse (as in the modernist theatrical experiments of T. S. Eliot) is read as continuing an antitheatrical legacy, with all the ramifications of its *somatophobia*. At the other extreme, however, is the reading of tragedy that sees it as the site of every possible quasi-Dionysian, hallucinatory, ecstatic experience that involves the body, individual or collective. This somewhat fetishist use of the body easily dissolves into a "neoprimitivism," with a long and distinguished history of its own in modernist performance, from the Gilbert Murray–Max Reinhardt production of *Oedipus Rex* in the early twentieth century,[8] to Pier Paolo Pasolini's version of *Medea* on film in the 1970s. However, as most interesting "neoprimitivist" productions underline, the two are interlocked. The high verse needs to be embodied (not simply recited as Eliot claimed) and the body of the actor, through the history of theatrical conventions no less, is also part of a material historical process. The emphasis on *hypocrisis* as both *crisis* (or *ecstasis*) and critique could allow for a modern engagement with tragic form that reads it beyond the binaries of metaphysical/historical, word/body, philosophy/theater, and possibly beyond one of the most formative binaries in modern performance theory, which sees Brecht and Brechtian aesthetics as defined against tragic form.

I.

Basic humanity, under too much pressure, explodes,
scattering everything with it into destruction.
Bertolt Brecht, 1948

The Antigone of Sophocles was to be the first production that Brecht directed upon his return to Europe in 1947 after years of exile, the final six of which were spent in the United States. The day after his appearance before the House Un-American Activities Committee, on October 31, 1947, Brecht left for Paris. His return to Europe, which he found "shabby and impoverished," also posed the challenge of the kind of theater appropriate for a postwar, post-Fascist Europe. In a sense Brecht revisits the questions already posed by Bloch and Lukács in the 1930s about the relationship between form and content and the efficacy of "committed art."[9] That he chose to do so by readdressing a text that is at once part of the classical canon and crucial to German Romanticism also needs underlining. While Brecht was working on *The Antigone of Sophocles* he was also formulating his *Short Organum for the Theatre*. These two projects need to be read in tandem. His version of *Antigone* emerges as an experimental exercise in Epic Theater but as an equally experimental proposition in modern tragedy.

Of course, *The Antigone of Sophocles,* with the conspicuous, almost ironic presence of the playwright in the title, is not really based on Sophocles at all but closely follows Friedrich Hölderlin's version of 1803. Significantly, Brecht seems to skip a generation of German Hellenism (bypassing the dominant presence of Wagner and Nietzsche) to go back to Hölderlin, whose translations were ridiculed when published and who had a reputation for being particularly obscure.[10] This difficulty was for Brecht part of the attraction, compounding his desired effect of distance and estrangement. In returning to Hölderlin he was performing two acts of recuperation, one for Germany (in reviving a type of classicism that wasn't tainted by Nazism) and the other for the whole of Europe (in reworking a model of tragedy for the purposes of modernity). This *Antigone* offers a platform for Brecht to reassess the role of art in the postwar era *and* to carve out a role for himself as a committed artist.

In reworking Hölderlin's translation Brecht could be seen as elaborating on a certain German Romantic sensibility that saw in Sophocles not the lyrical, measured poet of Athenian democracy but the Oriental, wild Dionysian version of the same project. Writing in the historical context of a new order, which would be republican and vital, Hölderlin was interested in making his adaptations relevant to his historical moment. David Constantine, the translator of both Hölderlin and Brecht, writes:

> That is the chief interpretative tendency in Hölderlin translations: to bring the ancient texts home in such a fashion that they will quicken hearts and minds in the torpid present. In translating like that, serving, as he thought, the present needs of his own countrymen, Hölderlin put himself ever more at risk. Always choosing the more violent word, so that the texts are stitched through with the vocabulary of excess, of madness, rage, he was also voicing those forces in his own psychology, which very soon would carry him over the edge.[11]

This fusion of the personal and the political makes Hölderlin a very intuitive reader of tragedy for Brecht. The madness, violence, and rage that permeate Hölderlin's translation is, in a way, historicized (or "rationalized," as Brecht claims) and becomes part of the political fiber of the play. Rather than reading the story in the familiar Hegelian terms of the individual against the law of the state, Brecht, following Hölderlin's lead, sees *Antigone* as a tale of destruction. He writes that "in *Antigone* the violence is explained by inadequacy. The war against Argos derives from mismanagement. Those who have been robbed have to look to robbery themselves. The undertaking exceeds the strength available. Violence splits the forces instead of welding them together; basic humanity, under too much pressure, explodes, scattering everything with it into destruction."[12] Admittedly Brecht makes major changes and additions to Hölderlin's version: he exaggerates the role of Haemon's brother, Megareus (offstage), and disposes of the mother, Eurydice, altogether; the war with Argos gets a "realistic" sheen and is fought over mineral wealth; Creon has total and absolute power and no rightful claim whatsoever. However, despite these attempts at "rationalization," I would argue that the text's main concern is with charting the "scattering of destruction" mentioned earlier. This fascination with catastrophe, which attracts Brecht to Hölderlin in the first place, is, I believe, the main structuring force of the adaptation. In a sense, the whole project is about finding a form to accommodate historical catastrophe.

In turn, the role of Antigone is radically rewritten to blend with this aesthetic. Rather than presenting her moral and heroic character (Brecht's epic mothers come to mind), as the antidote to the extreme and total power of Creon, she appears to be rather more implicated in the violence she supposedly opposes. "She ate bread baked in servitude, she sat comfortably in the shade of the strongholds of oppression. Only when the violence dealt out by the house of Oedipus rebounded on that house did she awake," writes Brecht.[13] So, this "rationalization" does not involve a transposition of the conflict between Antigone and Creon into the terms of his own postwar present, and in terms of all the usual binaries that the play is read as enacting. Rather, this reading of Antigone presents her as inextricably linked to the power structures she is trying to resist. For Brecht, the interest of the play is not so much in showing how one system of values might triumph over the other but how both systems are implicated in the violence of war. This reading also helps excavate the tensions in the original play between law and lawlessness, between civilization and barbarism. Hence the emphasis placed in his production on the aesthetic of barbarism: "In modelling the set Cas [Neher] and I stumble on an ideological element of the first order. Should we place the barbaric totem poles with the horses' skulls at the back between the actors' benches, thus indicating the barbaric location of the old poem, which the actors leave in order to act (the de-totemised version)? We decide to place the acting among the totem poles, since we are still living in the state of totemic class war. . . . *Antigone* in its entirety belongs with the barbaric horses' skulls."[14]

His own *Antigone,* however, firmly located between the old and the new, among the totem poles, was to underline the structural, dialectical relationship between the two. Like Hölderlin before him, Brecht sees in the Greek model of tragedy not the taming, civilizing *gestus* that leads to progress and civilization, nor does he see it solely as epitomizing the barbarism that results from empire and war. Rather, he sees both these themes bound together, implicated in each other's narratives, like Creon and Antigone. Rather than a paean to humanism, his *Antigone* is about the violence that humanism potentially engenders. The famous "Ode to Man," in addition to charting man's progress, becomes a catalogue of catastrophes framed by the word "monstrous" at the start and the end of the ode. This is Hölderlin's translation (which Brecht maintains) of the term *deinon* in Sophocles. It is a notorious term that has inspired much philosophical reflection and that roughly translates as "awesome," "wondrous," "extremely able," but also as "strange," "other," and "monstrous."[15] Like Hölderlin, Brecht highlights this bleaker aspect of the humanism that the ode celebrates. By the end of the ode the subject of this humanism that Brecht, quoting Hölderlin, explores becomes a stranger to himself:

> Monstrous, a lot, But nothing
> More monstrous than man.
> . . . .
> A measure is set.
> For when he wants for an enemy
> He rises up as his own. Like the bull's
> He bows the neck of his fellowmen but these fellowmen
> Rip out his guts. When he steps forth
> He treads on his own kind, hard. By himself alone
> His belly will never be filled but he builds a wall
> Around what he owns and the wall
> Must be torn down. The roof
> Opened to the rain. Humanity
> Weighs with him not a jot. Monstrous thereby
> He becomes to himself.[16]

This reading of *deinon* as both wondrous and monstrous punctuates the whole adaptation. It informs Brecht's decision to place the horse skulls among the actors and not behind them. In this way, rather than gesturing toward prehistoric ritual, these horse skulls become the emblems of historical violence. Although the adaptation uses ritual, and the discourse in the *Antigone-Model* is full of ritualized and medicalized language (fevered life, the consumptive), this ritual is never truly conceptualized within a primitivist framework. The violence in the text and on the stage is not a reference to any quasi-anthropological, prehistoric ritual that is able to redeem a crisis-ridden humanism (and humanity). For Brecht, as he clearly states in the *Model,* his adaptation of *Antigone* is a study of state power in crisis that "only becomes aware of its own laws of motion in a catastrophe."[17] (The term "crisis" is deliberately used in the Greek sense: fevered response, eruption, but also the possibility of critique.) The reading of humanism (and tragedy) proposed through this interpretation of *deinon* allows for both the wonder and the catastrophe to surface. Although the play uses the aesthetics of ritual, this ritual is never seen as prehistoric but rather as the bearer of historical catastrophe itself. The primitive, the barbarian, is not something that forms part of a humanist evolutionary trajectory that we have outgrown or "lost" and occasionally revisit in our search for experimental forms of performance ("the Greeks as the childhood of mankind," as Marx put it). For Brecht, as for Walter Benjamin, it has always run parallel to the movement for progress, light, reason, and civilization, and the two cannot be structurally separated; hence the decision to place the actors among the skulls.

In turning to Hölderlin, Brecht is also engaging with what Françoise Dastur calls his "speculative theory of tragedy."[18] Hölderlin's shift from writing his own modern tragedies (*Empedocles, 1798–80,* unfinished) to translating Sophocles has been interpreted by Philippe Lacoue-Labarthe as a "radical rupture . . . that opens onto the very root of theatre."[19] In other words, Hölderlin approaches Sophocles after the so-called failure of his own attempts at modern tragedy in search of a "model." "The 'return to Sophocles' does not, for Hölderlin, mean some sort of 'nostalgia for Greece.' It means a return to the ground of theatricality," as Lacoue-Labarthe claims.[20] In his essays on tragedy and "Remarks" on Oedipus and Antigone, Hölderlin presents a version of this theatricality, without which modern tragedy would be impossible. He suggests a speculative theory of tragedy as "the metaphor of an intellectual intuition." This use of the term "speculative," as Dastur claims, restores to it its original Greek meaning of *theoria,* which was translated as *specto/speculatio* into Latin by Boethius. We begin to understand how Hölderlin's quest for a speculative theory of tragedy actually translates into a quest for theatricality or for a language that theorizes theatricality.

In Christian theology the Greek sense of *theoria,* and the original meaning of *specto* (all connected semantically with looking, scrutinizing, and reflecting but also with the embodied and spatialized dimension of those original etymologies) and speculation become connected with *speculum,* the mirror. The theatrical act itself thus changes from potentially speculative to overwhelmingly spectacular. Once again we are in the familiar Platonic territory of the distorting effects of tragedy. This shift in meaning from *theoria* as a type of *speculative* thinking to *theoria* as representing a distorted image—indeed, one that can only be restored by the intervention of the divine [*visio Dei*]—bears all the traces of antitheatrical philosophy. So much so that Thomas Aquinas's derivation of *theoria/speculatio* from *speculum* (rather than *specto*) can be read as echoing the master of antitheatrical philosophy himself. In turn, the identification of things *spectacular* with distortion and corruption of the truth may account for the difficult relationship between Christianity and theater in general.[21]

Through his encounter with the theatricality of tragedy Hölderlin is searching for both a *speculative* and a *spectacular* approach to modern tragedy; at once textual and material, metaphysical and physical. He writes in the opening of his "Remarks on Oedipus":

> It will be good, in order to secure for today's poets, also at home, an existence in the city, to elevate poetry, also at home, given the difference of times and institutions, to the level of the *mechane* of the Ancients.
>
> When being compared with those of the Greeks, other works of art too lack reliability; at least, they have been judged until today according to the impression they produce rather than according to their lawful calculation and to the other methodical modes through which the beautiful is engendered. . . .
>
> As men, we must first realize that it is something, which can be known by means (*moyen*) of its manifestation, that the way in which it is conditioned may be determined and learned. Such is the reason why—to say nothing of higher reasons—poetry is in special need of secure and characteristic delimitations.[22]

This poetics of tragedy that is at once *techne* and *mechane* shifts the critical attention from the audience to the stage, from theories of reception [*katharsis*] to theories of theatrical production and performance. It foreshadows notions of embodiment (manifestation) and also the principle of reproducibility, later to be developed by Benjamin (whose *Origin of German Tragic Drama* provides a further layer of filtering in the relationships between Brecht and Hölderlin).[23]

Hölderlin's fascination with the image of the *mechane* is in line with his notion of tragedy as "the metaphor of an intellectual intuition," where metaphor is used in its Greek sense of *transport* or mediation. Tragedy itself is seen as such a form of *transport*, a *mechane* that acts as a bridge to combat the eternal and "limitless separation" between the earthly and the divine, between the word and the body, between subject and object. Also, it always transpires as self-reflexive:

> The tragic *transport* is actually empty and the least restrained. So, in the rhythmic sequence of the representations wherein *transport* presents itself, there becomes necessary *what in poetic meter is called caesura*, the pure word, the counterrhythmic rupture, namely in order to meet the onrushing change of representation at its highest point in such a way that very soon it is not change of representation which appears but representation itself.[24]

Hölderlin's notoriously dense term "caesura," with its mingling of physical and lexical qualities, its "counterrhythmic rupture," and its ever-present fixation on representation proves very attractive for Benjamin. The term also finds its way into Brechtian theory, particularly in his formulation of *gestus*—a crucial performative act, in which the body and language both posit and estrange the actor on stage and within a broader network of socio-historical interactions. *Gestus*, as a "counterrhythmic rupture," can both impersonate and demonstrate, making the natural seem strange and wondrous, yet always historical. Crucially the term "caesura," itself borrowed, rewritten from poetic theory, becomes the fundamental premise of theatricality. As Philippe Lacoue-Labarthe states, "the *caesura* is the condition of possibility for manifestation, for the (re)presentation [*Darstellung*] of the tragic. Such is the law or, if you prefer, the principle of its theatricality."[25] In tackling *The Antigone of Sophocles*, already rewritten by Hölderlin, Brecht continued an unfinished project. We begin to understand the inclusion of Sophocles in the title. He set out to rewrite *Antigone* as a piece of poetry *and* as an example of tragic *transport*. The *Antigone-Model*, produced with photographs by Berlau after the play-text, *The Antigone of Sophocles*, and significantly after the performance, could signify an attempt at such a tragic *transport*. Through its reliance on the principle of reproducibility (the *mechane*, as Hölderlin would have it) and the conspicuous use of photography (which Benjamin would have approved of), it emerges as a specifically modernist inflection on the idea of tragic *transport*.

II. Helene Weigel and the Door

The *Model* contains a photograph of Helene Weigel attached to a door, which she carries crucifixion-style on her back from the moment she is arrested by Creon's soldiers, from the moment the *peripeteia* begins to unravel. This is a striking image at once referring to the themes of the play but also, crucially, embodying them. The relationships between Helene Weigel, the performer (in her first German-speaking part in ten years), the role of Antigone as tragic heroine, and the theatrical object of "the door" form an intriguing *gestus*, one whose precedent can be found in Hölderlin's caesura.

The door draws attention to the themes of the play: the *oikos* and the *polis*, home and homelessness, inside and outside the law. It is, however, a door attached to the body of the performer, and it also signals a relationship between actors and objects on the stage. This intricate relationship between subject and object on the stage seems to be a fundamental aspect of the Brechtian *gestus*. It is also something that will later form a very specific part of the makeup of Helene Weigel, the performer (her relationship with the cart and her moneybag, for example, in *Mother Courage and Her Children*).

Unlike the image of the cross to which it also alludes, this wooden frame is never turned into a symbol in the *Model*. It never stands in for the body, which it has sublimated or sacrificed. It remains stubbornly attached to the performer as a kind of *transport* rather than as a substitution. Indeed, one carries the other, as the image of Helene Weigel attached to the door proposes an interchangeability between subjects and objects on stage. Rather than presenting the door—a potent image in its own right—as the main symbol of the play, separate and distinct as a stage "prop," this dynamic and contingent reading at once highlights the Hegelian binaries within which the play has been read and critiques them. As a theatrical *gestus* it is also citing a particular theatrical convention, its history, and its political efficacy.

In attaching Antigone to the door, the *Model* cites a number of theatrical traditions: the reading of the Passion of Christ as a tragedy and the medieval Mystery Cycles among them. In addressing these, the *Model* is also engaging with the difficult relationship that these traditions exhibit with the body of the actor. Unlike the Christian drama, which turns the wooden cross into a symbol of redemption, eradicating the presence of the body in the process (although this axiom is constantly challenged

Helene Weigel as Antigone and Hans Gaugler as Creon in Bertolt Brecht's *Antigone-Model 1948*. Stage design by Caspar Neher; photography by Ruth Berlau. Courtesy Bertolt-Brecht-Archiv, Akademie der Künste, Berlin/Hilda Hoffmann.

in every theatrical and ritualistic re-enactment of the Passion of Christ), this *gestural* drama confuses the line between actors and objects, granting neither the privilege of agency, ascension, or sublimation. However, this intermingling does not necessarily resort to primitivism, where people are reduced to inanimate things, nor does it revel in a postmodern, ahistorical, ecstatic substitution of people by things. For this door is definitely a ruin. Brecht writes:

> If theatre is capable of showing the truth, then it must also be capable of making the sight of it a pleasure. How then can such a theatre be created? The difficulty about ruins is that the house has gone, but the site isn't there either. And the architects' plans, it seems, never get lost. This means that reconstruction brings back the old dens of iniquity and centres of disease. Fevered life claims to be particularly vital life; none steps so firmly as the consumptive who has lost all feeling in the soles of his feet.[26]

The door emerges as such a ruin and Weigel/Antigone as a figure of the consumptive who is nevertheless walking very firmly on her feet.

Brecht's reading of the function of theater at a "time of reconstruction" is that of a *pharmakon* (as both poison and cure). The excavation that reconstruction implies helps to bring to the surface the centers of disease, and the moment of drama (crisis/hypocrisis) brings together the fevered life and the vital life. As Brecht implies, life is at its most vital when it is flaring up with fever. This reading of theater, very close to Antonin Artaud's idea of theater as the plague, is at once ritualistic and historical. The relationship it proposes between actors and objects is an extension of this view. The relationship between Antigone and the door is not a comment on her lost humanity (her thingness) or her inability to control the world around her. Rather, it points toward the materiality and the theatricality of this relationship, where, in a moment of historical catastrophe, disease and vitality, people and things, life and death become interchangeable. For Brecht, following Benjamin, this moment is also a moment of truth;[27] a truth, however, that needs to be manifested through strangeness, like the consumptive who steps firmly only after he has "lost all feeling in the soles of his feet."

"*Things* have a life," says Winnie in Samuel Beckett's *Happy Days,* herself buried up to the neck in a mound.[28] In "Helene Weigel and the door" this "life of things" creates the main *gestus* of the *Model,* in many ways manifesting that "counterrhythmic rupture" that Hölderlin saw as essential to the *caesura.* Lacoue-Labarthe cites Hölderlin's Tiresias's few lines of speech as the "moment of the *caesura*": "In both pieces [*Oedipus* and *Antigone*], it is the speeches of Tiresias which form the *caesura*. He enters the course of destiny as the custodian of the power of nature which, tragically, tears man from his own life-sphere, the mid-point of his inner life, transporting him into another world and into the eccentric sphere of the dead."[29] Interestingly, this reworking of the caesura is not solely linguistic/poetic; it is arrived at through the encounter between the textual and the material, poetry and stage prop, actor and object. "Helene Weigel and the door" becomes such a form of transport, which enacts all the themes of the play in a manner that is at once a performance *and* a philosophical debate. This reworking of the caesura through Brecht's *gestus* posits the possibility of a "philosophical theatre," one that dramatically recasts the agonistic relationship between tragedy and philosophy.[30]

This "transport," as Hölderlin claims above, leads us to "another world and into the eccentric sphere of the dead." Crucially this "another world" is not the same as the "sphere of the dead," as the paratactic use of "and" clearly shows. Arguably, it is the world of the stage, the in-between world, the world of mediation, where the *mechane* is exposed and theatricalized, and truth potentially revealed. The "eccentric" nature of the "sphere of the dead" guarantees that the encounter with their world is tangible and formative. This is a reading of the stage as a site of mediation and also of mourning. This door becomes the rupture between the "sphere of the dead" and the stage. It is not simply standing in for any number of doors (exile, tombstone, stage, bed, etc.) that could symbolize the themes of the play. Through its theatrical relationship with the body of the performer, it is *attempting* to embody them, as the speculative nature of this enterprise is endemic. In this sense the figure of Antigone, as tragic protagonist, enacts the tensions between embodiment and monumentalization, tensions that are also thematically played out in the text. Is the performer of such a "tragic protagonist" an *actor* (with all the notions of character and psychology that it implies) or a *hypocrite* (a *mechane*, an acting machine)? "Helene Weigel/Antigone and the door" does not necessarily resolve this binary but sets to tease it out, significantly *transporting* it from the "world of poetry" to the "world of the stage."

Ruth Berlau continues this *transport* with her photographs in the *Model*. The image needs to be read as also negotiating relationships between Brecht the director and Berlau the photographer. Is it significant that the "gaze" is female? And is it significant that Helene Weigel is inhabiting a theatrical role that in Athenian tragedy had no female performers? In other words, how is the *Model* addressing the *difficulty* that tragic form has always had with the female performer?

More than a case of making the female performer visible or "correcting" a historical form, the modern encounter with tragedy throws into crisis some of its fundamental representational economies. The convention of men playing women is endemic to tragedy and at once nods to the exclusion of women from the civic sphere and toward a male homosexual sublime.[31] The physical presence of a female performer in the role of Antigone (while important historically and politically) does not in and of itself constitute a reading of Antigone. Nor is it a case of the female performer having access to a "real" Antigone. In many ways, the presence of the female performer highlights the role as a "performing machine," a non-character, as a modern performer would intertextually be inhabiting a role that was written for a male hypocrite and is associated with a long history of female impersonation.

Interestingly, female impersonation plays a significant role in the formation of Brecht's *Verfremdungseffekt,* which is clearly articulated by Brecht only after his formative encounter with the Chinese *dan* (female impersonator) actor, Mei Lan-fang at the Writers' Conference in Moscow in 1936. Contemporary feminist performance theorists have revisited this event and have criticized Brecht for exhibiting a classic Marxist "blind spot" when it comes to gender.[32] The tradition that he had found inspiring in its ability to separate performer from role was also one that had no female performers. Furthermore, this separability, so desirable for the activation of the V-effect, relied on a fundamental separability of female "essence" and female "performance." It is fascinating to note that in the history of performance conventions the ideas of estrangement, otherness, and unhomeliness are usually linked with the specific representation of the female (always performed by men). Brecht saw in Mei Lan-fang's performance a fine example of his alienation effect. We could say that the form performs a similar function in Athenian tragedy. In both cases the first "thing" that is "alienated" is the female. Read in a psychoanalytical framework this function of impersonating the female becomes a prerequisite of tragic form, in the same way that the female body (reflecting Plato's cave *and* his antitheatricality) becomes a prerequisite of representation.[33]

Helene Weigel inhabiting the role of Antigone forms part of a huge and varied cast of female performers within modernism who rewrote theatrical conventions in order to make their presence visible as artists.[34] From Naturalism's "New Woman" to the daring experiments in Modern

Dance (the pioneers of which were mostly women),[35] the specific representation of the female performer poses both a thematic and a formal challenge. This epic rendition of the "New Woman" goes beyond the aesthetic and political parameters of Naturalism. It views the "woman problem" as part of the "capitalist problem," in a tradition of philosophical reflection from Engels to Trotsky (after all, as Marx said, "social progress can be measured exactly by the social position of the fair sex, the ugly ones included"). The work of the Russian/Soviet director Vsevolod Meyerhold and his actress wife, Zinaida Reich, is also a fine example of constructivist readings of this structural relationship between capitalism and gender oppression. Sometimes, the "woman question" comes to metaphorically stand in for and redeem "the capitalist question," utilizing the genre of classic epic and romance, in a long and distinguished literary tradition from classic epic's use of Helen of Troy to Brecht's own "Epic mothers."[36] In this scheme of things the female protagonists of Brecht display significant attachments to "things": to a door in *Antigone,* to a cart in *Mother Courage,* to a "child" in *The Caucasian Chalk Circle,* to a "gift" from the gods in *The Good Person of Szechwan.* However, the obsession with "things" that these roles exhibit can be seen to result from an approach that reads the female protagonist as tied up with the world around her and its history. It can also be found in the fascination with objects that we see in Heiner Müller's work (*Hamletmachine, Medea Material*) or in contemporary feminist performance (as the recent interface between feminist performance theory and Brechtian theory clearly indicates).[37] In both these examples, the work of Brecht is built upon but also "supplemented," at once homage and betrayal, to paraphrase Müller. ("To use Brecht without criticizing him is betrayal.")[38]

In this context, Weigel's Antigone can be read as inflecting Naturalism's tradition of the "New Woman" through an epic aesthetic that has its roots in both modernist poetic drama and the European avant-garde. In opening up to this level of experiment and critique, the epic tradition in tragedy that we have been sketching out so far is also forced to encounter another difficulty: that between Marxism and feminism. In the case of the *Model,* one could say that it is also enacted through the relationships among Weigel, the performer, Berlau, the photographer, and Brecht, the director. Weigel, the performer, reconfigures a set of conventions that historically deny her presence, and Berlau documents the event through the most modern of media, photography. The *Model* begins to emerge as a very modernist rendition of tragedy indeed, complete with New Woman on and off the stage and technologies of reproduction. The figure of Brecht himself begins to fade; or rather his work—that of the playwright/adaptor/director—becomes a type of mediation, *transport,* between the stage, the lens, and the book of the *Model.* The *Model* would have a similar impact, as he had hoped: "The idea of making use of models is a clear challenge to the artists of a period that applaud nothing but what is 'original,' 'incomparable,' 'never been seen before,' and demands what is 'unique.'"[39]

In rejecting the quest for newness, Brecht turns to the oldest form of theater available in the European canon. In doing so he is also re-igniting the battle between the ancients and the moderns, ushering in a specifically modernist type of Hellenism, akin to the "neoclassical" experiments undertaken by James Joyce, Gertrude Stein, Stravinsky, or the Cubists. At the same time, he is making a contribution to a long-standing debate about the efficacy of tragedy in modernity. This contribution, it could be argued, consists mainly of the *Model* itself. The textual reworking follows Hölderlin more or less faithfully (in its attitude to language and to "the Greeks"). The *Model,* on the other hand, comes into being through the contributions of a performer, Helene Weigel, and a photographer, Ruth Berlau. As versions of the "New Woman" and in an amalgamation of the personal and political (that was to become a hallmark of later feminist performance), they are constitutive of the *Model* and the versions of modern tragedy it proposes.

The quest for modern tragedy is usually read within a literary history that starts with the Greeks and ends with "high," modernist poetic drama, via the Elizabethan stage and German Romanticism. Almost invariably this analysis focuses on a literary theatrical tradition and not on instances of performance or indeed on historical performance conventions. It seems that this *Model* follows what Benjamin called "a secret smugglers' path" in theater history (through the Mysteries, through the history of performers, and through Baroque drama).[40] In negotiating a relationship between tragedy and modernity, it is also raising questions of tragic form beyond the function of high verse. At the same time, it forms part of a general modernist Hellenism that views the "Greeks" as embodied, situated, and historical (the work of the Cambridge Ritualists, for example, forms part of this trend).[41]

Brecht's and Berlau's *Antigone-Model* can also be read within a literary history that seeks to rework tragic form within modernity. Rather than polarize and somewhat caricature these diverse experiments in modernist drama as either failed Christian or failed Marxist tragedies, they could be seen as negotiating different approaches to the embodiment, theatricality, and reception of modern tragedy. The contribution of this particular *Model* also opens up the debate between the ancients and the moderns to the historical avant-garde. In revisiting Sophocles and Hölderlin through the incorporation of the theatrical experiments of the avant-garde, the *Antigone-Model* allows us to read the "quest" for modern tragedy beyond its manifestations as literary drama.

This "quest" is always shadowed by a discourse of failure. And to read the *Model* within this trajectory is both to highlight its differences/contrasts and also to unravel its failures, or its attitude toward failure. In a sense failure is already inscribed in the speculative/spectacular nature of the enterprise. This is the difference between what Jameson calls Brecht's "method" (or model in this instance) and "other philosophical methods or world-views." "Method" would appear to have a strong attachment to the "speculative" [*theoria*]. The use of the term "method" easily translates into the ancients' *mechane,* albeit via Hölderlin. And the Brecht-Berlau *Antigone-Model 1948* can be read as such a form of transport [*mechane*], which puts forward a "speculative concept" of modern tragedy "by virtue of its unique form," as Jameson phrases it.⁴² This "unique form" in this instance (and I would claim throughout the Brechtian project) is "profoundly related" to tragic form. This speculative failure embodies a type of negativity, at once physical and metaphysical, that doesn't readily translate into quasi-existential nothingness. It relates theatrical practice to a tradition of critical philosophy (Brecht's "philosophical theatre") and injects the Brechtian project with that "pessimism of the intellect" that some critics believe it desperately needs. This attachment of Epic Theater to tragic form that I have tried to sketch out in this analysis gets an added modernist sheen through the use of photography in the *Model.*

It also posits the possibility that the failures of the avant-garde could be read as modern tragedies. The way the *Model* appears as an aesthetic object owes as much to the literary experiments of German Romanticism as to the spatial/performative experiments of the avant-garde. As a *mechane* it can be read as inflecting the idea of the ready-made, the discarded and used but also utopian object. As work of mourning the *Model* is both commemorative of the theaters of the past *and* a form of *transport* for the theaters of the future, where the use of photography compounds the impact of commemoration/mourning. As a model for modern tragedy it displays a profound attachment to discourses of death, in a sense rewriting the German Romantic/Idealist tradition, which constantly mourns the "death of tragedy." The whole "death of tragedy" thesis—one that also reads Brecht's work as part of its trajectory—comes to formally and thematically inform the *making* of the *Model*. With a nod to German Idealism (through its radical strand, Hölderlin) but also with a keen engagement with avant-garde experiment, the *Model* emerges as Brecht's and Berlau's paradigm for the engaged work of art. That this work of art is itself a modern tragedy is significant. It challenges the impossibility of modern tragedy and the ways we as audience or scholars respond to tragedy; that is, it also proposes a modern *theoria* of tragedy. This is one that is driven by a *hypocritical* imperative and displays a profound attachment to speculative and spectacular thinking. Either way, the literary/philosophical model of approaching tragedy is seriously challenged. In addressing this challenge the Brecht-Berlau *Antigone-Model 1948* also inevitably fails, but it *fails spectacularly,* or to paraphrase Samuel Beckett, it "Fails again. Fails better."[43]

Notes

1. The texts from the *Model* have been translated by David Constantine as "Texts by Brecht," in *Brecht, Collected Plays,* ed. Tom Kuhn and David Constantine, vol. 8 (London: Methuen, 2003); here see 203.

2. Fredric Jameson, *Brecht and Method* (London: Verso, 1998).

3. For an analysis of Plato's repudiation of mourning see Henry Staten, *Eros in Mourning* (Baltimore: Johns Hopkins University Press, 1995). Staten claims that a similar thanatoerotic drive to that which informs Plato's antimourning can be read into Lacanian psychoanalysis, with both exhibiting similar ambivalence toward the feminine. This ambivalence, in turn, translates into antitheatricality, as Lacan's essay on Antigone exemplifies. Appropriately, his essay, "The Splendour of Antigone," appears in his seminars on ethics. See Jacques Lacan, *The Seminar of Jacques Lacan,* vol. 7, *Ethics of Psychoanalysis 1959–1960,* ed. Jacques-Alain Miller, trans. Dennis Porter (New York: Norton, 1992).

4. For the interesting interface between classics, anthropology, and psychoanalysis on the issue of mourning, see the work of Margaret Alexiou, Gail Holst-Warhaft, Richard Seaford, and Nicole Loraux.

5. Kuhn and Constantine, "Texts by Brecht," 204.

6. On gender and representation in Athenian tragedy, see the work of Nicole Loraux, Froma Zeitlin, and Helene P. Foley.

7. See Stathis Gourgouris, "Philosophy's Need for Antigone," in *Does Literature Think? Literature as Theory for an Antimythical Era* (Stanford: Stanford University Press, 2003).

8. On the impact of Max Reinhardt's production of *Oedipus Rex,* with Gilbert Murray's translation, at Covent Garden in 1912, see "Greek Tragedy and the Cos-

mopolitan Ideal," in *Greek Tragedy and the British Stage, 1660–1914,* ed. Edith Hall and Fiona Macintosh (Oxford: Oxford University Press, 2005), 521–54. The authors with Oliver Taplin have founded the APGRD (Archive of Performances of Greek and Roman Drama) at the University of Oxford, a hugely significant project that will contribute to a new understanding of Greek tragedy in performance.

Epigraph: Kuhn and Constantine, "Texts by Brecht," 199.

9. Ernest Bloch, George Lukács, Bertolt Brecht, Walter Benjamin, and Theodor Adorno, *Aesthetics and Politics,* trans. Ronald Taylor, Afterword by Fredric Jameson (London: Verso, 1980).

10. The translator of Hölderlin, David Constantine, notes that contemporary scholars have found more than one thousand errors in Hölderlin's versions of *Oedipus* and *Antigone.* Even if these are all random and not systematic (proposing in themselves a reading), they surely portray a consistent irreverence toward "the Greeks."

11. *Hölderlin's Sophocles' Oedipus and Antigone,* trans. and intro. David Constantine (Newcastle-upon-Tyne: Bloodaxe Books, 2001), 11–12.

12. Kuhn and Constantine, "Texts by Brecht," 199.

13. Ibid., 217.

14. Ibid., 198–99.

15. For a discussion of the philosophical debates surrounding the translations of *deinon* from Hölderlin to Heidegger (who translates the term as *Unheimliche*) see Gourgouris, "Philosophy's Need for Antigone," in *Does Literature Think?,* 134–37.

16. Bertolt Brecht, *The Antigone of Sophocles: A Version for the Stage after Hölderlin's Translation,* in Kuhn and Constantine, *Brecht, Collected Plays,* 8: 17–18.

17. Kuhn and Constantine, "Texts by Brecht," 203.

18. Françoise Dastur, "Tragedy and Speculation," in *Philosophy and Tragedy,* ed. Miguel de Beistegui and Simon Sparks (London: Routledge, 2000), 78–87.

19. Philippe Lacoue-Labarthe, "Hölderlin's Theatre," in ibid., 118.

20. Ibid., 118–19.

21. In "Tragedy and Speculation," Dastur writes, "the word *speculatio* comes, of course, from *specto,* to look at, to scrutinise, and was used by Boethius to translate the Greek *theoria* into Latin. But in Christian theology the meaning was forgotten, especially by Thomas Aquinas, who derives *speculatio* from *speculum,* mirror, and relates the word of God whom we see now confusedly as 'in a mirror' but whom later, that is to say, after death, we will see 'face to face'. *Speculation* means, therefore, partial and confused knowledge, as indirect and unclear as the image of oneself in the metal mirrors of these early times, and it is this meaning of the word that will be used by the German mystics. . . . Thus speculation is connected with the *visio Dei,* the vision of the supersensible, or with what Kant calls 'intellectual intuition,' an intuition which is refused to finite things, which are only able to have 'sensible intuition,' that is, an intuition of what is already given to them through their senses" (de Beistegui and Sparks, *Philosophy and Tragedy,* 78–79).

22. Friedrich Hölderlin, *Essays and Letters on Theory,* trans. Thomas Pfau (Albany: State University of New York Press, 1988), 101.

23. Walter Benjamin, *The Origin of German Tragic Drama* (1928), trans. John Osborne (London: Verso, 1998).

24. Hölderlin, *Essays and Letters on Theory,* 101–2.

25. See Lacoue-Labarthe, "Hölderlin's Theatre," in de Beistegui and Sparks, *Philosophy and Tragedy,* 130.

26. Kuhn and Constantine, "Texts by Brecht," 204.

27. Brecht writes, "But mere catastrophe is a bad teacher. One learns hunger and thirst from it, but seldom hunger for truth and thirst for knowledge. No amount of illness will turn a sick man into a physician; neither the distant view nor close inspection makes an eye-witness into an expert" (Kuhn and Constantine, "Texts by Brecht," 204).

28. Samuel Beckett, *Happy Days* (London: Faber & Faber, 1963), 40. In terms of literary history Beckett's obsession with "thingness" has been read as deriving primarily from the experiments in Anglophone poetic drama. Yeats's famous aphorism that calls for actors to be pushed about in barrels ("The barrels, I thought, might be on castors, so that I could shove them about with a pole when the actors required it," W. B. Yeats, *Explorations* [London: Macmillan, 1962], 86–97), and Eliot's view of the stage as a physical correlative of the poet's voice (T. S. Eliot, *Poetry and Drama* [London: Faber & Faber, 1950]) are cited as Beckett's main predecessors. However, Beckett's lineage might be more through the theatrical experiments of the historical avant-garde—where Brecht also gets his obsession with materiality and thingness rather than from the experiments in verse drama.

29. Lacoue-Labarthe, "Hölderlin's Theatre," in de Beistegui and Sparks, *Philosophy and Tragedy,* 130.

30. Brecht is not oblivious to the significant position occupied by German philosophy in this endeavor, as he writes as early as 1929: "At present it's Germany, the home of philosophy, that is leading in the large-scale development of the theatre and the drama. The theatre's future is philosophical," in "Last Stage: Oedipus," in *Brecht on Theatre,* ed. John Willet (London: Methuen, 1964), 24.

31. This male homosexual sublime is punctuated by the discourses of male-to-male *philia* and *philoxenia* (hospitality), which come with their own politics and economies of exchange. For a genealogy of the politics of *philia* from Aristotle onward, see Jacques Derrida, *The Politics of Friendship* (London: Verso, 1997), where he writes, "What relation does this domination maintain with the *double exclusion* we see at work in all great ethico-politico-philosophical discourses on friendship: on the one hand, the exclusion of friendship between women; on the other, the exclusion between a man and a woman? This double exclusion of the feminine in this philosophical paradigm would then confer on friendship the essential and essentially sublime figure of virile homosexuality" (279). For an analysis of the function of *philia* and *philoxenia* in Athenian tragedy, see Olga Taxidou, *Tragedy, Modernity, and Mourning* (Edinburgh: Edinburgh University Press, 2004), 64–69; 119–25.

32. See Carol Martin, "Brecht, Feminism, and Chinese Theatre," *Drama Review* 43, no. 4 (1999): 77–85. She writes, "Brecht's emphasis on the form of Chinese acting at the expense of its interior processes, and his choice to ignore the significance of men playing women, could only have occurred because he ignored two of his own main concerns: an understanding of the historical conditions that produced traditional Chinese acting, and an inquiry into the assertion that the actor could and should quote the character played" (79–80).

33. See Joan Copjec, *Imagine There's No Woman: Ethics and Sublimation* (Cambridge, MA: MIT Press, 2002), especially the chapter entitled "The Tomb of Perseverance: On Antigone," 12–47.

34. See Penny Farfan, *Women, Modernism, and Performance* (Cambridge: Cambridge University Press, 2004).

35. See Sally Banes, *Dancing Women: Female Bodies on Stage* (London: Routledge, 1998).

36. See Iris Smith, "Brecht and the Mothers of Epic Theatre," *Theatre Journal* 43, no. 4 (1991).

37. See Elizabeth Sakellaridou, "Feminist Theatre and the Brechtian Tradition," in *Where Extremes Meet: Rereading Brecht and Beckett,* The Brecht Yearbook 27, ed. Antony Tatlow (Madison: University of Wisconsin Press, 2002), 179–98.

38. Heiner Müller, *Germania,* trans. Bernard and Caroline Schütze, ed. Sylvère Lotringer (New York: Semiotext[e], 1990), 133.

39. Kuhn and Constantine, "Texts by Brecht," 209.

40. Benjamin writes, "This important but poorly marked road, which may here serve as the image of a tradition, went via Roswitha and the mystery plays in the Middle Ages, via Gryphius and Calderon in the Baroque age. . . . It is a European road, but a German one as well—provided that we may speak of a road and not of a secret smugglers' path by which the legacy of the medieval and Baroque drama has reached us. It is this mule track, neglected and overgrown, which comes to light today in the dramas of Brecht" (Walter Benjamin, "What Is Epic Theatre," in *Illuminations,* trans. Harry Zohn, intro. Hannah Arendt [London: Fontana Press, 1992], 146).

41. See Robert Ackerman, *The Myth and Ritual School* (New York: Garland, 1991). For a full bibliography of the group's work, see Arlen Shelley, *The Cambridge Ritualists: An Annotated Bibliography* (Metuchen, NJ: Scarecrow Press, 1990).

42. Jameson, *Brecht and Method,* 168–69.

43. Samuel Beckett, *Worstward Ho* (1984) (London: Calder Publishers, 1999), 7: "Ever tried. Ever failed. No matter. Try again. Fail again. Fail better."

Transforming Polities and Selves
Greek Antiquity, West African Modernity

Timothy J. Reiss

Western thinkers have long stressed tragedy's uniqueness to Western culture, its absence from and inaccessibility to others. Against other Western practices, tragedy gives an extreme standard of judgment, a limit-case scale of comparison, a site where human freedom and fate, exaltation and angst, self and servitude, reason and unreason, individual and universe jostle each other. Against non-Western cultures, it offers a not just symbolic way to name invasive conflicts as "tragic" outcomes of fated historical processes for which the invader is thus not responsible, indeed, by which, as agent of these processes, he then "rightly" controls, even possesses, the "tragic" victims (mulatto, Indian, African, or other) of this noble "tragedy" of cultural conflict. Such notions have ruled Western thinking on tragedy since the late eighteenth century. They have done so because Western thinkers largely agree in their suppositions about the nature of a person and of being human in the world, so that, as Rita Felski says in her Introduction to this collection, even "critics of differing methodological and political stripes concur that tragedy undermines the sovereignty of selfhood and modern dreams of progress and perfectibility."[1] She thus accents that this thinking needs less a specific body of "tragedy" than local understandings and experiences of "self" and "subjectivity." These have a private self lodged in "homelessness and despair," a subject foiled in its desires, an individual in agonistic and agonized conflict with the universe, the gods, social ties, communicative incapacities, or psychological aporias.[2] Such ideas have been possible only since the late European seventeenth century, when this sense of an individual agent self became the dominant Western experience of a person, of how people knew their "who-ness."[3] So "rethinking tragedy" means rethinking this thinking no less than tragedy. Otherwise, our questions are repetitions and our answers, however seemingly diverse, tread the same ground. We must see the *locality* of thinking, and doing, before hoping to change them.

To alter the ground in times of political and epistemic fret is the more necessary apropos of tragedy. Its great eras have been those of social turmoil, political challenge, invention of new beginnings: ancient Athens and the ensuing thought of Socrates, Plato, Aristotle; sixteenth- and seventeenth-century Europe, with Hobbes and Locke; Romantic northern Europe with Hegel and Marx . . . In parts of the world tragedy is enabling anew vital debate and new futures. To approach these requires thinking within and without those European traditions: within, because historically they have been the sites of tragedy; without, because each time and place has its own horizons, possibilities, and assumptions of idea and act. Only of the West now or lately past can one write with C. L. R. James that Aeschylus and Shakespeare, Griffith and Chaplain "give three stages in the development of the individual man to his social environment which is the true history of humanity" or, with David Scott of James's concern that "tragedy both constitutes and enables a distinctive reflection upon subjectivity in moments of historical crisis."[4] Like Felski's, these formulations signal both tragedy's general seriousness and its local interpretation inside a particular, quite recent European horizon. Such expressions capture formally the need for rethinking that their authors emphasize.

Here, I first propose rethinking Greek tragedy, misapprehended via the application of modern Western forms of subjectivity, and through this to try to see why the demise of tragedy as playing a chief role in the self-understanding of the Athenian *polis* and so in the actual construction of fifth-century Greek political conditions coincided with the rise of the powerful political theorizing of Plato and Aristotle. Plato, we shall see, and the historical timing of tragedy's great moments suggest that the idea and practice of tragedy coincide with the event and thinking of new social and political beginnings. To follow this in the case of the Greeks, I rely on a different experience of the person from what is taken typically to be that of Western modernity. Second, bracketing five centuries of European practice of tragedy and thinking about tragedy and the tragic that do assume familiar Western "subjectivities," I turn to practices of tragedy adopted in Africa and the African diaspora since the 1960s, notably as ways to imagine the predicaments of colonization and the post-colony that rework elements of Greek tragedy in not dissimilar ways. They suggest, too, experiences of who-ness that may share more with that of the Greeks than modern Western ones, even as, by their historical context, they write against later Western tragedy and its assumptions of being and identity. Here, too, tragedy gives ways to understand events and offer new beginnings in fraught times of social turmoil and political challenge. Seeing African tragedy with that of ancient Athens illuminates the goals of both. Inasmuch as the Greeks, and Europeans into the eighteenth century (some even later), always acknowledged their debt to African culture, there may be deeper historical reasons for these proximities (which is not to reify African histories into some atemporality, but to recognize *longue durée* continuities).

A place to start is Plato's *Laws* 7.817b, with which George Steiner begins his essay in this collection. Reiterating *Republic*'s repudiation of art, especially drama, the Athenian tells Clinias that writers of tragedy are not needed in the good *polis,* for "we are ourselves authors of a tragedy, and that the finest and the best we know how to make. In fact, our whole polity has been constructed as a dramatization [*mimesis*] of [the] noble[st] and perfect life; that is what *we* hold in truth to be the most real of tragedies." As Steiner says, the passage raises serious questions. What does Plato mean by saying that the legislators of his new city are "authors of a tragedy," that this city is "the most real of tragedies" *because* it is "a [*mimesis*] of the noblest and perfect life"?

The word *mimesis* is key, crucial to the *polis* of *Laws* (and *Republic,* whose ostracism of theater *Laws* glosses here) as it is, too, to the idea of tragedy and to why as theater it is *therefore* unwanted in the city. The most noble and perfect life, charted in Plato's city, was always that of the philosopher seeking to regain that knowledge of Ideas whose intimate acquaintance was lost to the soul [*psuchè,* or life force] when it split from the ensouled substance [*ousia*] of the universe to enter a body. The new *polis* to be created reflects and embodies that search at the level of the collectivity, which is why the city is truly philosophical, and hopeful. But however hopeful, it is also a tragedy, since the search ineluctably sets the seeker against the limits of human possibility. For, since soul *is* embodied, it can never surmount its mimetic remove from the Idea of a noble and perfect life. Even such a life lived or *polis* realized is a distant *mimesis* of its reality as Idea. Texts like *Laws* and *Republic* are at a second mimetic remove: imitations of imitations of Ideas, at the same remove from Idea as any theatrical tragedy. Still, the goal of such political-theoretical texts is to give a direct model for real practice. It is the case that even if they enabled their *polis* to be achieved, it could only ever be an imperfect rendition, like the life of the perfect polity of Idea. Nonetheless, such a *polis,* because lived in the actual, would be "the most real of tragedies" possible in life, nearer the ideal than theatrical tragedy could ever be, itself always only a *mimesis* of such real action. This may explain why theatrical tragedy yielded, historically speaking, to political theory: the latter offers not just a clearer *mimesis* of the city but also a model for making the city a first order *mimesis,* an actually experienced search for the good life.

Political theory, in *Laws* as in *Republic*, makes the ideal polity a communal quest for the ideal personal life. This imbrication of the personal and the communal is also essential to tragedy as form—and practice: tragedy in fifth-century Athens being public, popular trial, and festival of its religious and political life by and before all its citizens. *Pace* Adorno, it is hard to think of a Western art practice that was less "the origin of the idea of aesthetic autonomy."[5] It involves, further, an unfamiliar apprehension of personhood, who-ness, itself webbed in community and the mimetic imperfection that I have just suggested was central to Plato's idea of city and tragedy alike. For ancient Greeks and others this imperfection was part of life. It was also what is *human* about life, which is why Seneca, half a millennium after Plato, called the ever-ongoing striving toward the good life a quest to be *humanior,* more human. It was a quest to establish a more harmonious balance between the many facets that composed a person, a quest that by definition could never come to an end.[6]

From before Plato, a person was felt as webbed in crowded surroundings. A person's presence in these surroundings was basic to being human, just as their combined presences were mutually essential elements of what it was to be a person. In Greco-Roman tradition until much later (ignoring other changes, and the probability that this was the principal rather than the only experience of who-ness), material world, society, family, rational mind (the being of *psuchè,* life force, soul), the divine and universal, named some of the "circles" that were a person. These circles, or "spheres"—as Cicero, Seneca, Hierocles, and Plutarch called them, cued by tradition reaching beyond Plato's *Republic, Timaeus,* and *Statesman*—did not "surround" a person who "fit" into them. They *were* what a person was: integral to my substance. At the same time they were public and collective, common to everyone qua human. They named existential spheres to which the person enlaced in them was in a *reactive* relation. I have detailed this relation and the sorts of experience involved in *Mirages of the Selfe,* using their Latin name of "passibility."[7] This is not passivity. Passibility names experiences of being whose common attribute is a sense of being *embedded in and acted on by* these circles—including the material world, biological, familial, and social ambiences, the soul's (or "animate") being, and cosmic, spiritual, or divine life. These circles "preceded" the person, which acted as *subjected to* forces working in complex ways from "outside." But because of the embedding, that "outside" imbued all aspects and elements of "inside"—of being a person.

Human agency, for example, entailed "acceptance" of actions preceding and enveloping their doer, acceptance due to anything from imperative constraint to rational consent. Reasoning and knowing meant slotting oneself into reasons and knowledge already present in the universe, having "one's life shaped by a pre-existent rational order," writes Charles Taylor of Plato.[8] Such experiences of doing and knowing grounded perceptions of the human capacities taken to enable them. "Will" did not name a capacity of an agent subject responsible for acts it alone chose. "Choice" did not name a solitary act of judgment founded on personal rights preceding collective intention. "Intention" did not name a purposive individual claim on rational enunciation or instrumental action. Intelligence of the terms translated as "will," "choice," and "intention"—as if essential to Western experiences of the subject (and concepts of tragedy)—involved a communally embedded sense of being human. As to "will," for example, the Greek terms always translated as denoting willed or unwilled actions, *hekousia* and *akousia,* denote not an agent's independent mental decision but such actions and their actor being in or out of kilter with *ousia,* the soul's or universe's "essence," or "substance." For human body and material world, embedding was physically literal: they were made of the same matter flowing between them. Too, this body was of "divine design," subjected to purposes whose study was for Aristotle a "cosmic inquiry" and on which Galen's *Usefulness of the Parts* was "an epic meditation" inspired by "awe."[9] Embeddedness was essential to these experiences of a person, different from anything familiar in the modern West—if not from other cultures' experiences. In this sense of who-ness, political society, family, cosmos, biological nature, and material world were ground and nature of personal being. A person, we shall see, could be torn apart by the final incommensurability of these spheres but could not be set against them as an "individual," integral as they were to the concept and experience of personhood.

In Plato, the circles or spheres of being began with the Demiurge's "eternal auto-rotation" (*Statesman* 269e5), continued in the circles and musical harmonies of stars and planets (*Republic* 616–17), and wended through the world and human souls, forms and motions, to include all *circum*stances that were what it was to be human (*Timaeus*). Fulfillment of human *logos* required all these; fulfillment of simple humanity required trying to keep them in balance; that trying made one *humanior,* especially as one knew it could never end. This was so not just because humans were mimetically distant from perfection; such perfection would itself make one inhuman. If you could, for instance, achieve a balance among the spheres of your being so perfect as to enable you to be unmoved by the emotional and material consequences of violence and evil, you would simultaneously cut yourself off, by this lack of feeling, from all that constitutes human society, losing the empathy also essential to being human. To attain the impassibility of total harmony, of Idea itself or of the demiurge, would be to deny humans' passible nature, that nature by which the person was its suffering from and reaction to the slings and arrows of its many spheres. It would also deny the reciprocity of services, exchanges of giving and receiving, and transfer of benefits essential to the welfare and stability of society. It would deny the dialectic of person, community, and world. Actually to attain the "noble and perfect life" would be to become inhuman, literally *unworldly.* It would mark a breach with and of personal and communal being that "is a tragedy every time."[10]

This sense of a person makes it wrong to apply modern psychological and moral concepts like self, will, intention, or independent action to antiquity and its auto-representations. Scholars have shown that for the Greeks one's sense of who-ness came largely from *being seen, subjected to, suffering* another's gaze. To be human was to be present *for* others. Like embeddedness in general, *presentness* for others was no chance property of being human, a relation to be chosen or not. It was essential to being (grounding all possible "choices"). This is how Froma Zeitlin can show that *Oedipus the King* insisted in plot and language on the multiplicity of Oedipus' "self": he is *there* for and by many others.[11] So when Oedipus shreds his eyes he marks, makes, not just exclusion from kingship, Thebes, and family love (especially using the pin of Jocasta's brooch), but from humanity. He knows at last that while he may have rivaled the famously impassible Sphinx, as a human he cannot *be* impassible, in perfect harmony. Nor can he will knowledge as his own. The seeing and *logos* in which he put repeated faith were ever imperfect imitations of knowledge received (suffered) from "without." Like all, he could assent to certain "*re*actions," but the actions *suffered* were processes into which the actor was absorbed, to which he was fitted. Thus his blinded cry:

> Apollo, friends, Apollo—
> he ordained my agonies—these my pains on pains!
> But the hand that struck my eyes was mine,
> mine alone—no one else—
> I did it all myself! (ll.1329–33)[12]

The protagonist of *Oedipus at Colonus* glosses this *acceptance* of action experienced as *reaction*: "my acts / were sufferings [*pathea*] more than actions outright" (ll.266–67).[13] His recognition that striving to be *humanior* is accession to "external" constraints and acts as much as or more than personal governance and that their (im)balance is humanity's condition is why Theseus can adopt *this* Oedipus in pity as the city's protection against terror.[14] Not just in pity: Oedipus at Colonus knows the embedded nature of the human, knows that imperfect action is the human condition, always, therefore, a *process* toward an always-distant perfection. Such knowledge is needed for the city's welfare and well-being. The new Oedipus does not just protect against external terror, he wards off future King Oedipoi.

The experience of being acted on in the spheres that compose whoness is one with being tied to those whose looks and speech make him who he is—as his do them. This is the sense of his cry and his blinding, one the messenger's report deepens. He names not eyes but the "joint of the spheres" [*arthron tôn kuklôn*], a phrase troubling to translators, who make it "eyeballs," "eye sockets," or some such. But Sophocles named not just the eyes Oedipus destroyed. He named disarticulation of his very spheres of being. This phrase and its intractability to any simple or brief translation sharply underscore that language is medium and container of complex cultural memory and understanding, experience and tradition. As the phrase becomes comprehensible only when one sees the assumptions about person, world, and community that it embraces, so it also reminds us that tragedy, whatever its continuities, is always embedded in particular local horizons, possibilities, and assumptions of experience, idea, and act.

Oedipus had thought to put an end to the process of striving for the noble and perfect life, in the form of knowledge assuring the city's, people's, his family's, and his own welfare. In the issue, the good of the knowledge, the good of the city, the good of the House of Thebes, even the good of Oedipus' initial confidence in their conjunction, are shown in tension, needing to be *balanced*—which is exactly why humans can never reach impassible harmony: the goods of the many spheres that I am differ in their perfections. These differences characterize our whoness, as "plural" as Kathleen Sands holds truth to be—and for the same reasons.[15] They are why the noble life is ever process, never end. To erase the differences is to become inhuman, to accept them, *humanior*—as is the struggle for the deepest consonance of being's spheres. It is also human to forget that this consonance and these spheres are always imitations of ideals and therefore necessarily imperfect. *Oedipus the King* is exemplary of how tragedy heightens mimetic imperfection. Still, like all tragedy, it *shows* and so *contains* that imperfection, its implications and consequences: it does not just nonplus its audience but shows how striving for the noble life, in Oedipus what would be balance of deed, knowledge, and "character"—*praxis, logos, ethos* (the last always a *result, a construct,* of *praxis*)[16]—conflicts with communal practice, custom, and credence (in explicit opposition to those voicing collective acts, beliefs, warnings: Creon, Tiresias, Jocasta, the Chorus) and brings exile from the city. Depicting humans caught *in their essential being* between incommensurable and ever-imperfect goods, tragedy was always political, showing effects of human action on the *polis.* But the nature of who-ness and conditions of possibility for that who-ness to be and to *re*act make the politics and the effects quite other than those of later tragedy, enabling something new, but not in the same way as would a Shakespeare, or differently again a Melville, or yet again modern writers in altogether different cultural contexts.[17]

Tragedy was not rare, not for Plato, Aristotle, or ancient Greece generally, with its many tragic authors and vastly more tragedies, though a decimal point percentage of them survives—and the idea of "absolute tragedies" excludes most of these, making "tragedy" indeed "rare"! Even if we did not know these numbers, Plato's repeated exclusion of tragedies from the *polis* would be inexplicable were they so rare. On the contrary, tragedies were as many as they were capacious: the striving to be more human *could* end in catastrophe; it could also end in good fortune (tragedy is not "tragic because someone dies").[18] I suggest that Plato feared tragedy in the city not because of its extremity, but because it *showed* that human striving for the good and noble life, to become *humanior,* was ineluctably limited, and that striving and limit alike were basic to human life. Made of plural spheres, a person could never reconcile their diverse goods. Living in a world of mimesis, a person could never attain final truth (hence, perhaps, Aristotle's preference for tragedies ending fortunately). That tragedies explored and showed these limits through a form that amplified and made more aesthetically moving not just what Aristotle called their terror and pity but their possible exalted grandeur—the paradox imaged in Oedipus—made them the more attractive. Oedipus' reasoned quest for knowledge broke royal power and the spheres of his being, disjoined the bonds that made him human. To think to be *humanissimus* was in fact to be less human. Thus, to perform tragedy in the city striving for human perfection could subvert its stated goal, just as, the discussants agreed in Book 2 of *Republic,* it could be subversive to tell anything about the gods that might mislead, above all that god was author of anything but the good. To reject evil from the city, whose citizen's indivisible bonds with divine *ousia* we have just seen, is of a piece with the rejection of tragedy.[19]

I say "could," though, because the performance or the telling undermines the *polis* only to the extent that imperfection is confused with hopelessness or evil, a confusion whose correction was a task of *Republic*'s education in *harmonia:* then we grasp that to set person and community in harmony—at *all* possible levels—is always a process. It can never end: "imperfection" is a statement about human becoming. What tragedy shows then, as the fifth-century festivals implied, was that the *polis* was at its best when in a state of continual debate and process. In tragedy, and not just for Aristotle, the mutability of human *praxeis* was more crucial than misfortune.[20] Hope depicts becoming; hopelessness posits an end that humans fail in trying to reach. But if you could reach that end, you would be inhuman, cutting yourself off from human community (the two are one). The thought saps Plato's ideal: ending becoming, his city would embody inhumanity. Tragedy was not deprivation of hope. Rather was it promise, fear, exaltation of the possibilities of change and becoming, ever marked by mimetic distance from absolutes. In art as in the city, such *mimetic* distance, defining human making and ideal truth, seems a version, fitted to a different conception of the human, of the subject/object tension that Adorno held vital to genuine art.[21] Not accidentally did Aristotle begin the *Poetics* by asserting *mimesis* as the first activity characterizing humans: *mimesis,* especially that taking the form of tragedy (setting aside Plato's injunctions, let's recall that the *Poetics* is chiefly about tragedy),[22] was as basic to humans as being rational, endowed with language, and sociable. For humans were humans, too, as a particular community. Tragedy shows us what kind, as it shows us how person and community fit. That Plato's rejection aims to benefit community is crucial in showing that *his* community was not the one whose rupture Oedipus' wracking of his spheres so terribly underscored. Plato's community would be something new. So would be those of later "organic" tragedy, that which, grounded in its local culture and moment, responded to and changed thought and experience.

Greek tragedy supposes a personhood and community not readily identifiable, let alone experienced, by modern Westerners. It also supposes mimesis as a constant striving toward action in the world. If, for Aristotle, *mimesis* was perhaps even more basic to human nature than reason and language, it was so because it provided the creative power the other two required for worldly action. It enabled *poiesis,* founding

271

in turn all human becoming. Tragedy was the supreme poetic form of such *mimesis,* giving a *"mimesis* of [human] action and life," out of which flow *ethos, logos,* and all aspects of human becoming. Tragedy itself imaged that becoming, developing from the dithyramb and earlier mimetic forms. In the process of that development it became a way to create and understand the life of the *polis.* I want to suggest that the practice and thinking of tragedy in Africa and its diaspora since the early 1960s explicitly echo this creative idea of tragedy, grounding tragedies of the postcolony that write back against Western claims for tragedy and Western claims *tout court* in an understanding of mimesis, who-ness, and community that has many analogies with Greek ideas and experiences.[23] Reworkings of or intertextual references to Greek tragedy give ways to think about social conditions and renew society, echoing the goals and power of ancient tragedy in new ways and with new applications. Certainly, these cases come from and are aimed at an elite, often a university, colonial-language audience, but that may also be the audience that has the best chance at real political and cultural action.[24]

Here, I shall name only a few widely performed tragedies to suggest how their producers' conception of mimesis, community, and who-ness does overlap with and renew the Greek patterns just suggested, turning them to give meaning to critical contemporary dilemmas, at the same time using them to set those meanings in local traditions and ways of understanding. This last is not to assert an atemporal realm of tradition possessed of some imaginary purity and somehow "truer" to the "African spirit" than the overlay of Western modernity to which colonization submitted it. Nor is it to suggest that all peoples of Africa are the same or differ in like ways from peoples of Europe (or other continents). It is to say with Amilcar Cabral that people's self-understanding requires that "they return to the upward paths of their own culture" even as they recognize and adapt "contributions from the oppressor's culture." It is to say with Aimé Césaire that cultures mingle their histories. It is to say with Achille Mbembe that at issue is "an *interlocking* of presents, pasts, and futures that retain their depths of other presents, pasts, and futures, each age bearing, altering, and maintaining the previous ones."[25] I shall return to this at the end, for it is important to understand that we have not to choose between "modernity" and myth, history and tradition. The issue is that of different histories and of modernities that differ *because* inflected by these histories. As Mbembe again puts it, from the fifteenth century African societies have been "embedded in times and rhythms heavily conditioned by European domination" (9). There is no "distinctive historicity," if by that we mean a still-existing original "purity." But nor is this to suggest that everyone inhabits the same modernity. Indeed, tragedies can show just how they do not.

Plays like the Nigerian John Pepper Clark-Bekederemo's 1961 *Song of a Goat* and 1964 *The Masquerade* refer generally to Greek tragedy. The very title of the first makes it a meditation on tragedy, its themes of fertility and procreation recall the Spring festival of Dionysus, many of its characters echo those of familiar Greek plays, Tiresias, Cassandra, Oedipus . . . The play offers ways to understand local villagers' lives, actions, and their results, invoking the dilemmas created for the community by one acting individually against collective interests. The curse of impotence laid on the hero for having contravened traditional demands by returning his leprous father's body for burial in the village means that he no longer plays his part in his people's survival and growth. The fatal consequences of incest and suicide, continued as murder to *The Masquerade*'s next generation, overlays its traditionalist construal with a warning about all such confrontations: actual cultural conflicts, even in the heady postindependence year of 1961 but especially by 1964, whether from European or local differences, might have mortal consequences. By the second play's date the real political tensions were growing that within two years would lead to a disastrous crisis and a year later to civil war when Biafra sought to secede. In 1964, too, Clark wrote *The Raft,* another play deeply inflected by the Greeks, again bedded in the land, sea, and sky immensities of the playwright's Niger Delta homeland and again meditating on Nigeria's drift toward catastrophe, as was immediately apparent to its spectators and commentators.

The irony, but appropriateness, of referencing a profoundly European cultural form to show these dangers might not have been lost on Wole Soyinka, one member of these plays' original audiences, who was to produce his own riff on a Greek tragedy in his 1973 *The Bacchae of Euripides,* a play subtitled *A Communion Rite,* and one that he required be played as "a tumultuous celebration of life."[26] Three years after the end of the Biafran War in 1970, Soyinka still had an optimistic take on the political and cultural future, as he explored decolonization (the destruction of Pentheus as that of political domination and slavery). The end of his *Bacchae,* gathering its protagonists to celebrate a new beginning around Pentheus' head, now spurting blood that turns out to be wine, is not just an upturning of Euripides' bleak ending. It also reworks the Eucharist to that new celebration, Eucharist that had been one of the major sacraments of that missionary Christianity central to the imposition of European dominion. Reworking cultural artifacts to new ends (and beginnings) is also central to these uses of tragedy.[27]

Soyinka's optimistic future may yet be proven only deferred, but political and cultural facts on the ground now make the romance of his *Bacchae* inadequate, like that of James's 1938 *The Black Jacobins:* there will be no linear accession to "progress" by ready transferral of a familiar past into a fortunate future. Neocolonial disaster demands new ways to tell how people might "integrate in the present [their] conceptions of [their] past and [their] expectations of the future."[28] There must be acknowledgment and consequences of imperfections, past and present moving toward "possible futures [that] seem less certain than they once did."[29] Scott argues that tragedy might offer such a new way, and he shows that from the 1938 to the 1963 edition of *The Black Jacobins* James altered his narrative from romance to tragedy, refiguring his understanding of Toussaint Louverture and offering, even enabling, different cultural and political futures. In Soyinka's *Bacchae,* Pentheus' wine may be a ritual turning of an imposed Eucharist but it is also wine whose grapes the now ex-slaves have harvested, making their once-tormented labor a vital element of a new society, where they are as indispensable as its rulers. Where before nature was exploited for luxuries for the elite, now its products forge a more harmonious society. No longer is nature "a background to men's activity or something to be conquered and used. It is part of man, at every turn physically, intellectually and emotionally, and man is part of it."[30] At the play's outset nature was part of the slaves' torture; at the end it is part of a new community.

For tragedy in Africa, like much art in the Third World, is rooted in the sociopolitical—*making,* not allegorizing it. It mimics it in Plato's or Aristotle's sense, with images that are *not* that world but that use its live continuities and connections to set "real-life events . . . in the emotionally and philosophically charged discourse of literary tragedy," enabling reflection on them by *ordering* their contingent events and thus advancing understanding and so action within them—the very understanding and action that Plato feared, bringing people to "engagement with their history."[31] These histories involve cultural realities very different from the modern West, and in their mutual articulation lie these tragedies' power and meaning. Soyinka argues that traditional Yoruba drama inspects "harmony in the universe," its ever incompleteness, and human challenges to it; but also that those challenges demand that the universe reorder itself in a "cosmic adjustment."[32]

Conceptions of human and cosmic incompleteness and adjustment recall the Greeks, as they help us read Ola Rotimi's redoing of *Oedipus*. *The Gods Are Not to Blame* (1968) opens at Ogun's shrine, where Baba Fakunle, "oldest and most knowing/of all Ifa priests," is to divine "the future that this boy/has brought/with him," telling King Adetusa and Queen Ojuola "what it is that the boy has brought/as mission from the gods/to carry out on earth." Like Oedipus, Rotimi's Odewale has a specific future, but he has it as a "mission from the gods." It aims to open deeper springs of humanity and renew the spirit. Breaking "taboos," it may "compel the cosmos to delve deeper into its essence," to repeat Soyinka. The unborn has knelt before Olodumare, father of the gods, to choose this mission freely from among the many possible futures the deity offers, although the soul cannot yet know the trajectory the choice will give to its embodied life. Nor can anyone know if a mission is good or bad, because no human can measure the needs of the cosmos. It is a destiny that cannot be altered, although it can be subject to some negotiations by the person, by ancestors, by deities, by certain communal interventions. But anyone who tries actually to prevent a mission by killing its bearer will be punished by the Creator.[33] Belief that a person's life is directed by such a destiny chosen by the soul and approved by a creator deity is shared by many West African cultures.

In Odewale's case the mission will mean killing his father and wedding his mother. Adetusa and Ojuola aim to avert it by "sacrificing" Odewale to the gods.[34] Seeking to annul his mission, his parents oppose divine decision and we know they will be punished for it. Odewale himself constantly invokes Ogun as god of the roads, of lightning, of iron implements (whether warrior's sword or farmer's plough), of jointure of human and divine. Indeed, as a farmer shaping the land, as a healer using its products to heal the village community from sickness, and as a soldier-king defeating their enemies in war to renew the collectivity, Odewale not seldom is close to being identified with Ogun. Unlike Oedipus, always at odds with Apollo's intent (and messages), Odewale embodies Ogun and, we must therefore suppose, the will of the gods. A person's coming into life as bearer of some divine will, his or her carrying it out as a small means of adjusting the cosmos, embedded always in the land (as farmer and healer), in the community in many different ways cannot but remind us of Greek experiences of personhood. They may not be like, but they are certainly analogous to the "multiple" and "embedded" who-ness of ancient persons.

This itself may be a reason why Greek tragedy can be so readily taken over and transformed to such effect. I am reminded here of *Edufa,* a play by the Ghanaian playwright Efua Sutherland that rewrites Euripides' *Alcestis.* Here, Edufa (the Admetus figure) sacrifices Ampoma (Alcestis) in order to live and enjoy his wealth longer, wealth that he has acquired by Western capitalist means, thinking that his "modern"-ness can defeat the claims of past, present, and future, of the ties that bind the human and the divine, of those that establish community. At a crucial moment in this play, when Kankam, Edufa's father, has been demanding that his son tell the truth about the evil trick he played on his now-dying wife to obtain her choice to die in his place, Edufa accuses him of lying and asks whether he is not mad. Kankam falls silent in shock and then exclaims: "*Nyame* above! To say father and call me mad! My *ntoro* within you shivers with the shock of it!" The appeal to the supreme divinity (*Onyame*) and to his *ntoro,* one of the four elements of the soul in Akan belief, this one passed through the father and embodiment of inherited traits, is again a reminder of a local sense of person and community.[35]

In Sutherland's rewriting of *Alcestis,* Ampoma remains dead and Edufa ends up mad himself. Edufa has flouted traditional experience too far.[36] This seems a very different ending from *The Gods Are Not to Blame.* To be sure, Odewale blinds himself and leaves the village. But he does so in the company of his four children and noting that he is taking to the road again, as he has done so many times before in his life in a gesture epitomizing his embodiment of Ogun, god of the roads. He heals himself and the village, reaffirming ties between humans and the divine, person and community. But in *Gods,* Rotimi also sought to intervene directly in critical political debate. Rotimi himself and many others interpreted the play's title as referring to the Biafran War, which had broken out in July 1967 and was by now increasingly savage and bitter. The unblamable gods would be the super- and not-so-superpowers whom many held guilty of the outbreak and continuance of war. Elechi Amadi (a novelist and member of a minority group in Biafra hostile to the Ibo-led secession) writes of the "countless protest marches . . . made against Britain, the Soviet Union and even the United States of America" in eastern Nigeria by May 1967.[37] To split Biafra from Nigeria would diminish a potentially supremely powerful African state, remove its most educated and technically skilled population, and put a land rich in raw materials yet more at the mercy of Western economic and political interests. Too, Nigeria's collapse would show Western racists that "the black man cannot run a big, prosperous state." Majority Ibos saw independent Biafra, "with its manpower resources and the revenue from oil" (eastern Nigeria having all the country's reserves) as a nation able soon "to compete with the developed nations in economic and technological advancement," ignoring the contrary wish of their many minorities.[38] Biafra's secession could be a gain to petroleum multinationals, keeping Nigeria together was of equal interest to Britain, the state's creator, one-time colonial ruler, and neocolonial leaders' Svengali. Even if it failed, civil war would leave furies to utterly divisive effect—as the case proved. The continuing intervention of colonial oppression is also that of individualist tyranny and of effectively totalitarian economic, military, and political demands.

To all this, Odewale opposes not just the idea but also the act of a single person *within,* as essentially *part of,* what James calls a now fundamentally *"panoramic"* world, "one of constantly increasing multiplicity of relations between [the person], immense mechanical constructions and social organizations of world-wide scope." James finds it in *Pequod*'s crew's "ever-present sense of community," whose success depends on people doing mutually necessary "types of work . . . It is this specific type of work which determines their social characteristics."[39] In *The Gods Are Not to Blame,* what makes Odewale's world panoramic is rather the experience of the multiple relations between the born and unborn, gods and humans, person and community. These relations and the "unified encounter" they posit are why some hold *all* African drama to be the "celebration" Soyinka insisted on for his *Bacchae.* They are also why, by 1974 for performance, Rotimi had accentuated this aspect of *Gods,* suffusing the play "with a good number of dances, songs and dirges borrowed from [the] indigenous artistic repertoire," especially dirges at the play's end.[40] The subliminal presence of Western oppression and its culture gives *this* panorama special force. Himself half Ijaw and half Yoruba, Rotimi was always attuned to the necessities of diversity and community, whatever its difficulties. The Biafran breach perhaps had its echo in the play not just in the wars and soldiering so central to it but also in the broken taboos, whose breach and healing have led to a deeper sense of a community of humans, the world and the gods, even as they show human imperfection in achieving life's mission and all efforts to imitate ideals, the gods.

These imperfections and contradictions are grave. Inside, within Odewale's cultural horizon, not only is knowledge of life's mission bound to remain imperfect, but two social and cultural compulsions, one positive, one negative, directly contradict each other. Custom dictates that the new king wed the widowed queen. But Ojuola is Odewale's mother (as no one knows), and obeying that peremptory claim breaches incest taboos. The human world is always ethically ambiguous, and that is also a reason why one cannot know if a destiny is good or bad. Outside Western impositions build further contradictions of freedom and fate (in the form of economic coercion and underdevelopment, greater technological provision and military capacity), mastery (Odewale's, for instance) and contingency (just *who* is to "blame"?), invulnerability (Ogun's and that of what he represents) and fragility (the enduring threat of Western intervention), knowledge and ignorance.[41]

This returns us to Plato and others for whom mimesis recreates nature's work, remakes cultures torn by oppression. It is the mimesis of origin. Toward the beginning of *The Birth of Tragedy,* Nietzsche recalls Silenus, Dionysus' companion, captured by Midas and replying under duress to the king's question as to what would be best and most desirable for humans, laughing: "What would be best for you is quite beyond your reach: not to have been born, not to *be,* to be *nothing.*"[42] No one can be in this state because being cannot be nonbeing. But inasmuch as the world (or God, or the demiurge, of Onyame, or Olodumare) creates being from nonbeing, so humans, through mimesis, create not just art but community and history. Indeed, that humans dwell in histories is another reason why Nietzsche's "nothing" has no location. He was echoing the Chorus of *Oedipus at Colonus:*

> Not to be born is best
> when all is reckoned in, but once a man has seen the light
> the next best thing, by far, is to go back
> back where he came from, quickly as he can.[43] (ll.1224–27)

The Chorus speaks as Oedipus is about to meet and damn Polynices for setting out to destroy Thebes and before we know Oedipus' final apotheosis as protector of a renewed Athenian society. However equivocal a hope that might have been as Athens was going down to defeat in the wars against the Spartan alliance, *that* is nonetheless what the tragedy was showing its audience. As Hannah Arendt observed of this same passage, it was this future *polis,* the new "space of men's free deeds and living words, which could endow life with splendour."[44]

Like Greek tragedies, these recent African ones anticipate this future, via experiences of mimesis, community, and who-ness that strikingly resemble those we saw through Plato (to say nothing of these dramas' often vital use of music and dance). They are as deeply embedded as were those ancient ones in their contemporary polities and the modernity that is these polities' necessary context. At the same time, local histories come into play to inflect that modernity in particular ways. This is the opposite of belief in a realm of African tradition outside the influence of modernity. What Clark-Bekederemo, Rotimi, Soyinka, Sutherland, Sylvain Bemba (in his *Noces posthumes de Santigone*), and others advance is to re-establish not an autonomous "authentic realm" fixed in static atemporality, an Other of Western history, but traditions that are *part of* African modernity—more precisely, of African and other modernities. They do not oppose Africa to the West, a stance that a cultural (as opposed to political) version of Negritude serves to warn against. They avoid both the problems of homogenizing claims of hybridity and those of "opposition."

In the third lecture of his 1999 *The Burden of Memory, the Muse of Forgiveness,* entitled "Negritude and the Gods of Equity," Soyinka revisited some of the issues, concluding luminously with a story of the royal balafon captured around 1230 by the army of Soundiata Keita, founder of the empire of Mali, from his enemy Soumare Kante, king of Soso. Guarded for the next eight centuries by the family of Soundiata's griot, Bala Fasseke Kouyate, this famous instrument, the Sosso-Bala, was taken outside the now Republic of Guinea for the first time in 1996 to be played in Paris at Léopold Sédar Senghor's ninetieth birthday celebrations. This balafon, "born out of conflict, of a bloody struggle for power and the travails of nation building" was "at once an embodiment of history, yet insulated from it, giving off its own statement of harmony and resolution." This "simple, unassuming xylophone" was both an embodiment of history, one that includes violent African wars and nation-building and later slavery and colonization, and a metaphor for the power of art and thought to create harmonies that retain "the near intolerable burden of memory" even as they produce analyses and understandings that go beyond it.[45]

There is nothing inauthentic about the Sosso-Bala or the female griot who performed with it in Paris. The histories that instrument, performance, and performer make present are as authentic as the mission Odewale accomplishes and as exact as the commentary on the Biafran War that the representation of that accomplishment simultaneously enables. *This* authenticity of multiple histories establishes clear cultural and political distinctions while leaving room for transcultural interchange (something that Fanon and Cabral, among others, argued for long ago). Such "authenticity" means neither stasis nor singularity of meaning. What Soyinka does not say is that different versions of Soundiata's epic, all equally "authentic," may capture different histories and analyses: the common proposal that Soundiata defeated an essentially evil, purely imperialist Soumare, for example, is upturned by a version performed by Wâ Kamissoko, who gave Soumare's reason for going to war his desire to stop the slave trade of the regional kings that was destroying their victim peoples.[46] That Kamissoko comes from the lands that were Sosso explains the difference. Authenticity, that is, has nothing to do with stasis or any singular history, geography, or economy. Nor does it set some African atemporality against any Western modernity. On the contrary, it provides ways of understanding the specificity of histories that have to be conceived as elements of modernity, building contemporary social and political actualities from local "linguistic affinities, economic reality, and geographic proximity" grounded in their own histories and "patterns of consumption."[47] This is what Soumare's balafon does, no less than Clark-Bekederemo's *Song of a Goat,* Rotimi's *The Gods Are Not to Blame,* Soyinka's *Bacchae of Euripides,* or Sutherland's *Edufa.* Their tragedies show that the understanding and creating of new spaces and places can always only ever be a work in progress, building the new imperfectly out of many histories, geographies, and economies. Undivine reason has no other way to create; so rational creation is always also doomed to the imperfection the Greeks perceived and whose perils and paradoxes their and these modern tragedies perform.

Notes

1. Rita Felski, "Introduction," *Rethinking Tragedy: New Literary History* 35, no. 1 (2004): xii. I thank Patricia Penn Hilden and Rita Felski for their careful readings of this essay.

2. The quoted phrase partly describes Ishmael of *Moby Dick,* in C. L. R. James's study of it as *the* representative novel of Western modernity: *Mariners, Renegades, and Castaways: The Story of Herman Melville and the World We Live In,* 2nd ed. (1978; rpt. London: Allison & Busby, 1985), 47. I shall return to James and his strong thinking on the uses of tragedy.

3. Timothy J. Reiss, *Mirages of the Selfe: Patterns of Personhood in Ancient and Early Modern Europe* (Stanford: Stanford University Press, 2003).

4. "Popular Art and the Cultural Tradition," in *The C. L. R. James Reader,* ed. Anna Grimshaw (Oxford: Blackwell, 1992), 251; David Scott, *Conscripts of Modernity: The Tragedy of Colonial Enlightenment* (Durham, NC: Duke University Press, 2004), 12. That tragedy has historically reflected on and furthered sociopolitical crises is a main theme of my *Tragedy and Truth: Studies in the Development of a Renaissance and Neoclassical Discourse* (New Haven: Yale University Press, 1980), especially 2–4, 282–302, and of the entry "Tragedy," in *The New Princeton Encyclo-*

pedia of Poetry and Poetics, completely revised, ed. Alex Preminger and T. V. F. Brogan, with Frank J. Warnke, O. B. Hardison Jr., and Earl Miner (Princeton: Princeton University Press, 1993), 224–28. For James this is a major aspect of tragedy: see, for example, "Whitman and Melville," "Letters to Literary Critics," in James, *Reader,* 214, 231; and James, *Mariners,* 124.

5. Theodor W. Adorno, *Aesthetic Theory,* trans. and ed. Robert Hullot-Kentor (Minneapolis: University of Minnesota Press, 1997), 6. James, too, is insistent that Athenian tragedy "was first and foremost a popular drama" which the entire community of the "whole city-state" glossed and judged: "Letters to Literary Critics," in James, *Reader,* 221, cf. 232; "Popular Art" in James, *Reader,* 250–51, 257; *American Civilization,* ed. Anna Grimshaw and Keith Hart (Oxford: Blackwell, 1993), 149–58.

6. These aspects of Seneca are the matter of chapter 5 of *Mirages of the Selfe.*

7. This paragraph and the next are adapted from *Mirages* to this new context of tragedy.

8. Charles Taylor, *Sources of the Self: The Making of the Modern Identity* (Cambridge, MA: Harvard University Press, 1989), 124.

9. Shigehisa Kuriyama, *The Expressiveness of the Body and the Divergence of Greek and Chinese Medicine* (New York: Zone, 1999), 157, 123.

10. Jacob Burckhardt, *Judgments on History and Historians,* trans. Harry Zohn (Indianapolis: Liberty Fund, 1999), 6. Burckhardt judges the difference of personal being to be why "today's 'educated man' can no longer understand Antiquity" (5). I found these remarks only after writing this essay, though they will not surprise those who know Burckhardt's *Civilization of the Renaissance in Italy,* with its claims about the very different humanity of the Middle Ages.

11. Froma Zeitlin, "Thebes: Theater of Self and Society in Athenian Drama," in *Greek Tragedy and Political Theory,* ed. J. Peter Euben (Berkeley: University of California Press, 1986), 111.

12. Sophocles, *The Three Theban Plays: Antigone, Oedipus the King, Oedipus at Colonus,* trans. Robert Fagles, intro. and notes Bernard Knox (Harmondsworth, UK: Penguin, 1984), 241.

13. Fagles's translation, with minor adjustments, 299. The line numbers (as before) and the Greek are from the Loeb *Sophocles,* ed. and trans. Hugh Lloyd-Jones, 3 vols. (Cambridge, MA: Harvard University Press, 1994–96).

14. Cf. Terry Eagleton's concluding paragraph to his "Commentary" in this volume.

15. Kathleen M. Sands, "Tragedy, Theology, and Feminism in the Time After Time," in *Rethinking Tragedy: New Literary History* 35, no. 1 (2004): 44.

16. Only by and *after praxis* is *ethos* developed and clarified, only when ended do "actions take on their true significance and agents, through what they have in reality accomplished without realizing it, discover their true identity": Jean-Pierre Vernant and Pierre Vidal-Naquet, *Myth and Tragedy in Ancient Greece,* trans. Janet Lloyd (New York: Zone, 1990), 45.

17. The subject phrase of this sentence is a reworking, against the idea of "volitional subjectivity," of a phrase from David Scott, *Conscripts of Modernity: The Tragedy of Colonial Enlightenment* (Durham, NC: Duke University Press, 2004), 107.

18. Simon Critchley, "I Want to Die, I Hate My Life—Phaedra's Malaise," *Rethinking Tragedy,* 34. That tragedies end in catastrophe is also Steiner's view. This inaccuracy is unhelpful: Reiss, *Tragedy and Truth,* 1–39 and passim.

19. Jean de Serres, early translator of Plato, glossed the Book 2 passage precisely in terms of telling god as author of evil: *Platonis opera quae extant omnia,* [trans. and ed.] Joannis Serrani, [corr.] Henrici Stephani, 4 vols. (n.p.: Henr. Stephanus, 1578), 2:379, where he added in the margin that the good of the commonwealth required that some other topos offset "these lying tales . . . that make God evil."

20. John Jones, *On Aristotle and Greek Tragedy* (New York: Oxford University Press, 1962), 47. His exact remark is quoted here by Page duBois, "Toppling the Hero: Polyphony in the Tragic City," *Rethinking Tragedy,* 68. Many of this collection's authors agree.

21. Adorno, *Aesthetic Theory,* for example, 346–52. The *different conception* of the human lies in how the tragedy of Ahab (embodiment of the totalitarian mind) is that he individualistically "cut himself off from all humanity," in an "isolation . . . so complete that he no longer has any sense of relation with other human beings at all" (James, *Mariners,* 65, 68).

22. If we accept the tenth-century *Tractatus Coislinianus* as a genuine epitome of the "lost" second half of the *Poetics,* it then seems that Aristotle described comedy as a formal echo of tragedy, exchanging pleasure and laughter for terror and pity.

23. In *Against Autonomy: Global Dialectics of Cultural Exchange* (Stanford: Stanford University Press, 2002), 133–49, and rather differently in "Using Tragedy Against Its Makers: Some African and Caribbean Instances," in *A Companion to Tragedy,* ed. Rebecca Bushnell (Oxford: Blackwell, 2005), 507–10, I have shown how Derek Walcott takes off from Nietzsche to propose this connection.

24. African critics distinguish popular and university ("elite") drama. The distinction concerns indigenous versus colonial languages as much as it does performance practices. Performance may cross more often than language, although dramatic multilingualism is not uncommon.

25. Amilcar Cabral, *Unity and Struggle: Speeches and Writings,* trans. Michael Wolfers (London: Heinemann, 1980), 143; Aimé Césaire, *Discourse on Colonialism,* trans. Joan Pinkham (New York: Monthly Review Press, 1972), 11; Achille Mbembe, *On the Postcolony* (Berkeley: University of California Press, 2001), 16 (his italics).

26. Wole Soyinka, *The Bacchae of Euripides: A Communion Rite* (1973; rpt. New York: Norton, 1974), "Production Note" (unpaginated). But see also below, note 40 and accompanying text.

27. These and other plays are explored at greater length in "Using Tragedy,"

in Bushnell, *A Companion to Tragedy,* 505–36. Here my goal is not introductory or close analysis but showing how these plays enable rethinking what tragedy is about.

28. James, "Popular Art," in *C. L. R. James Reader,* 247. For James all great art creates the new (e.g., "The Artist," 185–86, and "The Olympia Statues, Picasso's *Guernica* and the Frescoes of Michelangelo in the Capella Paolina," in *The Future in the Present,* 226–34), but tragedy especially does (e.g., *Mariners,* 124).

29. Scott, *Conscripts,* 20.

30. James, *Mariners,* 93.

31. Ato Quayson, *Calibrations: Reading for the Social* (Minneapolis: University of Minnesota Press, 2003), 58, 74. This is Scott's argument, too.

32. Wole Soyinka, *Myth, Literature, and the African World* (Cambridge: Cambridge University Press, 1976), 156.

33. William R. Bascom, "Social Status, Wealth, and Individual Differences among the Yoruba," *American Anthropologist* 53, no. 4 (1951): 492; Michael Etherton, *The Development of African Drama* (New York: Africana Publishing, 1982), 124; Ola Rotimi, *Understanding the Gods Are Not to Blame* (Lagos: Kurunmi Adventures Publication, 1984), 3–4; Barry Hallen, *The Good, the Bad, and the Beautiful: Discourse About Values in Yoruba Culture* (Bloomington: Indiana University Press, 2000), 51–52, 63–64.

34. Ola Rotimi, *The Gods Are Not to Blame* (London: Oxford University Press, 1971), 2–3.

35. A "reminder" for outsiders, of course. The African spectator already lives it: Efua T. Sutherland, *Edufa* in *The Marriage of Anansewa and Edufa* (1975; rpt. Harlow, UK: Longman, 1987), 111. The other parts of a person are *ôkra,* living soul from *Onyame,* whose leaving is death; *sunsum,* the specific person you are; and *mogya,* from your mother, fixing clan identity: Kwasi Wiredu, *Philosophy and an African Culture* (Cambridge: Cambridge University Press, 1980), 47.

36. As in the case of Rotimi's play, I have discussed Sutherland's at much greater length in "Using Tragedy" (in Rebecca Bushnell, ed., *A Companion to Tragedy*).

37. Elechi Amadi, *Sunset in Biafra: A Civil War Diary* (London: Heinemann, 1973), 40.

38. Amadi, *Sunset,* 89, 41.

39. "Popular Art" in Grimshaw, *The C. L. R. James Reader,* 246; James, *Mariners,* 54, 86.

40. Kole Omotoso, "Concepts of History and Theatre in Africa," in *A History of Theatre in Africa,* ed. Martin Banham (Cambridge: Cambridge University Press, 2004), 9 (he also cites Hubert Ogunde and Joel Adedeji to this effect); Dapo Adelugba, "Wale Ogunyemi, 'Zulu Sofola and Ola Rotimi: Three Dramatists in Search of a Language," in *Theatre in Africa,* ed. Oyin Ogunba and Abiola Irele (Ibadan: Ibadan University Press, 1978), 214–15.

41. The abstract oppositions are from Scott, *Conscripts,* 192; I take their concrete manifestations from Rotimi's play.

42. Friedrich Nietzsche, *The Birth of Tragedy and the Genealogy of Morals,* trans. Francis Golffing (Garden City, NJ: Doubleday Anchor, 1956), 29.

43. Sophocles, *The Three Theban Plays,* 358 (see nn. 11 and 12, above).

44. Hannah Arendt, *On Revolution* (1963; rpt. Harmondsworth, UK: Penguin, 1973), 281. I am indebted to Scott for this reminder: *Conscripts,* 211–12, 267.

45. Wole Soyinka, *The Burden of Memory, the Muse of Forgiveness* (Oxford: Oxford University Press, 1999), 187–94.

46. Youssouf Tata Cissé and Wâ Kamissoko, *La grande geste du Mali,* 2 vols. (Paris: Karthala, 1988–91), 1:27, 155, 191–201, 207.

47. Manthia Diawara, *In Search of Africa* (Cambridge, MA: Harvard University Press, 1998), 162.

Tragedy, Film, Popular Culture

Femme Fatale—
Negotiations of Tragic Desire

Elisabeth Bronfen

Tragedy is the image of Fate, as comedy is of Fortune.

Susanne Langer

One of the old themes of tragedy, Stanley Cavell argues in his reading of Shakespeare's *King Lear,* is "that our actions have consequences which outrun our best, and worst, intentions . . . the *reason* consequences furiously hunt us down is not merely that we are half-blind, and unfortunate, but that we go on doing the thing which produced these consequences in the first place." If Cavell thus locates a repetition compulsion at the heart of the tragic theme he is concerned with, he does so because at stake for him is not simply the moral lesson we are to learn from tragedy but also the question what leaving the scene of tragedy might imply. For this reason, he goes on to claim that "what we need is not rebirth, or salvation, but the courage, or plain prudence, to see and to stop. To abdicate. But what do we need in order to do that? It would be salvation."[1]

By distinguishing between a salvation which results from seeing and stopping and one that results from rebirth, Cavell raises two interrelated questions. Firstly, what exactly is it that we keep on doing to sustain tragedy? And, secondly, what would putting a stop to the repetition compulsion underlying tragic desire imply? For Cavell both questions revolve around the human proclivity to avoid attending to the specificity of the person before one, as this comes to be coterminous with failing to attend to one's own specificity. "Recognizing a person," thus his claim, "depends upon allowing oneself to be recognized by him" (AL 279) in a dialogic gesture where self-revelation implies self-recognition as well. If, for Cavell, tragic action serves to prevent one from seeing the other (and thus oneself), then the knowledge being staved off is, furthermore, precisely that referring to one's humanity—in the sense of acknowledging one's fallibility and imperfection, which is to say, one's mortality. For what is being avoided, as a perpetual sustenance of tragic misrecognition prevents one from stopping to see the world at hand, is an acknowledgement of one's irrevocable limitedness.[2]

Implenitude thus comes into play in the sense that one can never know the other, but only acknowledge her or him as embodying precisely the limit to one's knowledge, and thus one's existence; as marking an obstacle which can only be overcome by recognizing it as such. At the same time, the refusal to acknowledge the other brings a further aspect of mortality into play. For the tragic corpses, whose production is the inevitable conclusion of a refusal to put a stop to a narrative of avoidance, only cement the fact that not seeing the other is tantamount to denying his or her humanity. The logic of denial at work can be formulated as follows. A recognition of one's own mortal implenitude is staved off by virtue of turning the other into a figure whose function is to sustain an illusion of self-empowerment. Yet, as Cavell claims, tragedy not only enacts the fatal consequences of refusing recognition of the other and of the self, but also comes to be the place where the heroes and heroines—and, implicitly, we as the audience—are not allowed to escape these consequences. For if the dead bodies at the end of a tragic text give evidence of the denial of the other's humanity, they also signify the death of our capacity to acknowledge, which is to say, the denial of our own.

In what follows I want to take the theme of fatal misrecognition, the consequences this entails, as well as the possibility of putting an end to their haunting, as a way of discussing a genre—*film noir*—which is usually ignored by tragic theorists. In so doing, I follow the proposal made by Rita Felski for this volume, namely, to think of tragedy not just as a narrowly defined dramatic genre, but as a mode, sensibility, or structure of feeling.

As Vivian Sobchack notes, "It is now a commonplace to regard *film noir* during the peak years of its production as a pessimistic cinematic response to volatile social and economic conditions of the decade immediately following World War II."[3] Indeed, the heroes of *film noir* repeatedly find themselves penetrating into the darkness of a fascinating, and at the same time threatening, counterworld of corruption, intrigue, betrayal, and decadence from which they can escape only by death. Yet the sense of a paranoid world transmitted in *film noir* need not be conceived exclusively as a cinematic refiguration of the political instability of the postwar period, especially when one takes into consideration its transformation since the 1980s into *neo-noir*. Rather, the fantasy scenarios *film noir* celebrates, with its protagonists fatefully entrapped in a claustrophobic world and unable to master their destinies, can just as fruitfully be understood as an example of the resonance tragic expression continues to maintain, particularly in the realm of popular cinema. Indeed, if one follows Felski's suggestion that tragedy be thought of less as a genre than as an attitude which addresses the limits of modern dreams of perfectibility, then the *femme fatale* can be understood as a particularly resilient contemporary example of tragic sensibility. For in the world of a *film noir* like *Double Indemnity,* where actions occur "accidentally on purpose," she functions both as the screen for fantasies of omnipotence and as the agent who, by ultimately facing the consequence of her *noir* actions, comes to reveal the fragility not only of any sense of omnipotence that transgression of the law affords, but, indeed, of what it means to be human.

At issue for me in tracing the question of tragic sensibility in Billy Wilder's *Double Indemnity* (1944) is the way the *femme fatale* emerges as the figure who comes to perform tragic acceptance in the manner Stanley Cavell understands it, namely, as "an enactment not of fate but of responsibility, including the responsibility for fate" (AL 310). For a character like Phyllis Dietrichson, this means insisting to her lover that, once they have embarked on their transgressive action, "it's straight down the line for both of us." Insofar as it was fate that they should have met, to play their criminal game (killing her husband, cheating his insurance company) to the end ultimately means acknowledging that each is responsible for the fatal consequences their transgression will have. What is, however, particularly significant about Wilder's *femme fatale* is that, in contrast to the lover she ensnares, she chooses destruction at every turn, and in so doing draws attention to the question of inevitability in a tragic sequence. Given that she is radically and continuously free to make a choice against sacrificing others and, ultimately, herself, her embrace of death calls upon us to ask why, if one could avoid death, should one choose it. Following Cavell's suggestion that "tragedy grows from the fortunes we choose to interpret, to accept, as inevitable" (AL 318), my own interest in the *femme fatale* is a two-fold engagement with the vexed interface between agency and fate. For even if in the classic *film noir* Phyllis Dietrichson chooses to interpret her demise as inevitable, significantly she comes to discover her freedom precisely in her embrace of the inevitability of causation.

To focus on the *femme fatale,* of course, also means introducing the question of gender difference into a discussion of tragic sensibility, in the sense that, while she comes to acknowledge her responsibility for her fate, the hero she involves in her transgressive plot is characterized by the exact opposite attitude, namely, a desire to stave off knowledge of his own fallibility at all costs. In the classic *noir* plot, the hero quite coincidentally meets the alluring *femme fatale*—in *Double Indemnity* he happens to pass by her villa and enters to ask her husband to renew a car insurance policy. Yet their meeting follows the fateful logic of a love at first sight. As Mladen Dolar notes, what seemingly happened unintentionally and by pure chance is belatedly recognized as the realization of an innermost wish: "the pure chance was actually no chance at all: the intrusion of the unforeseen turned into necessity."[4] From the moment the hero catches sight of the *femme fatale,* both find themselves caught in a sequence of events which can go only one way. Both are tragically framed within a narrative of fate and can only come to accept the law of causation. Yet if the contingent turn from free choice to inevitability is aligned with a masculine gaze appropriating a seductive feminine body, one must not overlook the fact that as bearer of the hero's look, it is the *femme fatale* who manipulates the outcome of their fatal meeting. It may be a coincidence that this particular man has caught her in his field of vision, but she has been expecting someone like him to do precisely that. She knows all along that she is fated and can, therefore, turn what is inevitable into a source of power. Indeed, the classic *femme fatale* has enjoyed such popularity because she is not only sexually uninhibited, but also unabashedly independent and ruthlessly ambitious, using her seductive charms and her intelligence to liberate herself from the imprisonment of an unfulfilling marriage. Furthermore, though she gains power over the *noir* hero by nourishing his sexual fantasies, her own interest is only superficially erotic. She entertains a narcissistic pleasure at the deployment of her own ability to dupe the men who fall for her, even as she is merciless in manipulating them for her own ends. Duplicity thus emerges as her most seminal value, insofar as she is not simply willing to delude anyone in order to get the money and the freedom she is after, but because she will never show her true intentions to anyone, especially not the hero she has inveigled, even if this entails not only his death but also her own.

One can speak of tragic sensibility in conjunction with the *femme fatale* in part because she inevitably comes to recognize that her radical insistence on independence is a delusion, which was meant to stave off a recognition of her own fallibility. As Paula Rabinowitz notes, "she is false, a double-crosser, so even if she is after the goods, they will elude her."[5] Indeed, she becomes fully tragic at the moment of *anagnorisis,* because it is here that she can recognize her desire for freedom as attainable only in death. At the same time, in that she uses her seductive powers to lead the *noir* hero from the sunlit exterior into a nocturnal world of transgressions, betrayals, and, ultimately, his demise, she also embodies the death drive, albeit in a highly ambivalent manner. On the one hand, one could speak of her as a figure of male fantasy, articulating both a fascination for the sexually aggressive woman, as well as anxieties about feminine domination. As Joan Copjec argues, in order to indemnify himself against the dangers of sexuality, the *noir* hero treats her as his double, to which he surrenders the fatal enjoyment he cannot himself sustain.[6] On the other hand, the *femme fatale* is more than simply a symptom of the hero's erotic ambivalence. She sustains his self-delusion, but also gives voice to a feminine desire that may include him in order to attain its aim, but also exceeds his fantasy realm. In her insistence that "it's straight down the line for both" of them, she can be understood as moving towards an ethical act meant to radically undercut the blindness of self-preservation her lover seeks to entertain at all costs.

Owing to this function of duplicity within *noir* narratives, Slavoj Zizek suggests that the *femme fatale* functions as a symptom of the *noir* hero's fatal enjoyment in such a way that, by destroying her—Walter Neff will shoot Phyllis Dietrichson in the heart—he hopes to purify himself of the desire she inspired and the guilt this entailed. In so doing, however, the *noir* hero not only does not recognize her as separate from him (thus denying her humanity), but also remains blind to the encrypted message about the fragility of his existence that she embodies for him. However, as a feminine subject taken by herself, the *femme fatale* assumes the death drive in a "radical, most elementary ethical attitude of uncompromising insistence, of 'not giving way.'"[7] The retreat of the *noir* hero from the *femme fatale,* Zizek adds, "is effectively a retreat from the death drive as a radical ethical stance" (156). For the *femme fatale* to fully assume the death drive is ultimately to show that the pursuit of power and money is inevitably thwarted, as it also means acknowledging that we can never purify ourselves from the consequences of our actions by shifting guilt onto the other. My point is that both in her function as a symptom within a male fantasy, as well as in her function as a subject beyond male fantasy, the *femme fatale* emerges as a figure of tragic sensibility. In the first case, she is denied humanity in the fantasy scenario of the hero, whose aim is to avoid an acknowledgment of mortality and guilt by transferring death exclusively to her body. In the latter case, she is the figure who accepts her death as the logical consequence of her insistence on a radical pursuit of personal freedom—the money and death of her husband at all costs. As such, she embodies tragic sensibility in the manner Felski proposes, namely, in opposition to a strand of American optimism that sees individuals as masters of their own destiny, with a right to pursue happiness at all cost without paying the price.

Double Indemnity has come to figure as the prototype of *film noir,* not least of all because it performs the rhetorical duplicity connected to the *femme fatale,* staging Phyllis Dietrichson (Barbara Stanwyck) both as the symptom of Walter Neff (Fred MacMurray) and as a female subject who will not give way and thus exceeds his narrative of the fatal consequences of their mutual transgression. We only hear the confession he makes to his superior Barton Keyes (Edward G. Robinson) after having shot his partner in crime; a self-justifying narrative, establishing the tragic code of failure. It begins with the statement, "I killed Dietrichson. I killed him for money and for a woman. I didn't get the money and I didn't get the woman. Pity isn't it," and continues as a voice-over throughout the film. Yet, at key moments in the fatal sequence resulting in the production of two corpses, Wilder also offers close-ups of Phyllis's face, visually articulating a different perspective than that of her *noir* lover. In so doing, Wilder brings a further duplicity into play. By encouraging Walter's vain narcissism for her own ends, willingly acting as his fetish object of desire, Phyllis is complicitous with his refusal to acknowledge her. The initial scene of seduction is staged in such a manner as to set the tone for the fatal misrecognition that subtends the entire *noir* tragedy. Wilder foregrounds the fact that, because each treats the other as though they were a character in the play they are living, even while the two fantasy scenarios do not coincide, the protagonists are not actually in the presence of each other. As Walter walks through her front door, Phyllis emerges at the top of the staircase, clad only in a towel. The erotic banter that follows signals to us not only that she has been cast by him into an object of prey he will seek to win for himself, but also that she knows this and will use the fact that she, in turn, has hooked him with the way she looked at him, in order to introject her scenario of death into his romantic one. Once she walks down the stairs, Wilder's camera zooms in on her feet to highlight the bracelet around her left ankle, before we see her entire body, now fully covered by a white dress, walking toward him, as she teasingly closes the top button. They have come together on a stage where each will ultimately seek to double-cross the other, because their desire was always at cross-purposes. As Walter Neff will explain to her during their final confrontation, "We were talking about automobile insurance, only you were thinking about murder, and I was thinking about that anklet."

By focusing on Phyllis's anklet, the camera invokes the code of fetish-

ism, and in so doing offers an image of this body part as a transition between the glance at her almost naked upper body and the fully dressed
woman Walter can visually enjoy without a staircase between them. This
visual fragmentation foregrounds the *noir* hero's willful blindness. As
Laura Mulvey notes, "Fetishism is born out of a refusal to see, a refusal
to accept the difference the female body represents for the male. These
complex series of turnings away, of covering over, not of the eyes but of
understanding, of fixating on a substitute object to hold the gaze, leave
the female body as an enigma and threat," as a symptom of anxiety, a
figure on the viewer's mind screen.[8] For the question of tragic sensibility
at stake in my own argument, one might add that the ambivalence of
feeling Wilder establishes with this initial scene of seduction is that his
noir hero wants the thrill of transgression, even while refusing to understand the woman inspiring this desire as another person, rather than assuming her to be an enigmatic figure of fantasy who will dupe and elude
him. "How could I have known that murder can sometimes smell like
honey-suckle," his voice-over asks, as we see him driving away from the
house, "I didn't. I felt like a million." The self-blindness he thus articulates need not only be read as a belated attempt at exoneration. The fact
that he has been tragically caught in the *femme fatale*'s trap also indicates his desire to be deluded, which, put in other terms, means his desire—at all costs—not to look at her, to fixate on a substitute so as not to
put himself in her presence. Even when, several days later, he comes to
accept her proposition, he does so because it supports his vanity. Again
Wilder's mise-en-scène makes visual the tragic aspect of his *noir* couple
in the way they do not share a fantasy space. Phyllis has come to Walter's
apartment, using her seductive powers to win him over. After an initial
kiss, Walter quite expressly disentangles himself from her arms and sets
a chain of narratives in motion. He tries to assure her that if someone
who has accident insurance with his company suddenly dies, his super-
visor Keyes will do everything to vilify the surviving wife. After Phyllis
has responded by sketching her fantasy about a fatal accident happening
to the husband who mistreats her and has written her out of his inheritance, Walter takes her into his arms, suddenly smiling as he presses her
face against his shoulder. In doing this, significantly he avoids looking
at her. So as to underline once more that these two fated lovers are not,
in fact, present to each other, Wilder has the camera draw back cutting
to the frame narrative, with Walter speaking his confession to Keyes into
his Dictaphone. Here he explains that he accepted Phyllis's proposal not
because of any erotic desire for her, nor out of pity, but rather out of pro-

fessional vanity. All these years he had been wondering how he could "crook the house," but "do it smart." Phyllis's entering his apartment that night was simply an embodiment of the opportunity for which he had been waiting.

The kiss that seals their pact is nothing other than an empty gesture that allows them to deny their avoidance of the other, because Wilder has also shown us that on the one hand, Walter's fetishism covers over any understanding of Phyllis's situation in favor of his hubris, while on the other hand, the *femme fatale*'s game of seduction is all about actually seeing something. After their first kiss, while Walter is telling her about a woman who ended up in prison after the death of her husband because his insurance claim was investigated by Keyes, Wilder includes a brief close-up of Phyllis's face as she mournfully replies, "Perhaps it was worth it to her." This is the first of a series of close-up shots we get of the *femme fatale,* visually expressing that while she is playing with Walter, she also stands emotionally apart from him. While Stanwyck's skillful performance of Phyllis's contrived gestures of seduction calls upon us to notice how ruthlessly she manipulates Walter, these close-ups invoke our pity in a way her narrative about domestic malaise does not. They transmit a tragic sensibility not only by foregrounding how utterly alone she is, but also by insisting that we must do what Walter avoids doing, both in his dealings with her, as well as in his frame narrative. We must look at her, and then, because we never see the object her thoughts are directed at, we follow her gaze into an abstract realm. In so doing we move away from treating her as a fetish image and instead share her mental space as one of conjectures about the inevitability of her fate. While Walter's fetishism allows him to go on doing something—hatching the perfect plot to kill Mr. Dietrichson and then, when faced with the fact that he may be found out, devising a scheme to have Phyllis take the fall for his own fallibility—these close-ups call upon us to take the opposite course. In each case we are shown Phyllis as she stops and looks, but—and therein resides the tragic sensibility of her side of the story—not at her *noir* lover, rather, prophetically at the consequences her deeds will have.

If one follows these close-ups and, in so doing, reads *Double Indemnity* against the grain of Walter's self-justifying confession, the entire film can be read as a tragic scenario transforming a question of free choice—my husband's death and his money—into a recognition that all choices are forced ones, where the issue is assuming the responsibility for one's fate. After watching her husband sign the accident insurance policy, thinking it is simply a car insurance renewal, we see Phyllis leading Walter to the door, and for a brief moment, after he has left her, Wilder shows us her face, glowing with anticipation at the thought that a train accident will mean twice the insurance sum. At the supermarket, where she complains to Walter how hard the waiting is for her (explaining, "It's so tough without you, it's like a wall between us"), he simply walks away from her, averting her eyes, with his own eyes covered by the shadow of his hat. We see her looking after him mournfully, aware that he is avoiding her. Most significantly, the actual murder of Mr. Dietrichson is presented indexically, by virtue of the changes in her facial expression. While Walter, hiding in the backseat of the Dietrichson car, strangles the husband, Wilder offers us a close-up of Phyllis's face, tracing her subtle shift in emotion, as determination initially turns to a sad acceptance of the death she has provoked and then becomes a quiet joy that indicates her own satisfaction at the completion of her plan. Finally, the night after the inquest, where the coroner confirms her husband's death to have been an accident, she goes to visit Walter in his apartment. Realizing that Keyes is there with him, she waits behind the door. As Walter opens it so Keyes can leave, she takes hold of the doorknob to indicate her presence to him. If, in the supermarket, she had tried to make Walter recognize the emotional wall separating them, the door, now literally between them, confirms her suspicion. Walter wants to put her behind him, turn his back on her. As she overhears Keyes confessing how he wants to send the police after her, we see her face registering, for the first time, a certain astonishment at the risk she has taken. Read as a sequence, these close-ups of Phyllis indicate the gradual unfolding of her tragic reading of the chain of causation she has set into motion, which is to say, her reading these events in relation to an inevitable tragic outcome.

Walter arranges another meeting at the supermarket to convince her that, because Keyes has figured out their scheme, he wishes "to pull out." Now she responds by taking off her sunglasses. Looking at him directly with a sober and determined gaze, she insists, as we once more see her face in close-up, "We went into this together and we're coming out in the end together. It's straight down the line for both of us, remember!" This time she is the one to turn her back on him. If Walter's apartment door had shielded them from each other, she now shows him that such a turning away is impossible, even if the end she is speaking about is not a life with money, but death. My intuition is to read the gesture of removing sunglasses as a moment of true, if tragic, self-recognition along the lines proposed by Jacques Lacan. He argues that it is precisely in situations of false choice, with the subject forced to make a choice that is inevitable, that she or he acknowledges their irrevocable fallibility. One prototypical scene would be that of a hold-up, where, faced with the choice of one's money or one's life, one can choose only the latter. Another, more poignant, scene is that of a revolutionary action, where the choice between freedom or death inevitably requires one to choose death, "for there, you show that you have freedom of choice."[9] For a discussion of the tragic sensibility embodied by the *femme fatale*, this formulation is particularly fruitful, for she consciously introduces a lethal factor into the question of choice, and, in so doing, undertakes an ethical act that allows her to choose death as a way of choosing real freedom by turning the inevitability of her fate into her responsibility.

To prepare herself for her last confrontation with Walter, Phyllis places her revolver under the living room sofa, correctly assuming that he, too, will come armed. When, after implicitly threatening to kill her, he goes to the window to close it, she fires her first shot. If she had initially turned to Walter because she wanted an unencumbered life and her husband's money, she now makes a different choice. The freedom she so relentlessly pursues emerges as an assumption of the death drive in its purest form, with all endeavors of avoidance dropped. As the wounded Walter walks toward her, she lowers her gun and embraces him one last time, choosing not to fire the second shot that would save her life. Once more we see a close-up of her face as she explains, "No, I never loved you nor anybody else. I'm rotten to the heart. I used you just as you said, until a minute ago, when I couldn't fire that second shot. I never thought that could happen to me." One could read this as a gesture of abdication, because at this moment she actually stops her seductive game to see both her lover and herself. She acknowledges him by directly acknowledging how she had used him, and, in so doing, she asks for him to attend to her. Walter, however, responds laconically, "Sorry, I'm not buying." While she suggests an exchange, which is not about economic gain but mutual recognition— "I'm not asking you to buy, just hold me close"—he holds onto his fetishistic avoidance to the end. By killing her rather than putting himself in her presence, he hopes to repress both his own desire for destruction as well as his complicity with her. That she, in turn, willingly accepts the death he is giving her not only renders visible the incompatibility of their two fantasy scenarios. It also allows us to decide whether we will privilege Walter Neff's misogynist description of the *femme fatale* in his voice-over narrative, or recognize her as a separate human being, exceeding his appropriation of her and, in so doing, exhibiting an agency of her own.

On the one hand, the self-justifying narrative Walter offers corresponds to a gesture of psychic and moral relief. Sacrificing his partner in crime allows him to abdicate both his sense of guilt as well as his responsibility for their mutual transgressions. If, upon seeing her the first time, he had come to recognize that he could not escape his fate, her sacrifice allows him to relieve himself of his desire for an erotically encoded death. Instead, he can now give himself up to a symbolically encoded death drive—the death penalty of the law. On the other hand, Phyllis Dietrichson emerges as a subject of radical tragic sensibility precisely because she directly accepts the death drive inscribed in the *noir* narrative she has been performing throughout. She explicitly gives a name to the obscene kernel at the heart of her being ("rotten to the core"), while refusing all moralizing excuses for her transgressions. By choosing not to shoot a second time, Phyllis Dietrichson performs an act in which she actively and consciously accepts her own fallibility. As the culmination of all the close-ups of Phyllis Dietrichson, we see first a look of astonishment and then pain, before we hear the two shots Walter fires straight into her heart; her death, like that of her husband, is registered only indexically, as a facial expression. We are, thus, left with a two-fold sense of tragic sensibility. On the one hand, the incompatibility between their fantasies has become cemented in her corpse, and with it Walter's tragic avoidance of self-recognition. On the other hand, it is precisely the way her facial expression at the moment of death captures her final tragic acceptance that evokes our pity for Wilder's *femme fatale* and endows her last image with an affective power that resonates beyond the end of the film. For she has undermined the fetishistic quality of Walter Neff's fantasy, has rendered it groundless, and offered something else—a relentless acknowledgment of her own vulnerability—in its place. It is this gesture of seeing and stopping that we ultimately remember.

According to Janey Place, *film noir* should be read as a "male fantasy" and the *femme fatale,* as the mythic "dark lady, the spider woman, the evil seductress who tempts man and brings about his destruction" and who has been haunting our image repertoire since Eve and Pandora.[10] Yet Place stresses a poignant contradiction. Even while *film noir* offers a stage for the dangerous woman, embellishing her seduction and her desire for power, it also relentlessly plays through her demise. This is because "the myth of the strong, sexually aggressive woman first allows sensuous expression of her dangerous power and its frightening results, and then destroys it, thus expressing repressed concerns of the female threat to male dominance" (WFN 36). Yet one might also say that even though, in the course of each cinematic narrative, the *femme fatale* loses her power both on the diegetic level (she dies) and on the visual level (she falls into shadows, diminishes in size, has no voice-over of her own), the disturbing power she embodies remains through the end. The restitution her sacrifice is meant to bring about is inevitably riddled with fissures. After all, the *femme fatale* successfully undermines the hegemonic morality of family values prevalent in the postwar period. So that, even though she is punished in the end, her transgressions against masculine authority—killing her husband, cheating the insurance company, bringing about the demise of her disloyal lover—is what tarries in our memory. As Sylvia Harvey notes, "Despite the ritual punishment of acts of transgression, the vitality with which these acts are endowed produces an excess of meaning which cannot finally be contained. Narrative resolutions cannot recuperate their subversive significance."[11]

Within feminist film criticism, the *femme fatale* has thus emerged as a fundamentally unstable figure. Not only will she not allow herself to be dominated by the men who fall for her charms, but also the meaning she assumes in any given text refuses to be fixed. In the same manner that she will not assume an unequivocal place in the fantasy life of the *noir* hero, no single interpretation can be imposed on the disturbance posed by her resilient feminine power. Mary Ann Doane understands the fact that she is usually declared to be an embodiment of evil, and punished or killed, as a "desperate reassertion of control on the part of the threatened male subject."[12] Her ability to seduce the *noir* hero into undertaking actions that undermine his self-interests renders visible a radical fallibility of the masculine subject. For this reason, Doane claims that the *femme fatale* should not be read as a modern heroine, endowed with an agency of her own, but rather as a "symptom of male fears about feminism" (2–3). Yet given the duplicitous manner in which Billy Wilder stages a prototypical *femme fatale* like Phyllis Dietrichson in *Double Indemnity* I would offer a counter claim. The *femme fatale* has resiliently preserved her position within our image repertoire precisely because she forces the spectator to decide whether she acts as an empowered modern subject or is simply to be understood as the expression of an unconscious death drive, indeed, whether we are to conceive of her as an independent figure or merely as a figure of projection for masculine anxiety. Given that she has no fixed place and no unequivocal meaning within the narratives of the classic *films noir,* a film like *Double Indemnity* can be read either as misogynist nightmare scenario (Walter Neff's narrative of how he was ensnared by an evil woman) that re-empowers a masculine subject in crisis, or as an ironic demontage of such masculinist anxieties (Phyllis Dietrichson's gaze) that renders visible to us that the *noir* lover only wanted to use the *femme fatale* and will frame her so that she can take the fall for him. Indeed, as Elizabeth Cowie notes, the *femme fatale* has come to serve as "a catchphrase for the danger of sexual difference and the demands and risks desire poses for the man. The male hero often knowingly submits himself to the 'spider-woman'—as Neff does in *Double Indemnity*—for it is precisely her dangerous sexuality that he desires, so that it is ultimately his own perverse desire that is his downfall."[13]

Yet the problem with reading the *femme fatale* as a stereotype of feminine evil, as a symptom of male anxiety, or as a catchphrase for the danger of sexual difference is that it treats this tragic feminine heroine as an encoded figure who exists only as the phantasmic emanation of others, who is acted upon and, when necessary, extinguished, rather than treating her as a separate subject who has agency and is responsible for her decisions. In so doing, feminist critics unwittingly imitate precisely the gesture of fetishism performed by Walter Neff at the very beginning of *Double Indemnity,* when he fixes his gaze on the golden bracelet Phyllis Dietrichson is wearing around her ankle, rather than acknowledging her as a separate human being. For they, too, find themselves caught in a complex series of turnings away, of covering over, not of the eyes but of understanding, when in reducing her to a symptom or a catchphrase they read the *femme fatale* either as an embodiment of threat or as a textual enigma and, in so doing, avoid actually seeing her as separate not only from the fantasies of the *noir* hero, but also from any critical preconceptions informing one's reading of a given text. Using the resilient power of the tragic sensibility embodied in the *femme fatale* as a point of departure, however, one might ask: what if, rather than treating her as a fetish, projection, or symptom, one were to treat her instead as the subject of her narrative? What if one were to follow the cue Wilder offers and read the confession his *femme fatale* makes about her own "rottenness" as a self-description we should take seriously? This would mean ascribing feminine agency to the *femme fatale,* seeing her as an authentic modern heroine, and insisting that in her actions she is everything but blind. For, if fetishism, as Laura Mulvey claims, consists in a refusal to see, Phyllis Dietrichson in her final confession pits against such self-delusion an unmitigated gaze at the destructive power of her desire.

The decision is thus ours as to whether we want to follow Doane and other feminist critics in reading the *femme fatale* as a symptom of patriarchal anxiety about feminism, or whether we want to follow Zizek and read her as a symptom for the ambivalence in feeling on the part of the *noir* hero and his retreat from the death drive. Another option would be to treat her as a prototypical instance of modern feminine subjectivity. This would lead one, along the lines Stanley Cavell proposes for tragedy, to acknowledge her precisely by recognizing that, far from being a victim who is punished for her transgressions or for the desires she elicits, the *femme fatale* chooses to accept the tragic consequences of her actions. In so doing, she becomes the figure *par excellence* for the recognition of human fallibility which, according to Cavell, tragedy teaches us. Yet recasting her in this sense not only affects our semantic encoding of her as a protagonist in a narrative, but also foregrounds the way we are implicated as viewers of films like *Double Indemnity*. For, as Cavell notes, in tragedy, "people in pain are in our presence, but we are not in their presence. Tragedy shows we are responsible for the death of others even when we have not murdered them" (AL 332). With this description of tragedy in mind, a film like *Double Indemnity* could be seen as posing the following question. What would it mean for us to put a stop to the series of turnings away which revolve around the *femme fatale,* to abdicate the gesture of fetishism, which supports the refusal to see her as a separate human being and the refusal to accept her difference?

As I have proposed in my reading of the sequence of close-ups of Phyllis Dietrichson's face, looking first at her and then with her implicates us in our viewing, in the sense that we find ourselves called upon to put our own avoidance of seeing her aside. We can put ourselves in her presence on the level of an aesthetic response—in the affective third space that opens up between what occurs on the film screen and the emotions this elicits in the audience—precisely by refusing a refusal to see her, which is what reducing her to the status of a symptom or a catchphrase amounts to. To acknowledge her as a subject of her actions means no longer being blind to the way she is anything but a victim, and, in her conscious choice for death, gives voice to the way suffering, loss, and fragility are inescapable. It also means overcoming a critical prejudice which, by treating her as a symptom of masculine anxieties and not as a subject of feminine desire, allows us as critics to avoid the tragic message she relentlessly embodies. As Cavell notes, tragedy is about a particular death that is neither natural nor accidental. Even though death is inflicted, "it need not have happened. So a radical contingency haunts every story of tragedy." At the same time, he continues, a radical necessity also haunts every story of tragedy, so that it is precisely the murky interface between contingency and necessity, which produces "events we call tragic: necessary, but we do not know why; avoidable, but we do not know how" (AL 341). If the perseverance of the final image of Phyllis Dietrichson in *Double Indemnity* resides in the fact that she has come to accept as her responsibility the fate of a death she did not know how to avoid, this is so precisely because she has recognized that to be hidden, silent, and not in the presence of the other is a question of choice. One can also abdicate this illusory safety, even if this means accepting the death one has been courting all along. It is her mode of salvation.

Notes

1. Stanley Cavell, "The Avoidance of Love: A Reading of *King Lear,*" in *Must We Mean What We Say?* (Cambridge: Cambridge University Press, 1976), 310; hereafter cited in text as AL.

2. As Cavell, in "Avoidance," argues, an acceptance of human limitedness implies recognizing, "There is nothing and we know there is nothing we can do. Tragedy is meant to make sense of that condition" (330).

3. Vivian Sobchack, "Lounge Time: Postwar Crises and the Chronotope of Film Noir," in *Refiguring American Film Genres: Theory and History,* ed. Nick Browne (Berkeley: University of California Press, 1998), 130.

4. Mladen Dolar, "The Object Voice," in *Sic 1: Gaze and Voice as Love Objects* (Durham: Duke University Press, 1996), 131.

5. Paula Rabinowitz, *Black & White & Noir: America's Pulp Modernism* (New York: Columbia University Press, 2002), 143.

6. Joan Copjec, "The Phenomenal Nonphenomenal: Private Space in Film Noir," in *Shades of Noir,* ed. Joan Copjec (London: Verso, 1993), 193.

7. Slavoj Zizek, *Enjoy Your Symptom! Jacques Lacan in Hollywood and Out* (New York: Routledge, 1992), 154.

8. Laura Mulvey, *Fetishism and Curiosity* (London: BFI, 1996), 64.

9. Jacques Lacan, *The Four Fundamental Concepts of Psycho-Analysis,* ed. Jacques-Alain Miller, trans. Alan Sheridan (New York: Norton, 1973), 213.

10. Janey Place, "Women in film noir," in *Women in Film Noir,* ed. E. Ann Kaplan (London: BFI, 1980), 35; hereafter cited in text as WFN.

11. Sylvia Harvey, "Women's Place," in *Women in Film Noir,* ed. E. Ann Kaplan (London: BFI, 1980), 31.

12. Mary Ann Doane, *Femmes Fatales: Feminism, Film Theory, Psychoanalysis* (New York: Routledge, 1991), 2–3.

13. Elizabeth Cowie, "Film Noir and Women," in *Shades of Noir,* ed. Joan Copjec (London: Verso, 1993), 125.

Spectacular Failure
The Figure of the Lesbian in *Mulholland Drive*

Heather K. Love

The trap, at this last moment, is the wrong kind of emphasis on the un-doubted fact that it could indeed be otherwise. To make it already otherwise, by selecting the facts and by subtly reducing the pressures, is to go over into propaganda or to advertising. . . . We have to see not only that suffering is avoidable, but that it is not avoided. And not only that suffering breaks us, but that it need not break us.

Raymond Williams, Modern Tragedy

Although the modern subject may imagine himself capable of the meta-physical heroics of Oedipus or Antigone, his suffering tends to be ordi-nary, banal—a disgrace rather than a catastrophe. Tragedy survives into the modern era, but it loses its patina of sublimity. The model of tragic ex-perience is no longer Icarus's spectacular plunge into the sea, but rather a slow sinking into disillusion and immobility. Even the supremely tragic "event" of modernity—the death of God—feels like a disappointment, not a disaster. Subjects are increasingly hardened against a world that seems at once brutally rational and completely meaningless. Given that this "state of exception" is now the rule, the fact that modern subjects are no longer able to experience the full intensity of tragic feeling should be taken not as a sign that tragedy has disappeared, but rather that it has become so widespread as to be unrecognizable.

In his 1966 study *Modern Tragedy,* Raymond Williams considers the rapid expansion of tragedy in the twentieth century. In the gas chambers and killing fields that served as tragedy's theater of operation in the mod-ern era, the scale of tragic suffering went beyond all known limits. At the same time, tragedy was democratized: while classical tragedy treated only the fall of gods and heroes, modern tragedy takes seriously the wreckage of even the most undistinguished lives. While Williams applauds this leveling of tragedy in one sense, he is attentive to its costs. While modern tragedy has overcome the elitism of classical tragedy, there is a sense in which we can only understand it *as tragic* that, in modernity, everyone is exposed to tragic suffering.[1] The modernization and democratization of tragedy means that suffering is multiplied even as the reasons to suffer become more and more obscure. Henri Lefebvre describes this state of affairs in "What is Modernity?" when he writes, "Our era is trying to eliminate the tragic, while all the while it is slipping deeper and deeper into tragedy."[2] Williams particularly laments the *individual* and *isolated* nature of tragic suffering in the modern era, a state of affairs linked to the profound atomization of modern society. For Williams, this breakdown of an integrated community is a disaster, because no alliance can be forged between modernity's tragic subjects.[3]

Terry Eagleton takes up this point in his recent book, *Sweet Violence*. Eagleton sees as tragedy's greatest potential its ability to rally a "community of suffering"[4] that would be grounded in the universality of human pain. Both Eagleton and Williams ground their dream of a tragic community of suffering in Marx's notion of a universal class, a class "which is the dissolution of all classes, a sphere of society which has a universal character because its sufferings are universal, and which does not claim a particular redress because the wrong which is done to it is not a *particular* wrong but a wrong in general."[5] In discussing the end of tragic heroism, Eagleton writes, "[U]nder democracy, tragic protagonists do not have to be heroes to be tragic. The only qualification for being a tragic protagonist is that you are a member of the species" (94). What is crucial in this tragic collective is that each member of the species should be interchangeable with any other member.[6] Eagleton interprets Marx's call for a universal class in the context of contemporary debates about identity politics: his argument for the political usefulness of the concept of modern tragedy is pitched explicitly against what he calls the "glib particularism" of contemporary left politics.

Eagleton concludes his book by arguing that there are in fact no minorities, that what we tend to think of as oppressed minorities in fact constitute a single majority. Discussing the figure of the scapegoat in classical tragedy, he writes,

> In the current preoccupation with minorities, one vital insight is in danger of being obscured. The astonishing fact about global capitalism is that it is the majority who are dispossessed. There are, to be sure, degrees of dispossession, and shipyard workers are by no means destitute. But while the idea of a social order which excludes certain vilified minorities is familiar enough, and these expulsions are visibly on show, the mind-shaking truth of a class analysis is that the social orders have always invisibly shut out the majority. This is so paradoxical a fact, as well as so

impalpable a one, that we have failed to be sufficiently struck by it. It carries a double message: that a system entranced by success is in fact a miserable failure; and that there is more than enough of this failure for it to convert itself into power. The classical *pharmakos* can be thrust out of the city because its rulers have no need of it, other than as an object on which to off-load their collective guilt. It is also terrible to look on, too hideous to tolerate within one's walls. But the modern-day scapegoat is essential to the workings of the very polis which shuts it out. It is not a matter of a few hired beggars or gaolbirds, but of whole sweated, up-rooted populations. (296)

Eagleton's argument against minority politics is a familiar one; at this point, it is at least as familiar as the narrative of the "exclusion of vilified minorities." Yet Eagleton does not take into account the extent to which modernity is bound up with the specific exclusions he dismisses here. Key aspects of modernization, such as commodification, global migra-tion, and the breakdown of social hierarchies, went hand-in-hand with the development of new technologies for the classification and manage-ment of populations. In this sense, modernity *produced* its own tragic others. While Eagleton is certainly right to suggest that the majority of the world's population is made up of "the dispossessed," the dispos-sessed are dispossessed in particular ways.[7] Simply "seeing through" the ideology of race or gender will not do away with the damage that these concepts have done. As in classical tragedy, the moment of recognition comes too late.

Eagleton's concept of the *pharmakos*—the scapegoat who visibly suf-fers the guilt of an entire population—is crucial to understanding the nature of modern tragedy and to imagining a tragic collectivity that does not operate under the sign of the universal. As Eagleton writes, the scape-goat is "symbolically loaded with the guilt of the community"; chosen from the "lowest of the low," this "desolate, abandoned figure is a nega-tive sign of social totality" (278). The *pharmakos* is crucial in Eagleton's defense of modern tragedy; in his view, this outcast figures the possibil-ity of a radical challenge to the existing order. Yet he also insists that this figure should be unmarked: "When it comes to victimage," he writes, "anyone will do" (278). The modern scapegoat, however, is by definition *marked*. Constituted as a sign of spectacular difference, he can be easily identified by his characteristic morphology as well as by his psychologi-cal profile. Modern tragedy cannot be separated from the tragedy of the so-called minorities: implicit in the concept of the *pharmakos* is the modern tragedy of *social types*.

Modern tragedy is equal opportunity tragedy: everyone is exposed to tragic suffering, but some people are more tragic than others. Modernity's others suffer losses and violence like everyone else—but a seal of seeming inevitability is added to their suffering. Their experience appears determined by their being. Nothing *befalls* them: because their very existence seems tragic, not only every catastrophe but every passing disappointment takes on the character of a curse and seems to arise from within rather than from without. The tragic condition of the scapegoat underlines his suffering, making it appear obvious, even natural. What George Steiner describes as "absolute tragedy," "the image of man as unwanted in life," is a general condition and a typical experience of modernity.[8] Yet this experience is overdetermined in material and psychic ways for modernity's others, who represent these losses for the community as a whole. The modern *pharmakos* stands in for a sense of loss that is widely shared: this figure embodies and literalizes what are in fact more general features of modernity. Registering the death of the universal on his overly particular body, he takes the blame for the losses of modernity, among which must be counted the death of tragedy itself.[9]

Recently, a few critics have suggested how we might rethink modern tragedy by drawing attention to some of modernity's excluded others. In an essay on the tragic mulatto, Werner Sollers suggests that we might understand this clichéd figure as actually tragic, an embodiment of tragic conflicts in the concept and deployment of race in America.[10] In her work on tragic women, Rita Felski suggests that women, by representing the contradictions of modernity, may be its exemplary tragic figures.[11] Such reflections on modernity's tragic others inform my own attention, in this essay, to the figure of the tragic lesbian. Like the tragic mulatto or the tragically suffering woman, this is a figure thought to be unworthy of serious attention. For one thing, she can appear to be profoundly anachronistic, an outdated figment of the homophobic imagination. In addition, her suffering, which most often takes the form of disappointment in love, does not really register as tragic, but as simply sad or pathetic. I argue that it is a mistake to dismiss this figure as a mere specter of ideology. Her suffering, apparently so far from modernity's mainstage, is significant precisely as modernity's remainder. As banal and pitiable as the tragic lesbian's experience is, it makes sense to name it as tragic: this is what modern tragedy looks like.

A genealogy of the modern lesbian turns up some outlandish characters. Like the modern homosexual, her origins can be found in the medical and criminal literature of the late nineteenth century. In the writings of the sexologists, the female invert is an unfortunate creature, a woman whose desires, habits, and sartorial choices conflict tragically with her biological sex. The invert, however, is not the only precursor for the modern lesbian, who can also lay claim to a more scandalous set of ancestors. These perverse schoolgirls, vampires, and poetesses appeared in works by authors such as Théophile Gautier, Honoré de Balzac, and Charles Baudelaire, but also in any number of less distinguished literary and pornographic texts. This wicked sisterhood tended to have more fun than the mannish women of the sexological case histories; however, they paid for their indiscretions, meeting fates ranging from abandonment to dismemberment.

While the gory antics of these hollow-eyed vixens may seem old-fashioned, it would be a mistake to think of them as irrelevant to contemporary lesbian representation and experience. While lesbian chic is getting a lot more press these days than lesbian vampirism, it is nonetheless the case that the figure of the lesbian remains an object of collective longing and loathing. A spur to acts of phallic virtuosity both on-screen and off, the lesbian sits at the crossroads, charged with unspeakable secrets of desire. While such phantasmic images of the lesbian should not be confused with the "reality" of contemporary lesbian existence, neither should they be written off too quickly or too completely.

David Lynch's 2001 film *Mulholland Drive* takes up several of the most powerful and persistent images of the lesbian. That Lynch had hit a vein was clear from the inordinately enthusiastic reviews that appeared in mainstream media and on the Internet. Reviewers rhapsodized in particular and at length about the film's sex scenes, as if there were a contest to see who could enjoy this representation of female same-sex desire the most. However, I happened to talk to several people who told me that they were disturbed by Lynch's representation of lesbians as objects of "male fantasy." These well-meaning viewers expected to find a sympathetic audience in me—as a lesbian, as someone who works on "lesbian representation." I was irritated by this assumption and found myself perversely defending male fantasy: "Hundreds of years of experience have gone into making those fantasies . . . those are *quality* fantasies!" Of course, these viewers were in one sense right—*Mulholland Drive* is awash in male fantasy. This in itself is not so shocking, though, since we can find traces of such fantasies in any representation of lesbianism—and in "real life" as well. Given that the lesbian is so overwritten by cliché, the central criterion for judging lesbian representation tends to be whether it challenges reigning clichés of the lesbian or capitulates to them. Lynch is not interested in challenging lesbian clichés; instead, he works almost exclusively through such clichés, exploring both the sweeping vistas and the back alleys of this stereotyped world.

Hollywood—the Dream Factory—is the perfect setting for Lynch's reflection on the relation between individual and public fantasy. If Hollywood cinema is without rival as the site for collective dreaming, it is no less true that it is an industry that passes off clichés as dreams. The film's universe is populated by a range of "walking clichés," from the promising young starlet to a maverick director to the gangster powerbrokers. As hackneyed as these tropes are, Lynch never gets to the bottom of them: while their ideological role is obvious, they are at the same time the source of mystery in Lynch's film. The film moves between different levels of fantasy, treating the relation between unconscious, structuring fantasies; dreams and daydreams; and shared, public fantasies (generic features, character types, verbal and visual clichés). While it is possible to read this film as a depiction of a confrontation between fantasy and real life, fantasy, in fact, has a much more diffuse presence in the film, underwriting "real life" at every moment. *Mulholland Drive* is both a film "about" fantasy and a film permeated by fantasy at every level: in its setting, its narrative structure, and its visual techniques, the film reflects constantly on the experience of the fantasizing subject. Lesbianism operates in the film as a site for the exploration of fantasy—it occupies a strange twilight realm, somewhere between a dream and a cliché.

The first part of the film traces the adventures of Betty (played by Naomi Watts), a young hopeful just in from Canada who is trying to make it as an actress in Hollywood. On her first day in town, Betty arrives at her aunt's apartment, where she encounters a noirish beauty recovering from a car accident (this character, played by Laura Elena Harring, calls herself Rita after seeing Rita Hayworth's name on a poster for the movie *Gilda*). In her purse, Rita has no clues to her identity: just a lot of cash and a blue key. As Betty attempts to get her career under way, the two women embark on a series of adventures in order to try to discover Rita's true identity. At the same time, the film traces other plots, including the story of a young director (Adam Kesher, played by Justin Theroux) who is losing control of his film to the gangsters who "really" run the film industry.

Betty misses an opportunity to audition for the director's movie in order to go with Rita to the apartment of a woman named Diane Selwyn. After snooping around the complex for a while, they are horrified to discover a woman's rotting corpse in Diane's bed. Back home, they create a disguise for Rita that makes her look like Betty; Betty then invites Rita to spend the night in bed with her, and the two women have sex. In the middle of the night, Rita wakes up and asks Betty to take her to Club Silencio, a theater where they see a series of simulated performances, including a Spanish-language version of Roy Orbison's "Crying," sung by Rebekah del Rio. The scene in the club serves as a hinge in the film: while they are there, Betty reaches into Rita's purse and finds a blue box, a match with the key from early in the film. The two women return home, Rita opens the box, and both women disappear from the frame and from the film.

The rest of the movie takes place in a world that has a lot in common with the first part: settings (Diane Selwyn's apartment, the diner Winky's, the director's house on Mulholland Drive), plot elements, and the use of the same two main actresses. Pointedly missing from this part of the film, though, are the characters of Betty and Rita. We finally meet Diane Selwyn in person—she is played by Watts, who is now almost unrecognizable as the perky, radiant blonde from the first half of the film. Diane is a failed actress; she is haggard, bitter, and sunk in depression. Harring reappears, playing the role of Camilla Rhodes, the actress whom Adam Kesher was forced to cast in the lead role of his film. In this reconfiguration, it appears that Camilla and Diane are both aspiring actresses; that Camilla has had a brief affair with Diane and dropped her; and that Camilla has become a star and is now engaged to the director. Furthermore, we come to understand that Diane has hired a hit man to have Camilla murdered. In the end, Diane, driven mad by remorse, retreats to her bedroom and shoots herself—thus setting the scene for the discovery of her corpse by Betty and Rita earlier in the film.

In *Mulholland Drive,* Lynch draws on not one lesbian cliché but two, as he juxtaposes the two most familiar lesbian plots of the twentieth century. In the romance between Betty and Rita, Lynch presents lesbianism in its innocent and expansive form: lesbian desire appears as one big adventure, an entrée into a glamorous and unknown territory. This fantasy both compensates for and functions as a screen for the story's other lesbian narrative. In the story of Diane and Camilla, Lynch offers us a classic lesbian triangle, in which an attractive but unavailable woman dumps a less attractive woman who is figured as exclusively lesbian. Just as it is necessary that there should be no man in the first, positive scenario, it is crucial that the betrayal in this second story should come in the form of the inaccessible woman's "ending up" with a man. Within such a narrative, the woman who discards a woman for a man stands in for the glamour of mobile desire, while the "committed lesbian" represents the horror of a fixed but impossible object choice. The continuing resonance of this plot of triangulation is legible in the fact that lesbianism is popularly understood as both the hottest thing on earth and, at the same time, as something fundamentally sad and not at all erotic. The lesbian is at once the sexiest possible woman and at the same time an abject and unwanted creature. Just as the innocent, schoolgirl plot floats magnificently free of the imperatives of the phallus, reproduction, and social reality itself, so in the classic lesbian triangle the heterosexual order asserts itself with crushing effects for the abandoned woman.

In *Mulholland Drive,* Lynch scrambles these two plots, refusing to respect the distance between the comic and the tragic versions of female same-sex desire. By casting Naomi Watts as both Betty and Diane, Lynch shows schoolgirl capers and abject lesbian longing to be two aspects of a single fantasy. Diane offers a resonant image of the tragic lesbian as the couple's abject remainder: unable to resist the totalizing logic of heterosexual romance, she is condemned to futile rage, jealousy, and self-destruction. In showing Betty as Diane's imaginary alter ego, Lynch reveals the idealized image of the lesbian to be a ghostly effect produced by the social impossibility of lesbianism. It appears that Diane, the ultimate loser, can hardly do without her fantasized twin, the woman who won the jitterbug contest and walked away from the prize. But at the same time, Betty cannot exist without Diane's longing for her: her victory is meaningless without Diane's loss. In this sense, the tragic lesbian stands behind the shimmering image of the lesbian-as-fantasy-object—a dark shadow she cannot shake.

In their essay "Fantasy and the Origins of Sexuality," Jean Laplanche and Jean-Bertrand Pontalis attempt through a rereading of Freud to restore fantasy as the "fundamental object of psychoanalysis."[12] They argue that we cannot understand fantasy simply as the opposite of reality, pointing out that, in a psychoanalytic view, fantasy is "more real" than reality, because it supports and structures the very appearance of reality. Furthermore, Laplanche and Pontalis do not understand fantasy as a way of seizing on an object of desire: rather, they describe it as the "setting of desire" and see neither the subject nor the object of desire as fixed in the fantasy scene. "Fantasy, however, is not the object of desire, but its setting. In fantasy the subject does not pursue the object or its sign: he appears caught up himself in the sequence of images. He forms no representation of the desired object, but is himself represented as participating in the scene although, in the earliest forms of fantasy, he cannot be assigned any fixed place in it . . . As a result, the subject, although always present in the fantasy, may be so in a desubjectivized form, that is to say, in the very syntax of the sequence in question" (26). Laplanche and Pontalis describe fantasy that is not attached to an object, but that is organized as a scene. The dreamer may be a character in this scene, but he is not guaranteed to be its protagonist; his identification may be with any of the characters in the scene, or, in fact, with the "very syntax of the sequence in question."

In her 1984 article "Fantasia," film critic Elizabeth Cowie takes up Laplanche and Pontalis's work to consider the relation between public and private fantasy and the role of gender difference in structuring fantasy. "Conventions are thus the means by which the structuring of desires is represented in public forms, inasmuch as . . . fantasy is the mise-en-scène of desire. What is necessary for any public forms of fantasy, for their collective consumption, is not universal objects of desire, but a setting of desiring in which we can find our place(s). And these places will devolve, as in the original fantasies, on positions of desire: active or passive, feminine or masculine, mother or son, father or daughter" (87).[13] Cowie argues that conventions—generic conventions, conventions of filmic representation, or the conventions of narrative—structure desires into public forms that allow for multiple identifications. These identifications are not completely unbound (as we might think of desire before its representation in fantasy) but rather are structured according to more or less fixed "positions." Gender difference is crucial in such positioning: though gender cannot determine precisely how one will identify, it determines the places that are available. Or, as Cowie writes, "While the terms of sexual difference are fixed, the places of characters and spectators in relation to those terms are not" (102).

This version of fantasy can, I think, help us read the opening moments of *Mulholland Drive*. The film begins as a few shadows move in slow motion across a blue screen; these blurry shapes will become visible as parts of human bodies only later. As the music hits full swing, several figures emerge, some shadows, some realized in full color, dancing an exuberant jitterbug, still against the backdrop of an electric blue screen. These figures overlap and play against each other, moving in and out of cut-out "blank" or "empty" silhouettes of dancing couples. (There are no "intermediate types" here.) The wild profusion of couples suggests that, as a viewer, it is not necessary to choose just one of these positions. The total effect is of a scene, a fantasy in which every image on the screen is potentially available as an object of desire and/or identification. The clichés of gender do not disappear in such a scene, but rather they are scattered across the screen. As a result, the spectator's investment here is in sequence, in the exuberance of gesture, and in the pleasure of moving imaginatively across the boundary between male and female, as well as across the boundary of the human form. Out of this depthless field, the triumphant face of Diane/Betty emerges in a halo of white light, the apparent winner of this contest. Her ghostly appearance as the protagonist of this scene signals a turn from an unfixed fantasy to a first-person wish-fulfillment dream that sets the film's narrative in motion.

The jitterbug contest is taken up again the second half of the film, when Diane describes how she came to Hollywood at Adam and Camilla's dinner party. In this scene, Diane emerges as a familiar figure—the tragic or failed lesbian, destined to lose her lover to a man. Late in the film, her story finally congeals, as she delivers it in a bitter, tearful, and subdued voice: "I won this jitterbug contest. That sort of led to acting. To wanting to act. When my aunt died, she left me some money." In this version, the blissful elasticity of the earlier fantasy drains away. As this early scene resolves into a story, we see that it is already a narrative of failure, with Diane cast as its abject protagonist. Diane's speech finds no audience, as the bored and intolerant guests at the dinner table have trouble making even the most rudimentary sense of her life story. Diane's speech in this scene is contrasted with the over-authorized speech of Adam and Camilla. The party turns out to be the occasion for the announcement of Adam and Camilla's marriage; however, this event turns out to be so legitimate, so expected, that the actual announcement is redundant. Adam is so busy kissing Camilla that he barely gets the words out; he only ever says, "Camilla and I are going to . . ." and the rapt audience and his guests fill in the blank.[14]

By contrasting these two versions of the jitterbug contest, Lynch underscores the difference between desubjectivized fantasy and fantasy as wish fulfillment. He also suggests that fantasy in its expansive, scenic form may not be able to survive its translation into narrative: the dream scene, itself a playful cliché, hardens into a different and more devastating kind of cliché. Lesbianism in *Mulholland Drive* represents both the utopian possibility of doing without a fixed sexual object as well as the disastrous consequences of fixing on an object that is by definition lost.

In the dinner party scene, Camilla with her perverse heterosexuality is allied with mobile, scenic fantasy; as an exclusively lesbian woman, Diane's desire is understood as tragic from the start. For her, the stakes are impossibly high: the difference between these two forms of fantasy means the difference between success and failure, between sexiness and abjection, even between life and death.

Lynch explores the volatility of cliché in the film's remarkable sex scenes. The first of these pictures the happy moment when Rita and Betty "get together"; the second scene pictures a "failed" erotic encounter, in which Diane "discovers" that Camilla is leaving her for Adam. Both scenes are deeply engaged with the stock images of lesbian representation: they pile up lesbian clichés quite freely, sometimes incoherently, and with effects that are both funny and moving.

The first scene occurs shortly after Betty and Rita have seen Diane's corpse. We find Betty musing in bed, modestly attired in pink pajamas. Rita appears in the doorway, wearing a towel and the blond wig that they have fashioned for her. Though the opening of the scene is played like an outtake from a college dormitory, Rita's dark eyes smoldering beneath her platinum hair suggest she may have wandered in from a different picture. The generic dissonance of this scene is the source of its comic effect as well as the reason for the constant misunderstandings between the two characters. Both the schoolgirl and the femme fatale are stock lesbian characters, but they are not supposed to end up in bed together. Betty's opening invitation to have Rita join her in the bed recalls a tradition of boarding school romances that walk a fine line between innocence and experience, between cuddling and depravity. Rita nearly passes for a character in such a drama at the beginning of this scene, though by the time she drops the towel it is clear where the scene is heading. Before climbing into bed, Rita pauses, striking a classic pin-up pose: we see almost her entire body, centered in the frame, lit from behind, and punishingly voluptuous.

As the scene gets going between these two women, it reflects a very familiar idea of what sex between women looks like—very breasty, very kissy. The mother-daughter "plot" of lesbian romance is invoked here as well: her torso looming up out of the bedclothes, Rita appears for a moment as a "noir mom" come to tuck in her daughter. The familiar but slightly "off" quality of this scene is underlined after the women start to kiss. Betty pauses to give voice to that ultimate cliché of the lesbian encounter: "Have you ever done this before?" In response to this naive (or faux-naive) question, Rita's honestly amnesiac response is "I don't know.

Have you?" The intense pleasure and surprise of this line is difficult to account for. It shines more brightly for being set against a background of hardened clichés. It also seems to point to a kind of utopian plenitude in the midst of this more or less predictable scene. Rita's response is striking in its insistence that what matters is not memory but desire. Her innocence here loosens the bonds between the past and the future and insists that the future is still in the making. It does not matter if we have done this before, or if we even know what it is (Have you done this before? What is *this,* anyway?). Together with Betty's next response ("I want to with you"), this line suggests that what we have done and who we are does not count for much—what matters instead is what we are about to do, what we want to do.[15]

The later scene between Diane and Camilla works according to a much different logic. It occurs in the morning, just after Diane has been awoken from a deep depressive sleep. Perhaps one of the most striking features of *Mulholland Drive* is the physical transformation of Naomi Watts from the beginning to the end of the film. After she "wakes up" in the second part of the film, Watts's perky slim body appears too skinny, ragged—as if hollowed out by desire. While we might read the scene between Betty and Rita as Diane's fantasy, it reads much less clearly as "sexual fantasy" than Diane's later encounter with Camilla. The iconography of this brief encounter is drawn from soft-core pornography, and the proximity of Diane's masturbation scene to this one suggests that this may be a more "straight," end-oriented erotic fantasy.

In this scene, Camilla, the focus of all Diane's longing, appears more radiant than ever. As Martha Nochimson points out, it is as if she has literally sucked the life out of Diane.[16] The life has certainly been sucked out of the dialogue in this scene, which proceeds from cliché to cliché. Diane's cheesy, slightly '80s line ("What was that you were saying, Beautiful?") is matched for pure woodenness by Camilla's response ("I said, 'You drive me wild!'"). Camilla plays the part of the femme fatale to the hilt, following "You drive me wild!" almost immediately with "We can't do this anymore," and, more emphatically, "Diane, *don't!*" These characters mouth their lines without conviction, their speech entirely devoid of the hesitation and surprise that characterize dialogue in the earlier scene. The possibilities for multiple identification and the improvisation opened in the first section of the film are shut down here, as each of the women plays her assigned role in a familiar—all too familiar—drama of lesbian triangulation and betrayal ("It's him, isn't it?"—but of course it is!).

In *Mulholland Drive,* cliché can be as deadening as Betty's "Have you ever done this before?" or as expansive as Rita's "I don't know." In the first half of the film, reality is structured by cliché but is nonetheless thickly studded with surprise. In the second half of the film, that reality hardens to the point of total immobility. Fantasy in part one gives reality a wonderful texture, a dazzling appearance that recalls the luminous world of the jitterbug dream in the beginning of the film. It also loosens the hold of cliché, making available stock genres and roles for shifting identifications. In the second part of the film, we alternate between a grim reality (with no trace of fantasy in it) and a compensatory world of fantasy in which desire is closely tied to an object that is always already lost. The object of desire is lost in both worlds—but the first part of *Mulholland Drive* points to the possibility of a kind of fantasy in which the loss of the object is not played in a tragic register.

The hardening of fantasy in the second half of the film has particularly dire consequences for Diane, because the role she takes up is a tragic one. While Camilla's utterly clichéd role still allows for some mobility and transgression, Diane turns into a cliché without any "give," without any "play." She reaches the depths of abjection in the masturbation scene, when on the couch she touches herself, tears rolling down her face. As Diane stares at the stony surface of the fireplace opposite, the rough, variegated surface of the chimney blurs in and out of focus. Lynch uses this technique several times during the film, and in this case it seems particularly closely tied to Diane's point of view. As her tears repeatedly blur this irregular surface into a smooth screen, it seems that Diane is willing herself into fantasy. But in this scene, her powerful fantasy-machine has run down; she manages for an instant, but the same stony reality keeps returning.

Camilla's betrayal of Diane is the oldest story in the book, a classic in the genre of homosexual tragedies of betrayal. Perhaps the best known is Oscar Wilde's trial and death: both Wilde and Diane make the mistake of expecting extraordinary things from people who turn out in the end to be quite ordinary. Anyone can make such a mistake, but it is because the homosexual already occupies the position of the scapegoat that his sacrifice looks so natural. For "someone like Diane," love fails because it must, because Sapphic promise *inevitably* founders on the rocks of homosexual impossibility. It can be counted as a tragedy that for modern subjects, having impossible desires means that you become an impossible person. Given that homosexuality is considered a tragic state of being, it is difficult for any individual homosexual life-story to signify as tragic.

Diane's abject longing for Camilla Rhodes is at some distance from the sublime defiance of Antigone. While Antigone's refusal of Creon's injunction makes her an enemy of the state, Diane's love for Camilla puts her outside the norm. Her state of exile does not have the dignity of rebellion. To add insult to injury, her desire for a "normal woman" makes her appear nothing more than a poor wretch, panting after goods that she cannot have. *Mulholland Drive* is remarkable in that it takes Diane's tragedy seriously. By linking Diane to Betty, her radiant alter ego, Lynch manages to make her suicide count as tragic action. Her rotting corpse is at the center of the film, the "content," if there is any, of the blue box.

Many gays and lesbians consider dwelling on such tragedies to be counterproductive in the extreme. According to this view, "homosexual tragedy" belongs to a different era, to a time when living as a homosexual was nearly impossible. Given that social circumstances have changed so profoundly in the last thirty years, they argue for the need to get over this past, not eroticize it. Such a view does not account for the ways in which lesbians and gays, despite the new possibilities that are open to them, continue to be positioned as modernity's others. Such structural facts are slow to change, as are the feelings that circulate around them. For contemporary subjects whose identities and desires are bound up with this past, this injunction to "get over the past" can sound like bullying.[17] As masochistic fantasies were off-limits for second-wave feminists, so for contemporary lesbians socially regressive desires—fantasies about lesbian abjection and glittering femmes fatales—are perhaps the greatest taboo. Our desires are supposed to lead the way to a different future, not fasten us to the image of the past.[18] Such forward thinking, however, cannot address structural inequalities or the real complexities of desire. Instead, we need a politics that goes "all the way down," that is attentive to the dark places of affective and erotic life.

A crucial debate about the political uses of tragedy has considered the question of whether tragedy is absolute, or whether it can be ameliorated through social change. The fact that homosexuality is tragic is a social rather than a natural fact. But it is not necessary to imagine that homosexual life will *never* change in order to experience it as tragic in the present. This vision of homosexuality is a product of ideology, but ideology has real effects: simply recognizing its illusory nature is not enough. (Such a point seems to be at the heart of the central sequence in the film, the "live" performance in Club Silencio. Although the emcee continually describes the scene on the stage as an illusion, this illusion has palpable effects: the stage lightning induces an epileptic fit in Betty; Rebekah del Rio's faked death elicits real tears from both women.)

Mulholland Drive depicts lesbian fantasy as inextricably bound up with lesbian tragedy. While Betty and Rita's unscripted antics gesture toward an escape route, the film keeps circling back to a dead end. The film supports Slavoj Zizek's suggestion that "fantasy does not simply realize a desire in a hallucinatory way: rather, . . . a fantasy constitutes our desire, provides its co-ordinates; that is, it literally 'teaches us how to desire.'"[19] The fact that fantasy does not follow after desire, but rather constitutes it, means that there is in the subject no pure wellspring of desire. (Or, as Zizek puts it, *there is no secret treasure in me* [10].) Recognizing the structuring function of fantasy means giving up on the dream of lesbian authenticity, which in this light looks like just another cliché. In a related sense, we might say that psychic injury is not a threat to subjectivity but rather constitutive of it. It is for this reason that we cannot blame Diane's death on a lack of optimism or a lack of nerve. As long as lesbianism is socially denigrated, her corpse will continue to turn up in the midst of even the dreamiest lesbian fantasy. Diane Selwyn is a *structural effect* of homophobia, one of the tragic others that modernity produces with such alarming regularity.

Notes

1. See Raymond Williams, *Modern Tragedy* (Stanford: Stanford University Press, 1966), 202–3. Terry Eagleton extends this point in *Sweet Violence,* arguing that "tragedy, that privileged preserve of gods and spiritual giants, has now been decisively democratized—which is to say, for the devotees of gods and giants, abolished. Hence the death-of-tragedy thesis. Tragedy, however, did not vanish because there were no more great men. It did not expire with the last absolutist monarch. On the contrary, since under democracy each one of us is to be incommensurably cherished, it has been multiplied far beyond antique imagining" (94). For Eagleton, as for Williams, the multiplication of tragedy in the modern world is hardly cause for celebration, for, in such a world, "absolutely nobody is safe" from its effects (95). For more on Eagleton's view of modern tragedy, see below (*Sweet Violence: The Idea of the Tragic* [Oxford: Blackwell, 2003]).

2. Henri Lefebvre, *Introduction to Modernity: Twelve Preludes September 1959–May 1961,* trans. John Moore (London: Verso, 1995), 190.

3. In *Modern Tragedy,* Williams argues that in classical drama, only the suffering of kings mattered, but this was largely because they suffered on behalf of the community as a whole. The modern tragic hero cannot be representative in the same way, for in classical drama what was important was "the general status of the man of rank. His fate was the fate of the house or kingdom which he at once ruled and embodied. In the person of Agamemnon or of Lear the fate of a house or a kingdom was literally acted out." In bourgeois tragedy, as it began to develop

in the eighteenth century, "the individual was neither the state nor an element of the state, but an entity in himself. There was then both loss and gain: the suffering of a man of no rank could be more seriously and more directly regarded, but equally, in the stress on the fate of an individual, the general and public character of tragedy was lost" (50). Now we live in an era in which no individual's suffering is bound up significantly with anyone else's: everyone has a "right" to tragedy, but each must go it alone.

4. Eagleton, *Sweet Violence*, xvi.

5. Karl Marx, "Contribution to the Critique of Hegel's Philosophy of Right," in T. Bottomore, ed., *Karl Marx: Early Writings* (London, 1963), 58. Quoted in Eagleton, *Sweet Violence*, 288.

6. Eagleton continues, "What category of member, as far as rank, profession, provenance, gender, ethnicity and the like go, is a supremely indifferent affair. As with censuses, there are certain questions which one need not ask" (94). Evincing a "supreme indifference" toward the specificities of gender and race, Eagleton appeals to the life of the species as the ground of tragic suffering. It is striking he dismisses such questions by means of an analogy with the census, which gathers information in these same categories.

7. A global coalition that would unite all of these outcasts is a powerful dream, and it may be that a tragic "community of suffering" is the best way to make this dream come true. But the fact that a universal revolutionary class has not emerged at the beginning of the twenty-first century cannot simply be blamed on the missteps of the cultural left, nor can a global coalition be built on a false sense of sameness or on a moribund concept of universalism. For an account of the political potential of universalism that is more attuned to its exclusions, see the debates between Judith Butler, Ernesto Laclau, and Slavoj Zizek, in *Contingency, Hegemony, Universality: Contemporary Dialogues on the Left* (London: Verso, 2000).

8. George Steiner, *The Death of Tragedy* (New Haven: Yale University Press, 1961), xi.

9. These "minorities" are of course also routinely blamed for the fragmentation of the Left and for the non-emergence of a viable revolutionary class.

10. Sollers argues that the mulatto is "a most upsetting and subversive character who illuminates the paradoxes of 'race' in America" (234). In addition, Sollers argues that given the importance of blood kinship, flawed heroes, the clash of moral orders, and secret plotting in narratives of the tragic mulatto, we may want to take seriously the idea that this figure is tragic in a sense contiguous with the classical meaning of this term. Werner Sollers, *Neither Black Nor White Yet Both: Thematic Explorations of Interracial Literature* (Cambridge, MA: Harvard University Press, 1997), 234.

11. Felski argues in an unpublished manuscript that modernity's most characteristic and ambivalent subjects may be those who stand to gain the most from its transformations. "The modern world speaks to women in compelling and contradictory ways, brandishing promises and inciting desires that it often fails to

fulfill. It is precisely because women feel themselves addressed by the hopes and ideals of the Enlightenment that they are so acutely aware of its failings." In addition, Felski considers the ways in which women embody both the promises and the failures of modernity. She writes, "[W]omen register the seismic tremors of modernity with uncanny sharpness. The contradictions of the modern world are writ especially large on female bodies." Rita Felski, "Tragic Women" (manuscript, Department of English, University of Virginia, 2003).

12. Jean Laplanche and Jean-Bertrand Pontalis, "Fantasy and the Origins of Sexuality" in *Formations of Fantasy,* ed. Victor Burgin, James Donald, and Cora Kaplan (London: Methuen, 1986), 14.

13. Elizabeth Cowie, "Fantasia," *m/f* 9 (1984): 71–105.

14. In a reading of J. L. Austin's *How to Do Things with Words,* Eve Kosofsky Sedgwick points out that "I do" is Austin's "most inveterately recurrent and . . . most influential example" (3) of the performative. Sedgwick discusses the marriage ceremony as a crucial site for socially authorized speech. In the dinner party scene in *Mulholland Drive,* Lynch suggests "We are going to be married" as a kind of super-performative utterance, a phrase that is so authorized that it does not even have to be spoken. See Sedgwick, "Queer Performativity: Henry James's *The Art of the Novel,*" *GLQ: A Journal of Lesbian and Gay Studies* 1.1 (1993): 1–16.

15. The lack of subjective coordinates in this scene seems to indicate that this is a fantasy that does not work through a logic of possession. Even Betty's next approach to Rita—"I am in love with you! I am in love with you!" (which we *might* read as the breaking through of Diane's character in this scene) does not sound much like an attempt to seize and hold the object of desire. This outburst registers a moment of shattering affective intensity, but one that does not necessarily lead toward the possession of the object. (We might contrast it with the final sex scene in *Lost Highway,* in which Bill Pullman says "I want you!" over and over.)

16. Camilla's name also evokes Sheridan Le Fanu's vampire story "Carmilla."

17. Although Andrew Sullivan's is the loudest voice in the "get over it" chorus, this sentiment is widely shared. See, for instance, the following e-mail, which Chris Castiglia cites in his article "Sex Panics, Sex Publics, Sex Memories." The author of the e-mail is a self-identified member of "Generation Q." He writes, "It has finally occurred to Generation Q that [in order] to make any significant progress in our own lives (call it greedy, if you like) it's time for gay men to stop thinking with their dicks . . . and start thinking about the future." *boundary 2* 27.2 (2000): 152.

18. See Elizabeth Freeman, "Packing History, Count(er)ing Generations" on the concept of temporal drag as a critique of the future-time of queer performativity. Freeman offers a fascinating reading of lesbian butch-femme practices as eroticizing not only gender difference but temporal difference as well. *New Literary History* 31 (2000): 727–44.

19. Slavoj Zizek, "The Seven Veils of Fantasy," in *The Plague of Fantasies* (London: Verso, 1997), 7.

The Return of the Tragic
in Postmodern Societies

Michel Maffesoli

Translated by Rita Felski, Allan Megill,
and Marilyn Gaddis Rose

The tragic is unthinkable, and yet it is incumbent on us to think it. Let us also remember that the spirit, like the wind, blows where it will. Perhaps in this way we can understand the astonishing return of archaic values to the forefront of the social scene. Tribalism and nomadism, in particular, undermine our mental convictions and ways of being. Like the wind, they swirl up around us; this renders them disturbing, as well as the values they bring with them.

But there is little talk of all this in the organs of established thought. Denial is mandatory; we dare not speak of what frightens us. The tragic belongs to this category. It is a deafening unsaid, for if there is anything that is lived empirically on a day-to-day basis, it is indeed "the tragic sense of life." There is a tendency to think of everyday life, which was terra incognita until recently, only in anecdotal and superficial terms. Commenting on the saying from the gospel, "Give us this day our daily bread," Jung observed that it was difficult to translate because the term "daily" occurs only in this passage, and he notes that St. Jerome proposed the Gnostic expression "suprasubstantial bread." This linkage is enlightening, for it emphasizes that the daily is the true principle of reality—indeed, of "superreality" (*surréalité*).[1]

Without being put into so many words, everyday facts and experience are there, inescapable. There is something fated about them and it is with this fatum that we must wrestle. This means integrating, on an individual as well as a collective level, the role of the unpredictable or the incalculable in causing decisive events. This is something like the "objective chance" (*hasard objectif*) of the surrealists, not limited to the happy few but widely lived by the whole of society.

This is a translation of part of the introduction and first chapter of Michel Maffesoli's *L'instant éternel: Le retour du tragique dans les sociétés postmodernes* (Paris: Denöel, 2000). Translated by permission of the author.

319

Unquestionably, if we know how to recognize all the features of the tragic, we will be able to understand a number of social practices, particularly among the young, that otherwise appear meaningless. Let me be direct: in the tragic sensibility, time comes to a halt, or at least it slows down. Speed in its diverse forms characterized the drama of modernity. Scientific, technological, or economic development is the most visible result. By contrast, we are seeing an emerging panegyric to slowness, indeed to idleness. Life is now no more than a concatenation of motionless moments, eternal moments, from which one must be able to draw the greatest amount of pleasure.

It is this inversion of the polarity of time that gives presence to life and accords value even to what is stifling in the present, that promotes the sense of tribal belonging, and that allows us to view ordinary life under the sign of destiny. Ordinary life, banal life: this is the mulch from which communal renewal comes.

The great paradigm shift that is taking place, thanks to this presentism, is indeed the slippage from an "ego-centered" to a "place-centered" (*loco-centré*) worldview. In the former instance of a modernity that is now ending, primacy is given to the rational individual living in a contractual society. In the latter instance, of an emerging postmodernity, it is groups that come into play, "neotribes" that lay siege to specific spaces and harmonize with them.

In the drama of modernity one finds an optimistic claim to totality: totality of the self, the world, the state. In the tragedy of postmodernity there is a concern for *entirety* leading to the loss of the individual ego in a greater self of natural or social otherness. The narcissism of the individual is dramatic; the primacy of the tribal is tragic. . . .

The importance of Greek tragedy for Western culture is in fact deeply rooted, frequently emphasizing everything that humanity owes to *Tyche* (Fortune) and *Moira* (Fate). There are many Greek poets, such as Archilochus, who show how the gods bring low and then in turn raise up human beings, countries, parties, and institutions. However conscientious, logical, or rational it may be, all human effort is precarious, even more so when it is moved by passion and affect.[2] There is something irrational about the trajectory of fortune. Or rather, its rationality lies precisely in its precariousness, in its not discriminating among those upon whom it acts. No one, mighty or lowly, rich or poor, escapes its blows. Everyone can await its blessings.

The vanity of human actions, the sense of their precariousness and of the brevity of life, are more or less consciously expressed in the latent tragic mood or the fervent hedonism that characterizes this fin de siècle. For there is a strong link—it will be necessary to show how it is articulated—between the tragic and hedonism. Both concern themselves with living intensely what offers itself to be experienced. Life is avidly lived. It is no longer a question of mere consumption, but of intense consummation. This "society of consummation" can be seen especially clearly in the practices of the young, who no longer recognize themselves in the postponed pleasures of political action or professional achievement but who want everything and want it now, even if this "everything" does not amount to much, even if it is—whether religious, cultural, technical, or economic—quickly rendered obsolete. It is this avid desire that allows us to understand the predominance of the "fashionable" mode of everything, or even the surprising instability that characterizes the political, ideological, and indeed the emotional relationships that make up the social bond. The sense of fate underlying all this expresses a way of life, an *ars vivendi* that accords with the world such as it is because it is the only one that we have, the only one that is given to live. An art of living that is no longer based on a search for absolute freedom, but rather for small freedoms that are interstitial, relative, empirical, and lived from day to day.

It is a matter, to be sure, of a general analytical framework. This framework serves to emphasize that the tragic, a secret or unobtrusive structural presence during the last two or three centuries which were largely dominated by a dramatic notion of the world, is now tending to assert itself ever more vigorously. Film, music, clothing, and above all music, forcefully evoke the return of necessity. This *Ananke,* which, according to the sages, did not have a face, nowadays, by contrast, wears a multitude of faces.

That things are felt to be inescapable, that we see the recurrence of the same phenomena, that everything mysteriously takes its course without there really being the possibility of intervention, the turn to fortune-telling or other forms of prediction, just like the religiosity that surrounds us—all this is indeed the sign of a kind of acceptance of fatality, the indication of the replacement of history, whose rational path we can influence, by a destiny which we must take on. There are moments, as Virgil says, when destiny finds the way: "Fata viam invenient."[3] Something of this sort is now under way. . . .

We need to reflect at length on this theme of the cyclical return of things. For the moment, let us note that it clearly underscores the predominance of fate, a fate with which one must reckon both in terms of individual life and of social life as a whole. The importance that the pursuit of pleasure is taking on—or taking on again—is illuminating in this regard. It is indeed true that, traditionally, the culture of pleasure goes hand in hand with the tragic sense of destiny. We can say, moreover, that the theatricality of everyday life, the pursuit of the superfluous, even the frivolous, and of course the importance given to *carpe diem,* not to mention the cult of the body in its diverse forms, are all expressions of such a tragic consciousness.

We often see social commentators puzzling over the violent character of some news item, taking note of the suicide of an adolescent seeking to emulate the rock singer who was his model. But this is not at all surprising. Such an excessive action simply reveals a latent state of mind that sees in paroxysmal revolt, in a death that is really enacted, the only alternative to a sanitized existence where the certainty of not dying is countered by the certainty of dying of boredom. Hard rock in its various forms, decadent styles in painting and dress, in short the nomadism that is around us, all reveal the return of the barbarians inside our gates, that is to say, the bursting apart of the civilized universe that modernity, over the course of three centuries, has patiently established.

There is a kind of wisdom at the disposal of the young who know, to paraphrase Aeschylus, how to yield to fate. This new tragic wisdom, which can go so far as suicide, and which in any case favors excess, is a form of heroism. A heroism that, while recognizing the irrevocability of love affairs, ideological commitments, and sudden acts of revolt, does not think of instituting them in the form of "family, faith, party," all forms that are sclerotic and potentially deadly.

In short, what once was—passions, ideals, enthusiasms—cannot be abolished, but one does not want to turn them into a constraining yoke. The culture of pleasure, the sense of the tragic, the confrontation with destiny, are both the cause and the effect of an ethics of the moment, of an emphasis on experiences lived for their own sake, that exhaust themselves in the very act and that no longer point forward into a future that is predictable and controllable at will. This is the outcome of "necessity" in its philosophical sense: it creates heroes, the new knights of postmodernity, capable of risking their lives for a cause that can be both idealistic and perfectly frivolous. Such a risk may be imaginary, belonging to the order of simulation, or, with brutal consequences, completely real. But in every instance we can understand it as an affirmation of life that is sufficiently polymorphous to include death.

In the confrontation with fate there is thus a passion for life that can only shock staid minds and other administrators of knowledge who are only capable of locating and analyzing thoughts and lifestyles that approximate the average. Fate reminds us that being is event, indeed advent. To return to the modernity/postmodernity opposition, one can say that in the framework of the former, history unfolds, whereas in the latter, the event arrives. It intrudes, it compels, it wreaks violence. Hence its brutal, unexpected, always startling quality. Here again we find the difference of tonality between the drama or the dialectic, which postulates a solution or a possible synthesis, and the tragic, which is aporetic in structure.

The advent is singular, but its singularity is rooted in an archaic atemporal substratum. Of course, it is a matter of "archaisms" that are rethought in relation to the present, that are lived in a specific manner, but that retain nevertheless the memory of their origins. The event-advent, as I have said. Certainly, whatever is experienced qualitatively and with intensity works to bring about the resurgence of what is already at the very heart of individual or collective being. Here we can refer to Heidegger and his concern for postmetaphysical thought, in that he strives to bring out the more "simple" that underlies human existence, but we can also refer to Leibniz, who through his "principle of indiscernibles" seeks a middle way between absolute difference and the return of the same.[4] Between these two, romanticism or *Lebensphilosophie* accentuates the tragic side of the present, as well as its demands, its passion for life, and the sense of urgency it exudes.

Does not all of this typify the surprising contemporary attitudes of young people and others who show little or no concern for the consequences of their acts? Plural families or serial and ephemeral love affairs exemplify this phenomenon in the affective domain, as do political fickleness or ideological changes in public life. The acceptance of the anarchic laws of production and at the same time the extraordinary suspicion of them attest to what we might call economic disorder. In all of this there is an air of nonchalance that encourages not concern for tomorrow but, on the contrary, a desire to live in the present, in reference to a mode of being that has progressively constituted itself over the course of centuries.

If we try to define this mood, we can link it with an eternal paganism, a paganism striving to seize hold of life, to seize what life offers and what presents itself. This pagan exuberance is determined to make use of the pleasures of the present, leading a bold, audacious life, a life permeated by the freshness of the moment—insofar as the latter is provisional, precarious, and therefore intense. Fichte refers to the "general impiety" to be found in Machiavelli's opposition to Christianity.[5] It seems to me that we can extrapolate from what Fichte says about this paganism. For it is indeed the essence of Christianity that we find in the political project, in the economic conception of existence, or in the search for security that is advocated by various social institutions.

It is against this form of Christianity that the impiety of the present is in revolt. The youthful quality of its effervescences, the freshness of its acts of revolt, the heightened search for polymorphous pleasure in the present, all lead it to see the "ancient world" as its country of origin. Of course, we have to understand "ancient world" metaphorically, that is, as meaning everything that contravenes the various categorical imperatives formulated by modern moralism, whether sexual, economic, or ideological. What distinguishes postmodernity is indeed this return to antiquity, to the archaic. It is as if, beyond the parenthetical episode of modernity, for better or for worse, in ordinary life or in paroxysmal frenzy, in subdued fashion or in destructive excess, the sublime aspect of the beauty of the world were being rediscovered. Only this would be important, to take pleasure in it for what it is, even if this means submitting to terrible and dangerous laws that must indeed be accepted. This is of course to evoke the theme of *amor fati,* whose major social consequences one can evaluate in a Nietzschean spirit.

Marx observes that men make history without knowing what history they are making. More generally, the whole of modernity sets up an equivalence between self-realization and mastery over one's self and the world. There is a kind of pleasure in activity, whether work in the strict sense or the activity of politics. People are very often outraged by the slogan that was inscribed on the gate of the Nazi concentration camp at Dachau: "Arbeit macht frei" (work makes you free). But this is not at all a gloomy antiphrasis; the concentration camps were only the paroxysmal form of the "camp" that is contemporary society, where the injunction to do one thing or another (work, political or conjugal duty, educating one's children, vacations, and so forth) offers an illusory freedom in exchange for a real slavery, that of "modern times." To give Marx his due, modern people have indeed made their own history, but what a strange history! In any case, if they had known what history they were making, perhaps they would have refrained!

Waking up with a hangover from this bacchanal of promethean activity, more and more people are adopting a stoic attitude. It is a generalized stoicism, whereby those things that people can do nothing about become unimportant to them. This is the *amor fati* which ensures that fate is not simply meted out but is accepted, even loved, for what it is. This leads to a form of serenity that can seem paradoxical, but that is the basis of the numerous expressions of generosity, mutual aid, volunteering, and various humanitarian activities that are not uncommon in society and that are tending to proliferate. For the acceptance of what is can go hand in hand with a wish to become involved—not to master a given situation, but to go along with it in order to induce it, should the occasion arise, to give the best of itself. Thus the realization of the self or the world no longer takes the form of straightforward economic action but opens out into an ecological interaction. Perhaps this is how we move from the Hegelian-Marxist "mastery" that typifies modernity to what Bataille calls "sovereignty," which operates in terms of structural reversibility and would be the trademark of premodern and postmodern societies.

This stoic sovereignty, to be sure, reminds us of the thought, sensibility, and attitudes of the Far East (for example, those of Japan or China) which tend—if I may refer here to François Jullien—to privilege the "propensity of things." Which is to say that things, the world—we might add social situations and why not even individual or tribal situations—develop according to their own dispositions. Hence there are no grounds for projecting desires, values, and convictions of whatever kind upon them; rather one must "harmonize" with their development and the necessity that is theirs.[6] Here again, the initiative no longer belongs to the isolated individual or a collectivity formed on the basis of a social contract; rather it is conjoined, shared between the world and humanity, between things and the words that are spoken about them. . . .

Indeed, being attentive to necessity, to the propensity of things, to fate requires us to view individuals in their globality, in their context. That is to say, they are not ruled only by reason, as was the case in modernity, but are equally moved by emotions, feelings, moods, all the nonrational dimensions of what is given in the world.

To take up again a well-known theme revived by Eric Dodds, we can recall the role of the *daimon* in Greek tradition. Socrates, of course, openly displayed his own *daimon,* and we can assume that this was a widespread belief from which no one was exempt. But in the context of the present argument, it is interesting to underscore the close link between the *daimon* and *Tyche*—that necessity which played such an important role in the framework of ancient culture. In short, we can say that much more depended on necessity than on the particular character of the individual. It is precisely this which is expressed in various ways in the tragedies; one is acted upon more than one truly acts. Fate is there, all-powerful and pitiless, and in spite of the will of the subject it guides the action in the direction of what is written. Here again we are dealing with a form of predestination. To cite just one example among many, the entire myth of Oedipus is constructed on such a necessity, with its well-known paroxysmal outcome.

In fact, the force of destiny only serves to accentuate the growing power of the impersonal. What is at stake in this return of fate is the very negation of the philosophical foundation of the modern West: free will, the decisions of individuals or social groups acting together to make history. The great fantasy of universality was the result. By way of contrast, the affirmation or reaffirmation of cyclical systems makes such free will null and void.[7] The diverse mythic visions of the East that intrude into postmodernity renew their bond with impersonal forces and with the ineluctability of their actions. Whether we are talking about the various philosophies, or more simply the techniques, of Buddhism, Hinduism, Taoism, of an African clairvoyance in direct contact with the forces of the earth, of African-Brazilian possession cults, not to mention the many New Age practices, or simply the fascination exercised by astrology—all this essentially underscores that individuals are at worst mere toys and at best the partners of forces that exceed them and to which they must adjust.

As expressions of contemporary mythology, science fiction films, many video-clips, and sometimes even advertisements, show very clearly this relativizing of free will by a supraindividual "force." To be sure, great minds make mockery of such things but their meaningfulness cannot be denied. It bores into the social imaginary, assures the success of folkloric displays and historical reenactments, sends crowds off to pilgrimage sites and turns novels of initiation into bestsellers. In all these cases, and the list is far from complete, it is indeed a matter of a collective mind, a mass subjectivity—what the initiatory tradition calls the "egregore," that is to say, a social bond that no longer relies on pure reason but on a global interaction saturated with pathos. We could call this an "ethics of the aesthetic," which is another way of asking the same question as those medieval alchemists puzzling over the *glutinum mundi,* the glue of the world which brings it about that, whatever else is the case, there is something rather than nothing, and that this something is coherent. This "glue of the world" would thus be an impersonal force, a vital flux in which everyone and everything participates in a mysterious attracting correspondence.

Numerous poets, artists, and utopian thinkers have celebrated this attraction, which it is possible to read in a socio-anthropological sense. This is what I have tried to do through my use of the term "orgy," by which I mean communal passion, social empathy. Or, to slightly modify a phrase used by Durkheim, we could speak in this regard of an organic solidarity that causes everyone, willing or not, to be essentially part of a whole that at the same time makes each person what he or she is. In short, I exist only because the other who is my neighbor, or the Other who is the social world, grants me my existence. I am such and such a person because the other recognizes me as such. Such a claim may well appear shocking, but is this not, empirically, how societies function, from the smallest entity to the largest wholes? In her book *How Institutions Think,* Mary Douglas ably describes such a "structural effect."[8] This same phenomenon allows us to understand that whoever does not submit to such a recognition will be rejected, stigmatized, or marginalized. This exclusion stems from the fact that he or she does not have the "clan scent" or did not want to acquire it.

Thus, beyond individualism, whether theoretical or methodological, empirical social life simply is the expression of successive feelings of belonging. One is a member, one belongs, one joins with others, one participates, or to put it more trivially, one is "in." Even if this could be so in the best moments of modernity, nowadays autonomy, distinctiveness, and the affirmation of individual or class identity are all no longer anything more than a lure, an illusion, a simulacrum. The "sociology of the orgy," I have called it—that is to say, an order of fusion, indeed of confusion, whereby every person exists according to a principle of heteronomy.[9]

Keeping this in mind, we can understand the wholesale return and resonance of emblematic figures and other archetypes of everyday life. The phenomenon of fan groups among the younger generation is simply the paroxysmal form of these multiple attachments that are lived without even being consciously noticed. In this way one magically "connects" with such and such a rock singer, sports idol, religious or intellectual guru, or political leader, a participation that produces a quasi-mystical communion, a shared feeling of belonging. In a subtle observation, Gilbert Durand, alluding to such great tragic figures as Don Giovanni, emphasizes that they become "pure objects." They are objects more than subjects since they only exist in the minds of others; they become "ideal types."[10]

We can pursue this line of analysis by noting that these "grand abstractions" or archetypes are tending to multiply, indeed to become more democratic. More and more, we see small grand figures. In the final instance, every postmodern tribe will have its emblematic figure just as each tribe, in the strict sense, possessed and was possessed by its totem. In every case, identity, free will, decision-making, and individual choice can, to be sure, be affirmed or claimed, but these are in fact dependent on the identities, decisions, and choices of the group to which one belongs. Let us note, moreover, that these archetypes are regaining force and vigor at the same time that the tragic mood of the present asserts itself. This correlation merits our attention.

Indeed, within the context of the mechanism of the saturation of cultural values so well described by Pitirim Sorokin, it is because belief in the individual's absolute mastery over himself and nature is waning that we are seeing the resurgence of grand emblematic figures who exercise a powerful attraction. In short, whether it is acknowledged or not, we need to reckon with powers that go beyond us. We might recall—and this complicates our analysis somewhat—that the Judeo-Christian tradition, or even Western culture, rationalized such powers to some degree. The notion of a unique, omnipresent, all-surveying God, and the rational theodicy or theology which served to justify it, are among these rationalizations. It is the same with the unified State, guarantor of the social contract, and the political models that serve as its theoretical foundation. Let us recall in this regard the formula that Marx uses in *The Jewish Question* to define politics: "the profane form of religion." God and the State have thus been "economic" ways of thinking and organizing the forces that transcend the individual. These forces were inscribed into a dramatic, rational, and potentially controllable process.

At other moments these forces are again diffracted—they become plural, wild, and hence tragic once more. We master them less than they rule us. We must, for better or worse, deal with them. With regard to Goethe's exemplary work *Wilhelm Meister's Apprenticeship,* it was possible to speak of an "intertwining of destinies and characters," a judicious comment that alerts us to the interaction between the "vital force" belonging to a given individual and "external circumstances," that is to say, what is determined by fate.[11] This is the eternal problem that defines the formation of human beings, but also their existence in society—the problem of the relationship between individual subjectivity and the importance of environment, whatever it may be.

In the final analysis, the long initiation that is human existence consists of finding an equilibrium between character (let us remember the etymology of character: imprint) and the necessities with which this character is confronted. In tragic epochs the archetype can offer a useful way of reaching this equilibrium. As an all-embracing model, as an informing type, it can serve as a matrix—it brings into being and is the condition of possibility for modes of individual and social life. We can illustrate this statement with an observation by Thomas Mann taken from that other great Bildungsroman, *Joseph and His Brothers:* "[T]he transparency of personality, the fact that it was the repetition and return of an established type: this basic idea was part of Joseph's flesh and blood."

Instead of being irreducibly opposed to each other, instead of being sublated into a reassuring synthesis through a dialectical and dramatic mechanism, at certain moments freedom and necessity are lived in contradictory tension (*tension contradictorielle*), what I have called conflictual harmony. This is of course reminiscent of the mystical tradition or of Hindu philosophy, but also of the process of individuation, well described by C. G. Jung, where the I acts and considers itself as the object of a subject that encompasses it. This is an experience of the Self that does not destroy the empirical individual, the I, but that, on the contrary, elevates it—that is to say, raises it up into a greater unity. This is indeed the intensity and exultation of the tragic condition, the condition, let us remember, of Nietzsche's *amor fati:* being free in a necessity filled with love.[12] In short, it is a form of dependence full of serenity, in that individuals fulfill themselves in a "surplus being" (*plus être*) that reveals them to themselves.

We can easily see how this condition of "surplus being" manifests itself nowadays. Huge rallies, crowds of all kinds, collective trances, fusion through sport, ecstacy through music, religious or cultural effervescences, all raise the individual up to a form of plenitude that is not provided by the grayness of economic or political functionality. In each of these phenomena there is a kind of magical participation in what is foreign, in what is strange, in a globality that transcends the singularity of the individual. This globality, whereby everyone is in communion, is of the order of the sacred. Is this the irony of the tragic or the "cunning" of the collective imaginary, putting back into the social circuit that numinous dimension that modernity thought it had evacuated from social life? A reenchantment of the world? Certainly this is the case insofar as we are undeniably witnessing a transcending of mere utility, indeed of instrumentality, whether it be individual or social.

From such a viewpoint, the world and the individual do not progressively become what they ought to be in the light of a predetermined telos, but rather, one might say, they arrive at what they are. The archetype is, in some way, simply an aid to this unveiling, a revelatory mechanism that highlights what is already there. In this sense there is a close link between the tragic dimension of the archetype and the emphasis on a cyclical view of time.

The structural proximity between the archetypal procedure, the collective unconscious, and cyclical time stems from the fact that, as Jung puts it, "every vital process follows its own internal laws." Take, for example, the unconscious: we cannot force what will come to light in its own good time. Like a spring that spurts forth, wells up again, or dries up according to its own rhythm, one can never predict with certainty the emergence of unconscious flux.

One can likewise compare this to what is circular—or better, spiral—in the creation of images in alchemistic thought or in the dynamic of the unconscious. This creation is not governed by the mechanical linearity of pure reason, but is highly convoluted, rendering its interpretation especially complicated. There is indeed a labyrinthine structure both in the unconscious and in the world of images. And if intellectual interpretation has made extensive inroads into the unconscious, the same cannot be said of the world of images, which continues to be ignored, belittled, or marginalized by thinkers, at least by those who defend a strictly rationalist point of view.

It is certain that convolutions, or even, if we refer to Jungian theory, "circumambulations," describe the slow circular work that everyone must undergo in order to accede, little by little, to the realization of what I previously called "surplus being." This is the work of a lifetime.[13] The Tibetan mandala illustrates this idea well in the Eastern tradition, just as the quest for the holy grail expresses it in the tradition of the West. In both cases there is repetition, cyclical movement, and a tragic conception of life. Archetypal figures always employ redundancy, they always refer to a mythical time, the undatable time of our myths and legends: the "once upon a time" of *illud tempus*.

This is noteworthy with mythic examples in the strict sense, of which there are many in literature, film, theater, and song. But this phenomenon of atemporality, of cyclical or tragic emphasis, can likewise be located in the everyday, or often spectacular, mise-en-scène of contemporary stars. The eternal boy (*puer aeternus*) represented by Michael Jackson, the repentant fallen woman embodied by Madonna, or, more prosaically, the holy rascal represented by Bernard Tapie, not to mention the warlike heroes exemplified in so many sports figures—all this stems from a reenchantment of the world that reverberates powerfully in the collective unconscious. These figures do not create anything specific, they only repeat, rearticulate, characters and ways of being that are anthropologically rooted. It is this cyclical aspect, moreover, that carries them to the pinnacle. And it is by communing with these redundant mises en scène, by identifying with them, that after a long and largely unconscious initiation, one goes beyond oneself, one "explodes" into something that transcends the confinement or the constriction of the small individual ego.

Precisely this is the question in the cyclical notion of time: the possibility of living a plural self or of getting beyond the self and becoming part of a much greater entity. This could be the Self, as suggested by various Eastern philosophies, or the conjunction of yin and yang in the same tradition. With regard to Western culture, we can note the two columns of Solomon's temple: Jachin and Boaz, metaphors of a kind of *coincidentia oppositorum,* namely, the conjunction of such opposites as passivity and activity, freedom and necessity, and, of course, self and nonself. In short, it is a matter of the globality, the organic character of all things.

It is important to highlight a fundamental redundancy, whether in the actual expressions of contemporary art, or—in an area not necessarily very far removed—in the contradictions of myth. Both Lévi-Strauss and Gilbert Durand have insisted that repetition, and the "bricolage" that goes along with it, are at work in the great spiritual works of humanity.[14] This repetitive quality, whether it be the Nietzschean return of the same, the idea that obsesses the writer, the characteristic phrase of the musician, the "hand" of the painter, the eternal theoretical digression of the thinker, even the recognizable refrain of the singer, all underscore, in a certain sense, the presence of the nontemporal in history, of a kind of immobility in the midst of movement.

It is by keeping in mind the redundancy of myth and the repetitiveness of daily creation, without, to be sure, forgetting the repetition at work in contemporary life, that we will come to understand the part played by the intimate emotions occasioned by familiar phenomena, situations, ideas, and so forth that regularly return. As Thomas Aquinas has shown, *habitus* emphasizes the structuring character of established custom. The metaphor of the "fold" proposed by Deleuze is a way of actualizing the resonance of habit. Contrary to what modern theories of education have claimed, everything shows that individual or collective improvement is not necessarily part of a progress without end. Rather, it can realize itself at certain moments in accordance with that which recurs: uses and customs, myths and rituals, the habitual practices of a given society. Such was the claim of premodern society; it is possible that it is regaining importance in postmodernity.

To put it another way, education gives way to initiation, with improvement drawing on internal resources and not as a function of what is imported or imposed from outside. All this is highlighted by the prevalence of the cyclical instead of the linear, the confrontation with fate rather than a history that one fashions as one wills. The relation to politics is certainly the clearest expression of such a paradigm shift. Thus it is no longer a matter of taking the place of the master via a struggle unto death, as the Hegelian dialectic of master and slave has it, but rather of recognizing, when one is ready, a master who presents himself. This might be a master in the strict sense, or it might take the form of inescapable events, of the tribe to which one belongs, or even the adversity that is accepted for what it is.

This is what initiation means: to use an external constraint in order to achieve an inner perfection. We could link such an initiation to Jung's commentary on an epitaph that appears in the cloister of Basel cathedral: "eadem mutata resurgo": to reappear transformed and yet the same.[15] This is, of course, the process of the unconscious turning in spirals around a center. But there are many social examples of this movement, resting less on a historical and progressivist notion than on a cyclical and more progressive one. It is a matter here of the return of a traditional attitude that is especially evident in the many syncretic practices that characterize postmodernity. We can easily locate this traditional attitude in Eastern philosophies, but it is also expressed in the Etruscan doctrine of "the Ages of the World." Henri de Lubac's analysis of Vico's claim that there is a regular rotation of the ages of the world is relevant here. Under the watching eye of Providence, peoples replay, always and anew, the eternal problem of life and death.[16]

It would be interesting to clarify, in the light of such a doctrine, the astonishing circular succession of social phenomena, as well as the no less surprising attitude of the ever greater number of individuals eager to perfect themselves through religion, fusion with nature, or merging with the group. In all these cases it is not the fact of being master (of oneself, of the world, of society) that is important, but, on the contrary, of acceding to the status of a disciple and adhering to the demanding servitude implied by such a status.

There is a form of fatalism that we could stigmatize and consider regressive, but which at the same time underlines a possible renaissance, the necessary renewal of all things. The spirit of the times, to be sure, inclines toward melancholy, toward a nostalgia for an indistinct elsewhere that is hard to locate in time and space. But this "thirst for the infinite," to take up Durkheim's expression, by virtue of the anomie that it causes, will encourage sudden acts of revolt and inspire multiple social effervescences that do not follow the established schema of historical reason, but that take the chaotic path of those utterly unpredictable *corsi e recorsi,* just like the surging pulse of life reacting against the multiple constraints of the forms of death. Like the fabulous phoenix that is reborn from its ashes, social life depends on surprising "regressions" (*regrédiences*) in order to surge up anew where one no longer expected it. What is indeed striking is the circularity of this movement, even while, thanks to the development of technology, it has affinities with a spiral process.

What is underlined by the doctrine of "the ages of the world," what is emphasized by the cyclical conception of time and highlighted by all the repetitive acts of everyday life, is a vital need for regeneration, an anthropological need grounded in the belief that life always begins anew. Here one finds the theme of the affirmative attitude that is characteristic, for example, of Nietzschean philosophy but that is also expressed in the Zen sensibility as it appears in this koan: "What is the ultimate word for expressing truth? Joshu replies: yes." To affirm existence is difficult for theories grounded in the meaning of history, whether divine or profane, that look for the significance of life in a finality that is to come and that is never attained. The Judeo-Christian and Hegelian-Marxist vulgates have based their waiting for the future coming on the negation of life "here" in relation to a life "over there" that would be better and free of all vicissitudes. The dramatic tension toward another life is their driving force.

The tragic sensibility, that of the cycle, is completely different, wisely accepting what is and applying a form of intensity to living it. We can allude here to a phrase from St. Augustine taken somewhat out of context: "[T]he measure of love is without measure." Precisely this is underscored by the intensity of the tragic: the measure of life is to live without measure. The confrontation with destiny that can be found in many youth practices, in the search for a life of quality, in the concern for the present, in an ecological sensibility, is, quite simply, a way of living with intensity what offers itself, what arrives—in short, what is rather than what should be or could be. As I have said, it is an ethics of the moment in that it means, obstinately and in spite of everything, to live this existence that is shot through by vicissitudes but that remains attractive in spite of this or because of it.

The tragic sense of life, whether acknowledged or not, whether conscious or unconscious, reminds us that the grayness of the everyday could not exist without moments of rupture that periodically illuminate it. These underscore the fact that a life that does not project itself into the future is obliged to take seriously the orgiastic pleasures of the unbridled senses, whether the pleasures of taste, smell, hearing, touch, or sexuality. Rooted in this chthonian foundation, that of the emblematic figure of Dionysus, the emphasis placed on the cycle makes it possible, when faced with apologists for the future and those nostalgic for the past, to relive the serenity of the Greek *kairos,* that is, to seize hold of the many opportunities of contemporary life.

We are talking here about a true revolution, one which, like the revolutions in the heavens, consists of a return to the forefront of the social scene of what we had thought we had left behind. This is what Pierre-Simon Ballanche calls "palingenetic cycles," which is to say that human affairs proceed less by evolution than by revolution. Palingenesis as "the law of repair" ensures that humanity grows on the ruins of what collapsed. Cataclysms are no more avoidable in the social order than they are in the natural order. Empires are born, flourish, then disappear. Other empires are born in their turn. But suffering and sorrow are educators of humanity in giving value to what is lived. "There can be no resurrection without the cross."[17] This saying belongs to a specific culture, but its meaning is general in establishing an equivalence between the precariousness of all things and the exalting of the world in its successive moments.

Confrontation with destiny and cyclical return—these are indeed the essential elements marking the fundamental change now taking place in the notion of social time. Let us recall that this is not an abstractly philosophical problem but rather the basis of a new relationship to others and to the world. Is it the turn of a millennium that reactivates the hopes and fears belonging to the arrival of a world to which we have not been accustomed? Historians have often made the point that millenarianism brings with it ideas of catastrophe, but also the hope for a "New Age." Let us keep in mind that the "New Age" of our own time is only a version of an older structure that sees in cyclical temporality an opportunity to change everything and every one of us. The idea of a millennium that changes everything has existed since the dawn of modernity, and as with Joachim of Fiore and Savonarola, it will not fail to find new forms of expression at this end of modern times.[18]

334

These could be the celebration of the image of the hero, or indeed the big-hearted bandit, or quite simply the delinquent whose exploits are discussed in detail on television and in the news. Serial dramas, documentaries, and human-interest stories on the television news—all these only awaken in everyone the desire for an intensely lived fate.[19] In communing with these anomic destinies one magically participates in the very idea of Destiny. The fascination that such destinies exert on the "man without qualities" forces us to recognize that the tragic is again the order of the day and that the antiseptic society that has gradually imposed itself may not be as solid as it appears. In each of us slumbers a bandit who does not fear death and who is willing to put his life on the line. This may well occur only by proxy, but even as fantasy it expresses a need for the Shadow, a desire for the "accursed share" that modernity thought it had well and truly eliminated.

Indeed, we must insist that there are moments when History writ large gives way to the small histories that are lived from day to day. At such moments, History exhausts itself in myths. At such moments, the tragic rises up again. It is the moment when death is no longer denied, but is deliberately confronted and publicly embraced.

Notes

1. *C. J. Jung parle: Recontres et interviews* (Paris: Buchet-Chastel, 1995), 286. Cf. Michel Maffesoli, *Du nomadisme* (Paris: Livre de poche, 1997).

2. On this topic, see Werner Wilhelm Jaeger, *Paidea: The Ideals of Greek Culture* (New York: Oxford University Press, 1965). On the Dionysian myth, see Michel Maffesoli, *L'ombre de Dionysos: Contribution à une sociologie de l'orgie* (Paris: Livre de poche, 1991); *The Shadow of Dionysus: A Contribution to the Sociology of the Orgy,* trans. Cindy Linse and Mary Kristina Palmquist (Albany: State University of New York Press, 1993).

3. Virgil, *Aeneid* 3.395.

4. See Gianni Vattimo, *L'ethique de l'interprétation* (Paris: La découverte, 1991), 21. On Leibniz, see the commentary by René Guénon, *Autorité spirituelle* (Paris: Trédaniel, 1984), 79.

5. J. G. Fichte, *Machiavel et autres écrits philosophiques et politiques de 1806–1807,* trans. Luc Ferry and Alain Renaut (Paris: Payot, 1981). For an example of the "excessive" life, see the research of H. Houdayer, *Le défi toxique* (Paris: Harmattan, 2000) and M. Xiberras, *La société intoxiquée* (Paris: Armand Colin, 1997).

6. François Jullien, *La propension des choses* (Paris: Seuil, 1992), 37–38. See also Maurice Pinguet, *La mort volontaire au Japon* (Paris: Gallimard, 1994); *Voluntary*

Death in Japan, trans. Rosemary Morris (Cambridge: Polity, 1993). On co-presence, see Anthony Giddens, *The Constitution of Society: Outline of the Theory of Structuration* (Los Angeles: University of California Press, 1986).

7. For elaborations of this point, see Ernst Jünger, *Graffiti fontalières* (Paris: Bourgois, 1977), 27, and Eric Dodds, *The Greeks and the Irrational* (Berkeley: University of California Press, 1951). See also J. Vanaise, *L'homme univers* (Brussels: Le cri, 1993), and Elizabeth Teisser and Henri Laborit, *Étoiles et molecules* (Paris: Grasset, 1992).

8. Mary Douglas, *How Institutions Think* (Syracuse: Syracuse University Press, 1986). On the inversion of organic solidarity in Durkheim, see Michel Maffesoli, *La violence totalitaire* (Paris: Desclée de Brouwer, 1999), 233. On attraction, see the analysis of Patrick Tacussel, *L'attraction social: Le dynamise de l'imaginaire dans la société monocéphale* (Paris: Libraire des Méridiens, 1984).

9. Maffesoli, *The Shadow of Dionysus.*

10. Gilbert Durand, "Le retour des immortels," in *Le temps de la réflexion* (Paris: Gallimard, 1982), 207.

11. See the Körner-Schiller correspondence cited by Louis Dumont, *L'ideologie allemande* (Paris: Gallimard, 1991), 25; *German Ideology: From France to Germany and Back* (Chicago: Chicago University Press, 1996).

12. See the remarkable analysis of Luigi Aurigemma, *Perspectives jungiennes* (Paris: Albin Michel, 1992), 250.

13. See Jung, *Mysterium conjunctionis* (Paris: Albin Michel, 1980), 145; and also Aurigemma, *Perspectives jungiennes,* 112, and Durand, "Le retour des immortels," 206.

14. See Gilbert Durand, *L'Âme tigrée* (Paris: Denoël, 1980), 130; and Jean-Pierre Bayard, *Symbolisme maçonnique traditionnel,* vol. 1 (Paris: Edimaf, 1982), 12.

15. C. G. Jung, *Psychologie et alchimie* (Paris: Buchet-Chastel, 1970), 285.

16. See Henri de Lubac, *La postérité spirituelle de Joaquim de Flore* (Paris: Le Thielleux, 1987), 230–231.

17. See de Lubac, *La postérité spirituelle de Joaquim de Flore,* 314; and also Michel Maffesoli, *La conquête du présent* (Paris: Desclée de Brouwer, 1998), 116.

18. See Donald Weinstein, *Savanorola and Florence: Prophecy and Patriotism in the Renaissance* (Princeton, NJ: Princeton University Press, 1970).

19. See Roberto da Matta, *Carnivals, Rogues and Heroes: An Interpretation of the Brazilian Dilemma,* trans. John Drury (South Bend, IN: Notre Dame University Press, 1991).

Commentary

Terry Eagleton

We live in an age of terror, which like many an apparently antique phenomenon—the Scottish kilt springs bathetically to mind—is in fact of fairly recent vintage. Of course people have been dismembering and disemboweling each other since time began; but terror as a political concept, Terror as an *idea* worthy of upper-case signification, is no older than modernity itself. Indeed, it is twinned at birth with what for some is the very source of later modernity, the French Revolution. There can be no modernity without its attendant terror.

It was Hegel who showed us how terror springs straight from the heart of the bourgeois social order. The absolute freedom of that society—"freedom in a void," as Hegel scathingly called it—acknowledges no bounds, and is thus doomed to a raging, unappeasable fury. For all its materialism, it harbors a virulent hatred of finitude. In an essay here which boldly overleaps the customary bounds of commentary on tragedy by taking a look at African tragic art, Timothy Reiss suggests that Plato was similarly shaken by what he saw as tragedy's revelation of the limits of human endeavor. If it seems to yearn for the carnal world, stuffing more and more colonies, conquests, and commodities into its insatiable maw, it is really only because it wishes to pound that world to pieces in its murderous infantile aggression. Like Conrad's crazed professor in *The Secret Agent* it is the ultimate anarchist, wishing to wipe the slate clean and start again *ex nihilo,* in a demonic reversal of divine creation. Like God, it is entirely self-causing and self-originating, confessing no dependency beyond itself. Like all desire (a phenomenon which some dewy-eyed postmodernists oddly regard as positive), it is in love only with itself. For how can any of its various self-realizations not seem wretchedly trivial in contrast to its own boundlessness? The various objects of this furious freedom are thus also obstructions to it. So it is logical, as Hegel sees, that it will end up by consuming itself, confronting itself as its own worst enemy and disappearing into its own sublime nothingness. Operation Infinite Freedom has been tried once already and failed. It is known as the Faust legend.

The freedom of modernity is not, to be sure, merely nothing. Only the

George Steiners of this world, in their monotone way, regard everything that happened from the Enlightenment onward as a disastrous declension, while naturally taking full advantage of many of that epoch's precious bequests (free speech, plastic bags, redress against torture, central heating, and the like). As the essays in this volume make ironically plain, the George Steiners of this world include, on this count at least, some of those who look with most disfavor on Steiner's own elitism. There are some curious bedfellows between these covers (or "weird," as the American neo-Gothic jargon has it), as the anti-Enlightenment rhetoric of cultural reaction joins forces from time to time with the language of the more radical and right-on. As far as the latter goes, one might allude to the essay by Michel Maffesoli, of which one might charitably remark that something has no doubt been lost in the translation.

The truth, however, is that for millions of previously dumped and discarded men and women, modernity has been an enthralling emancipation. Some on the cultural left tend to forget that democracy, equality, socialism, feminism, trade unionism, and anti-colonialism are as much products of modernity as profiteroles or the panopticon. The ontological homelessness which George Steiner sees as the curse of our condition is also the source of our creativity—which is to say that our *culpa* is *felix,* our Fall fortunate, our disabilities enabling. Without this divorce from the sensuous at-homeness of our fellow animals, we would indeed not endure most of the privations and oppressions that we do, but neither would we be able to compose sonnets or symphonies, or write distinguished essays in US journals about our not-at-homeness. Our fall up from the creaturely innocence of the beasts into history, language, and power is as much loss and gain as modernity itself. But to register this requires a habit of thought known as the dialectical, which we now know to be totalizing and tyrannical.

If there remains at least one good reason to be a Marxist, other than the pleasures of sheer perversity, it is because no other discourse of which I am aware claims in the same breath that modernity has been a revolution in human happiness and well-being and one long nightmare. And each, moreover, in terms of the other. This is one reason why Marxists differ from Joshua Foa Dienstag, who is out to press the claims of pessimism against optimism, whereas Marxism is pessimistic and optimistic at the same time. If indeed these terms have much political meaning, which I doubt. It is Marxists—those who wish to abolish the bourgeois order—who pay the most admiring homage to that regime's erstwhile revolutionary character, a character which the middle classes themselves, understandably enough, seek to thrust into oblivion once they are safely ensconced in power. They are aided in this enterprise by the postmodernists, who being a little shaky on their history were never aware that the middle classes were revolutionary in the first place. The fact that there was no indigenous aristocracy in America to be toppled may have something to do with this postmodern myopia.

Yet this dimension of human existence, which is at once traumatizing and liberating, is of course much older than the modern, and perhaps lies somewhere near the root of the tragic. One of its ancient names was the Dionysian, in which an obscene enjoyment or fearful *jouissance* enraptures us even as it shatters us maliciously to pieces. For the middle ages, the chief title for this dangerous ambivalence was God, whose ruthlessly unconditional love will burn us up (God himself is the fire of hell) unless we have hijacked for ourselves some of its power, a power which knows no bounds in its mercy and tenderness and which is therefore terrible to look upon. For Aquinas, God is at once quite other to us, and closer to us than we are to ourselves; and this is true of all the various manifestations of this perilously ambiguous force, which inhabits our bodies like some alien creature whose purposes are in no sense our own, yet which, lying as it does at the very root of our subjectivity, is more intimate to us than breathing.

Freedom was a name for this destructive creativity when the capitalist order was still in its infancy, and the political going was good. Later on, when that order had outlived its youthful buoyancy, freedom turned into that negative version of itself known as desire, which constitutes our very being but which is absolutely nothing personal. As Simon Critchley argues about *Phèdre,* in an essay which stands out in this issue for its elegance, stylishness, and subdued humor, desire is an anonymous field of force into which we fall as into a sickness, a monstrous fatality or ontological malaise into which we are born and which chooses us far more than we choose it. It is a "virus of Venus in the veins," and one of the more traditional names for this guilt without a crime is original sin. How can we not be guilty simply by existing, when, given that we are bound up with each other as intimately as breathing, the most innocent of our actions may breed dire consequences in the lives of others? Only the human animal of a Hobbes or Rousseau, gloriously autonomous of its fellows, could escape this creative sickness, whose "originality" has nothing to do with a paradisal garden and everything to do with the root or source of our creaturely existence.

Before Freud, however, we have the age of Enlightenment, for which this strange Janus-faced force returns in the form of the sublime. (This, I confess, is a rather potted kind of history of ideas, and one which will doubtless be deeply suspect to those who champion what one might call the Goldfish Theory of History, namely history as a discontinuous series of uniquely particular presents.) The sublime elevates and intoxicates us even as it chastens and chastises, reminding us with Kantian severity of our creaturely limits while finding an answerable infinity in our bosoms. Foremost among the various signifiers of the sublime in the eighteenth century is the Law itself, which as Edmund Burke recognized is a holy terror whose illicit origins are not to be investigated with too indecent a curiosity. For Burke, as for Pascal, Hume, and Kant, an arbitrary act of violent imposition lies at the origin of the Law, social order being no more than the name for our merciful oblivion of this primordial crime. The Law for Burke, the man who gave us the word "terrorist," is a kind of traumatic horror which works only by cloaking itself in the decent drapery of civility and consent, a decorous veiling which he calls beauty. In Burke's view, women are beautiful, while men are sublime—which is to say that the Law for him is a cross-dresser, a sublimely coercive male power beguilingly veiled in female drapery. (Our modern term for this fusion of coercion and consent is hegemony.) When, however, the Law is brought into disrepute, as it is today when it is used by the West as a cover for flagrantly illegal actions, the terror which it softens and dis- tances in symbolic form reappears in the Real, in the shape of atrocities of terrorism.

If the sublime is one modern name for the ambiguity in question, and the superego a late-modern reworking of it, then the Lacanian Real, in the sense of the obscenely enjoyable cat-and-mouse game between *Eros* and the death drive, is a familiar postmodern equivalent. But one might just as well claim that this ambivalence is inherent in the whole Promethean late-capitalist system as such, which is tragically self-undoing exactly in so far as it has materially speaking produced the means of emancipation, while politically speaking thwarting that end at every turn. Like any sys- tem which refuses the constraints of the flesh, it is in perpetual danger of overreaching itself and bringing itself to nothing. If tragedy has returned (and Elisabeth Bronfen gives us an excellent analysis on one of its latest manifestations in *film noir*), it is among other things because late moder- nity has recreated in its own way some of the conditions which gave birth to this scapegoat song in classical antiquity. Rita Felski argues just this in her lucid, illuminating Introduction. The fragility and self-opaqueness of the once-sovereign subject, its exposure to enigmatic, impenetrable forces, its lack of agency and quickened sense of mortality, the inevitable conflict of goods in a pluralist culture, the complex density of a social order in which human damage spreads like typhoid: all these are reasons why the very epoch which for George Steiner spells the death of tragedy has in fact witnessed the renewal of it, however many languages Steiner may tell us his thesis has been translated into. You do not render your case more persuasive by having it repeated in Slovenian or Bulgarian.

The tragic hubris of a capitalism which acknowledges no bounds, and which is therefore bound to be self-blinded, is not especially to the fore among these deft, suggestive pieces. In the very belly of the beast, the talk on the cultural left is far more of gender and ethnicity than it is of the death-ridden corporate capitalism which might end up destroying the lot of us. One or two misunderstandings between such New World contributors, and a Marxist dinosaur from Donald Rumsfeld's old Europe like myself, are therefore perhaps unavoidable. Heather K. Love interprets my book *Sweet Violence* as claiming that there are no minorities, a claim which would be as absurd as suggesting that there are no Milanese. My point was not that on the last count there were no gay Chinese (though I was once solemnly informed that this was the case on a visit to the country), but that the postmodern cult of minorities (some of which, needless to say, are noxious and abhorrent, and should be abolished as soon as possible) tends to overlook the astonishing fact that in the class-societies of bourgeois democracy, the actual majority of men and women are excluded from power. One might expect minorities to be given short shrift, but hardly the logical paradox of a sidelined majority.

My point was also that such postmodern particularism defuses another sort of scandal: the radical-Enlightenment insight that anyone whatsoever has in principle a claim on us by virtue of their sheer raw humanity, not by virtue of their being arch-dukes, Portuguese lesbians, mulattos, one-legged cosmetic surgeons, or even Canadians. It is this revolutionary universalism, reflected in the truth that any old body can be a tragic protagonist, which postmodern particularism passes over. Of course, if I do not attend to you *as* a one-legged cosmetic surgeon, then I am not attending to *you*. But it is not the fact that you are what you contingently are which *motivates* my attention. If it were, then I would feel perfectly free not to come to the aid of other cultural types, like Spanish social democrats. I would also feel free to endorse Richard Rorty's extraordinary comment that the best reason to feel outraged at the existence of poor Americans is because they are poor *Americans*.[1] This is not to suggest that our attentions should be distributed with impeccable even-handedness: being on the political left means backing the interests of some against the interests of others. But one does this in the name of a future justice, one which may or may not come to birth, in which human particularity would be seen as a way of living a common humanity, not as an alternative to it.

One of the pleasures of commentaries such as this is that they allow one to give vent to various whinings and bleatings about others' readings of one's work. It is not a pleasure which I have the spiritual self-discipline to renounce, though (since complaining is a two-way street) I stand corrected by Martha Nussbaum, in a piece which ranges all the way from Sophocles to Adam Smith, for having misinterpreted a point she has made previously. Joshua Foa Dienstag chides me with setting the value of pessimism too briskly aside—an odd upbraiding, given that far too much of *Sweet Violence* is devoted to poking fun with my usual tiresome facetiousness at those critics of tragedy who regard it as the most robustly affirmative of forms, just the right cure for a bout of the blues. Even so, it is refreshing to see such a spirited apologia for pessimism in a country for which the negative, downbeat, sardonic, or satirical are viewed by the sovereign Can-Do ideology, with its insane voluntarism, as thought-crimes only mildly less heinous than zoophilia. The United States is a profoundly anti-tragic culture which is now having to confront tragedy on an epic scale. In a lively contribution, David Scott sees the self-determining agent of history as an anti-tragic animal; but the effects of this strenuous autonomy can always undo him and bring him to nothing, as indeed is happening as I write in Iraq.

Dienstag, however, sees pessimism in a Nietzschean vein as a sense of the transience and perishability of things, whereas my own eccentric view is that the perishability of George Bush is one of the most positive facts about him. It is neither the case that all transience is *ipso facto* negative (as Samuel Johnson considered), nor that it is *ipso facto* positive (as Bertolt Brecht believed). By the end of his essay, Dienstag has subtly redefined pessimism as an openness to mutability, thus rendering it wellnigh indistinguishable from optimism. As J. L. Austin once observed, there is the bit where you say it, and the bit where you take it back. An initially startling defense of pessimism turns out to be a championing of our old postmodern friend "instability" in thin disguise. In any case, the claim that suffering must be embraced as inseparable from growth and change is embarrassingly close to the affirmative sorts of tragic theory which Dienstag finds most distasteful.

Sacrifice, I comment in *Sweet Violence,* is commonly understood as "relinquishing one's own desires in the service of a master's. It has unpleasant overtones of self-repression and self-laceration, of bogus appeals to tighten one's belt in the general interest. It is what women do for men, infantrymen do for generals, or what the working class are expected to do for the benefit of all."[2] These sentences must have fallen out of the US edition of the book, since Page duBois accuses me of advocating an ethic of sacrifice of exactly this oppressive, masochistic kind. She cannot free herself from the sway of this conventional, puritanical notion of sacrifice (which she naturally rejects, as I do myself) to the point where she might allow herself to make more interesting political sense of the notion. She is like those leftists who reject, say, the idea of tradition as a ruling-class ploy, thus unwittingly ditching everything from the Levellers to the Suffragettes. Sacrifice concerns the passage of the reviled thing from humiliation to power, and thus has a bearing upon our contemporary politics rather more insistent than the question of Athenian slaves, about whom, after all, there is little we can do now. For duBois, this is all "very Christian," a phrase which is clearly intended to be as self-evidently pejorative as "very silly." I wonder if she would write "very Islamic" or "very Jewish" to the same effect? Or is it only their homegrown religion which intellectuals tend to revile? What form of homogenizing is at work here, as the anti-essentialists (of whom I am assuredly not one) might piously inquire? The pope is very Christian, to be sure, but so was Father Camillo Torres, who along with others of his kind was killed fighting in the name of his faith as a guerilla in the jungles of Latin America.

Even Kathleen M. Sands, in a rich meditation which reveals a far surer understanding of such matters, can grasp the idea of otherworldliness only as an escape from the political status quo, rather than as a transformation of it. Even Simon Goldhill, in an otherwise typically erudite, incisive piece, speaks of Christianity as "revalorizing" human suffering, apparently unaware that the New Testament regards suffering as an evil to be abolished, not a condition to be heroically endured. Jesus never once counsels a sufferer to be reconciled to his or her illness. There are, to be sure, false Christian conceptions of otherworldliness in abundance, as with the man who remarked that when religion began to interfere with one's daily life it was time to give it up. Even so, it is hard to see how any reasonably sensitive soul can read the newspapers and not believe devoutly in the need for another world. The other world of the Judeo-Christian heritage is the realm of justice, mercy, and loving fellowship, not some pie in the sky. Simon Critchley makes a similar sort of mistake in believing that Christian faith (as opposed to Jansenist versions of it) rejects the world. It is odd that God should have gone to the trouble of fashioning one just so that his creatures could spurn it, their thoughts piously fixed on higher things even than their Creator's.

In a characteristically burnished, commanding piece of rhetoric, George Steiner rehearses his familiar case (now broadcast in no less than seventeen languages) that the mildest whiff of hope is fatal to tragedy. Even the author of the last act of *Lear* fails to be glum enough to qualify for kosher tragic status. It is worth noting to begin with how highly un-traditionalist a thesis this is, given the traditionally minded nature of its author. Most theorists of tragedy have indeed been at one with Steiner over its numinous, auratic character as an aristocrat among art forms; but most of them have held that for just this reason it has no truck with anything as drably prosaic or quotidian as pessimism. On the contrary, as Steiner himself has occasionally argued, it is a bracing, chastening, edifying affair, quite distinct from mere common-or-garden misery.

It is not only that such a dogmatic stance constrains one to dismiss as nontragic a ridiculously large sector of distinguished tragic art, not least the *Oresteia*. It is also that it is in a certain sense illogical. Pure tragedy, Steiner claims, must be immune to hope; but hope is bound up with human possibility, which is in turn bound up with value. And without some sense of value there can be no tragedy. Nor, for that matter, can there even be pessimism. One could not be a pessimist about the human condition if one could not even conceive of its being other than it is. It would be like being pessimistic about the fact that badgers have snouts. If *Waiting for Godot* is pessimistic, it must be because the idea of Godot's coming must always have been conceivable. What makes for tragedy, often enough, is exactly the fact that we can indeed conceive of a more humane condition. The immense political scandal of our world is that things could be *feasibly* a good deal better than they are. The red herring of utopian perfection is cynically intended, among other things, to distract us from this outrage. This does not, *pace* Steiner, necessarily involve some grand Blochian Hope. One can hope without clinging to Hope, just as most people, even postmodernists, believe in progress but not in Progress. Tragedy is not always about despair; it can also be, to adopt Yeats's splendid lines, a matter of recognizing that nothing can be sole or whole that has not been rent. The fact that it may be made whole does not diminish the tragedy of the rending—of the fact that only by a passage through hell is redemption conceivable. The final, infinitely tremulous, exquisitely tentative note of hope beyond hope (if that indeed is what it is) of Adrian Leverkuhn's last composition in Thomas Mann's *Doctor*

Faustus does not cancel out the catastrophe of the composer's demonic life.

Steiner's literary style—gnomic, mandarin, prophetic, magisterial, imperious, resonantly authoritative—has always been an exact imprint of his ideology. Rarely have form and content in a critic been so precisely matched. His dazzlingly erudite range of cultural allusion is one which the rest of us can only find daunting (it is intended to be so, barely concealing an aggressive *hauteur*), even if the phrase "coruscating on thin ice" could have been specially invented for him. But it is a cultural authority which pays an enormous price in its sacrifice of the flesh. It is an austerely patrician world constructed so as to exclude common feeling, which is why it is all the more ironic that Steiner should insist on the theological basis of tragic art. For there is, as he seems not to appreciate, theology and theology. As a kind of *ersatz* theodicy, not to speak of a displaced religious critique of secular modernity, tragic theory has for the most part been theological in all the wrong ways. Its displaced religiosity is in an exact sense bad faith, since it generally has no actual belief in religion whatsoever, which is why it needs tragic art in its place. The Judeo-Christian wisdom which Steiner would no doubt find intolerable is the outrage that the mundane is not the opposite of the transcendent but the very locus of it—that transcendence lies for this heritage not in the first place in ritual and hierarchy, but in the outstretched palm of a starving child. Christianity, as Charles Taylor has argued in *The Sources of the Self,* is the first movement to take the common life with absolute seriousness. In her wide-ranging contribution, Wai Chee Dimock captures something of this quality, as does Stanley Corngold's somber reflection on the theme of destruction in the fiction of W. G. Sebald. Similarly, it is the lesson of a good deal of tragedy that only by an unutterably painful openness to our frailty and finitude—to the material limits of our condition—can we have any hope of transcending it. Steiner insists on the littleness of humankind, but not on its preciousness; whereas in a good deal of tragic art, the collision of the two terms lends the phrase "precious little" a new, paradoxical meaning.

In his jealous demarcation of the sacred from the profane, Steiner shows up by contrast as pagan. He would, I am sure, dismiss such comments as "pseudo-Marxist chatter," a phrase of which by far the most revealing term is "pseudo." Roughly translated, the phrase means: "These comments are Marxist nonsense; but in case that should appear excessively complimentary, since it does after all imply that you have some grasp of such an intellectually demanding body of work as Marxism, I hereby append the qualifier 'pseudo' to 'Marxist,' as philistines do to the word 'intellectual,' thus suggesting that you are not even a proper Marxist and that it would be preferable if you were (which I do not in fact believe). In any case, I have been translated into no less than seventeen languages, which I very much doubt is the case with you."

Oedipus, broken and blinded, stands before Colonus. As he once returned an answer to the Sphinx, so his presence now poses a question to the nearby city of Athens. Is it to gather this unclean thing to its heart, or cast it out as so much garbage? Is it to dismiss this beggarly king as a monster, or find in his disfigured visage an image of the monstrosity of the human, which is to say of itself? Can it bring itself to pity what it fears? Will it discern in the death-in-life condition of the dispossessed the shadowy outline of a new way of living, one which preserves a pact with failure and mortality?

Then Theseus, ruler of Athens, deciphers the riddle. He knows that by making this obscene thing into the cornerstone of the *polis,* a great power for good will inevitably follow. The terror which threatens to undermine civility will be turned outward to protect it. *Thanatos* will be harnessed to the service of *Eros,* but only in the perilous, reverent awareness that it can always blow it apart. The West has yet to learn this tragic lesson. It cannot recognize in the fury at its gates its own monstrous violence come home to roost. It is unable to decipher the symptoms of weakness and despair in that annihilating rage, and is therefore capable only of terror rather than pity.

Notes

1. Richard Rorty, *Contingency, Irony, and Solidarity* (Cambridge: Cambridge University Press, 1989), 191.

2. Terry Eagleton, *Sweet Violence: The Idea of the Tragic* (Oxford: Blackwell, 2003), 275.

Notes on Contributors

ELISABETH BRONFEN is Professor of English and American Studies at the University of Zurich. Her publications include *Home in Hollywood: The Imaginary Geography of Cinema* (2004) and *Over Her Dead Body: Death, Femininity, and the Aesthetic* (1992).

STANLEY CORNGOLD is Professor of German and Comparative Literature at Princeton University and Adjunct Professor of Law at the Columbia University Law School. He has recently translated and edited a new Norton Critical edition of *Kafka's Selected Stories* (2007) and is at work on a volume titled *Kafka before the Law,* which will relate Kafka's office writings as an executive in workmen's compensation insurance to his stories and novels. His recent books are *Lambent Traces: Franz Kafka* (2004; 2006), *Complex Pleasure: Forms of Feeling in German Literature* (1998), *The Metamorphosis: Translation, Backgrounds, and Contexts of Criticism* (1996), *The Fate of the Self: German Writers and French Theory* (1994), and *Franz Kafka: The Necessity of Form* (1988).

SIMON CRITCHLEY is Professor of Philosophy at the New School for Social Research and at the University of Essex. During 2007 he is a scholar at the Getty Research Institute in Los Angeles. He is author of many books, most recently, *Things Merely Are* (2005) and *Infinitely Demanding* (2007).

JOSHUA FOA DIENSTAG is Professor of Political Science at the University of California, Los Angeles. He is the author of *Pessimism: Philosophy, Ethic, Spirit* (2006) and *Dancing in Chains: Narrative and Memory in Political Theory* (1997). He is currently working on film and temporality.

WAI CHEE DIMOCK is William Lampson Professor of English and American Studies at Yale University. She is the author, most recently, of *Through Other Continents: American Literature Across Deep Time* (2006), and co-editor of *Shades of the Planet: American Literature as World Literature* (2007). She is now at work on a book on genre: *Elemental Harm: Greek Tragedy and Modern Catastrophes.*

PAGE DUBOIS teaches classics, comparative literature, and cultural studies in the Literature Department of the University of California at San Diego. Her publications include *Centaurs and Amazons* (1982), *Sowing the Body* (1988), *Torture and Truth* (1991), *Sappho Is Burning* (1995), and *Trojan Horses: Saving the Classics from Conservatives* (2001). Her most recent book is *Slaves and other Objects* (2003).

TERRY EAGLETON is Professor of Cultural Theory and John Rylands Fellow at the University of Manchester and a Fellow of the British Academy. He is the author of more than forty books of literary criticism and political and cultural theory, the most recent of which are *The English Novel* (2004) and *How to Read a Poem* (2006). He has also written stage, television, and radio plays produced in Ireland and London and is the author of the screenplay of Derek Jarman's film *Wittgenstein* (1993).

RITA FELSKI is William R. Kenan Jr. Professor of English and Chair of Comparative Literature at the University of Virginia. She is the author of *Beyond Feminist Aesthetics* (1989), *The Gender of Modernity* (1995), *Doing Time: Feminist Theory and Postmodern Culture* (2000), and *Literature After Feminism* (2003). Her account of the uses of literature is forthcoming as a Blackwell's manifesto in 2008.

SIMON GOLDHILL is Professor of Greek at Cambridge University and Fellow of King's College. His books include *Language, Sexuality, Narrative: The Oresteia* (1984), *Reading Greek Tragedy* (1986), *Aeschylus' Oresteia* (1992), *Who Needs Greek? Contests in the Cultural History of Hellenism* (2002), and most recently, *Love, Sex and Tragedy: How the Ancient World Shapes Our Lives* (2004) and *The Temple in Jerusalem* (2004). *How to Stage Greek Tragedy Today* will be published in 2007.

HEATHER K. LOVE is the M. Mark and Esther K. Watkins Assistant Professor in the Humanities at the University of Pennsylvania and the author of *Feeling Backward: Loss and the Politics of Queer History* (2007). She is currently at work on a book on social stigma, tentatively titled *Marked for Life*.

MICHEL MAFFESOLI is Professor of Sociology at the University of Paris (V) and Director of the Centre d'Etudes sur l'Actuel and le Quotidien. He is the author of *The Shadow of Dionysus* (1975; 1993), *The Time of the Tribes*

(1988; 1996), *The Contemplation of the World* (1993; 1996), and many other books.

MARTHA C. NUSSBAUM is Ernst Freund Distinguished Service Professor of Law and Ethics at the University of Chicago, appointed in the Philosophy Department, Law School, and Divinity School. She is an Associate in the Departments of Classics and Political Science. Her most recent book is *Frontiers of Justice: Disability, Nationality, Species Membership* (2007). Her book about religious violence in India, *The Clash Within: Democracy, Religious Violence, and India's Future,* will also appear in 2007.

TIMOTHY J. REISS is Professor of Comparative Literature at New York University. His most recent books are *Against Autonomy: Global Dialectics of Cultural Exchange* (2002) and *Mirages of the Selfe: Patterns of Personhood in Ancient and Early Modern Europe* (2003), and the edited collections *Sisyphus and Eldorado: Magical and Other Realisms in Caribbean Literature,* rev. ed. (2002), and *Music, Writing, and Cultural Unity in the Caribbean* (2005). He is completing a book on Descartes and the beginnings of the "modern" era, a collection on *Ngugi in the Americas,* and working on rethinking the "Renaissance" as a process of cultural circulation between Africa, the Americas and Europe. He published *Tragedy and Truth* in 1980 and since then has continued to write extensively on tragedy in Europe and in different cultures.

KATHLEEN M. SANDS is Associate Professor and Director of Religious Studies at the University of Massachusetts, Boston. She is author of *Escape from Paradise: Evil and Tragedy in Feminist Theology* (1994) and editor of *God Forbid: Religion and Sex in American Public Life* (2000). She is currently writing a book that brings critical studies in religion to bear on church-state relations in the United States.

DAVID SCOTT teaches at Columbia University, where he is Professor of Anthropology. He is the author most recently of *Conscripts of Modernity: The Tragedy of Colonial Enlightenment* (2004), co-editor of *Powers of the Secular Modern: Talal Asad and His Interlocutors* (2006), and editor of the journal *Small Axe.* He is currently at work on two projects: one, an exploration of Third World sovereignty through a genealogy of self-determination and nonalignment; and the other, an exploration of trauma, memory, law, and repair in thinking through the aftermaths of New World slavery.

GEORGE STEINER is a Fellow of Churchill College, Cambridge, and Emeritus Professor of the University of Geneva. In 2000–2001, he was Charles Eliot Professor of Poetics at Harvard University. His most recent book is *Lessons of the Masters* (2003).

OLGA TAXIDOU is a Reader at the University of Edinburgh, where she teaches performance studies. She has written *The Mask: A Periodical Performance by Edward Gordon Craig* (1998) and *Tragedy, Modernity and Mourning* (2004). She is also co-editor of *Modernism: An Anthology of Documents and Sources* (1998) and *Post-War Cinema and Modernity* (2000). Her most recent book is *Modernism and Performance: Jarry to Brecht* (2006). She also enjoys writing adaptations of Athenian tragedies, some of which have been performed.

Index

action: and African culture, 274; and
Aristotle, 134; consequences of,
291, 300; in *Double Indemnity,* 289;
in Euripides, 57, 58; and femme
fatale, 291, 300; in Greco-Roman
culture, 266–67, 268; and ritual, 83;
in Sophocles, 159, 162, 270; and
time, 209
actors, 133, 140, 243, 250, 253, 254.
See also chorus
Adorno, Theodor, 13, 88, 144n25, 266
Aeschylus, 33, 37, 53, 68, 149, 218;
Agamemnon, 55; and Aristotle, 130;
Choephori, 58; *Eumenides,* 55; and
Euripides, 58; and fate, 322; Gilligan on, 94; and James, 206, 264;
language in, 39; *Libation Bearers,*
137; Nietzsche on, 107; *Oresteia,* 40,
43, 55, 56, 57, 58, 94, 191, 192, 344;
Prometheus Bound, 211; *Seven Against
Thebes,* 35, 40, 60; and social context, 39
aesthetics, 10, 17; in Aristotle, 54; and
Athenian tragedy, 266; and Brecht,
241, 246, 258; and creation, 34; in
Double Indemnity, 300; of Hegel,
51; of Kant, 50–51; pagan, 178; and
pessimism, 104; and philosophy, 3;
and ritual space for trauma, 83; in
Sebald, 219, 221; and suffering, 86
affliction, 115, 178. *See also* suffering
Africa, 220–21, 236
African culture, 20–21, 264–65, 272–
80, 326, 337
agency: in African culture, 21; in
Double Indemnity, 21, 289, 296; and
fate, 11–12; of femme fatale, 298,

299; in *film noir,* 6; in Greco-Roman
culture, 266–67; and Greek tragedy,
20; and hurricane Katrina, 68; and
James, 204; lack of, 341; limits of,
12; and reason, 210; and resistance,
200–201; and slavery, 202; sovereign, 200; and West African drama,
20; in Western culture, 20, 263
alienation, 15, 30–31, 32–33, 255. *See
also* estrangement
Amadi, Elechi, 276
Améry, Jean, 231, 232, 236
Amores Perros (film), 118
amor fati, 114, 325, 329
anagnorisis, 49–50, 193, 290. *See also*
recognition
anawim, 88, 95
Anaximander, 108, 122n21
Anderson, Paul Thomas, 184
Anderson, Perry, 130
Anselm, St., 86
Antigone, 18, 51, 243
Apollonian spirit, 59, 122n19
Apollonius of Tyana, 56
Aquinas, Thomas, 249, 260n21, 331,
339
archetypes, 14, 328, 329, 330
Archilochus, 320
Arendt, Hannah, 18, 116, 117–19, 199,
215, 278; *The Human Condition,*
118–19
aristocracy, 37–38, 133, 140, 164, 165.
See also hierarchy
Aristophanes, 47
Aristotle: and Aeschylus, 130; and
African culture, 274; and Athens,
131; body in, 267; and Brecht, 241,

Aristotle (*continued*)
242; context of, 129–30; on contingent disaster, 33; and democracy, 131, 133; and Dionysus, 132; and Euripides, 40, 47, 57, 78–79, 130; fault in, 152–53; and fortunate endings, 270; and great man, 132; and history, 131; and James, 210, 212; language in, 47, 48; and legitimacy of tragedy, 32; mimesis in, 271–72; *Nicomachean Ethics,* 154; Nietzsche on, 108; *peripeteia* in, 66; pity in, 149, 152–53, 154, 157; and Plato, 40, 54, 131, 132; *Poetics,* 30, 47–48, 49–50, 54, 78–79, 130, 131, 133–34, 271; and politics, 132, 264; and Racine, 193; *Rhetoric,* 47, 149, 152–53; and ritual, 131; and Sophocles, 78–79, 130, 133; and tragic form, 2; truth in, 132
Arnold, Matthew, 51
art, 16, 50, 51, 111–12, 265
Artaud, Antonin, 35, 253
atheism, 34, 35
Athens, 4, 54, 66, 69, 71, 118, 119, 127, 130–31, 132, 264, 266
audience/spectator, 70, 109, 133, 139, 140, 151, 158, 160, 164, 311
Augustine, St., 91–92, 93, 333; *Confessions,* 170, 177–78, 186, 187
Austin, J. L., 342

Bach, Johann Sebastian, 34
Badiou, Alain, 129
Ballanche, Pierre-Simon, 334
Balzac, Honoré de, 306
barbarians, 137, 138, 142. *See also* other, the
barbarism, 13, 20, 199, 215, 246
Baroque drama, 257
Barthes, Roland, 172, 179, 227
Bataille, Georges, 325; *Le bleu du ciel,* 187
Batson, C. Daniel, 162, 165, 166
Baudelaire, Charles, 306
beauty, 50, 52, 55, 86–87

Beckett, Samuel, 30, 33, 190, 259; *Endgame,* 10, 37; *Happy Days,* 253; *Molloy,* 220; *Waiting for Godot,* 10, 37, 44, 180–81, 344
Beethoven, Ludwig van, 29
Bemba, Sylvain, *Noces posthumes de Santigone,* 279
Benjamin, Walter, 32, 226, 230, 235, 242, 248, 250, 253, 257; *Origin of German Tragic Drama,* 249
Berlau, Ruth, 20, 241, 254, 256, 257; *Antigone-Model 1948,* 241–59
Berlioz, Hector, 29
Bernstein, Jay, 226
Bizet, Georges, *Carmen,* 117
blame, 12, 67, 92, 95, 149, 154, 278, 305. *See also* culpability; fault; guilt
Blanchot, Maurice, 180, 187
Bloch, Ernst, 244
body: in Aristotle, 267; in Brecht, 20, 250, 251, 254; in Christianity, 46; in *Double Indemnity,* 292–93; Eagleton on, 151; and femme fatale, 290; in Greco-Roman culture, 267; and modernity, 305; Nietzsche on, 113; in Owen, 152; and Plato, 243, 265; in Racine, 19, 186; and Sophocles, 152, 153, 164. *See also* embodiment
Boethius, 248, 260n21
Boukman, 203
Bradley, A. C., 212
Brahms, Johannes, 29
Brecht, Bertolt, 4, 6, 35, 342; *Antigone-Model 1948,* 20, 241–59; *The Antigone of Sophocles,* 241, 244–48, 250; and Benjamin, 249, 253, 257; *The Caucasian Chalk Circle,* 256; *The Good Person of Szechwan,* 256; and Hegel, 243, 251; *Mother Courage and Her Children,* 251, 256; and Plato, 242, 243, 255; *A Short Organum for the Theatre,* 241, 244–45; and *Verfremdungseffekt,* 255
Bronfen, Elisabeth, 21, 340
Brooks, Peter, 7–8

Büchner, Georg, *Woyzeck,* 36, 37, 39, 43, 44
Bultmann, Rudolf, "The Problem of Sin in Luther," 188
Burckhardt, Jacob, 281n10
Burke, Edmund, 340
Bush, George, 342
Butler, Judith, 5, 18; *Antigone's Claim,* 135
Byron, George Gordon, Lord, *Manfred,* 35

Cabral, Amilcar, 272, 279
Calvinism, 33, 34
Camus, Albert, 18, 105, 116; *The Myth of Sisyphus,* 119; *The Plague,* 10
Carlyle, Thomas, 207
Casanova, Giovanni Giacomo, 236, 238n11
catastrophe: and Brecht, 241, 242, 246, 247, 248, 253; in *film noir,* 6; and Greek trilogies, 40; human conception of, 68–69; and melodrama, 7; and modern subject, 302; moral, 84; and proportionality, 67; Smith on, 156; social, 17; and time, 66, 67, 69; and tragic lesbian, 21. *See also* destruction
catharsis, 40, 48, 116, 131, 132, 242
causality, 11, 150, 204, 218, 289, 290, 295, 319
Cave, Terence, *Recognitions,* 49
Cavell, Stanley, 21, 287–88, 289, 300
Celan, Paul, 43
Cervantes, Miguel de, *Don Quixote,* 120
Césaire, Aimé, 272
Chalamov, Varlam, 43
chance, 200, 209, 210, 319. *See also* fortune
Chaplain, Charlie, 264
Char, René, 38
character, 133, 140, 141, 160, 163, 254, 270, 328–29
characters, 134, 135, 136, 139, 140, 141–42

Châteaubrun, Jean-Baptiste Vivien de, 150
choice, 142, 210–11, 213, 214, 267, 289, 290, 294, 295–96, 300
chorus: in Aristotle, 54, 78, 133; and citizens, 141; as collectivity, 140; composition of, 72; conventions concerning, 79; in Euripides, 71–72, 77–79, 192; foreignness of voice of, 71; in Freud, 134; as Greek public self, 109; and Homer, 72, 75; importance of, 136–37; language of, 140; and morality, 141; Nietzsche on, 109; as official voice, 71–72; in Sebald, 236; in Sophocles, 78–79, 138, 158, 159, 160, 163, 164; standpoint of, 69–70; status of, 71–72; strangeness of, 141; tension of characters with, 140; Vernant on, 80n10; and World War II, 76. *See also* actors
Christ, Carol P., 103n36
Christianity, 33, 34; and absolute tragedy, 41; body in, 46; and Brecht, 251, 257; counterstatement to, 39; and Eagleton, 82, 88, 145n28; and evasion of tragedy, 87–92; and feminism, 17, 93, 97, 98; and Goethe, 41–42; goodness in, 89; guilt in, 31; and Heidegger, 188–89; and limit experiences, 86–87; and Machiavelli, 324; Nietzsche on, 113, 114–15, 192; and Racine, 19, 171, 190; and rationality, 328; in Shakespeare, 41; in Soyinka, 273–74; Steiner on, 16, 82, 87, 115, 116; and subjectivity, 177, 178; and suffering, 46, 343; *theoria* and *speculum* in, 249, 260n21. *See also* theology
Churchill, Winston, 233–34
Cicero, 150–51, 266
citizens, 70, 71, 130, 131, 132, 141
city, 66, 67, 73, 74, 75, 85, 134, 139, 140, 142, 155, 179, 191, 269. *See also* polis
civilization, 206, 246, 248

Clark-Bekederemo, John Pepper, 21, 279; *The Masquerade,* 273; *The Raft,* 273; *Song of a Goat,* 273, 280
Claudel, Paul, *Le Partage de Midi,* 42–43
Coetzee, J. M., 238n9; *Elizabeth Costello,* 227–28
Coleridge, S. T., 35
collectivity: and Aristotle, 132; chorus as, 140; in Clark-Bekederemo, 273; and Dionysus, 18; Eagleton on, 303; and embodiment, 244; in Euripides, 61, 78, 128; and everyday life, 319; in Greco-Roman culture, 267; in Greek culture, 21; in Homer, 17, 72–76; and individual, 141; and lesbians, 306; in Nietzsche, 6; and original production of tragedy, 70; in Plato, 265; and relevance of Greek tragedy, 129; in Sebald, 236
colonialism, 202, 203, 208, 212–14, 220, 264, 273, 274
comedy, 47, 48, 70, 120, 189
community: in African culture, 272, 278; in Aristotle, 271; in Butler, 135; duBois on, 151; in Greco-Roman culture, 267, 268; and Greek culture, 2, 21; and original production of tragedy, 71; and *pharmakos*/scapegoat, 304; recognition exceeding, 140; in Sophocles, 270; as unstable characteristic, 218
conflict, 53, 134, 210, 212
Connolly, William, 116, 199
Conrad, Joseph, *The Secret Agent,* 337
Constant, Benjamin, 10
Constantine, David, 245
contingency, 4, 17, 33, 200, 209–10, 300
Copjec, Joan, 291
Corneille, Pierre, 39, 52
Corngold, Stanley, 20, 345
Cowie, Elizabeth, 299; "Fantasia," 310
crisis, 7, 244, 248, 264
Critchley, Simon, 2, 19, 339
Cubism, 257

culpability, 31, 35, 172. *See also* blame
culture, 14, 45, 116, 128, 221. *See also* African culture; Greek culture; Roman culture; Western culture
cyclicity, 321, 326, 330, 331, 332, 333, 334. *See also* repetition

Dante Alighieri, 30, 32
Dastur, Françoise, 248
d'Aubigné, Agrippa, *Tragiques,* 29
death: Cavell on, 300; in *Double Indemnity,* 289, 295, 296, 297, 300, 301; and femme fatale, 21, 290, 291, 298, 300; in *film noir,* 288; of God, 302; in Heidegger, 181; in Homer, 73–74; Lacan on, 134, 135; and modernity, 322; in *Mulholland Drive,* 307, 312, 315, 316; Nietzsche on, 113; in Racine, 174, 179, 182, 186, 189, 191, 193; in Sophocles, 153. *See also* mortality; suicide
death drive, 134, 186, 291, 296, 297, 298, 300, 340
Death in Venice (film), 8
Deleuze, Gilles, 331
de Man, Paul, 135, 235
democracy: Arendt on, 118, 119; and Aristotle, 131, 133; in Athens, 130, 131, 132; as context, 60; and death of tragedy, 8–9; and decline of tragedy, 37; dilemmas of, 13; Eagleton on, 151, 303, 316n1; and Euripides, 57; and Gilligan, 98; and Greek culture, 2; Hall on, 142; in Homer, 75; modern, 4; Nietzsche on, 110; and original production of tragedy, 71; ritual and political institution of, 131; and Sophocles, 152, 164; Steiner on, 87; R. Williams on, 302–3
Democritus, 108
demonic, the, 9, 33, 38, 40, 88, 93, 95, 181, 325, 337, 345
Derrida, Jacques, 235
desire, 5, 9–10, 11, 19, 87, 94, 219, 291, 292, 307, 339

Dessalines, Jean-Jacques, 203, 213
destiny, 13, 22, 41, 278, 288, 292, 320, 321, 322, 326, 333, 334, 335
destruction, 17, 20, 111, 112, 118, 177, 246, 289, 291, 296, 299. *See also* catastrophe; violence
Dickens, Charles, *Bleak House,* 229
Diderot, Denis, 213
Dienstag, Joshua Foa, 17, 338, 342
difference, 137, 138, 141, 142
Dimock, Wai Chee, 15, 16, 345
Dio Chrysostom, 168n4
Dionysian, the, 13, 59, 85, 107, 109, 110, 112–13, 114, 116, 122n19, 231, 244, 245, 339
Dionysus, 17–18, 29, 105, 115, 127, 128, 132, 139, 273, 334. *See also* Great Dionysia
disinterestedness, 50, 52, 55, 62, 64, 65
Doane, Mary Ann, 8, 298, 299
Dodds, Eric, 325
Dolar, Mladen, 290
domestic life, 7, 8, 35, 78, 138. *See also* family
Dostoyevsky, Fyodor, 106, 112; *Crime and Punishment,* 117
Double Indemnity (film), 21, 289–301
Douglas, Mary, *How Institutions Think,* 327
drama, 2, 6, 29, 46, 48, 49
Dreiser, Theodore, *An American Tragedy,* 29
Driscoll, Kevin, 237n6
duBois, Page, 18, 151, 343
Durand, Gilbert, 327, 331
Durkheim, Émile, 327, 333

Eagleton, Terry, 3, 9, 21, 82, 85, 87–88, 91, 105, 145n28, 153, 316n1, 317n6, 342, 343; *Sweet Violence,* 151, 303–4, 342–43
Eastern thought, 325, 326, 329, 330, 331, 332
economics, 32, 288, 323, 324, 325

education, 49, 54, 56, 127, 331–32, 334
Eliot, George, 51–52
Eliot, T. S., 43, 244; *Family Reunion,* 39; *Murder in the Cathedral,* 39; *Poetry and Drama,* 261n28
elite/elitism, 8, 105, 110, 116, 119, 164, 165, 338. *See also* hierarchy
Elizabethan drama, 39, 257
Ellison, Ralph, 10
Elsaesser, Thomas, 7
emancipation, 19, 338, 340
embeddedness, 266, 267, 268
embodiment, 3, 20, 21, 243–44, 257, 291. *See also* body
emotion, 47, 48, 49, 59, 108, 148–49, 155, 162, 163, 268, 294, 295, 325
Engels, Friedrich, 256
Enlightenment, 13, 34, 106, 116, 200, 210, 211, 213, 214, 241, 339–40
epic, 17, 38, 39, 59, 72, 75, 131, 133, 241, 256
Epictetus, 158
Epic Theater, 241, 245, 258
equality, 38, 87, 90
Equiano, Olaudah, *Interesting Narrative,* 207
estrangement, 32, 35, 245, 255. *See also* alienation; strangeness
ethics/morality: in African culture, 278; and Aristotle, 54, 133; Cavell on, 287; certainties of, 17; and chorus, 141; and Christian feminism, 98; in *Double Indemnity,* 297; and dualism and privation theory, 91; examination of, 140; and fault, 85; and feminism, 93–94; and femme fatale, 291, 298; in *film noir,* 6; Frye on, 11; in Greco-Roman culture, 268; in Hegel, 134; and incompatible goods, 85–86; insight into, 1; and James, 207; Kant on, 50; Lambropoulos on, 3; and melodrama, 7; and metaphysics, 93–94; and modernity, 322; Nietzsche on, 108, 110; of pity, 157; in Plato, 49, 271;

ethics/morality (*continued*)
and politics, 12; in Racine, 177; in Rousseau, 106; in Sebald, 230, 235; in Sophocles, 18, 163, 164; and suffering, 84, 86. *See also* evil
Euben, Peter, 12–13; *The Tragedy of Political Theory,* 209
Euripides, 13, 33, 35, 39, 47, 56, 71–72, 107, 130, 149, 164, 276; *Alcestis,* 276; *Andromache,* 76–78; *Bacchae,* 5, 12, 32, 40–41, 44, 128; *Electra,* 56–58, 59; *Hecuba,* 40, 76–78, 136–37; *Heracles,* 40; *Hippolytus,* 40, 192; *Medea,* 40, 52–53, 244; *Phoenician Women,* 55, 137–38; *Trojan Women,* 40, 44, 60–61, 76–78
Europe, 4, 150, 151, 155, 157, 220, 222, 232, 244, 245, 264–65, 272–73, 274
European avant-garde, 241, 256, 258
everyday life, 115, 319, 320, 322, 327, 330, 333, 334
everyman/common man, 10, 38, 132, 234
evil: and Aristotle, 133; in Christianity, 17; and distortion, 92; in *Double Indemnity,* 21; and falsehood, 89; and femme fatale, 298, 299; in Greco-Roman culture, 268; Nietzsche on, 109; in Plato, 271; privation theory of, 89–90, 91, 92; problem of, 89; and reason, 85; in Sebald, 236; and suffering, 84; women as, 93. *See also* ethics/morality; goodness
existence, 170, 179, 182, 183, 186, 190, 305

fall, 18, 32, 34, 94, 128, 188, 234, 235
fallen world, 17, 91–92
family, 5, 47, 55, 60, 85, 134, 135, 138, 155, 266, 267, 298. *See also* domestic life
Fanon, Frantz, 279; *Les damnés de la terre,* 204
fantasy, 309–10, 311, 313, 314, 315–16
fatalism, 34, 332–33

fate: acceptance of, 325; and agency, 11–12; and aristocracy, 38; and Aristotle, 133, 134; and choice, 142; and context, 325; and disproportionate suffering, 232; in *Double Indemnity,* 289, 294, 297; Eagleton on, 87; and everyday life, 319; and fallen world, 92; and femme fatale, 290; in *film noir,* 6; and freedom, 12, 87; and history, 332; and hurricane Katrina, 68; intensely lived, 335; and modernity, 321–23; and necessity, 326; Sands on, 219; in Sebald, 220, 221, 236; in Sophocles, 11; in Western culture, 263
Faulkner, William, 10
fault, 84–85, 92, 94, 152–53, 219. *See also* blame; guilt; responsibility; sin
Faust, 9, 33, 337
Felski, Rita, 166, 219, 263, 264, 288, 289, 291, 305, 340
feminism: and Antigone, 243; and Brecht, 255, 256; and Christianity, 17, 93, 97, 98; and *Double Indemnity,* 21, 299; and evasion of tragedy, 82, 93–99; and femme fatale, 298; and history, 99; and Marxism, 256; and metaphysical dualism, 89, 90–91, 92, 97, 98; and perfectibility, 17, 96; religious, 94; and women's weepies, 6. *See also* women
femme fatale, 21, 289–301, 312, 313
fetishism, 292–93, 294, 296, 299
Fichte, Johann Gottlieb, 324
film, 6, 8, 29, 34
film noir, 6, 21, 288–301, 340
flaw, 18, 127, 128, 133, 134, 210. *See also* hamartia
fortune, 33, 47, 133, 134, 155, 156, 160, 161, 163, 210, 289, 320, 321. *See also* chance
Foucault, Michel, 13, 116, 178
Fowler, Alistair, 14
fragility, 11, 61, 151, 152, 219, 278, 289, 291, 300, 340

Frankfurt School, 208
freedom: and desire, 339; and differ-
	ence, 142; in *Double Indemnity,* 289,
	294, 296; Eagleton on, 9, 87; and
	fate, 12, 87; and femme fatale, 290,
	291; in Heidegger, 184; illusory,
	324; and James, 207, 212, 213, 214;
	in Levinas, 170; and modernity,
	321; and necessity, 329, 331; and
	pessimism, 117, 120; progress of,
	82; in Racine, 186; Sands on, 219;
	Schelling on, 11; and terror, 118;
	vanishing, 92; in Western culture,
	263
French Revolution, 203, 207
Freud, Sigmund, 5, 9, 10, 16, 31, 32,
	40, 94, 114, 134, 186, 243, 309, 339;
	"Mourning and Melancholia," 99
Frye, Northrop, 8, 11
Fugard, Athol, *The Island,* 13, 43
future, 22, 66, 114, 117, 199, 200, 203,
	204, 208, 209, 215. *See also* time

Galen, *Usefulness of the Parts,* 267
Gaugler, Hans, 252
Gautier, Théophile, 306
gaze, 21, 268, 290, 293, 299
Gellrich, Michelle, 134; *Tragedy and
	Theory,* 135–36
gender, 5, 20, 242, 243, 255, 256, 289,
	311, 317n6. *See also* women
generalization, 16, 45, 52, 56, 59–60,
	61, 165
German Hellenism, 245
German Idealism, 52, 243, 258, 259
German Romanticism, 2–3, 60, 245,
	257, 258
Giacometti, Alberto, 43
Gilligan, Carol, 82, 96, 97, 98, 99–100;
	The Birth of Pleasure, 94, 95
God: as all good and powerful, 89; in
	Aquinas, 339; in Augustine, 178;
	and Beckett, 37; and Büchner, 36, 37,
	39; and creation, 34–35; death of,
	99, 302; as *deus absconditus,* 36, 186;
	Goldmann on, 193; in Jansenism,
	189; and justice, 89; in Marlowe,
	42; and privation theory of evil, 89;
	in Racine, 19; and rationality, 328;
	and salvation, 95; and theodicy, 89,
	100n5; and truth, 90; will of, 89. *See
	also* theology
gods: in Aeschylus, 58, 191; and aris-
	tocracy, 38; cruelty of, 33, 40; in
	Euripides, 41, 192; Lessing on, 150;
	malignity of, 40; in Plato, 270–71;
	in Racine, 189, 190; in Sebald, 234;
	Steiner on, 9; R. Williams on, 302
Goethe, Johann Wolfgang von, 16, 40,
	237; *Conversations with Eckermann,*
	151; *Faust I,* 39; *Faust II,* 34, 36,
	41–42; *Wilhelm Meister's Apprentice-
	ship,* 328
Goheen, Robert, 138
Goldhill, Simon, 16, 70, 132, 343
Goldmann, Lucien, 176, 189, 193
goodness, 89, 90. *See also* evil
goods, 84, 85–86, 92, 154, 155, 156,
	158, 160–61, 219, 221, 270
Gordon, Paul, 105
Gorra, Michael, 240n36
Gould, John, 71
Great Dionysia, 46, 54, 70, 71, 132. *See
	also* Dionysus
great man/woman, 5, 10, 18, 127, 128,
	129, 132, 136, 151, 234, 316n1
Greek culture: and African culture,
	264–65, 272, 275–76; and Brecht,
	241; in Freud, 134; and human
	beings, 265, 266; and modern trag-
	edy, 257; Nietzsche on, 6, 107, 110,
	111; otherness of, 3; pity in, 155;
	Schelling on, 51; slaves in, 18; suf-
	fering in, 150; tragedy in, 2, 46; and
	West African drama, 20–21; world-
	view of, 16
Greek tragedy, 9, 12–13, 20, 52, 54,
	129, 191–92, 242–43, 247, 278, 302
grief, 99, 100, 139. *See also* lamenta-
	tion

Griffith, D. W., 264
Griffith, Mark, 142
Grünwald, Matthias, *Crucifixion,* 34
guilt, 16, 31, 33, 35, 96, 170, 177, 179, 185, 188, 291, 297, 304, 339. *See also* blame; fault

Habermas, Jürgen, 13
Hadot, Pierre, 122n22
Haitian Revolution, 19, 203, 205, 210, 214
Hall, Edith, 5, 141–42, 143n12
Halliwell, Stephen, 47, 48, 149
hamartia, 31, 133, 210. *See also* flaw
happiness, 10, 11, 110, 114
harmony, 266, 267, 268, 269, 271, 274, 279
Harris, Sir Arthur "Bomber," 233–34
Hartmann, Edouard von, 106–7
Harvey, David, 199
Harvey, Sylvia, 298
Heaney, Seamus, 152; *The Cure at Troy,* 151
Hegel, G. W. F., 1, 45, 142, 264; *Aesthetics,* 134; and Bradley, 212; and Brecht, 243, 245, 251; and character, 134; on competing rights, 7; conflict in, 210, 212; and history, 55, 210, 211; on human existence, 2; and legitimacy of tragedy, 32; and master-slave dialectic, 332; mastery in, 325; on middle class, 337; and negation of here, 333; *The Philosophy of History,* 207; protagonist in, 18; and Racine, 190, 191; and Schelling, 50; and Sophocles, 40, 51, 55, 135; and time, 200
Heidegger, Martin, 19, 30, 32, 185, 188–89, 191, 218, 224, 225, 237, 323; *Sein und Zeit,* 170, 178, 181, 183–84, 185, 226
Heilman, Robert, 7
hero: and Aristotle, 132–33, 133, 134; commoner as, 165; Eagleton on, 303; and Euripides, 57; and fate, 322; in *film noir,* 288, 291, 293, 298, 300; focus on, 136; Frye on, 8; and Homer, 66, 75; and James, 207, 213, 214; Lessing on, 150; Promethean, 5, 38; in Racine, 170, 176, 180, 189; in Sophocles, 164, 165; in Stoicism, 158; Vernant on, 80n10; R. Williams on, 302. *See also* protagonist
hierarchy: in Aristotle, 49; and chain of being, 90, 92; and cosmology, 4; Eagleton on, 87; and feminism, 93, 94, 95, 96, 97; and Judeo-Christian tradition, 345; and modernization, 304; and pity, 149, 165, 167; social, 39; in Steiner, 87; and suffering, 46. *See also* aristocracy; elite/elitism
Hierocles, 266
Hinduism, 329
history: and African culture, 272, 274, 279, 280; and Aristotle, 131; and Brecht, 242, 248, 250, 253; context of, 16; and destiny, 321; and fallen world, 92; and fate, 332; and feminism, 99; and Hegel, 55, 210, 211; and James, 204, 206–7, 212, 214, 264; and justice, 97; and knowledge, 324; Marx on, 324; and modernity, 323; Nietzsche on, 112; and pessimism, 119; and postmodernity, 323; and post-1914 period, 43; progressivist view of, 19; in Sebald, 220, 223, 231; and time, 199, 200, 202, 204; and tragedy, 243; and truth, 61; in Western culture, 263
Hobbes, Thomas, 264, 339
Hofmannsthal, Hugo von, 51
Hölderlin, Friedrich, 31, 38, 50, 247, 250, 251, 257, 258, 259; "Blödigkeit," 226; *Empedocles, 1798–80,* 248; "Poetic Courage," 226; "Remarks on Oedipus," 249; version of Sophocles' *Antigone,* 20, 241, 245–46, 248, 253–54
Holly, James Theodore, *A Vindication of the Capacity of the Negro Race for*

Self-Government, and Civilized Progress, 207

Holocaust, 220, 229, 230, 232

homelessness, 3, 15–16, 19, 30–31, 251, 263, 338

Homer, 29, 38, 49, 56, 59, 72; *The Iliad,* 16–17, 66, 72–76

homosexuality, 21–22, 255, 305, 306, 314, 315

hope, 32, 33, 34, 41–42, 60, 61, 109, 201, 219, 271, 344

Hopkins, Gerard Manley, 35

Horkheimer, Max, 13

human beings: in Aristotle, 272; Cavell on, 287; claims of, 341; control of destiny by, 13; in *Double Indemnity,* 289; duBois on, 151; and femme fatale, 291; as flawed and blameworthy, 92; and fragility, 11; in Greco-Roman culture, 265, 266, 267, 268; in Greek culture, 20–21; and Rotimi, 275; Schiller on, 2; in Sophocles, 269, 270; as theater, 38; in Western culture, 263

human condition: Nietzsche on, 109, 112; and pessimism, 118, 120; in Plato, 265; in Rousseau, 115; in Sophocles, 152; and suffering, 46

humanior, 266, 267, 269, 270

humanism, 20, 99, 200–201, 247, 248

Hume, David, 32, 340

hurricane Katrina, 16, 67–68

Hussein, Saddam, 129

Ibsen, Henrik, 52, 53, 106, 176–77; *Brand,* 39; *Ghosts,* 188; *Hedda Gabler,* 11

Imitation of Life (film), 8

individual: in African culture, 21; Arendt on, 117, 118, 119; and Aristotle, 132; Badiou on, 129; and chorus, 70; in Clark-Bekederemo, 273; and collectivity, 141; and destruction, 118; and Dionysus, 18; and embodiment, 244; in Euripides, 78, 137; and everyday life, 319; focus on, 136, 142; in Freud, 134; in German Romanticism, 2–3; in Greco-Roman culture, 267; and Greek culture, 2; and Hegel, 55; Maffesoli on, 22; modern, 5, 142; Nietzsche on, 109, 111; and other, 320; as part of whole, 327, 328; and pessimism, 120; protagonist as, 71; and relevance of Greek tragedy, 129; transcendence of, 331; in Western culture, 263; R. Williams on, 303

initiation, 326, 328, 331, 332

innocence, 32, 84–85, 92, 219

intention, 21, 200, 209, 268. *See also* will

Jackson, Michael, 330

Jacobean drama, 35, 39

James, C. L. R., 264, 276, 281n5; *Beyond a Boundary,* 211; *The Black Jacobins,* 19, 203–9, 210–15, 274; *Notes on American Civilization,* 208; *State Capitalism and World Revolution,* 208; *World Revolution,* 205

Jameson, Fredric, 258

Jansen, Cornelius, 177

Jansenism, 19, 39, 42, 171, 176, 177, 180, 189, 193

Jaspers, Karl, 45

Jerome, St., 319

Joachim of Fiore, 334

Johnson, Samuel, 41, 342

Jones, John, 130, 132–34, 136

Joyce, James, 257

Judeo-Christian tradition, 328, 333, 345

judgment, 50, 51, 153, 166, 263, 267

Jullien, François, 325

Jung, C. G., 319, 329, 330, 332

justice/injustice: and Churchill, 234; content of, 98; and cruelty of gods, 40; Eagleton on, 9, 342; in Euripides, 41; and everyman, 40; and false-

justice/injustice (*continued*)
hood, 97; and feminism, 17; and
God, 89; in Greek tragedy, 192; and
hierarchy, 95; and metaphysics, 97,
98; and Nietzsche, 108, 115; and
outrage, 12; and pity, 149, 153; and
politics, 46; and proportionality,
67; and sacrifice, 95; in Sophocles,
163, 164, 166; and suffering, 83; and
tragic fault, 85

Kafka, Franz, 10, 30, 222, 223, 229,
231, 236, 239n18; *The Castle,* 220;
parable of the Law, 32; "Reflections
on Sin, Pain, Hope, and the True
Way," 229
Kane, Sarah, *Phaedra's Love,* 190–91
Kant, Immanuel, 16, 50–51, 52, 55,
162, 193, 210, 340; *Critique of Judgement,* 50
Keats, John, 205
Kierkegaard, Sören, 2, 32, 40, 45
Kiernan, Victor, 212
Kleist, Heinrich von, *Amphitryon,* 35
knowledge: and African culture, 274;
Cavell on, 287, 288; in Euripides,
57, 58; in *film noir,* 289; in Greco-
Roman culture, 267; and history,
324; lack of, 86; Nietzsche on, 108,
109, 110; in Plato, 265; politics of,
13; in Sebald, 223, 226; in Sophocles, 268, 269, 270
Koselleck, Reinhart, 201, 202, 203
Kosinski, Jerzy, 232

Lacan, Jacques, 1, 18, 134–35, 141,
295–96, 340
Lacoue-Labarthe, Philippe, 248, 250,
253–54
La Harpe, Jean-François de, 150
Lambropoulos, Vassilis, 3
lamentation, 18, 99, 135, 139, 140,
218, 232. *See also* grief; mourning
Lamming, George, *The Pleasures of
Exile,* 211

language, 46–47, 48, 134, 140, 160,
223, 227, 229–32, 243–44, 248, 250,
269, 271
Laplanche, Jean, "Fantasy and the Origins of Sexuality," 309–10
law, 20, 70, 131, 134, 246, 289, 297, 340
Lawrence, D. H., 35
Leclerc, Charles, 203
Lefebvre, Henri, "What is Modernity?"
303
Leibniz, Gottfried Wilhelm, 89, 106,
323; *Théodicée,* 106
Lenin, V. I., 38, 207
Lenson, David, 10
Leopardi, Giacomo, 34; *Moral Essays,*
106
lesbians, 21–22, 305–16
Lessing, Gotthold Ephraim, 51, 160;
Laocoon, 150–51, 155
Levi, Primo, 43, 232
Levinas, Emmanuel, 19, 170, 179–80,
183, 184, 193; "De l'évasion,"
181–82
Lévi-Strauss, Claude, 16, 31, 331
Lloyd-Jones, Sir Hugh, 64n34
Locke, John, 264
Longo, Oddone, 70
Loraux, Nicole, 139, 140
loss: in Butler, 135; in Christianity, 89;
in *Double Indemnity,* 300; evocation
of, 140; Felski on, 219; finality of, 83;
and healing, 99; inescapable, 11; lost
sense of, 82, 99; meaning in stories
of, 96; and modernity, 305; moral,
99; and pity, 156; role of, 18; in
Sebald, 223, 230, 235; in Stoicism,
155
Louverture, Toussaint, 19, 203, 205,
206, 207, 210, 211–13, 214, 274
Love, Heather K., 21, 341
Lubac, Henri de, 332
Lukács, Georg, 244; *Soul and Form,* 176
Luther, Martin, 188, 189
Lynch, David, *Mulholland Drive,* 22,
306–16

Lyotard, Jean-François, *La confession d'Augustin,* 186–87

Machiavelli, Niccolò, 324
Maffesoli, Michel, 15, 22, 338
Magnolia (film), 184
Mann, Thomas: *Doktor Faustus,* 220, 344–45; *Joseph and His Brothers,* 329
Marlowe, Christopher, 35; *Doctor Faustus,* 33–34, 42
Marx, Karl, 16, 31, 32–33, 248, 264, 303, 324, 325; *The Jewish Question,* 328
Marxism, 20, 87, 88, 116, 129, 208, 212, 256, 257, 333, 338
Maupassant, Guy de, 180; "The Horla," 181
Mbembe, Achille, 272
McCulloh, Mark, 228
meaning, 2–4, 52–53, 83–87, 88, 96, 111, 231, 235, 298
Mei Lan-fang, 255
melodrama, 6–9, 12, 33, 35–36, 116
Melville, Herman, 206, 270; *Moby-Dick,* 10, 208
metaphor, 72–73, 74, 229, 230, 231, 250
metaphysics, 12, 16, 17, 32, 84, 89, 90–91, 92, 93–94, 97, 98
Meyerhold, Vsevolod, 256
Michelet, Jules, *History of the French Revolution,* 206–7
middle class, 46, 115, 316n3, 337, 338–39
Middleton, Thomas, *Timon of Athens,* 41
Miller, Arthur, *Death of a Salesman,* 10, 165
Milton, John, 41; *Samson Agonistes,* 191
mimesis, 34, 48, 49, 202, 204, 209, 265, 266, 269, 270, 271–72, 278
minority, 303, 304, 305, 341
modernism, 244, 255, 256, 257, 258
modernity: and African culture, 272, 274, 279, 280; and Aristotle, 133–34,

271; in Benjamin, 235; and Brecht, 241, 245, 257; and dualism, 90; Eagleton on, 9, 87, 303, 304; and emancipation, 338; and embeddedness, 267; and equality, 90; and fate, 321–23; and freedom, 321; in Greco-Roman culture, 267, 268; and individual, 5, 142; and James, 212–13; and limit experiences, 86–87; Maffesoli on, 15, 22; and Marxism, 338; and mastery, 325; and others, 304, 305, 315; and perfectibility, 289; and *pharmakos*/scapegoat, 304; and politics, 19, 55; and progress, 66; and protagonist, 18; questioning of, 13; and reason, 320; in Sebald, 20, 220, 236, 237; Steiner on, 9; and suffering, 302, 303, 305; and time, 320; R. Williams on, 302–3; and women, 305
modern tragedy, 9–10, 234–37, 241, 242, 255, 257, 259
Molière, *Don Juan,* 35
monstrous, the, 172, 173, 186, 247
Morrison, Toni, *Beloved,* 12, 82, 86
mortality, 151, 287, 288, 291. *See also* death
Most, Glenn, 2
mourning, 18, 20, 136, 139, 140, 142, 242, 243, 254, 259n3. *See also* lamentation
Mozart, Wolfgang Amadeus, *Cosí fan tutte,* 44
Mulholland Drive (film), 22, 306–16
Müller, Heiner, 243; *Hamletmachine,* 256; *Medea Material,* 256
Mulvey, Laura, 293, 299
Murray, Gilbert, 244
Mystery Cycles, 251, 257
myth, 14, 31, 38, 57–58, 59, 134, 207, 331

Napoleon I, 210, 213
narrative, 46, 48, 83, 200, 201, 202, 203, 204, 214, 225–26, 232

natural disasters, 16, 17, 67, 69, 74, 80
necessity, 11, 52, 83, 300–301, 321,
    322, 325–26, 329, 331
Neher, Caspar, 241, 246, 252
Nietzsche, Friedrich, 18, 45, 104–20,
    119; and *amor fati,* 114, 325, 329;
    and Beckett, 37; *The Birth of Tragedy,*
    104, 107, 108, 111, 117, 278; and
    Brecht, 245; on Christianity, 192;
    and cyclicity, 333; *Ecce Homo,* 178;
    and Euripides, 59, 60, 107; and
    legitimacy of tragedy, 32; and Maffe-
    soli, 22; pain in, 53, 113, 114; and
    pessimism, 17, 104–5, 106–11, 112,
    117; *Philosophy in the Tragic Age of the
    Greeks,* 108; pity in, 156, 159, 161–
    62, 163; return of same in, 331; and
    Sebald, 231–32, 234; and Sophocles,
    160; and strangeness, 128; thought
    of, 6; *Twilight of the Idols,* 113
Nochimson, Martha, 313
nonhuman actor, 16, 17, 73, 74, 75, 78
nostalgia, 88, 129, 142, 248, 333, 334
Novelli, Gastone, 231
Nussbaum, Martha C., 12, 18, 84,
    342; *The Fragility of Goodness,* 209;
    Upheavals of Thought, 153

Oedipus, 5, 18, 94, 326
O'Neill, Eugene, 43
opera, 6, 34, 117
optimism, 107, 110, 111, 113, 115, 116,
    292, 338
order, 108, 111, 112, 113, 115
other, the, 3, 17, 32, 33, 44, 46, 255,
    287, 288, 304, 305, 315, 320
Ovid, 29
Owen, Wilfrid, 152

paganism, 178, 190, 323–24, 345
pain: Eagleton on, 303; meaning in
    stories of, 96; Nietzsche on, 53, 113,
    114; and pity, 149, 154; in Plato, 48;
    in Racine, 177, 179; in Sebald, 231;
    Smith on, 156; in Sophocles, 149,

150, 152, 153–54, 158, 159, 160, 161,
    163, 164; in Stoicism, 155. *See also*
    suffering
Pascal, Blaise, 39, 42, 176, 193, 340
Pasolini, Pier Paolo, 244
past, 2, 20, 140, 199, 200, 201, 209; in
    P. T. Anderson, 184; in Euripides, 58,
    59; and James, 204, 205, 213–14; in
    Racine, 19; in Sebald, 222, 225, 230,
    231; in Sophocles, 59. *See also* time
Paul the Apostle, 31, 178
Peloponnesian War, 130, 139
perfection/perfectibility, 11, 17, 18, 96,
    263, 289, 344
peripeteia, 66, 67, 69, 77, 193
person, 17, 21, 266–67, 271, 287
pessimism, 84, 115, 117, 118, 119–20,
    338; Eagleton on, 105, 342; in *film
    noir,* 6; in Nietzsche, 17–18, 104–5,
    106–11, 112, 114, 116, 117; as term,
    106; and value, 344
pharmakos/scapegoat, 21, 95, 136,
    145n28, 303–4
philosophy, 1, 2–4, 14, 32, 33, 49, 104,
    131, 132, 243
Philostratus, 56
Picasso, Pablo, 34; *Guernica,* 43
Pinter, Harold, 30; *Homecoming,* 43
pity, 47, 148–67, 189; arguments
    against, 154–58; debate over, 148–
    52; in Sophocles, 18–19, 157–67
Place, Janey, 297
Plath, Sylvia, 38
Plato: and African culture, 274; and
    Aristotle, 54, 131, 132; banishment
    of tragedy by, 40, 54, 270; body in,
    265; and Brecht, 242, 243, 255; col-
    lectivity in, 265; on distortion, 249;
    human condition in, 265; knowl-
    edge in, 265; and language, 46–47,
    48; *Laws,* 29–30, 265–66; and legiti-
    macy of tragedy, 32; and limits of
    human endeavor, 270, 337; mimesis
    in, 265, 278; and mourning, 259n3;
    Nietzsche on, 107, 108, 110, 111;

Philebus, 48; pity in, 149, 151, 154, 155, 158; polis in, 265–66; politics in, 264, 266; *Republic,* 48, 49, 154, 155, 265–66, 270–71; and society, 264; *Statesman,* 266, 267; *Symposium,* 44; C. Taylor on, 267; *Timaeus,* 266, 267; and West African drama, 20

pleasure, 22, 48, 94, 96, 99, 100, 133, 222, 320, 321, 322, 323, 324, 334

Plutarch, 266

Poe, Edgar Allan, 180

polis, 5, 29–30, 41, 48, 54, 59, 69–72, 75, 130, 192, 243, 264, 265–66, 271, 272. *See also* city

politics: Arendt on, 117–19; and Aristotle, 132, 264; in Athenian tragedy, 59; avoidance of, 12; in Clark-Bekederemo, 273; as context, 16, 37, 60, 61, 131; Eagleton on, 88, 151, 303; in Euripides, 57; in Greco-Roman culture, 267; and Greek tragedy, 12–13; and historically specific readings, 5; of hope, 34; identity, 303; and James, 205, 208; Loraux on, 139–40; Maffesoli on, 22; and melodrama, 12; and modernity, 19, 55; and morality, 12; of nationalism, 51; in Nietzsche, 116; and pessimism, 18, 120; in Plato, 30, 264, 266; postcolonial, 19; in Racine, 191; and Simpson trial, 127; and social change, 315; in Sophocles, 152, 270; in Soyinka, 273; in Steiner, 55; of tragedy, 55; transcendence of, 4, 5, 9; in Western culture, 264

Pontalis, Jean-Bertrand, "Fantasy and the Origins of Sexuality," 309–10

postcolony/postcolonialism, 14, 19, 202, 203, 204, 208, 209, 264, 272

postmodernism, 87, 88

postmodernity, 90, 129, 142, 322, 324, 325, 326, 328, 332

present, 22, 114, 200, 202, 205, 209, 215, 320, 323, 324, 333. *See also* time

pre-Socratic philosophers, 107–8, 109

progress, 9, 11, 13, 18, 66, 87, 112, 114, 119, 248, 263, 274, 332

Promethean hero, 5, 38

Prometheus, 31

protagonist: aristocratic, 37–38; and Aristotle, 132, 133, 134; Eagleton on, 303; in Euripides, 78; in Ibsen, 11; individualized, 71; kinds of, 8–10; modern ideas of, 18; in modern tragedy, 234; and past, 2; pay for actors playing, 71; power of, 11; and self, 18; in Sophocles, 11, 78; Vernant on, 80n10. *See also* hero

psychoanalysis, 135, 242, 243, 255, 309

Quine, Willard Van Orman, 43

Rabinowitz, Paula, 290

Racine, Jean, 35, 37, 39, 43, 52, 68; *Bérénice,* 42; *Phèdre,* 19, 34, 38, 170–94, 339

rationality: in Brecht, 20; and dualism, 90, 91; in Euripides, 41, 57, 59; and fortune, 320; and God, 328; Nietzsche on, 107; politics of, 13; and privation theory of evil, 89; and Racine, 42; and redemption, 92; Steiner on, 87, 115

Raynal, abbé, 213

reason: absolute, 89; in Aristotle, 54, 271; and Brecht, 248; and Casanova, 238n11; and chain of being, 90; and chance, 210; compromised, 13; and contingency, 209–10; and emotion, 325; and Euripides, 57; and evil, 85; Felski on, 219; and fortune, 210; in Greco-Roman culture, 267; and hurricane Katrina, 68; and incompatible goods, 85; insufficiency of, 12; and James, 213; limits of, 11; and modernity, 320; and natural disasters, 67; progress of, 82; in Sebald, 233, 234; in Steiner, 115; and unconscious, 330; as unstable characteristic, 218; in Western culture, 263

recognition, 56, 288, 296, 327. See also
anagnorisis
redemption, 17, 19, 32, 36, 41, 88, 92,
115, 117. *See also* salvation
Reich, Zinaida, 256
Reinhardt, Max, 244
Reiss, Timothy J., 20, 337; *Mirages of
the Selfe,* 266
Renan, Ernest, 51
repetition, 83, 331–32. *See also* cyclic-
ity
responsibility, 16, 21, 96, 289, 294,
297, 300, 301. *See also* fault
Rezzori, Gregor, 232
Ricoeur, Paul, 202
ritual, 5, 46, 54, 71, 83, 131, 132,
145n28, 253, 274
Rocco, Christopher, 211; *Tragedy and
Enlightenment,* 209
Romance, 201, 202, 203, 206
Roman culture, 155, 266
Romantic Hellenism, 16, 51
Romanticism, 2–3, 4, 13, 52, 60, 117,
205, 207, 208, 214, 245, 257, 258,
264, 323
Rorty, Richard, 341
Roth, Joseph, 223
Rotimi, Ola, 21, 279; *The Gods Are Not
to Blame,* 275, 276, 277–78, 280
Rousseau, Jean-Jacques, 32–33, 115,
148–49, 152, 339; *Confessions,* 178;
Discourse On the Arts and Sciences,
106

sacrifice, 92, 94–95, 145n28, 219, 298,
343
Salih, Tayeb, *Season of Migration to the
North,* 13
salvation, 95, 287, 301. *See also*
redemption
Sands, Kathleen M., 17, 23, 219, 223,
232, 235, 269, 343
Santner, Eric, 226–27
Sartre, Jean-Paul, 32, 43

Savonarola, 334
scapegoat. See *pharmakos*/scapegoat
Schelling, Friedrich, 2, 11, 45, 50–51
Schiller, Friedrich von, 2
Schlegel, A. W., 122n17
Schlegel, Friedrich, 2, 51, 227, 228
Schmidt, Dennis, 11
Schoenberg, Arnold, 34
Schopenhauer, Arthur, 1, 2, 107, 108,
112, 120, 122n21; *Parerga and Parali-
pomena,* 106
Scott, David, 13, 19, 264, 274, 342
Searles, Harold, 231
Sebald, W. G., 20, 218–37, 345; *After
Nature,* 232; *Austerlitz,* 219, 228–29,
230–31, 240n36; *The Emigrants,* 219,
221, 227; *On the Natural History of
Destruction,* 219, 224, 228, 232; *The
Rings of Saturn,* 219, 223; *Vertigo,*
219, 221–22
secularism, 2, 4, 34, 35–36, 37
Sedgwick, Eve Kosofsky, 318n14
Segal, Charles, 140–41; *Tragedy and
Civilization,* 209
self: construction of, 140–41; Felski on,
219; in Greco-Roman culture, 268;
Lacan on, 135; modern Western
ideas of, 20, 142; in Nietzsche, 116;
and nonself, 331; plural, 331; and
protagonist, 18; realization of, 325;
in Sebald, 235; in Sophocles, 268;
thin or deontological, 201
self-awareness, 38–39
self-blindness, 293
self-command, 155
self-consciousness, 134
self-control, 49
self-delusion, 291, 299
self-destruction, 31
self-determination, 208
selfhood, 11, 219, 263
self-justification, 292, 294, 297
self-mastery, 185, 219, 332
self-perfection, 332

self-preservation, 291
self-punishment, 61
self-recognition, 287, 288, 295–96
self-shaping, 116
self-sufficiency, 185, 210
Seneca, 37, 39, 156, 157, 161, 266;
  Medea, 52–53
sexuality: in Augustine, 178; in Clark-
  Bekederemo, 273; in *Double Indemnity,* 297, 299; in Euripides, 137; and
  femme fatale, 290, 291; in *film noir,*
  299; Gilligan on, 94; and Greek tragedy, 5; in *Mulholland Drive,* 306–7,
  312–13, 314; Nietzsche on, 113–14;
  in Racine, 171–74, 177, 178, 182, 187,
  193; in Sophocles, 138
Shakespeare, William, 4, 5, 37, 42, 52,
  61, 68, 88, 206, 264, 270; *Hamlet,* 30,
  33–34, 36, 39, 41, 53, 134, 180, 183,
  199, 212–13; *King Lear,* 32, 33, 35, 41,
  43, 287, 344; *Macbeth,* 33, 36, 38, 41,
  180; *Othello,* 36, 41, 43; *The Tempest,*
  211, 212; *Timon of Athens,* 41; *Twelfth
  Night,* 44
Shelley, Percy Bysshe, 34; *Cenci,* 35,
  42; *Prometheus,* 35
Shostakovitch, Dmitri, 43
Silverblatt, Michael, 228–29, 230
Simon, Claude, 231
sin, 19, 30, 31, 91–92, 171, 179, 187,
  188–89, 192, 219, 339. *See also* fault
Singer, Ben, 8
Sirk, Douglas, 6–7, 8
Sisyphus, 31
slavery: and agency, 202; in Aristotle,
  133; in Caribbean, 203, 204; and
  colonialism, 203; debate over, 139;
  and difference, 142; duBois on, 151;
  in Euripides, 77–78, 137, 138; in
  Greek culture, 18, 132, 136, 141; Hall
  on, 142; and James, 203, 207, 210,
  211, 214; modern, 13, 142; in Sebald,
  236; in Sophocles, 138, 164, 165; in
  Soyinka, 273

Smith, Adam, 150, 157, 163–67, 165;
  Theory of Moral Sentiments, 155–56
Snell, Bruno, 141
Sobchack, Vivian, 288
social contract, 320, 325, 328
society: and alienation, 32; in Brecht,
  250; Constant on, 10; of consummation, 321; as context, 37, 39, 60,
  61; exclusion from, 30–31, 149, 152,
  153–54; and feelings of belonging,
  327; and *film noir,* 288; in Greco-
  Roman culture, 266, 268; in Homer,
  74; and James, 204, 207, 212; as
  limited and conflictual, 96–97;
  perfectibility of, 96; and pessimism,
  119; and pity, 148–49; and Plato,
  264; status in, 8–9; Steiner on, 9; in
  Western culture, 263–64; R. Williams on, 303
Socrates, 107, 108, 110, 111, 120,
  122n19, 131, 264, 325
Sollors, Werner, 13, 305
Sontag, Susan, 238n9
Sophocles, 13, 30, 37, 38, 39, 56,
  58–59, 68, 87, 88, 107, 110, 130, 241,
  245, 258, 275; *Ajax,* 40, 59–60, 118;
  Antigone, 5, 11, 32, 40, 51–52, 55, 71,
  78, 118, 134–35, 138–39, 191, 192,
  244–48, 314–15; *Electra,* 56; *Oedipus
  at Colonus,* 268–69, 278; *Oedipus Rex,*
  49, 59, 71, 78, 133, 134, 138, 145n28,
  211, 244, 268, 269–70; *Philoctetes,*
  18–19, 149–52, 153–54, 157–67; *Trachiniae,* 138
Sorokin, Pitirim, 328
Soviet Union, 276
Soyinka, Wole, 21, 275, 279; *The Bacchae of Euripides,* 13, 273–74, 277,
  280; *The Burden of Memory, the Muse
  of Forgiveness,* 279–80
Speer, Albrecht, 233
Stalin, Joseph, 205
state, 55, 71, 134, 191
Staten, Henry, 15, 259n3

Stein, Gertrude, 257

Stein, Peter, 55

Steiner, George, 9, 55, 60, 61, 67, 104, 118; on absolute tragedy, 15–16, 305; *Antigones,* 14; and being of world, 69; and Christianity, 82; and death of tragedy, 341; *The Death of Tragedy,* 4, 15, 32, 44, 66, 72, 115; desperation in, 87; and dramatic form, 14; and Eagleton, 87–88; *Grammars of Creation,* 34; and hope, 344; and Nietzsche, 115; and Oedipus myth, 5; and pessimism, 84, 115, 116; and post-Enlightenment culture, 338; and Romance, 201; on social status, 8–9; and R. Williams, 117; on worldview, 53

Stendhal, 222, 223, 236

Stoicism, 18, 52, 149, 151, 154–55, 156, 157, 158, 159, 160, 162, 163, 164, 324–25

strangeness, 128, 140, 141. *See also* estrangement

Stravinsky, Igor, 257

Strindberg, August, 35, 106

Strong, Tracy, 116

subjectivity, 19, 21, 170, 171, 176, 177, 178, 179, 192, 193, 220, 263, 264, 300

sublimity, 50, 52, 302, 340

suffering: absolute of, 88; and aesthetics, 86; ancient explorations of, 61; and aristocracy, 38; in Aristotle, 47; and Christianity, 46, 343; creaturely, 234, 235; and culture, 116; disproportionate, 218, 232–33, 234; in *Double Indemnity,* 300; Eagleton on, 87, 88, 151, 303; as education, 334; and evil, 84; Felski on, 219; and feminism, 17, 83, 84, 86, 87, 95–96; in Greco-Roman culture, 268; in Greek culture, 150; and historically specific readings, 5; inescapable, 11; and injustice, 83; innocent, 84; of Jesus, 95; justification of, 95–96; kinds of, 10; legitimation of, 83; of lesbians, 305; Lessing on, 150–51; meaning in, 83; in melodrama, 7; and modernity, 302, 303, 305; and morality, 84, 86; narrativization of, 46; and nationalism, 46; and necessity, 83; Nietzsche on, 109, 110, 113, 114, 115; and otherness, 46; in Plato, 48, 49; and power, 95–96; and progress, 87; in Racine, 182; and redemption, 88; rhetoric of, 46; Sands on, 219; in Sebald, 219, 220, 222, 226, 230, 232, 233, 234–35, 236, 237; shape of, 14; Smith on, 155; in Sophocles, 18, 149, 150, 160, 165, 268; Steiner on, 16, 201; substitutional, 102n30; telling of, 83, 100, 219, 235; trivialization of, 4; as unstable characteristic, 218; in Weil, 108; R. Williams on, 4, 302, 316n3; and worldview, 53. *See also* affliction; pain

suicide, 40, 161, 179, 273, 322. *See also* death

Sutherland, Efua, 279; *Edufa,* 276, 280

Swinburne, Algernon Charles, 236

Szondi, Pete, 52

Tacitus, 39, 156

Tantalus, 31

Tapie, Bernard, 330

Taplin, Oliver, 56

Taxidou, Olga, 3, 20

Taylor, A. E., 30

Taylor, Charles, 267; *The Sources of the Self,* 345

terror, 11, 117, 118, 120, 189, 337

Theognis, 32

theology, 17, 32, 33, 36, 37, 82, 84, 87–92, 98–99, 345. *See also* Christianity; God

Thomas, John Jacob, *Froudacity,* 207

Thucydides, 139

Tiepolo, Giovanni Battista, 34

time: and action, 209; in African culture, 280; in Anaximander, 108;

and archetypes, 330; and catastrophe, 66, 67, 69; and change, 117; compression and acceleration of, 199; cyclical, 330, 331, 333; and Dionysus, 109; and history, 199, 200, 202, 204; and James, 204, 205, 209, 214–15; Maffesoli on, 22; and modernity, 320; in *Mulholland Drive,* 313; and narrative, 202; Nietzsche on, 108, 112, 114, 117; and pessimism, 17, 106, 118, 120; as progress, 82, 86–87; in Racine, 185–86, 192; and redemption, 19; in Steiner, 116; as succession, 200; and trauma, 83; as unlimited, 66. *See also* future; past; present
Tolstoi, Leo, 34
Tourneur, Cyril, *An Atheist's Tragedy,* 35
tragedy: absolute/pure, 15–16, 32, 33, 39–41, 42, 43, 55, 270, 305, 315, 344; as attitude, 289; cast of, 69–70; death of, 8, 14; definitions of, 30, 133; and drama, 6; and epic, 75; as genre, 6, 10–11, 14, 30, 52, 56, 61, 83, 116, 219, 288, 289; Greek, 9, 12–13, 20, 52, 54, 129, 191–92, 242, 242–43, 247, 278, 302; as mode, 14, 30, 201, 209, 219, 288; modern, 9–10, 234–37, 241, 242, 255, 257, 259; original production of, 70, 71; performance of, 3, 66, 109, 132, 133; politics of, 55; scope of, 66, 68, 79, 104; as sensibility, 6, 9, 10, 19, 20, 82, 96, 100n5, 201, 214, 215, 219, 220, 224, 226, 288, 289, 290, 291–92, 293, 294, 296, 297, 299, 320, 333; as structure of feeling, 219, 288; as term, 29; as worldview, 16, 47, 48, 49, 53, 84, 93, 95, 96, 100n5
tragic, the, 2, 3, 4, 45, 46, 47, 48, 52, 60, 61, 83–87
trauma, 17, 83–84, 94, 96, 339
Trojan War, 73
Trotsky, Leon, 205, 256; *History of the Russian Revolution,* 206–7

Troy, 17, 34, 73, 137, 139
truth, 85, 89, 90, 192, 199, 221, 225, 226, 230, 235, 271

unconscious, 330, 331, 332
United States, 276, 342
universality, 15, 16, 50, 52, 55, 117, 303, 305, 341
utopianism, 120, 141, 344

Verdi, Giuseppe, *Othello,* 36
vernacular, 2, 3, 10, 68
Vernant, Jean-Pierre, 11, 71, 80n10, 131, 132, 140, 145n28
Vico, Giovanni Battista, 332
Vidal-Naquet, Pierre, 11
violence: in Aristotle, 47; in Brecht, 20, 246, 248; and disproportionate suffering, 232; in Euripides, 57, 59; and fallen world, 92; in Greco-Roman culture, 268; and hurricane Katrina, 67; and innocent fault, 94; in James, 214; love of, 95; and modernity, 305, 322; Sands on, 219; in Sebald, 220, 221, 223, 236; in Sophocles, 58. *See also* destruction
Virgil, 29, 321
Virilio, Paul, 199
Visconti, Luchino, 8
Voltaire, 170; *Candide ou l'Optimisme,* 106

Wagner, Richard, 117, 245
war, 72–76, 78, 79, 80, 246
Weigel, Helene, 20, 251, 252, 253, 255, 256, 257
Weil, Simone, 75–76, 108
Western culture, 13, 34, 37, 263, 272, 278, 279, 280, 320, 330, 331
Wharton, Edith, 10; *The House of Mirth,* 118
White, Hayden, 201
Wilde, Oscar, 314
Wilder, Billy, *Double Indemnity,* 289–301

will, 92, 111, 161, 201, 268. *See also* intention
Williams, Delores, 102n30
Williams, Eric, "Is Massa Day Dead?" 209
Williams, Raymond, 4, 5, 104, 117, 204; *Modern Tragedy,* 68, 302–3
Winckelmann, Johann Joachim, 51
Winkler, John J., 70, 71
witness, 222, 231, 232, 236
Wittgenstein, Ludwig, 227; *Philosophical Investigations,* 34; *Tractatus,* 36
women: African American, 102n30; in Aristotle, 133; in Brecht, 20, 254–56; as demonic, 93, 95; and difference, 142; in Euripides, 5, 77–78, 128, 137, 192; as evil, 93; and fallenness, 17; in Greek tragedy, 242–43; in Hegel, 134; as inferior, 93, 95; and misog-

yny, 296, 298; and modernity, 305; and New Woman, 255, 256, 257; and Oedipus myth, 94; in Racine, 192; in Sophocles, 138, 164, 165. *See also* feminism; gender
Wood, James, 238n9
Wooster Group, 182; *To You, the Birdie!* 190
Wordsworth, William, 205
World War I, 43, 242
World War II, 43, 75, 76, 208, 224, 242

Xenophon, 139

Yeats, William Butler, 235, 344; *Explorations,* 261n28; *Purgatory,* 36, 37

Zeitlin, Froma, 70
Zizek, Slavoj, 291, 299–300, 316